THE BRITISH ADMIRALS OF THE FLEET 1734–1995

"... behold
Upon the hempen tackle ship-boys climbing;
Hear the shrill whistle which doth order give
To sounds confused; behold the threaden sails,
Borne with the invisible and creeping wind,
Draw the huge bottoms through the furrow'd sea,
Breasting the lofty surge. O! do but think
You stand upon the rivage and behold
A city on the inconstant billows dancing;
For so appears this fleet majestical"

Chorus to Shakespeare's *King Henry V*, Act III, Prologue.

THE BRITISH ADMIRALS OF THE FLEET 1734–1995

A BIOGRAPHICAL DICTIONARY

by

T. A. HEATHCOTE

With a Foreword by

ADMIRAL SIR MICHAEL BOYCE, GCB, OBE, ADC

CHIEF OF THE DEFENCE STAFF

LEO COOPER

To the officers, midshipmen and cadets, past and
present, of the University Royal Naval Units

First published in Great Britain 2002 by
LEO COOPER
an imprint of
Pen & Sword Books Ltd
47 Church Street,
Barnsley,
South Yorkshire,
S70 2AS

Copyright © 2002 by T. A. Heathcote

ISBN 0 85052 835 6

A catalogue record for this book is
available from the British Library.

Typeset in 10.5/12pt Plantin by
Phoenix Typesetting, Burley-in-Wharfedale, West Yorkshire.

Printed in England by
CPI UK

CONTENTS

Tables:

Bibliography   317

Index   324

FOREWORD

Admiral Sir Michael Boyce, GCB, OBE, ADC
Chief of the Defence Staff

This is the second of Dr Tony Heathcote's biographical dictionaries of what are sometimes called 'five star officers'. For the Royal Navy, this means Admirals of the Fleet, those commanders whose privilege it was to fly the Union Flag in their flagship, and, in modern times, to serve on the Active List of Officers for life. The rank is currently in abeyance and, under normal circumstances, no more holders of this historic rank will be appointed.

The reader will note that some Admirals of the Fleet were awarded their honorary rank as a mark of enormous respect for their social position, rather than as a result of naval command, but these were relatively few and the accolade was usually reserved for the British Sovereign or those of the most distinguished friends and allies. Among these were Kaiser Wilhelm and his brother Prince Heinrich of Prussia, who, after the outbreak of the First World War in 1914, understandably felt then need to divest themselves of their British ranks.

The book includes some of the most illustrious names in Royal Naval History: Anson, Hawke, Jervis, Cochrane and Fisher and, more recently, Beatty, Jellicoe, Cunningham, Vian, Lewin and Fieldhouse. But some famous names do not appear: until the mid 19th Century Admirals of the Fleet not only had to be very young promotions to Captain, but also had to exhibit extraordinary longevity to rise to the top of the list. Tony Heathcote wryly reminds us that even Nelson, with all his experience and achievements in combat – had he not been killed in action – would have had to have lived until the age of 86 to have reached the top of this very sharp pyramid!

This volume is an excellent compendium of men who served their country with huge distinction over the last three hundred years. They contributed in large measure to the security provided by the Royal Navy, which enabled the country to prosper economically while avoiding the ravages of continental warfare that afflicted so many of our neighbours and competitors. Tony Heathcote has produced a succinct treasure trove of information in a highly-readable style with a light touch. It is a most valuable reference source for students of naval history.

PREFACE AND ACKNOWLEDGEMENTS

The aim of this book is to give an outline of the careers of the officers who held the rank of admiral of the fleet in the Royal Navy, with as many details of their domestic lives as space permits, so as to hoist the sails of personality on the masts of historical narrative. Entries generally contain information relating to their subjects' date and place of birth and death; their families; the dates of their appointments and promotions; the ships in which they served; the stations to which they were deployed and operations in which they took part. The dates of peerages, baronetcies and knighthoods are given when these awards involved a change in style or title, as are those of the award of decorations for brave conduct. Otherwise, for reasons of space, they are omitted, along with civic or academic awards, county lieutenancies, and similar distinctions of an honorary nature, following the principle established in *The Gondoliers* by W S Gilbert, himself a deputy lieutenant for Middlesex. ("On ev'ry side field marshals gleamed, small beer were lords-lieutenant deemed, with admirals the ocean teemed . . ."). Also for reasons of space, I have generally refrained from giving the ages of officers on their several appointments, even though by modern standards these were sometimes very young or very old. They can, however, be easily calculated from the information given in each entry. Numerals in **bold** within square brackets **[nn]** after each name indicate the place of an admiral of the fleet within the seniority list (Table 1) at the end of the book. In the main text, entries are arranged in alphabetical order according to the names by which the admirals of the fleet were known at the end of their careers.

I have assumed a general knowledge on the part of the reader of the major political events, wars and naval organization in the times in which the admirals of the fleet lived. To do otherwise would make the work not a collection of biographies, but a history of the British Fleet and of the British State in whose story it plays so great a part. Nevertheless, some background information has been included where this seemed helpful in placing each individual's story in an intelligible context. In accordance with the custom of the Service itself in ordinary usage, I have referred to the Royal Navy throughout as the Navy, and to other navies by their full titles. "Home", in context, means the United Kingdom.

Although all commanding officers of ships are their captains in the traditional usage of the sea, only those appointed to the command of rated (in modern terms, major combatant) ships were captains by rank, known in the terminology of the day as post captains. In this work, "captain" indicates "post captain" at the periods when the latter term was in common use. The commanding officers of unrated (ie minor) warships were "masters and commanders", or, more simply, "commanders". In the late 1820s the seconds-in-command of major warships (previously, as in all ships of the fleet, their first lieutenants) also became commanders by rank, so that after that time the term commander, depending on the context, indicates either the commanding officer of a minor unit or the second-in-command of a major one. Until 1861, when the rank of sub-lieutenant was introduced, midshipmen qualified for promotion to lieutenant, but below the required minimum age, could be appointed to the rank of mate. At the lowest extreme of the promotion ladder, "cadet" in this book means naval cadet, not sea cadet. The ranks of vice admiral, rear admiral and lieutenant commander are in modern usage each written as two separate words. During most of the period covered by this book they were hyphenated as vice-admiral, rear-admiral and lieutenant-commander, and I have therefore used this older form throughout the work.

The ancient office of Lord High Admiral was from November 1709 onwards executed by a commission, apart from the period in 1827–28 when it was held by the Duke of Clarence [11]. The Lords Commissioners of the Board of Admiralty, as its members were styled, were headed by the First Lord of the Admiralty, who was sometimes a professional seaman, but more usually (after 1806 invariably) a professional politician, and almost always, in the period covered by this work, a Cabinet Minister. The post was abolished in 1963. Boards of Admiralty always included at least one civil lord commissioner. Officers in the Navy who were lords commissioners are referred to in this work as naval lords up to the reforms of 1904, and thereafter as Sea Lords, the term which came into formal use at that time. From May 1915, the First Sea Lord was also Chief of the Naval Staff. Both titles remain in use despite the abolition of the Lords Commissioners of the Board of Admiralty and their replacement by the Admiralty Board in the Ministry of Defence set up in 1964.

I take this opportunity of expressing my gratitude to all those who have given me assistance or encouragement in the preparation of this book, especially to Matthew Midlane, Director of Studies at the Royal Military Academy Sandhurst and to Tony Clayton, Debbie Goodwin, Brian Jones, Andrew Lambert, Michael Orr, and Michael Ranson, past or present members of the RMAS academic staff; to my other correspondents, Robin Brodhurst; Paul Kendall; Nico Steffen; the Reverend D M B Mathers, vicar of Thurston, the Reverend R A Potter, rector of Broxbourne and the Reverend S J Smith, vicar of Swaffham; and to Surgeon Commander Sandy Cochrane, late Royal Naval Reserve, and Surgeon Lieutenant Commander Dennis Freshwater, Royal Navy, for their advice on naval medicine and their friendship over many years. I am particularly grateful to all those admirals of the fleet now living who so kindly spared their time to read and correct the draft entries relating to their own several careers. I also offer my thanks to Andrew Orgill and John K Pearce of the RMAS Central Library, Pam Bendall of the Conflict Studies Research Centre Library, Christine Mason of the Bodleian Library, Oxford University, and the staff of the municipal libraries of Portsmouth and Reading, and of the Institute of Historical Research, London. Most of all, my thanks are due to my wife Mary, herself an historian by training, who researched naval obituaries, accompanied me around churchyards, proof-read my typescript, and gave me all the support, moral and material, that any writer could desire. All errors of fact or interpretation remain the sole responsibility of the author.

Neither the MOD Naval Historical Branch nor the Royal Naval Museum, Portsmouth, were able to find a definitive list of the officers who held the rank of admiral of the fleet and I have therefore compiled my own, mostly from successive Navy Lists. In a number of cases officers died shortly after reaching this rank and so did not appear as such in the subsequent issue of the Navy List. I apologize for any omissions arising from this, and cordially invite any better-informed reader to send the necessary corrections of these or indeed any other errors. That many details of the lives of the admirals of the fleet have not been included was unavoidable, given the nature of a work that seeks to cover so extensive a period in a single volume. I can only plead, in extenuation, that even the greatest English writer was conscious of the problems of reducing much to little.

> *Thus far, with rough and all-unable pen,*
> *Our bending author hath pursued the story;*
> *In little room confining mighty men,*
> *Mangling by starts the full course of their glory.*

Chorus to Shakespeare's *King Henry V*, Act V, Epilogue.

T A Heathcote,
Camberley, April 2002

INTRODUCTION

In March 1995 an Independent Review of the Armed Forces' Manpower, Career and Remuneration, headed by an eminent businessman, Sir Michael Betts, included in its report a finding that the ranks of admiral of the fleet, field marshal, and marshal of the Royal Air Force were unnecessary because of the reduced size of the British Armed Forces, and because these ranks were not used by close allies of the United Kingdom. The Review therefore recommended that the practice of promoting the chiefs of staff of each service to their respective "five-star" rank on completing their tenure of appointment should be discontinued. The Ministry of Defence, in accepting this recommendation (the only one put into effect without delay), added the spin that these ranks were appropriate only for those who had commanded large fleets, armies or air forces in successful operations, or had been at the head of their service in a major war. Therefore, it declared, no more promotions to this level would be made, except in these or other special (unspecified) circumstances.

In fact, as the research undertaken in the course of preparing this volume and its companion *The British Field Marshals 1736–1997* shows, such conditions had never previously been necessary for promotion to these ranks in the British services. In particular, not every British admiral of the fleet had held high command in war, there had never been any direct correlation between the number of ships or men in the Navy and the number of admirals of the fleet, nor had the Navy's rank structure been influenced by that of Allied navies.

THE ORIGINS AND DEVELOPMENT OF THE RANK

The title Admiral of the Fleet originally indicated an appointment corresponding in many ways to the present-day C-in-C Fleet, rather than the permanent rank that it later became.

The Navy of the late seventeenth century was organized to form a single fleet, divided into three squadrons. These were distinguished in order of seniority by the colours Red, White and Blue, and formed respectively the centre, van and rear of the battle line. Each squadron was organized into three divisions, commanded respectively by an admiral, vice-admiral and rear-admiral. The position and grade of each of these officers was indicated

1

by a plain flag of the appropriate colour (red, white or blue respectively) and the masthead (main, fore or mizen) at which it was worn. All ships under a flag officer's command, including his own flagship, wore an ensign of the appropriate colour, with the national flag in the upper canton, at their stern. The admiral commanding the Red squadron, by virtue of being the senior officer of the senior squadron, was also the admiral of the fleet and flew the national flag, rather than a red flag, at his masthead. In practice, the concept of the navy operating as a single large formation was soon overtaken by changes in strategy, requiring the deployment of several separate fleets and squadrons in different theatres at the same time. It was not until the early 1740s, however, that the number of flag officers was increased from the original establishment of nine, and from then on there was a steady increase in the number of officers in each grade. There was no admiral of the Red, by that title, until 1805, when this rank was introduced to give admirals of the White a better opportunity of promotion than that provided by the single post of admiral of the fleet. Thereafter, the distinguishing flag of admirals of the Red was red at the mainmast.

In the early period, the post of admiral of the fleet was not invariably held by the longest-serving admiral, nor was it awarded for life. From 1718 promotion to and within the flag ranks was by seniority, according to the date of an officer's first commission as captain. The last admiral of the fleet to be appointed for the duration of a specific campaign was James, third Earl of Berkeley, who flew his flag as such from 13 March to 15 April 1719, during a brief war against Spain. Thereafter, during the "long peace" that followed, no admiral of the fleet was appointed until February 1734, when Sir John Norris [1] was given this rank, two years before the Earl of Berkeley's death. Norris was the first admiral of the fleet (apart from those drowned or killed in action) to retain his rank for life in the same way as field marshals of the Army, whose rank was created by George II two years later. It is therefore with Norris that the sequence of admirals of the fleet in this book begins. After 1734, with only one interval, the rank continued to be filled until the present time.

Promotion to this rank was thereafter normally (though not invariably) by seniority, through the lists of each squadron in turn. Thus the senior rear-admiral of the Red, when a vacancy occurred in the next higher rank, would become the junior vice-admiral of the Blue and so on up to the rank of admiral of the fleet, of whom there was, until 1821, only one at a time. This arrangement, and the titles that went with it, remained in existence until 1864, when the system of dividing flag officers between coloured squadrons was abolished. The admiral of the fleet's flag remained the national flag (the Union flag) worn at the mainmast. That of all other admirals was thereafter a white flag with the red cross of St George, differenced in the case of vice-admirals and rear-admirals by one or two red roundels respectively. At the same time all ships of the Navy adopted the white ensign, which from then on was allotted solely to warships, and the blue ensign was allotted to other vessels operated by the government. The red ensign, previously the national flag of all British ships except those in the White or Blue squadrons, was reserved for British-registered merchantmen, fishing boats and privately-owned vessels of all kinds.

As long as promotion was by seniority, and no provision was made for compulsory retirement on grounds of age or fitness, officers became admirals of the fleet at an advanced age. Nevertheless, some clung tenaciously to life and office. Sir John Norris [1], appointed at the age of seventy-four, lived to be eighty-nine. The Honourable John Forbes [8] was admiral of the fleet for fifteen years until his death in 1796 at the age of eighty-two. Sir Peter Parker [10], appointed in 1799, was seventy-eight when he died in 1811. On Parker's death, the vacancy thereby created was given to William, Duke of Clarence [11], admiral of the White and third son of George III. Clarence was only forty-six years old and in good health, so that a promotion blockage immediately resulted.

Not until the coronation of George IV (Prince Regent when his naval brother became admiral of the fleet) ten years later was this problem addressed. In the celebrations marking his accession, the two senior generals in the Army were promoted to field marshal, and the second senior officer in the Navy, the Earl of St Vincent [12], admiral of the Red, was made an admiral of the fleet on 19 July 1821. St Vincent's death two years later left Clarence once more the sole admiral of the fleet until his accession as William IV in June 1830. The new king then gave up his naval rank, but appointed three new admirals of the fleet, William Williams Freeman [13], Lord Gambier [14] and Sir Charles Pole [15], who died in 1832, 1833 and 1830 (three months after being promoted) respectively. In subsequent years, there were usually two admirals of the fleet in the Navy List, though at times the figure dropped to one, as it did on the death of Sir George Cockburn [20] in 1853. After Sir Thomas Martin [19] died in 1854, the rank was left vacant until 1857, when Sir Charles Ogle [21] was promoted. The reason for this interregnum appears to have been that the next senior officer to Martin was Admiral Thomas Gosselin, who had not been to sea since 1809 and was in poor mental health. The latter circumstance was held to disqualify him from being appointed head of his Service, but the Admiralty was reluctant to pass over him, so the post was left vacant for three years until his death in 1857.

The naval reforms of 1851, introducing a system of compulsory retirement for officers, stipulated that the number of active flag officers was to be gradually reduced to 99 exclusive of admirals of the fleet, for which no number was specified (there were in fact two in post at that time). In 1863 an establishment of three was authorized and, after 1870, all admirals of the fleet were required to retire on half-pay on reaching the age of 70, or (if earlier) ten years after last hauling down their flag. Admirals on the active list in 1870 could, if they so chose, be promoted to admiral of the fleet and placed permanently on half-pay, supernumerary to the three on the establishment, when they reached the normal retirement age of their rank. In some cases these rules resulted in admirals who elected for permanent half-pay being promoted to admirals of the fleet ahead of those senior to them who, though on half-pay, remained on the active list held against established posts. Thus Sir Henry Keppel [36], who was six years junior to Sir Provo Wallis [37] as an admiral, became an admiral of the fleet before him because Keppel was promoted on electing for permanent half-pay, and was held supernumerary to the three established posts, whereas Wallis chose to remain on the establishment.

Wallis's promotion arose from a special proviso allowing captains who had commanded a major (or "rated") combatant vessel, prior to the end of hostilities in 1815, to retain their existing right to be promoted by seniority, as vacancies occurred, up to admiral of the fleet. These officers were allowed to remain on the active list, irrespective of age, held against the posts established for their rank. As was the case with all other commissioned officers of the Navy at this time, they were placed on half-pay unless actually employed. Wallis became an admiral of the fleet in 1877 at the age of 86 and lived to the age of 101, blocking the promotion of his juniors in the meanwhile.

Retired admirals otherwise qualified for promotion to the rank could be promoted to admiral of the fleet on the retired list, subject to a maximum of three in this category at any one time. Promotion by special Order in Council allowed admirals, whose services in a particular post were required after they reached the age of sixty-five, to be promoted to admiral of the fleet in excess of the establishment, so that they could remain on the active list until the age of seventy. Both Lord Walter Kerr [56] and Lord Fisher [58] were promoted in this way

By 1914 there were three active and six retired admirals of the fleet. In addition, the King, George V [64], was an admiral of the fleet, and there were three honorary admirals of the fleet, viz, the Emperor Nicholas II of Russia [60], the German Emperor William II [47] and the latter's brother, Grand Admiral Prince Henry of Prussia [62]. Of these, the two Germans disclaimed their British appointments on the outbreak of war with the United Kingdom in August 1914 and the Emperor of Russia was murdered by the Bolsheviks in July 1918. With the promotion of Jellicoe [68] and Beatty [69] in April 1919, the number of admirals of the fleet on the active list was increased to five. On the outbreak of the Second World War in September 1939, there were five active and five retired admirals of the fleet. The Duke of Windsor [84], who had become an admiral of the fleet at the beginning of his brief reign as Edward VIII, was included among the five on the active list. His brother and successor, George VI [86], was also an admiral of the fleet, but listed separately. The five retired admirals of the fleet were then restored to the active list, where they and all their successors remained for life, in the same way as had always been the custom for field marshals in the Army and marshals of the Royal Air Force. At the end of the war there were eleven admirals of the fleet, among them George VI and the Duke of Windsor. In 1995, at the time of the Betts Report, there were nine officers in this rank, including the royal consort, Philip, Duke of Edinburgh [99], but none were in actual employment.

Of the 115 British admirals of the fleet, three, namely the Emperor Nicholas II of Russia [60], the German Emperor William II [47] and the latter's brother, Prince Henry of Prussia [62] (a Grand Admiral in the Imperial German Navy) held honorary rank. Another three, though they had been full-time naval officers (two of them taking part in major battles at sea), only became admirals of the fleet when royal duties obliged them to give up the sea. These were George V [64] and George VI [86], both of whom were younger sons who had not been expected to succeed to the throne, and Philip, Duke of Edinburgh [99], consort of Elizabeth II. Edward VII [44] was made an honorary admiral of the fleet when Prince of Wales, and his grandson Edward VIII [84] served briefly as a cadet at the Royal Naval College. The only British sovereign to become an admiral of the fleet before becoming heir to the throne was William IV (Duke of Clarence) [11]. Including this prince, but excluding the remainder of those listed above, there were 107 admirals of the fleet who reached their rank through the normal course of promotion in the period covered by this book, and it is only these 107 who are included in the analysis given below.

THE PATH TO PROMOTION

It is a truism that in any profession it is necessary to stay alive in order to achieve promotion, though this is never as easy for a sea officer as for a landsman. He is equally subject to the ordinary hazards of existence in the time at which he lives, with all the additional risks arising from the perils of the sea and the violence of the enemy. It is impossible to calculate how many potential admirals of the fleet never survived storm, battle or unhealthy climates to outlive or outperform their contemporaries. Of those that did, seven were in ships lost by storm, one in a ship lost by collision, and four in ships lost as the result of enemy action, including Sir Philip Vian [98], who had two ships sunk under him by air attack in the Second World War. At least ten suffered from illnesses serious enough to be recorded. About ninety were in combat either on land or at sea (some many times and several in both elements), and eighteen were wounded (eleven while serving ashore). Several became prisoners of war, though most of these were soon either rescued or released in accordance with the civilized practice of former times, by which captured officers were exchanged with those of equal rank. Ashore, they fought in naval brigades or landing parties in a list including China, the Crimea, Egypt, India, New Zealand, Spain, South Africa, the Sudan and the United States. Six took part in the relief of the International Legations at Peking (Beijing) in 1900. Afloat, they were present at most major engagements in the history of the Navy, though there was only one future admiral of the fleet at Trafalgar, compared with fifteen at Jutland. Of those that saw combat, three were awarded the Victoria

5

Cross, four the Distinguished Service Cross, twelve the Distinguished Service Order, and thirty-six were mentioned in despatches, some more than once, with the record being held by Sir George Cockburn, who was mentioned eleven times. Out of combat, three received awards from the Royal Humane Society for courage in saving life at sea.

Until the reforms of the mid-nineteenth century all that a captain had to do to become an admiral of the fleet was to outlive his contemporaries. Because promotion to the flag ranks was by seniority, it was demonstrably an advantage to become a captain at a young age. This was quite feasible in the period when promotion up to the rank of captain was by selection regardless of seniority. Of the first thirty admirals of the fleet, who reached this rank in the period between 1734 to 1868, the average age on promotion to lieutenant was eighteen years and eight months and, to captain, twenty years and six months. The youngest to become a lieutenant was Peter Parker [10], promoted not merely to lieutenant but also to commander at the age of fourteen, and the oldest was John Norris [1], promoted at the age of twenty-nine. Norris was also the oldest on promotion to captain, at the age of thirty-three, and it was only his remarkable longevity that brought him to the rank of admiral of the fleet some forty-four years later. The youngest to become a captain was Thomas Cochrane [28], who was then aged nineteen. Of the next thirty, who became admirals of the fleet between 1869 and 1913, the average age on promotion to lieutenant was twenty years and six months, and on promotion to captain twenty-nine years and six months. The final members of this group had become captains in the 1870s and 1880s, by which time their average age on promotion had risen to 35.

As long as this system was in force, not even the greatest achievements could bring promotion to admiral of the fleet. The reader will search these pages in vain for such major figures as Barham, Collingwood, Duncan or Rodney. Even Nelson would have had to survive another twenty-nine years after Trafalgar and reach the age of 86 before succeeding Sir Charles Nugent [16] in 1844. At all periods the limited establishment prevented the promotion of many deserving officers. So it is that several distinguished admirals of the Second World War period do not appear in this book, while many lesser-known ones, as well those British and foreign royal personages who were made admirals of the fleet for dynastic reasons, are included.

The Navy was some two hundred years ahead of the Army (where until 1870 only artillery and engineer officers were actually required to have any formal professional training) in demanding some evidence of technical competence in its officers. The requirement for midshipmen to have spent a specified period at sea and to have passed an Examination Board before becoming eligible for promotion to lieutenant dated back to the reforms introduced by Samuel Pepys. Even though it was possible for a well-connected individual to evade the letter of these regulations, or to count on the indulgence of his examiners, there was general agreement that ships and, more especially, fleets were too valuable to be entrusted to incompetents. As there were always fewer commands than there were officers qualified to fill them, it was not difficult for the Admiralty to select capable men to fill them, but the system of promotion by seniority meant that failure to be appointed to a ship or a squadron did not prevent an officer from continuing to rise in rank.

AIDS TO SELECTION

In all professions, patronage or "net-working" brings an advantage. Forty-four admirals of the fleet were the sons, grandsons or nephews (sometimes all three) of flag officers or captains, and twenty-eight stood in the same relationships to peers or baronets. Six were connected with the Royal Family. Of their wives, twenty-one were related to peers or baronets and ten were the daughters, granddaughters or nieces of captains or flag officers, with many falling into both categories. Several others came from wealthy families or had fortunes of their own.

Those who are favourably noticed inevitably have a better chance of promotion than those who, though otherwise equally well qualified, find themselves at some critical time under a spiteful or prejudiced superior. At the same time, those lucky enough to be in the right place at the right time need the additional quality of ambition to take advantage of their opportunities. From the second half of the nineteenth century, specialization brought a clear benefit and a total of twenty-five gunnery officers and twelve torpedo officers became admirals of the fleet. Appointment to a flagship, often at the nomination of the admiral concerned, generally carried the likelihood of further promotion. Fourteen future admirals of the fleet served as flag lieutenants (often to their fathers or uncles) and thirty-five as flag captains. Sixteen served in royal yachts. Ashore, twenty-one sat as Members of Parliament in the House of Commons and twenty-two, late in their careers, joined the House of Lords, all except two as peers of first creation.

Despite the statistical information presented above, this book is intended as a work of synthesis rather than analysis, reflecting the author's professional career as a museologist and his ivory-towered belief that the prime scholarly function of a curator (or curatrix) is taxonomy, the science of classification. Thus it is offered to historians and cataloguers as a convenient tool for use in research or study, as a supplement to existing knowledge and a guide to further areas for study. Other writers or researchers may find here ideas for fuller biographies, documentaries, screenplays or historical fiction. To members of the Royal Navy and its various reserves and auxiliaries, past, present and future, it is offered as a record of those who reached the highest rank their Service had to offer.

NOTE ON THE RATING
OF SAILING WARSHIPS

During the period covered by this book, major sailing combatant vessels of the Royal Navy, including those with auxiliary steam engines when these came to be fitted, were divided into six rates, according to the number of their guns. 1st, 2nd and 3rd-rates were ships of the line, carrying their guns on two or three decks. 4th-rates were generally considered too weak to stand in the line of battle, and were mostly employed as convoy escorts for protection against commerce raiders, or as ships of force on distant stations. 5th and 6th-rates were respectively large and small frigates, defined as ships that carried all their guns on a single deck.

THE BIOGRAPHIES OF THE ADMIRALS OF THE FLEET

ALFRED ERNEST ALBERT

HRH Duke of Edinburgh, Duke of Saxe-Coburg and Gotha, KG, KT, KP, GCB, GCSI, GCMG, GCIE, GCVO (1844–1900) **[49]**

Prince Alfred, the second son and fourth child of Queen Victoria, was born at Windsor Castle, Berkshire, on 6 August 1844. Destined for a naval career, he joined the frigate *Euryalus* as a cadet in February 1858 and served in this ship on the Mediterranean and Cape of Good Hope stations before returning home in August 1861. In June 1862 he was appointed a midshipman in the 86-gun screw ship *St George*, in which he spent the next few months in the Channel, West Indies and Mediterranean. In October 1862 a military coup deposed the unpopular King Otto of the Hellenes. His subjects held a national referendum and, by 230,016 out of the 241,202 votes cast, elected Prince Alfred to the vacant crown, hoping that a young British prince would rule as a constitutional monarch. A prior agreement between the United Kingdom, France and Russia that no member of their royal houses would become a candidate for the Greek throne obliged him to decline. In March 1863 the Greeks elected Prince William of Schleswig-Holstein-Glucksburg, whose father became King Christian IX of Denmark in November 1863. King Christian's daughter, Alexandra, married Prince Alfred's eldest brother, the Prince of Wales, later Edward VII **[44]**. In conjunction with these dynastic arrangements, the Prince of Wales renounced his right of succession to the childless Duke Ernest II of Saxe-Coburg and Gotha (Duke Ernest's previous heir had been his younger brother, Albert, the Prince Consort, the Prince of Wales's father, who died in December 1861). The succession to this German duchy was then settled on Prince Alfred, as next in line to the Prince of Wales.

Alfred returned to naval duty and was promoted to lieutenant on 24 February 1863, when he was appointed to the corvette *Racoon* as her fourth lieutenant. He left this ship on his promotion to captain on 23 February 1866, followed by a peerage on being created Duke of Edinburgh on 24 May 1866. In January 1867 Edinburgh was given command of the frigate *Galatea* and began a long cruise taking him to Brazil, South Africa and the Australian colonies, where, at Sydney, he was

9

shot and slightly wounded by an Irish nationalist, who was promptly arrested, tried and hanged. After returning to the United Kingdom in mid–1868, he spent a further year at sea in *Galatea* in which he visited India, China and Japan. On 23 January 1874, at St Petersburg, he married the Grand Duchess Marie, only daughter of Alexander II, Emperor of Russia. A second wedding, by Anglican rites, was held in Westminster Abbey, but the service was not attended by Queen Victoria, who disapproved of this alliance with the Romanov dynasty. Edinburgh, a heavy drinker in a time of heavy drinkers, was not one of his mother's favourites, though he tried to act as peace-maker between her and the Navy (which she never forgave for denying her consort, Prince Albert, the rank of admiral of the fleet). He also incurred his mother's displeasure for objecting to the behaviour of John Brown, the Queen's Highland Servant.

Edinburgh did not return to sea until 25 February 1876, when he was given command of the armoured ship *Sultan* in the Mediterranean, with Prince Louis of Battenberg [74] (a nephew of his sister, Princess Alice) as one of his junior officers. He served under Vice-Admiral Hornby [45] during the international crisis of 1878, when the Mediterranean Fleet was sent to Constantinople (Istanbul) to be met by a Russian army on the outskirts of the city. There, he found Louis's brother, Prince Alexander of Battenberg, serving with the Russians, and invited him aboard his ship. This brought him a rebuke from the Queen, who told him that everyone would say the Battenbergs were Russian spies, and accused him of "extreme thoughtlessness". In June 1878 Edinburgh became captain of the armoured ship *Black Prince*, in the Channel Squadron, followed by promotion to rear-admiral on 26 November 1878. From November 1879 to November 1882 he was admiral superintendent of naval reserves, based at Harwich, with his flag first in the corvette *Penelope* and then in the battleship *Hercules*. He was promoted to vice-admiral on 30 November 1882 and commanded the Channel Squadron, with his flag in the armoured ship *Minotaur*, from December 1883 to December 1884. Edinburgh was C-in-C, Mediterranean, with his flag in the armoured ship *Alexandra*, from March 1886 to March 1889, and promoted to admiral on 18 Oct 1887. Between August 1890 and June 1893 he was C-in-C, Devonport, and was promoted to admiral of the fleet on 3 June 1893.

The Duke of Edinburgh succeeded his uncle as Duke of Saxe-Coburg and Gotha on 22 August 1893. The duchy was by this time part of the German Empire, though it still retained autonomy in internal affairs. A special Order in Council allowed Duke Alfred to retain his place in the Navy List. Despite his own reserved and somewhat distant character, he overcame the resentment of his German subjects at the arrival of a British admiral to rule over them. He displayed an interest in local agriculture and industry, indulged his taste for sporting activities, and, himself an enthusiastic rather than a talented violinist, became a patron of music. His lavish life style (including the retention of a London residence) ran him into debt, and to satisfy his creditors he was obliged to sell his valuable stamp collection. It was bought by his brother, the Prince of Wales, the future Edward VII [44]. The Prince presented it to his own second son, the future George V [64], whose interest in this subject had been awakened when serving under Edinburgh as a young officer, and who went on to establish a philatelic collection of international importance.

Duke Alfred's declining years were marred by the death of his unmarried only son, Prince Alfred, who had never enjoyed robust health and shot himself in mysterious circumstances in February 1899. Duke Alfred himself died from cancer of the throat on 30 July 1900, at his palace of Schloss Rosenau, Coburg, and was buried in the family mausoleum there. Although all four of his daughters married and had issue, the Salic Law prevented them from succeeding to his throne. The succession therefore passed to his younger brother, Queen Victoria's third son, the Duke of Connaught. When Connaught disclaimed the title, it passed to the teenage Charles Edward, 2nd Duke of Albany, whose father, Leopold, had been Victoria's fourth and youngest son. The dukedom of Edinburgh became extinct until revived in November 1947 for the benefit of Lieutenant Philip Mountbatten [99], consort of the future Queen Elizabeth II.

ANSON
George, Lord Anson (1697–1762) [5]

George Anson, the second son of William Anson of Shugborough Hall, Colwich, Staffordshire, was born on 23 April 1697. His mother's sister was married to Thomas Parker, later Earl of Macclesfield and Lord Chancellor of England from May 1718 to January 1725. Anson served in the Navy as a volunteer during the War of the Spanish Succession, joining the 4th-rate *Ruby* on 2 February 1711 and subsequently moving to the 3rd-rate *Monmouth*. On 17 March 1716, while serving in the Baltic fleet under Sir John Norris [1], he was promoted to lieutenant in the 4th-rate *Hampshire*, where he remained until December 1717. Anson was appointed second lieutenant of the 4th-rate *Montague* in March 1718, in a fleet sent to the Mediterranean to prevent a Spanish occupation of Naples and Sicily. He was present at the battle of Cape Passaro (31 July 1718) and transferred to the flagship, the 2nd-rate *Barfleur*, on 2 October 1719.

Anson was in June 1722 appointed commander of the sloop *Weazell*, employed on anti-smuggling duties in the North Sea. In February 1723 he became captain of the 6th-rate *Scarborough*, operating against pirates and Spanish privateers around the Bahamas. In July 1728 he was given command of the 6th-rate *Garland* and served on the coast of South Carolina. He became a popular figure in the colony, where Anson County was named in his honour. In 1730–31 Anson was captain of the 5th-rate *Diamond* in the Channel, before going back to the Carolinas as captain of the 6th-rate *Squirell*. After returning home in June 1735, he was employed between 1737 and 1739 on commerce protection duties, first off the West

11

African coast and then in the West Indies, in command of the 3rd-rate *Centurion*.

On the outbreak of the War of Jenkins's Ear in October 1739, Anson, in *Centurion*, was appointed commodore of a small squadron of six warships and two auxiliaries, and tasked to attack Spanish settlements and shipping in the Pacific. Delays at the Admiralty resulted in his orders, drafted in January 1740, not reaching him until the following June. He was provided with a total of 1,900 men, made up of untrained marines supplied by the Army and pensioners from the Royal Naval Hospital, Greenwich. The expedition eventually left Portsmouth on 18 September 1740 and soon ran into bad weather. After rounding Cape Horn, Anson reached the island of Juan Fernandez in June 1741, where two of his ships later joined him. After several weeks' rest and refitting, he decided to put the survivors of the three crews (335 men out of 961) into *Centurion*, the only ship still sea-worthy. He then raided the Spanish port of Paita, Chile, before crossing the Pacific in 1742 to wait for the annual Spanish treasure ship from Manila, in the Philippines. Failing to make contact, he reached Macao on the Chinese mainland, with his crew reduced by scurvy to barely two hundred men. Finally, on 20 June 1743, he captured the treasure galleon *Nuestra Senhora de Cabadonga*, after which he sailed for home via the Cape of Good Hope. Anson arrived at Spithead on 15 June 1744, having circumnavigated the globe and acquired an immense quantity of bullion. This, valued at half a million pounds in the currency of the time (more than a quarter of the Royal Navy's annual vote), was then driven to London in a triumphant convoy of thirty-two wagons.

The prize money, with Anson entitled to one-eighth as commodore and two-eighths as captain, made him an extremely rich man and gave him a place in political circles. He was promoted to rear-admiral of the Blue on 19 June 1744, but refused the promotion because the Admiralty refused to confirm his first lieutenant as captain (originally denied on the grounds that Anson, although commodore, was at the relevant time in command of only his own ship). His conduct throughout the expedition was an inspiration to his crews. In an age of keen social distinctions, he helped in carrying the sick ashore, and worked as a carpenter when his ship was under repair. His navigational notes proved of great value to map-makers and he pointed out the potential value of the Falkland Islands as a British naval base.

The United Kingdom formally entered the War of the Austrian Succession on 11 April 1744. A change of ministry in November 1744 brought a new First Lord to the Admiralty (the Duke of Bedford) with Anson himself being appointed to the Board. On 19 June 1745, following an increase in the establishment of flag officers from the original nine, he was promoted from captain to rear-admiral of the White. In July, still a lord commissioner of the Admiralty, he became vice-admiral of the Blue and was given command of the Western Squadron, in the Channel, though the poor state of his ships delayed his sailing until November 1746. Flying his flag in the new 3rd-rate *Yarmouth*, he cruised off the northern coast of

France until returning to Portsmouth in February 1747 without having sighted the enemy. In April 1747 Anson again put to sea commanding the Western Squadron, in the Channel and off the French Atlantic coast, with his flag in the 2nd-rate *Prince George*. In a major fleet action off Cape Finisterre (3 May 1747), he captured six French men-of-war and six Indiamen, together with various other merchant ships and privateers. Their cargoes included the pay chests for the French garrison of Canada. With a major victory to his credit and prizes totalling around two million pounds, he was raised to the peerage as Lord Anson, Baron of Soberton and promoted to vice-admiral of the Red. He married Lady Elizabeth Yorke, daughter of the first Earl of Hardwicke, Lord Chancellor of England, and a political ally. The couple set up home at Carshalton before moving to Moor Park, Northwood, Middlesex (now a golf club).

Lord Anson was promoted to admiral of the Blue on 12 May 1748. He became First Lord of the Admiralty, in succession to his friend and supporter the Earl of Sandwich, on 22 June 1751 and retained this post until November 1756, when the Duke of Newcastle's ministry fell after a series of British disasters at the beginning of the Seven Years War. In June 1757 he became an admiral of the White. When Newcastle joined Pitt's ministry on 2 July 1757, Anson once more became First Lord and continued to hold this office until his death. While at the Admiralty, he did much to reform the Navy. He made a point of visiting and inspecting dockyards, and succeeded for a time in at least reducing the corruption invariably associated with defence contractors. He improved the standard of medical care in the fleet and encouraged research into the cause of scurvy. The Articles of War were revised. Dress regulations were issued for officers, introducing the blue coat with white facings later adopted by almost every navy as standard nautical wear. This combination of colours was said to have been taken from a riding habit worn by the Duchess of Bedford, whose husband had been First Lord of the Admiralty from 1744 to 1748. Fighting Instructions were revised, allowing commanders to act in accordance with the spirit rather than the letter of tactical doctrine. The Marines were established as a corps under Admiralty control, in place of the Army's marine regiments. An improved system of arranging warships into various rates, according to the number of their guns, was introduced.

In July 1758, after Sir Edward Hawke [7] had suddenly hauled down his flag in protest at an imagined slight, Anson felt obliged to take his place in command of the Western Squadron. With his flag in the 1st-rate *Royal George*, he continued the blockade of the French Atlantic naval bases. Though not in favour of Pitt's policy of raiding the French coast, he provided ships to cover descents on Cherbourg (August 1758) and St Malo (September 1758). Anson was promoted to admiral of the fleet on 30 July 1761. He died at Moor Park on 6 June 1762, two years after his wife, and was buried at his native Colwich. He had no children and his barony became extinct.

ASHMORE
Sir Edward Beckwith, GCB, DSC (1919-) **[109]**

Edward Ashmore was born at Queenstown, County Cork, Ireland, on 11 December 1919, the elder son of Lieutenant (later Vice-Admiral) L H Ashmore and his wife, Tamara Vasilevna, whom he had met and married while serving in Russia, survivors of whose family became refugees from the Bolsheviks. Like his younger brother, who also became an admiral, Edward Ashmore accompanied his parents as they moved to various stations, rather than being sent to boarding school as was more usual at that period. He was educated at various schools at Alverstoke (Gosport, Hants), Claremont (Cape Province, South Africa) and Yardley Court (Tonbridge, Kent), before joining the Navy as a cadet at the Royal Naval College, Dartmouth, in September 1933. He went to sea in the cadet training cruiser *Frobisher* from May to July 1937 and joined the battleship *Rodney*, flagship of the Home Fleet, as a midshipman on 1 September 1937. Ashmore was appointed in January 1938 to the cruiser *Birmingham* on the China station, at a time of increasing international tension with the Japanese. After returning home overland via Manchukuo (Manchuria), Siberia, Russia and Germany, he reached the United Kingdom on 26 August 1939 and was promoted to sub-lieutenant on 1 September 1939, just before the outbreak of the Second World War.

Ashmore joined the destroyer *Jupiter* on 3 January 1940 and took part in various operations in the North Sea, the Norwegian campaign, and in the Channel (with a brief detachment to Force H at Gibraltar in February 1941). He was promoted to lieutenant on 1 January 1941 and left *Jupiter* in June 1941 on appointment as first lieutenant of the destroyer *Middleton*. This ship, commissioned at the end of the year, spent most of 1942 as a fleet escort, covering the Atlantic and North Russian convoys, with a brief detachment to the Mediterranean in June 1942 to escort a relief convoy to Malta, where Ashmore gained the DSC. In August 1942, he was sent to North Russia to help organize the return of the survivors of the ill-fated convoy PQ17. In December 1942 he married Elizabeth Mary Doveton Sturdee, a second officer in the Women's Royal Naval Service, daughter of Rear-Admiral Sir Lionel Sturdee and granddaughter of Sir Doveton Sturdee **[73]**. They later had a family of a son and two daughters, the younger of whom was tragically killed in a rail disaster at Hither Green, London, in November 1967. Between February and May 1943 Ashmore served in *King Alfred*, Lancing, Sussex, training candidates for hostilities-only commissions.

Ashmore then decided to specialize as a signals officer and from June to December 1943 attended signals and radar courses. He was then posted to the staff of the C-in-C, Home Fleet, as Fleet Wireless Assistant in the battleship *Duke of York*, where he served until September 1944. He was then appointed Squadron Signal Officer of the 4th Cruiser Squadron and flag lieutenant of the rear-admiral commanding the Cruiser Squadron,

British Pacific Fleet, and took part in operations supporting the United States landing on Okinawa. Ashmore served in the aircraft carrier *Implacable*, conducting air attacks on the Japanese-held island of Truk, before returning to the flag in the cruiser *Swiftsure*. The flag was subsequently transferred to the cruiser *Newfoundland* which formed part of the British Carrier Task Group and came under kamikaze air attack during July and early August 1945. After the Japanese sued for peace, Ashmore, who was later mentioned in despatches for his services with the British Pacific Fleet, sailed into Tokyo Bay in company with *Duke of York* on 27 August and was on board the USS *Missouri* to witness the formal surrender ceremony.

Ashmore returned home in January 1945 to attend the School of Slavonic Studies, Cambridge University, and qualified as a First Class Interpreter in Russian. During 1946 and 1957 he was Assistant Naval Attaché at Moscow and Helsingfors. On 30 September 1947, he was appointed a lieutenant-commander on the staff of the Royal Naval Signals School *Mercury*, Petersfield, Hampshire, in charge of instruction in the technical aspects of wireless equipment. Ashmore was promoted to substantive lieutenant-commander on 1 January 1948. Early in 1949 he qualified at the Royal Naval Staff College, Greenwich.

On 15 October 1949 Ashmore joined the aircraft carrier *Vengeance*, flagship of the Third Aircraft Carrier Squadron, based at Portsmouth, as squadron communications officer. He was promoted on 31 December 1950. He then went to the Admiralty as Assistant Director (Communications) in the Radio Equipment Department, where he remained until appointed on 23 June 1953 to command the frigate *Alert*, despatch vessel of Sir Charles Lambe [103], C-in-C, Far East Fleet. He returned to *Mercury* in October 1954 as second in command. On 30 June 1955 Ashmore was promoted to captain, so becoming the youngest captain since Beatty [69]. He attended the Joint Service Staff College, Latimer, Buckinghamshire, before becoming Chief Signals Officer, HQ C-in-C Allied Forces, Northern Europe, Oslo. He returned to sea in October 1958, as Captain (F) of the Sixth Frigate Squadron, commanding the frigate *Blackpool* in the Mediterranean Fleet. From June 1960 to December 1961 he was at the Admiralty as Director (until November 1960, Deputy Director) of Naval Plans. Ashmore became Director of Plans, MOD, under the first Chief of the Defence Staff, Lord Mountbatten [102] in December 1961 and remained there as Chairman of the Service Directors of Plans until January 1963. At Mountbatten's insistence he was made a commodore in March 1962.

During 1963 and 1964 Ashmore was Commander, British Forces, Caribbean Area, Senior Naval Officer, West Indies, and NATO Island Commander, Bermuda, with the task of providing tri-service support to the local Commonwealth and colonial authorities and liaison with neighbouring United States and Netherlands commanders. He was extensively at sea, flying his broad pendant in a number of the ships under his command, including the frigates *Londonderry*, *Ursa*, *Whirlwind*, *Tartar*, *Leander*, *Rothesay* and *Defender*, and dealt with various periods of tension in the area, notably in British Honduras (Belize), British Guiana (Guyana) and the Bahamas. After returning home, he was promoted to rear-admiral on 7 January 1965 and was appointed Assistant Chief of Defence Staff (Signals) at the Ministry of Defence. In April 1967 Ashmore became Flag Officer, Second-in-Command, Far Eastern Fleet, based at Singapore. He flew his flag in a variety of ships in the Pacific and Indian Oceans, including *Kent*, *Victorious*, *Bulwark*, *Eagle*, *Albion*, *Hermes*, *Devonshire*, *Triumph*, *Defender*, *Fearless*, *Intrepid* and *Fife*, and commanded the substantial naval covering force off Aden at the end of British sovereignty there in November 1967. Ashmore was promoted to vice-admiral on 24 July 1968. Later that year he became Vice-Chief of the Naval Staff at the Ministry of Defence. He was promoted to admiral on 4 November 1970 and awarded the KCB in January 1971.

From September 1971 to December 1973 Sir Edward Ashmore was C-in-C Western Fleet (later renamed C-in-C Fleet when the Far East Fleet was abolished) and NATO C-in-C Eastern Atlantic (CINCEASTLANT) and C-in-C Channel (CINCHAN) with his HQ at Northwood, Middlesex. Once more he took every chance to fly his flag, both on exercises and ceremonial visits, in ships under his operational command, including *Antrim*, *Ark Royal*, *Albion*, *Fearless*, *Fife* and *Bristol*. Between March 1974 and March 1977 he was at the Ministry of Defence as First Sea Lord, where he had to deal with a major defence review by the Labour government of the day and the Turkish invasion of Cyprus. When the death in office of Marshal of the Royal Air Force Sir Andrew Humphrey in January 1977 created an unplanned vacancy as the Chief of the Defence Staff, Ashmore was appointed in his place, with promotion to admiral of the fleet on 9 February 1977. The post was reclaimed by the RAF with the appointment of Marshal of the Royal Air Force Sir Neil Cameron on 31 July 1977, and Sir Edward Ashmore went onto retired pay, remaining on the active list, on 1 August 1977. He returned briefly to active duty to represent the British Government at the ceremonies held in Honolulu in September 1995 to mark the Fiftieth Anniversary of the Japanese surrender at the end of the Second World War.

AUSTEN
Sir FRANCIS WILLIAM, GCB (1774–1865) [25]

Francis Austen was born on 23 April 1774, fourth son in a family of six boys and two girls. His father was the Reverend George Austen, at that time Rector of Deane and Steventon, near Basingstoke, Hampshire, and his mother was Cassandra, daughter of the Reverend Dr Theophilus Leigh, for some fifty years Master of Balliol College, Oxford. Warren Hastings, the first Governor-General of Bengal, was an influential friend of both families.

16

Francis's youngest brother, Charles, also joined the Navy and died on active service in October 1850 during the Second Burma War, as C-in-C, East Indies. Jane Austen, the younger of their sisters, became the most famous member of the family and her novels (especially *Persuasion* and *Mansfield Park*) contain many allusions to sea officers and their families, with details based upon the careers of her two naval brothers.

Francis Austen (known on his family first as "Fly" and later as "Frank") was educated at the Royal Naval Academy, Portsmouth, from April 1786 to December 1788, before being appointed a volunteer in the 5th-rate *Perseverance*. He served in this ship on the East Indies station, where in December 1789 he was appointed as a midshipman. From there he joined the 3rd-rate *Crown*, under Commodore the Honourable William Cornwallis, C-in-C, East Indies, and later transferred with him back to *Perseverance* and then to the 5th-rate *Minerva*. They were engaged in the blockade of the coast of Mysore and in November 1792 exchanged fire with a French frigate. Austen was promoted to lieutenant in the brig *Despatch* on 28 December 1792, where he served for a short time before returning to *Minerva* as a supernumerary. Earlier in 1792 the marriage of his eldest brother, James, made him a family connection of Captain James Gambier [14]. Austen returned home in 1793, after the outbreak of war with Revolutionary France.

In 1794 Austen was appointed to the sloop *Lark*, employed in the Downs and the North Sea. Through the influence of Rear-Admiral James Gambier he moved to the 5th-rate *Andromeda* in May 1795. Shortly afterwards he transferred to the 2nd-rate *Prince George*, where he was placed by the local admiral as eighth of her nine lieutenants, though by seniority he should have been third. He then moved to the 2nd-rate *Glory*, which sailed with a convoy for the West Indies in December 1796, but was driven back to Portsmouth by foul weather. Austen then joined the 5th-rate *Shannon*, only to find that her captain was a sadistic monster. He went on half-pay from June to September 1796, but was then appointed first lieutenant of the new 5th-rate *Triton*, under the command of an old shipmate from his days in *Perseverance*. They captured several small ships in the Channel, but Gambier felt that his protégé would have better prospects of promotion in the Mediterranean. He accordingly appointed him to the 5th-rate *Seahorse* in March 1797. After covering the unsuccessful British raid on Ostend, (19–20 May 1797), where rising surf made it impossible to re-embark the troops, Austen joined the Mediterranean Fleet under St Vincent [12]. In February 1798 he was appointed first lieutenant of the 2nd-rate *London* and a year later became commander of the sloop *Peterel*.

Austen commanded *Peterel* in the Mediterranean for the next eighteen months. He captured or destroyed some forty minor vessels, was present at the capture of a small French squadron on passage from Jaffa to Toulon (19 June 1799), drove two French vessels ashore off Marseilles and captured a third, the brig *Ligurienne* (21 March 1800). In recognition of this action he was mentioned in despatches and was promoted to captain on 13 May 1800. Austen took part in the blockades of Genoa (May 1800) and Aboukir (August 1800), and drove off a French prize-crew from a Turkish ship of the line stranded off the Egyptian coast. In October 1800 he gave up his command of *Peterel* and returned to England. He returned to sea at the end of August 1801 in command of the 2nd-rate *Neptune*, as flag captain to Vice-Admiral James Gambier, where he remained until hostilities with France ended in October 1801. In *Neptune* Austen maintained his reputation as a captain concerned with his men's welfare, and experimented with coating cheeses with whitewash as a preservative to improve his men's diet (justifying the expense on the grounds that it would avoid waste). He got on well with Gambier and, like the rest of the Austen family, shared his Evangelical views, though these made Gambier unpopular with many other officers. Like Gambier, Austen avoided the foul language used as a matter of course by many sea officers of his time.

When the war with France was renewed in May 1803 Austen was given the task of raising and commanding a body of Sea Fencibles (the Admiralty's inshore local defence troops), based at the fashionable resort of Ramsgate, Kent. On 7 May 1804 he was given command of the 4th-rate *Leopard*, as flag captain of Rear-Admiral Sir Thomas Louis, with whom he first served in the blockade of Boulogne, and then transferred to the 3rd-rate *Canopus* in the Mediterranean. He served under Louis in Nelson's pursuit of the French fleet to the West Indies and back in the summer of 1805 and in the subsequent blockade of the Combined Fleet at Cadiz, before being detached with Louis's squadron to the Straits of Gibraltar. They thus missed the battle of Trafalgar (21 October 1805), but then rejoined the main fleet to resume the blockade of Cadiz. In December 1805 the blockading squadron sailed in pursuit of a French force heading for the West Indies. Austen was present at the subsequent battle of Santo Domingo (6 February 1806), off Spanish-held eastern Hispaniola, in the last major fleet action of the Napoleonic wars, for which he received a gold medal and the thanks of Parliament. In June 1806 he went on half-pay and, in the following month, he married a gentleman's daughter, Mary Gibson, whom he had first met when at Ramsgate. They set up home, with his mother and sisters, in Southampton and later had a family of five daughters and six sons, three of whom entered the Royal Navy. Austen's sisters were not enthusiastic at this match, as they had hoped that he would marry their close friend, Martha Lloyd, daughter of the rector of Enborne, Berkshire

Austen returned to full pay on 23 March 1807, as captain of the 3rd-rate *St Albans*. He escorted convoys to the Cape of Good Hope and St Helena, and troopships to the Peninsular War. Off the Tagus, he watched through his telescope the smoke of the battlefield of Vimiero (21 August 1808), the future Duke of Wellington's first victory over the French, and then returned home carrying wounded and prisoners of war. At the end of January 1809 he supervised the disembarkation at Portsmouth of British troops evacuated from Spain after the retreat to Corunna (La Coruña). He then served on the East Indies station, escorting a convoy to Canton (Guangzhou). There, the Chinese governor demanded his assistance against local pirates as a condition of maintaining friendly relations. At the same time, members of the crew of an East Indiaman, who had murdered a Chinese national, evaded trial by sailing with their ship. In accordance with their normal procedure, the Chinese authorities held the entire local British community collectively responsible. Austen dealt diplomatically with both of these problems and succeeded in maintaining British prestige without alienating a valuable trading partner. He received the thanks of the Admiralty, with a more tangible reward of a thousand guineas from the East India Company.

Austen left *St Albans* in September 1810 to become flag captain to Gambier as C-in-C in the Channel, blockading the French coast in the 1st-rate *Caledonia*. When Gambier's command came to an end in 1811 Austen was appointed to the 3rd-rate *Elephant*, in which he served in the North Sea, blockading the mouth of the Scheldt. During the American War of 1812 he cruised off the Azores, where he captured the 12-gun United States privateer *Swordfish* after a chase of eleven hours. He then served in the Baltic, where in 1813 he incurred the displeasure of his superiors for the excessive level of punishments he awarded (mostly for drunkenness) to his crew. *Elephant* returned to pay off in May 1814, a month after Napoleon's first abdication.

In 1815 Austen settled with his growing family, first in the Great House at Chawton, Hampshire, and then at nearby Alton, where his wife died shortly after the birth of her last child in 1823. He moved to Portsdown Lodge, near Portsmouth, in 1828, when he married Martha Lloyd, in the match that his sisters had hoped for. He became a rear-admiral of the Blue on 22 July 1830, rear-admiral of the Red on 10 January 1837, KCB at the beginning of 1837, and vice-admiral of the Blue on 28 June 1838. His second wife died without offspring in 1843. Sir Francis Austen returned to sea in December 1844, when he was appointed C-in-C, North America and West Indies, with his flag in the 4th-rate *Vindictive*. During the Venezuelan civil wars and the war between Mexico and the United States (1846–48) his ships protected British trade from attacks by privateers and continued patrols against slave-traders sailing variously under the flags of Brazil or Portugal. He became a vice-admiral of the Red on 9 November 1846 and maintained his characteristic care for detail by, on one occasion, warning an officer who had gone into the sea to swim that he was in danger from a nearby shark, "of the Blue variety".

Austen hauled down his flag for the last time in June 1848 and was promoted to admiral of the Blue on 1 August 1848 and admiral of the White on 1 July 1851. On the outbreak of the Crimean War in 1854 he was offered the appointment of C-in-C, Portsmouth, but declined on account of his advanced age. He became an admiral of the Red on 3 July 1855 and an admiral of the fleet on 27 April 1863. He died at Portsdown Lodge on 10 August 1865 and was buried in the nearby churchyard of Saints Peter and Paul, Wymering.

BACKHOUSE
Sir ROGER ROLAND CHARLES, GCB, GCVO, CMG
(1879–1939) **[88]**

Roger Backhouse was born on 24 November 1878 at Middleton Dyas, Yorkshire, the fourth son (one of twin boys) of Jonathan Backhouse, later created a baronet, and his wife, the youngest daughter of Sir John Salusbury-Trelawny, ninth baronet. He became a cadet in the training ship *Britannia* at Dartmouth in 1892 and joined the battleship *Repulse* in the Channel Squadron in 1894, with promotion to midshipman on 15 September 1894. He was appointed in October 1895 to the cruiser *Comus* on the Pacific station, from where he returned home to become an acting sub-lieutenant on 15 March 1898 at the beginning of his promotion courses. He was promoted to lieutenant on 15 March 1899 and served in the battleship *Victorious* in the Mediterranean Fleet from November 1899 to October 1900. Backhouse then attended the gunnery school *Excellent* and subsequently rejoined the Mediterranean Fleet as gunnery lieutenant successively of the battleships *Russell* (from February 1903) and *Queen* (from April 1904) until being appointed to the permanent staff of *Excellent* in July 1905. He married in 1906 Dora Louisa Findlay, the sixth daughter of a Banffshire gentleman, and later had with her a family of two sons and four daughters.

In August 1907 Backhouse was appointed gunnery officer of the new battleship *Dreadnought*, flagship of the C-in-C, Home Fleet, Vice-Admiral Sir Francis Bridgeman, at the Nore. He was promoted to commander on 31 December 1909, and returned to the staff of *Excellent* in February 1910. Backhouse went back to sea in March 1911 as commander of the battleship *Neptune*, to which Bridgeman transferred his flag. He remained there when Sir George Callaghan **[67]** succeeded Bridgeman (who then became First Sea Lord) on 5 December 1911 and transferred with the flag to the new battleship *Iron Duke* in March 1914.

On the outbreak of the First World War in August 1914 Callaghan's command was remustered as the Grand Fleet, with Sir John Jellicoe **[68]** appointed as its new C-in-C. Backhouse remained in *Iron Duke* in which he became flag captain on promotion on 1 September 1914. He left the ship in November 1915, on appointment to the cruiser *Conquest* in the Harwich Force. From there he moved on 30 November 1916 to be flag captain of the battle-cruiser *Lion*, flagship of the Battle-cruiser Force, with special responsibility for gunnery training. Backhouse was relieved on medical grounds in May 1918. After sick leave he joined the Admiralty, where he remained after the end of the war in November 1918, and served as Director of Naval Ordnance. Between September 1920 and October 1922 he was captain of the battleship *Malaya* in the Atlantic Fleet, followed by two years at the Staff Officers' Technical Course, Portsmouth, where he was promoted to rear-admiral on 3 April 1925. From May 1926 to May

1927 he commanded the Third Battle Squadron in the Atlantic Fleet, with his flag in *Iron Duke*, and then became Third Sea Lord and Controller of the Navy, responsible for ship-building, dockyards and armaments. Backhouse was promoted to vice-admiral on 10 October 1929. He remained in the Admiralty during a period of severe retrenchment culminating in the economic crisis of 1931 and the formation of a National Government under Ramsay MacDonald. In April 1932 he was appointed as Vice-Admiral commanding the First Battle Squadron and second-in-command of the Mediterranean Fleet, with his flag in the battleship *Revenge*.

After being awarded the KCB in 1933 Sir Roger Backhouse (widely known simply as "RB") was promoted to admiral on 11 February 1934. He became C-in-C, Home Fleet, with his flag successively in the battleships *Nelson* and *Rodney*, in August 1935. Believing that a fleet commander should concentrate all decisions into his own hands, he was unable to establish good working relations with his chief of staff, Rear-Admiral Bertram Ramsay, an old shipmate in *Dreadnought*. When Ramsay prepared orders on his behalf, Backhouse considered that this was tantamount to usurping his own authority as C-in-C. Ramsay came to believe that Backhouse was trying to deny him the responsibility that went with the post of a chief of staff and was relieved at his own request in December 1935. Backhouse was appointed First Sea Lord in 1938, in the Board headed by Alfred Duff Cooper in Neville Chamberlain's Cabinet. Very tall, with a determined manner and presence, capable of great charm though also of harshness to subordinates who did not reach his standards, he soon established his authority as the head of his Service. Almost immediately after taking up office he was faced with the implications of the Munich crisis. Duff Cooper resigned and his successor, Earl Stanhope, accepted the Treasury view that, with Germany appeased, the rate of naval rearmament could be reduced.

As First Sea Lord Backhouse was willing to consider innovations, but his critics saw him as prone to indecision and over-centralization. He seems to have realized that the official British strategy of sending a major fleet to Singapore to protect Australia against any Japanese aggression was no longer viable, and hinted as much to his Australian opposite number. The establishment of a German protectorate over the Czech lands in March 1939 forced the Cabinet to face the need for greater defence spending, but Backhouse did not live to see the results. He became ill in the Spring of 1939 with what was at first thought to be influenza, but was later diagnosed as a brain tumour. As his health grew worse, he left office in May and retired in June 1939. He was promoted to admiral of the fleet from the retired list on 5 July 1939 and died in London on 15 July 1939.

BATHURST
Sir DAVID BENJAMIN, GCB (1936-) [115]

Benjamin Bathurst, the son of Group Captain and Lady Ann Bathurst, was born on 27 May 1936 and educated at Eton College. He entered the Navy as a cadet in 1953 when he joined the Royal Naval College, Dartmouth, and became a midshipman on 1 September 1955. He was promoted to acting sub-lieutenant on 1 January 1957 and served during 1958 in the coastal minesweeper *Woolaston* followed by promotion to lieutenant on 1 February 1959. In 1959 he married Sarah Peto and later had with her a son and three daughters. Bathurst specialized as a naval aviator and qualified as a pilot at No 1 FTS, Royal Air Force, Linton-on-Ouse in 1960. After completing a helicopter conversion course at the Royal Naval Air Station *Seahawk*, Culdrose, Cornwall, in 1961, he served during 1962 in the ship's flight of the guided missile destroyer *Devonshire*. In 1964 he was in 737 Squadron at the Royal Naval Air Station *Osprey*, Portland, at the Central Flying School, RAF Ternhill, where he qualified as an instructor, and 706 Squadron at RNAS Culdrose. During 1965 he was an exchange officer with the Royal Australian Navy, and was based at the Royal Australian Naval Air Station *Albatross*, Nowra, New South Wales, with the Australian 723 and 725 Squadrons. Bathurst was promoted to lieutenant-commander on 1 February 1967 on appointment as senior pilot of 820 Squadron in the aircraft carrier *Eagle*. From February to October 1969 he was the commanding officer of 819 Squadron. During 1970 he served on the staff of the Director General of Naval Recruiting in the Ministry of Defence, with promotion to commander on 30 June 1970.

Bathurst returned to sea as executive officer of the guided missile destroyer *Norfolk* from February 1971 to November 1972. In February 1973 he was appointed to the Directorate of Naval Air Warfare at the MOD, where he remained until promoted to captain on 31 December 1974. From March 1975 to April 1976 he commanded the frigate *Ariadne*, after which he rejoined the Navy Department at the MOD as Naval Assistant to two successive First Sea Lords, Sir Edward Ashmore [109] and Sir Terence Lewin [110]. Bathurst became Captain (Frigates) of the Fifth Frigate Squadron, in the frigate *Minerva* in September 1978. During 1981 he attended the Royal College of Defence Studies, followed by appointment as Director of Naval Air Warfare in 1982. He was promoted to rear-admiral on 10 October 1983 and subsequently served until 1985 as Flag Officer, Second Flotilla. Between 1985 and 1986 he was Director General, Naval Manpower and Training, at the MOD, followed by promotion to vice-admiral on 22 December 1986. Bathurst remained at the MOD from 1986 to 1989 as Chief of Fleet Support, with the award of the KCB in 1987.

Sir Benjamin Bathurst was promoted to admiral on 21 April 1989. Between 1989 and 1991 he was C-in-C Fleet, with the NATO commands of C-in-C, Channel (CINCHAN) and C-in-C, Eastern Atlantic

(CINCEASTLANT). He returned to the MOD in 1991 as Vice-Chief of the Defence Staff, and remained there from 1993 to 1995 as First Sea Lord. He was promoted to admiral of the fleet on leaving office on 10 July 1995, the last officer to be awarded this rank in normal peacetime circumstances.

BATTENBERG
Prince Louis of, see MOUNTBATTEN, LOUIS ALEXANDER [74]

BEATTY
Sir DAVID RICHARD, 1st Earl Beatty, GCB, OM, GCVO, DSO (1871–1936) [69]

David Beatty was born on 17 January 1871 at Howbeck Lodge, Nantwich, Cheshire. He was the second son in a family of five children of a former subaltern of the 4th Hussars who had been obliged to resign after eloping with the wife of a brother officer. Both parties came from Anglo-Irish squirearchy and on their marriage settled in Cheshire to train horses from their family estates in Ireland. Beatty joined the Navy as a cadet in the training ship *Britannia* in 1884. In February 1886, through the influence of his mother (a forceful women, who prophesied that one day England would ring with her son's praise) he was appointed to the battleship *Alexandra*, flagship of the Duke of Edinburgh [49] as C-in-C, Mediterranean. He became a midshipman on 15 May 1886 and an acting sub-lieutenant in May 1890, at the beginning of his promotion courses. On 19 January 1892 he was appointed sub-lieutenant in the battleship *Nile* in the Mediterranean. He joined the royal yacht *Victoria and Albert* in July 1892 and, on the completion of her summer cruise, was promoted to lieutenant on 25 August 1892. Thereafter he served in the Mediterranean, successively in the corvette *Ruby* until September 1893, the battleship *Camperdown* until September 1895, and the battleship *Trafalgar* until late 1897.

During 1896 Beatty was second-in-command of a flotilla of river gunboats on the Nile, in support of the Anglo-Egyptian expedition for the re-conquest of the Sudan. After passing the Third Cataract, Beatty (with his sun helmet hit by a Sudanese bullet) took over when his commanding officer was wounded, and pushed on upstream to reach Dongola with the Army. Beatty was awarded the DSO and went home on leave. He returned to the Nile campaign in 1897, in command of the Egyptian gunboat *El Teb*. The vessel capsized attempting to pass the Fourth Cataract, but Beatty escaped and went on to command a naval rocket battery at the battle of the Atbara (8 April 1898) and the gunboat *Fateh* at the battle of Omdurman (2 September 1898). He then proceeded up the river with the expedition commander, Sir Herbert Kitchener, to establish contact with a small

French party that had reached Fashoda from West Africa. The French officers were treated diplomatically and carried down the Nile to Egypt, but the Fashoda Incident inflamed French public opinion and for a time threatened to lead to war between France and the United Kingdom. Beatty, with special promotion to commander on 15 November 1898 (passing over nearly 400 lieutenants senior to him) returned home a hero. In his favourite pastime of foxhunting he met the twenty-three-year-old American society beauty, Mrs Ethel Field Tree, heiress to the Sears Roebuck fortune, as wilful as she was beautiful, and already growing estranged from her husband.

Beatty returned to sea in April 1899 as commander of the battleship *Barfleur*, flagship of the second-in-command on the China station. In 1900, during the Boxer Rebellion, he landed with reinforcements for the multinational garrison of Tientsin (Tienjin). He led a number of sorties, in one of which he was ambushed and wounded, and later took part in the relief of the naval brigade under Vice-Admiral Sir Edward Seymour [57] at Hsiku. His services were rewarded with promotion to captain on 9 November 1900. In May 1901 he married Mrs Tree, after her husband had obtained a divorce and the custody of their child, on the grounds of desertion. Marriage to a divorcee was frowned upon in the society of the time, and Beatty's family counselled him against this step, but the combination of Beatty's heroic reputation and his wife's riches made them acceptable at Court, and at first they were happy together. In June 1902 Beatty was given command of the cruiser *Juno*, in which he served successively in the Channel and the Mediterranean, where he transferred to the cruiser *Arrogant* in April 1903. From October 1904 to September 1905, still in the Mediterranean, he commanded the armoured cruiser *Suffolk*. His wife accompanied him and lived at Malta. When there was talk of Beatty being disciplined for damaging *Suffolk*'s engines when rushing back to join her, she offered to buy the Admiralty a new ship as a replacement. He subsequently returned to London where he was appointed a naval adviser at the War Office.

Beatty was appointed in December 1908 to the battleship *Queen*, in the Atlantic Fleet. Two years later he reached the top of the captains' seniority list, but his rapid promotion, and the fact that his wife's money had made it unnecessary for him to seek a ship, meant that he had not served the six years at sea required for promotion to flag rank. Nevertheless, the First Sea Lord, Sir John Fisher [58], wished Beatty to be promoted, and by a special Order in Council made him a rear-admiral on 1 January 1910, the youngest flag officer since Nelson. He declined the offered appointment as second-in-command of the Atlantic Fleet, based at Gibraltar, in the hope that he would be given a post in the more important Home Fleet. The Admiralty, where there was some feeling against Beatty because of his rapid promotion, was not accustomed to officers behaving in such a way, and his career might have languished but for a social encounter with Winston Churchill, who became First Lord of the Admiralty in October 1911. Despite official advice to the contrary, Churchill appointed Beatty to his staff as Naval Secretary in January 1912. In the manoeuvres of July 1912 Beatty commanded a cruiser squadron from the reserve fleet, with his flag in the armoured cruiser *Aboukir*. A former cavalry subaltern, Churchill was impressed by the dash and quickness of mind he believed Beatty had developed from his polo-playing and foxhunting, and which other naval officers seemed to him to lack. He decided that these attributes made Beatty an ideal choice over the heads of all other candidates for command of the Battle-cruiser Squadron. Beatty assumed command, with his flag in the battle-cruiser *Lion* in March 1913 and was awarded the KCB in June 1913.

Sir David Beatty was given acting promotion to vice-admiral on 2 August 1914, just before the outbreak of the First World War. His first sea combat was at the battle of Heligoland Bight (28 August 1914) where he emerged as the inheritor of the Nelsonian tradition of the offensive. He demonstrated the same offensive spirit at the battle of the Dogger Bank (24 January 1915), where he inflicted a defeat on the German battle-cruiser force, though *Lion* was badly damaged, so that the Germans escaped before Beatty could shift his flag to *Princess Royal* and re-establish control. At the battle of Jutland (31 May–1 June 1916) Beatty succeeded in drawing the German High Seas Fleet into contact with the Grand Fleet, but in the process suffered the loss of two battle-cruisers. Their destruction by sudden explosion led Beatty to remark to his flag captain, Alfred Chatfield [83] "There seems to be something wrong with our bloody ships today, and with our system". Some analysts later criticized Beatty's tactics at Jutland, though others defended his actions with equal vigour.

On 4 December 1916 Beatty succeeded Sir John Jellicoe [68] as C-in-C, Grand Fleet, with acting promotion to admiral. With his handsome appearance, flamboyant manner, cap worn at a rakish angle and jacket adorned with six buttons in place of the regulation eight, he was the antithesis of his austere and clinical predecessor. His own dash in command of the battle-cruisers at Jutland was widely contrasted with Jellicoe's cautious handling of the main battle fleet, and he was popular both with the British public and the King, George V [64]. Believing that the Germans had escaped destruction because the Grand Fleet had lacked tactical flexibility, he replaced Jellicoe's prescriptive fleet orders with fleet instructions that allowed captains greater freedom to use their initiative. Early in 1917, he transferred his flag from the battleship *Iron Duke* to the faster and newer battleship *Queen Elizabeth*. After the United States entered the war in April 1917 his fleet was reinforced by a battle squadron under Rear-Admiral Hugh Rodman, United States Navy. Despite two successes by German surface raiders against Norwegian convoys, the Grand Fleet retained its dominance of the North Sea until the end of the war, when the High Seas Fleet mutinied rather than put to sea. On 21 November 1918, in accordance with the terms of the Armistice, Beatty escorted it to internment at his own base, Scapa Flow and gave the order "The German flag will be hauled down at sunset and will not be hoisted again without permission". This was, in fact, an unlawful requirement, as the High Seas Fleet had been interned rather than captured, and remained the property of the German government, but, under Beatty's guns, the Germans were forced to comply. He was promoted to admiral on 1 January 1919 and to admiral of the fleet on 3 April 1919, prior to hauling down his flag when the Grand Fleet was dispersed on 7 April 1919.

In the post-war honours it was at first envisaged that Beatty should be granted a viscountcy, as had been awarded to Jellicoe. He held out for an earldom, such as had been given to Field Marshal Haig, C-in-C of the British Expeditionary Force at the time of the Armistice, and received this late in 1919. He also hoped for an immediate appointment as First Sea Lord, preferably combined with a role as C-in-C of the Navy, but the incumbent, Sir Rosslyn Wemyss [71], remained in post until 1 November 1919, when Beatty succeeded him. Earl Beatty was First Sea Lord for over seven and a half years, holding this post for longer than any other officer and serving under five successive First Lords, in one Coalition, one Labour and three Conservative administrations. During this period he had to deal with all the usual problems facing a post-war navy, including Treasury-led demands for reductions in the fleet. The long-standing British policy of maintaining absolute supremacy at sea had to be abandoned in the face of the emergence of the United States as a world power, with the wealth and will to build a large navy matching its new position.

Beatty attended the Washington Naval Conference of November 1921, where in accord with Cabinet policy, he accepted parity, at the lowest possible number, with the United States battlefleet, while retaining superiority over France, Italy and Japan. Nevertheless, he continued to argue that British dependency on seaborne trade required British supremacy in the number of cruisers. He saw Japan, a former ally, as a future rival, and pressed hard for funds to construct a naval base at Singapore from which fleet operations in the Far East could be mounted. He also pressed for the return of responsibility for naval aviation from the recently-formed Royal Air Force to the Royal Navy, on the grounds that this arm would play a vital part in future warfare at sea and could not be entrusted to another Service with its own doctrine and priorities. Indeed, he began by advocating the abolition of the Royal Air Force and the Air Ministry altogether, and promised financial savings in other branches of the fleet if given control of the RAF's maritime air assets. He failed in this, and the RAF's argument that the air was an indivisible element, so that the same Service should operate aircraft over the sea and over the land, continued to have Cabinet support. His only success was an agreement achieved in 1924 that observers and non-commissioned aircrews in aircraft carriers should be members of the Royal Navy rather than the Royal Air Force.

Beatty supported the creation of the Chiefs of Staff Committee and proved to be a fair-minded chairman. He encouraged the development of the Naval Staff College at Greenwich and the Imperial Defence College, London. He also used his position as First Sea Lord to alter the draft of the official record of the battle of Jutland, so as to maximize the achievements of his own Battle-cruiser Fleet and imply that Jellicoe and the Grand Fleet had arrived late and done little. This led to a controversy between rival adherents of the two admirals that outlived both of them. Beatty's greatest achievement in this period was to defend the Navy against even more drastic reductions than those it actually sustained. He ended his active career on leaving the Admiralty in July 1927. He maintained his reputation as a keen horseman, but two severe hunting accidents, following a car crash, left him badly injured. Edith Beatty had given her second husband two sons, but their marriage was increasingly unhappy, with each partner unfaithful to the other. Beatty himself later complained "I have paid a terrible price for my millions", while his wife blamed him for neglecting her in order to further his naval career. She grew steadily more unstable and restless, and travelled extensively to find cures for her ill-health. This, to a great extent psychotic in origin, ended with her death from cerebral thrombosis in July 1931. Beatty died of heart failure at his London home on 11 March 1936 and was buried in St Paul's Cathedral. He was succeeded in the peerage by his elder son.

BEGG
Sir VARYL CARGILL, GCB, DSO, DSC (1908–95) [105]

Varyl Begg was born on 1 October 1908 and educated at St Andrew's School, Eastbourne, and Malvern College, Worcestershire. He entered the Navy as a cadet under the Special Entry scheme in 1926 and was promoted to midshipman on 1 September 1927. He joined the cruiser *Durban* on the China station in October 1927, from where he was appointed to the battleship *Marlborough* in the Atlantic Fleet in April 1929. He became acting sub-lieutenant on 1 January 1930 at the beginning of his promotion courses, and a lieutenant on 1 December 1930. In April 1931 he was appointed to the cruiser *Shropshire* in the Mediterranean Fleet. Begg attended the gunnery school *Excellent* during 1934 and, after qualifying, served from December 1934 to November 1935 as gunnery officer of the battleship *Nelson*, flagship of the Home Fleet. He then completed the Advanced Gunnery Course before being appointed gunnery officer of the destroyer flotilla leader *Cossack* in November 1937, and subsequently going with her to the Mediterranean Fleet, with promotion to lieutenant-commander on 1 December 1938. In June 1939 he was appointed gunnery officer of the cruiser *Glasgow*, pendant-ship of the commodore of the South America division, where he was serving on the outbreak of the Second World War in September 1939. During 1940 the ship was part of the Home Fleet, escorting convoys in the North Atlantic and taking part in the Norwegian campaign and the occupation of Iceland.

In January 1941 Begg became gunnery officer of the battleship *Warspite*, flagship of the Mediterranean Fleet, in which he took part in a number of operations, including the battle of Matapan (28 March 1941). The commanding officer of *Warspite*, himself a gunnery specialist, greeted the direct hits scored by her first salvo (at the relatively short range of three miles) on the Italian cruiser *Fiume* with the surprised exclamation "My God, we've hit her! ". Begg was mentioned in despatches and awarded the DSC for this action. He remained in *Warspite* until damage sustained during the evacuation of Crete (May 1941) resulted in the ship going for repair in the United States. He was promoted to commander on 31 December 1942 and joined the Admiralty early in 1943, where he remained, in the Gunnery and Anti-Aircraft Warfare Division, until after the end of the war in 1945. In 1943 he married Rosemary Cowan, with whom he later had two sons. In May 1946 he was appointed to the cruiser *Phoebe* as operations officer of the destroyer flotillas in the Mediterranean Fleet.

Begg was promoted to captain on 30 June 1947 and commanded the gunnery school at Chatham from 1948 to 1950. He then commanded *Cossack* as Captain (Destroyers) of the Eighth Destroyer Flotilla between August 1950 and February 1952, in which he was again mentioned in despatches and awarded the DSO for services during the Korean War. He was captain of *Excellent* from 1952 to 1954 and commanded the aircraft carrier *Triumph* from December 1954 to December 1955. After attending the Imperial Defence College, Begg was promoted to rear-admiral on 7 January 1957. During 1957–58 he was chief of staff to the C-in-C, Portsmouth, and then served from 1958 to 1960 as Flag Officer commanding the Fifth Cruiser Squadron and second-in-command, Far East station.

Begg was promoted to vice-admiral on 21 May 1960. He was at the Admiralty as Assistant Chief of the Naval Staff from 1961 to 1963, with the award of the KCB in 1962. Sir Varyl Begg became an admiral on 8 March 1963 and served as C-in-C, British Forces, Far East, from 1963 to 1965. This period included confrontation with Indonesia in support of Brunei, in a successful campaign involving one-third of the Navy's surface fleet and half its aircraft carriers, and including a number of minor actions against faster Indonesian patrol boats (sold to them by the British). In August 1965 he was appointed C-in-C, Portsmouth. This period coincided with a far-reaching Defence Review conducted on the orders of Denis Healey, Secretary of State for Defence in the Labour Cabinet that took office under Harold Wilson in October 1964. The assumptions were made that the United Kingdom would never again go to war except as part of the NATO alliance, and that, east of Suez, there was no significant seaborne threat to British interests. This led to the decision in February 1966 that there was no longer any need for aircraft carriers in the fleet. These were to be phased out during the following decade, and the strike, reconnaissance and air defence functions of the Fleet Air Arm transferred to land-based aircraft of the Royal Air Force. Accordingly, the order for a new large carrier intended to come into service in 1973 was cancelled.

The Minister for the Navy, Christopher Mayhew, and the First Sea Lord, Admiral Sir David Luce, resigned in protest, and Begg was appointed in Luce's place. Begg had an open mind on the aircraft carrier question, but took a realistic view of what was acceptable to the Cabinet at a time of severe economic pressure. An austere and reserved character, he did much to reshape the Navy for its new role and to preserve morale in a time of reductions and withdrawals. He was promoted to admiral of the fleet on 12 August 1968, on leaving the Admiralty, and was appointed Governor of Gibraltar in 1969, where he was extended in office until 1973. He retired to his home in Chilbolton, Stockbridge, Hampshire, and, after suffering for many years from Alzheimer's disease, died on 13 July 1995.

BOWLES
Sir William, KCB (1780–1869) [31]

William Bowles, the eldest son of a country gentleman and the grandson of an admiral, was born in 1780 at Heale House, near Old Sarum, Wiltshire. He joined the Navy in September 1796, during the French Revolutionary War, as a first class volunteer in the 3rd-rate *Theseus* in which he served in the English Channel and off Cadiz until June 1797. He was then promoted to midshipman in the 3rd-rate *Captain*. During 1798 he was in the corvette *Daphne* in the North Sea and then went to the West Indies station, from which he returned in November 1800 in the 5th-rate *Hydra*. Bowles served successively in the 5th-rate *Acasta* in the Mediterranean and the sloop *Driver*, before being promoted to acting lieutenant on 22 July 1803 (confirmed on 30 August 1803) in the 4th-rate *Cambrian* at Halifax, Nova Scotia. He served on the coast of North America in the 4th-rate *Leander* and (after her capture from the French by *Leander* in 1805) the 5th-rate *Milan*, and was made a commander on 22 January 1806. He was given command of the bomb-vessel *Zebra* on 25 March 1807 and took part in the bombardment of Copenhagen (2–7 September 1807).

Bowles became a captain on 13 October 1807, with temporary command successively of the 5th-rate *Medusa* in December 1808 and of the 3rd-rate *Warspite* in June 1809. He again commanded *Medusa* from June to November 1810 and took part in operations along the north coast of Spain, co-operating with the Spanish partisans against French coastal defences and being mentioned in despatches for his leadership of a naval brigade in an attack on Santona, near Santander. In March 1811 he became captain of the 5th-rate *Aquilon* and was deployed against French-controlled commercial shipping in the Baltic. During 1813 he served on trade-protection duties off the River Plate, before returning home in April 1814. After the end of the Napoleonic Wars in 1815 Bowles was C-in-C and commodore, South America station, from 1816 to 1820, with his broad pendant successively in the 5th-rates *Amphion* and *Creole*. In 1820 he married the Honourable Frances Temple, sister of Viscount Palmerston (at that time Secretary at War and later Prime Minister). She died without offspring in 1838.

In 1822 Bowles briefly commanded the royal yacht *William and Mary* prior to appointment as Comptroller-General of the Coast Guard on 8 July 1822. In 1830, writing under the pseudonym "An Old Flag Officer", he recommended the creation of a gunnery training establishment, an idea that already had wide general support and led to the establishment of an experimental gunnery school in the hulk *Excellent* at Portsmouth later that year. He retained this post until 23 November 1841, when he was promoted to rear-admiral. From May 1843 to May 1844 he was at sea with his flag first in the 6th-rate *Tyne* and then the 1st-rate *Caledonia*. He then became third naval lord at the Admiralty, serving in the Board under first the Earl of Haddington and then the Earl of Ellenborough, in Sir Robert Peel's second ministry. Bowles left the Admiralty, when Peel (to whom he was related by marriage) resigned in 1846. Between 1845 and 1850 he sat as Conservative Member of Parliament for Launceston, Cornwall. He became a vice-admiral on 8 March 1852 and an admiral on 15 January 1857. He was made a KCB in 1869 and was promoted to admiral of the fleet on 15 January 1869. Sir William Bowles died on 2 July 1869.

BOYLE
Sir WILLIAM HENRY DUDLEY, 12th Earl of Cork and Orrery
GCB, GCVO (1873–1967) [87]

William Boyle, born with a twin sister at Hale, Farnham, Surrey, on 30 November 1873, was the second son in a family of nine children born to Captain (later Colonel) Gerald Boyle, of the Rifle Brigade. Captain Boyle was a grandson of the eighth Earl of Cork and Orrery, and his wife, Lady Theresa, was the daughter of the first Earl of Cottenham. "Ginger" Boyle, as he was commonly known, entered the Navy as a cadet in the training ship *Britannia* in 1887, and went to sea in December 1888 in the armoured ship *Monarch* in the Channel Squadron. He became a midshipman on 15 June 1889 and joined the battleship *Colossus* in the Mediterranean Fleet in March 1890. In July 1892 he transferred to the corvette *Active* in the Training Squadron from where, in June 1893, he became an acting sub-lieutenant on beginning his promotion courses. Boyle joined the gunboat *Lizard*, bound for the Australia station, in September 1894, and remained there, with promotion to lieutenant on 1 October 1895, until returning home with the ship in 1898. In July 1898 he was appointed to the cruiser *Furious* in the Channel, and in November 1898 to early 1902 was first lieutenant of the sloop *Daphne*, ordered to the China station.

In July 1902 Boyle was appointed first lieutenant of the torpedo gunboat *Hazard*. In the same year, he married Lady Florence Keppel, daughter of the seventh Earl of Albemarle. From August 1902 to October

1903 he was in command of the destroyer *Haughty* and subsequently returned to the China station as gunnery lieutenant of the cruiser *Astraea*, where he served from February 1904 to September 1906. Boyle was promoted to commander on 31 December 1906, followed by appointment as the commander of the battleship *Hibernia*, flagship of the second-in-command of the Channel Fleet, where he remained until January 1909. From 1909 to 1911 he was in the Naval Intelligence Division at the Admiralty and returned to sea in 1911 as commander of the armoured cruiser *Good Hope*, flagship of the Fifth Cruiser Squadron in the Atlantic Fleet, based at Gibraltar. In January 1912 he was given command of the scout cruiser *Skirmisher*, attached to the Fourth Destroyer Flotilla in the Home Fleet.

Boyle was promoted captain on 30 June 1913 shortly after being appointed naval attaché at the British Embassy in Rome. From there he visited the Second Balkan War in 1913. After the outbreak of the First World War he joined the Dardanelles campaign in February 1915, attached to the staff of Rear-Admiral Rosslyn Wemyss [71] in the gunboat *Hussar*. During the naval bombardment of 18 March 1915 he was present with the military commander, Sir Ian Hamilton, in the cruiser *Phaeton*. Boyle was ordered back to Rome in April 1915, shortly before the entry of Italy into the war on the side of the Entente Powers. He then visited the Italian naval brigades on the Isonzo front. His repeated requests to the Admiralty for a more active appointment brought the response that naval officers were expected to serve where their Lordships considered they were best employed and that another request would lead to his being placed permanently on the half-pay list. He considered joining the Army, but with the support of the British ambassador, who stated that he feared for Boyle's sanity if retained in Rome, was eventually found a sea-going appointment.

Boyle then saw active service in command of the light cruiser *Fox* to which he was appointed in September 1915, initially under the command of a French rear-admiral, in the Northern Red Sea Patrol. Forbidden, out of deference to Muslim opinion, to bombard Turkish positions on the coast of Hejaz (Hijaz), he landed a small raiding party at Aqaba in December 1915. In January 1916 he was given command of the entire Red Sea Patrol. He supported the Arab rebellion with a six-day bombardment of Jedda (Jiddah) in June 1916, though he was still forbidden from landing British officers to report the fall of shot, and suspected that many of the targets indicated to him by Arab representatives on board his ship were actually owned by their local rivals. He operated in the Red Sea and the Indian Ocean, and gave valuable support to Colonel T E Lawrence ("Lawrence of Arabia") in the Arab Revolt against Turkish rule. During October 1916 he commanded from a hired boarding steamer, *Suva*, and, early in 1917, from the Royal Indian Marine ship *Northbrook*. Boyle was given command of the battle-cruiser *Repulse* in November 1917 and served for the rest of the war in the Battle-cruiser Fleet of the Grand Fleet, as flag captain to Sir Henry Oliver [78]. In April 1919 he transferred to the battle-cruiser *Tiger*,

31

flagship of what then became the Battle-cruiser Squadron of the Atlantic Fleet. He was appointed commodore, 2nd Class, and chief of staff and, acquitted by court-martial after his ship collided with the battleship *Royal Sovereign* in Portland harbour in 1920, remained in post until March 1921. Between July 1921 and October 1923 he was in charge of the naval barracks at Devonport.

Boyle was promoted to rear-admiral on 1 November 1923. From May 1924 to May 1925 he was second-in-command of the Second Battle Squadron of the Atlantic Fleet, with his flag in the battleship *Resolution*. He subsequently attended the Senior Officers' war course at the Royal Naval College, Greenwich, prior to being given command, in September 1926, of the First Cruiser Squadron, with his flag in the cruiser *Frobisher*. Boyle served with this squadron first in the Mediterranean and then on the China station, until returning home on promotion to vice-admiral on 12 June 1928. In December 1928 he became Vice-Admiral commanding the Reserve fleet, with his flag in the light cruiser *Constance* at Portsmouth. From April 1929 to August 1932 he was President of the Royal Naval College and Vice-Admiral commanding the Royal Naval War College, Greenwich, with the award of the KCB in 1931.

Sir William Boyle was promoted to admiral on 1 November 1932 and became C-in-C, Home Fleet, with his flag in the battleship *Nelson*, in September 1933. In 1934, following the death of his cousin, he succeeded to the peerage as twelfth Earl of Cork and Orrery. In his maiden speech in the House of Lords he supported a motion to abolish the right of a peer to be tried by his peers. After completing his command on August 1935 Lord Cork expected no further employment, but, on the death in office of Admiral Sir William Fisher, was appointed C-in-C, Portsmouth, where he remained until June 1939. He was promoted to admiral of the fleet on 21 January 1938.

The outbreak of the Second World War in September 1939 found Lord Cork still on the active list and still full of energy. By sheer force of personality he persuaded the new First Lord of the Admiralty, Winston Churchill, to nominate him to command the naval element of a British force intended to support Finland against the Soviet Union in the Winter War of 1939–40. The idea of this expedition, intended to land at Narvik and cross the northern parts of neutral Norway and Sweden, was abandoned when Finland agreed to Soviet terms on 12 March 1940. Cork received a substitute command on 8 April 1940 when Germany invaded Denmark and Norway. The United Kingdom and France responded to Norway's request for assistance by sending troops, and Cork was appointed flag officer, Narvik, where Churchill intended the main effort to be made. In fact, the major landings took place further south, around Trondheim, where the Allies were forced to re-embark at the beginning of May.

Cork, with his flag in the cruiser *Aurora*, wished to land troops immediately on his arrival at Narvik on 14 April 1940, where the Germans were still recovering from the shock of being bombarded by the battleship

Warspite the previous day. Major General P J Mackesy, commanding the troops, had orders not to attempt an opposed landing and decided to wait for the arrival of his main force on 15 April 1940. When the two commanders met, they discovered that each had received conflicting orders and a violent disagreement ensued. The two were in accord neither tactically nor by temperament. Mackesy, an officer of the Royal Engineers, the intellectual elite of the British Army, was a meticulous planner, already convinced that, for lack of air power and artillery, the expedition was likely to end in disaster. He was faced by an admiral of the fleet (senior in rank to his own superior officer, the C-in-C Home Fleet, Sir Charles Forbes [90]) who was a nominee of the First Lord (the chief supporter of the Narvik operation) and, moreover, a man whose nickname "Ginger" referred as much to his personality as to the colour of his hair. Cork's active nature and desire for offensive action endeared him to Churchill, who was anxious for speed to prevail over caution. He made a personal reconnaissance of the terrain and, being of short stature, disappeared up to his waist in snow, losing his temper, his dignity and the monocle that he habitually wore. On 24 April 1940 he bombarded Narvik, but with the Germans still displaying resistance, the proposed landing was cancelled. On 12 May 1940, with his flag in the cruiser *Effingham*, he covered the landing of troops of the French Foreign Legion at Bjerkvik, as a first move towards Narvik.

The following day Mackesy was succeeded by Lieutenant General Auchinleck, an Indian Army officer with expertise in mountain warfare, with Cork becoming commander of all British forces at Narvik. The town was eventually captured on 28 May 1940, a day after Cork, with his flag in the cruiser *Cairo*, had covered another landing, but his ships were soon forced out to sea by German air attack. With the successful German offensive on the Western Front, the Allies had already decided to leave Norway. On 8 June 1940 Cork began a successful evacuation and, with his flag in the cruiser *Southampton*, returned home as the Norwegians concluded an armistice. The failure of this campaign played an important part in bringing about the fall of the Chamberlain ministry and the emergence of Winston Churchill as Prime Minister. Cork was sent by Churchill to Gibraltar in December 1940 to conduct an enquiry into the conduct of Sir James Somerville [93] in not pursuing an Italian fleet after the battle of Cape Spartivento (27 November 1940). His findings entirely exonerated Somerville, whom he saw as the victim of Churchill's impatience for dramatic results and disregard for practicalities. From February to November 1941, having failed to secure further employment from the Admiralty, he served in the Home Guard and became deputy commander of London Zone "B" with the rank of lieutenant-colonel until relinquishing this appointment on age grounds. Between1942 and 1953 he was president of the Shaftesbury Homes and the training ship *Arethusa*. Lord Cork died in London on 19 April 1967 and was succeeded in the peerage by his nephew.

BROCK
Sir Osmond de Beauvoir, GCB, KCVO (1869–1947) [79]

Osmond Brock, the eldest son and second child of a retired naval commander, was born at Plymouth on 5 January 1869 and joined the Navy as a cadet in the training ship *Britannia* in January 1882. He became a midshipman in the corvette *Carysfort* on 18 August 1884 and served in the Mediterranean Fleet, where he was lent to the barbette ship *Téméraire*. In March 1885 he joined the frigate *Raleigh*, flagship of the Cape of Good Hope and West Coast of Africa station and, while at the Cape, was awarded the certificate of the Royal Humane Society for rescuing a stoker from drowning. Brock joined the cruiser *Active*, in the Training Squadron, in November 1887 and became an acting sub-lieutenant at the beginning of his promotion courses on 14 August 1888. He was promoted to lieutenant on 14 February 1889 and appointed to the battleship *Trafalgar*, flagship of the second-in-command of the Mediterranean Fleet, in April 1890. After returning home in September 1891 he attended the gunnery training school *Excellent* at Portsmouth, where he qualified in 1894. Brock was appointed gunnery lieutenant in the battleship *Devastation*, port guardship at Devonport, in August 1894. From October 1894 to November 1895 he served in the new cruiser *Cambrian*, commanded by Captain Prince Louis of Battenberg [74] in the Mediterranean Fleet. He then became gunnery lieutenant of the battleship *Ramillies*, flagship of the Mediterranean Fleet, and left the ship on promotion to commander on 1 January 1900.

Brock was appointed commander of the battleship *Repulse* in the Channel Squadron in January 1901. From August 1901 to May 1902 he was commander of the battleship *Renown*, flagship of the C-in-C Mediterranean Fleet, Sir John Fisher [58]. After a period on half-pay, he was given command of the despatch vessel *Alacrity* on the China station in January 1903, where he remained until promoted to captain on 1 January 1904. He was appointed captain of the Admiralty yacht *Enchantress* in May 1904 and returned to the Mediterranean in May 1905 as flag captain to the C-in-C, Lord Charles Beresford, in the battleship *Bulwark*. At the end of 1906 Brock moved to the Admiralty as one of the three Assistant Directors of Naval Intelligence. He returned to sea in March 1909 as flag captain to the Vice-Admiral commanding the Second Division of the Home Fleet, in the battleship *King Edward VII*. In August 1910 he was re-appointed to the Admiralty as one of the two Assistant Directors of Naval Mobilization. He was given command of the new battle-cruiser *Princess Royal* in August 1912, in the Battle-cruiser Squadron under Rear-Admiral David Beatty [69].

After the outbreak of the First World War in August 1914 Brock served in *Princess Royal* at the battles of Heligoland Bight (28 August 1914) and the Dogger Bank (24 January 1915). While *Lion* was under repair after sustaining battle damage at the Dogger Bank, Beatty shifted his flag to *Princess Royal*, so that for a short while Brock was his flag captain. He was promoted to rear-admiral on 5 March 1915 and assumed command of the First Battle-cruiser Squadron with his flag in *Princess Royal*. At the battle of Jutland (31 May–1 June 1916), after *Lion*'s radio system was put out of action by German gunfire, *Princess Royal* became Beatty's radio link with the rest of the fleet, repeating messages to and from the flagship by visual signals.

Brock's analytical mind and studious disposition made him a perfect complement to the dashing and impetuous Beatty, and the two formed a high opinion of each other's abilities. When Beatty was appointed C-in-C, Grand Fleet, at the end of November 1916 he took Brock with him as his chief of staff, with the flag in the battleship *Queen Elizabeth*. In 1917, to Beatty's disapproval, Brock married the green-eyed, red-haired Irene Catherine Francklin, widow of Captain Philip Francklin, lost with all hands in the armoured cruiser *Good Hope* at the battle of Coronel (1 November 1914). She came from a naval family and was the daughter of one admiral and granddaughter of another. With her second husband, she later had a daughter of her own. At the end of 1917 Brock was awarded the KCVO. He became an acting vice-admiral on 17 January 1918, while remaining Beatty's chief of staff until the Grand Fleet dispersed in May 1919 after the end of the war.

Sir Osmond Brock was promoted to vice-admiral on 3 October 1919, following his appointment as Fifth Sea Lord and Deputy Chief of the Naval Staff at the Admiralty, where he remained until the end of 1921. In April 1922 he became C-in-C, Mediterranean Fleet, flying his flag in the battleship *Iron Duke* with promotion to acting admiral in July 1922. In August 1922 the forces of a renascent Turkey routed the Greek army in Asia Minor and recovered the old Ottoman port of Smyrna (Izmir). Many of the Greek inhabitants were massacred. Others escaped with the departing Greek troops under the protection of Brock's ships. The Turks pressed on to the neutral zone of the Dardanelles, held by a small British garrison at Chanak. The British Prime Minister, David Lloyd George, threatened war with Turkey, but gained little support at home or abroad, and was driven to resign office in October 1922. The Turks, correctly anticipating that the zone would be restored to them by international agreement, had already halted their advance. During the crisis Brock deployed his fleet to the Dardanelles, but was careful to avoid an armed clash, and was thanked in Parliament for his diplomatic conduct. He was given substantive promotion to admiral on 31 July 1924 and shifted his flag to the newly arrived battleship *Queen Elizabeth*. After handing over command of the Mediterranean Fleet in May 1925, he returned home to become C-in-C Portsmouth, where he served from 31 July 1926 to 29 April 1929. Sir Osmond Brock was promoted to admiral of the fleet on 31 July 1929 and retired on 31 July 1933. He died at Winchester on 14 October 1947.

BURNEY
Sir CECIL, 1st Baronet, GCB, KCMG (1858–1929) [72]

Cecil Burney, second son of a naval captain, was born on 15 May 1858 at his mother's family home in Jersey. He was educated at the Royal Naval Academy, Gosport (a private tutorial establishment or "crammer") and joined the Navy in July 1871 as a cadet in the training ship *Britannia* at Portsmouth. He became a midshipman in October 1873 in the battleship *Repulse*, flagship of the Pacific station. Burney became a sub-lieutenant on 18 October 1877 at the beginning of his promotion courses and was appointed to the Indian troopship *Serapis* on 6 January 1879. He subsequently served from June to August 1879 as a sub-lieutenant in the royal yacht *Victoria and Albert*. He was promoted to lieutenant on 30 August 1879 and appointed to the corvette *Carysfort*, in the Mediterranean Fleet, in September 1880.

At the beginning of the British campaign in Egypt in 1882 Burney landed in command of a Gatling gun section as part of a naval brigade. When the British advanced inland from the Suez Canal he accompanied the army with his guns drawn by mules, and brought them into action on the British flank at Tel-el-Mahuta (24 August 1882). He was with the naval brigade at the battle of Kassassin (28 August 1882) and subsequently joined an expedition against a group of Arabs who had murdered a party of British explorers. Burney also served in the Eastern Sudan campaign of February–March 1884, against the Mahdist forces threatening the Red Sea port of Suakin. He returned to Portsmouth in September 1884, to join the gunnery training ship *Excellent*. In the same year he married Lucinda Burnett, daughter of a London gentleman. They later had a family of two daughters and a son, who became a commander in the Navy.

After qualifying as a gunnery officer, Burney was appointed to the gunnery training ship *Cambridge* at Devonport in June 1886 as one of her two junior staff officers. He subsequently joined the North America and West Indies station, where he served as a gunnery lieutenant successively of the flagship, the battleship *Bellerophon*, from August 1887 to April 1889, and then of the cruiser *Comus* until 1891. He was gunnery officer of the armoured cruiser *Immortalité* in the Channel Squadron from 1 January 1892 to 1 January 1893, when he was promoted to commander.

From May 1893 until the end of 1895 Burney was commander of the cruiser *Hawke* in the Mediterranean Fleet. He became the commanding officer of the boys' training establishment at Portland in January 1896, where he was promoted to captain on 1 January 1898. After leaving Portland in 1900 he briefly commanded *Hawke* on manoeuvres. On 8 August 1900 he became captain of the cruiser *Sappho*, initially on the South Coast of America station, but detached during 1902 to the Cape of Good Hope station in the closing stage of the Anglo-Boer South African War. There *Sappho* struck the harbour bar at Durban, Natal, and was forced to return to the United Kingdom for repair. As the vessel had been under the supervision of a local pilot at the material time, Burney was exonerated from blame and in September 1902 was given command of the battleship *Empress of India*, flagship of the second-in-command of the Channel Squadron. In June 1904 he was appointed captain of the battleship *Triumph* in the Home Fleet and in July 1905 joined the training establishment *Impregnable*, at Devonport, as inspecting captain of all boys' training ships. He remained there until his promotion to rear-admiral on 10 October 1907.

In February 1911 Burney was given command of the Fifth Cruiser Squadron, in the Atlantic Fleet, flying his flag in the armoured cruiser *Good Hope*. He was promoted to command the Atlantic Fleet, as acting vice-admiral, with his flag in the battleship *Prince of Wales*, on 20 September 1911. In April 1912 this fleet became the Third Squadron of the Home Fleet, with Burney remaining in command but shifting his flag to the battleship *King Edward VII*. He was confirmed as vice-admiral on 20 September 1912, followed by the award of the KCB. In 1913 a renewed war in the Balkans resulted in the capture by Montenegro of the Turkish fortress of Scutari (Shkodar) in Albania. The Great Powers, in the interests of European peace, agreed that this region should be handed over to the newly-independent kingdom (former Turkish province) of Albania. Measures taken to enforce this collective decision included the despatch of a multi-national naval squadron to blockade the Montenegrin port of Antivari (Bar) on the Adriatic coast. Sir Cecil Burney, with temporary appointment as second-in-command of the Mediterranean Fleet and flying his flag in the light cruiser *Dublin*, commanded this squadron during the blockade (April-May 1913). He then commanded the multi-national peace-keeping force that occupied Scutari from April to November 1913. Burney's austere character, personal integrity and impressive physique (he had, earlier in his career, been noted for his strength and for his boxing skill) proved valuable in dealing both with local Balkan warlords and the various national contingents under his command, while arrangements were made for the Albanians to take over the Scutari area.

Burney returned home to become Vice-Admiral commanding the Second and Third Fleets in December 1913, with his flag successively in the battleships *Queen* and (after July 1914) *Lord Nelson*. On the outbreak of the First World War in August 1914 his command mobilized to form the Channel Fleet, responsible for protecting the coasts of southern England and ensuring the safe passage of the British Expeditionary Force to France. In December 1914 he became second-in-command of the Grand Fleet with his flag in the battleship *Marlborough*. At the battle of Jutland (31 May–1 June 1916) *Marlborough* was the first ship of the main battle fleet to engage the Germans. She was later torpedoed and forced to return to base, with Burney's flag transferred to the battleship *Revenge*.

Burney was promoted to admiral on 9 June 1916. He remained under the command of Sir John Jellicoe [68] in the Grand Fleet until November 1916, when both went to the Admiralty, as First and Second Sea Lords respectively. Burney left the Admiralty to become C-in-C, Coast of Scotland, on 13 October 1917 and remained there until 30 March 1919, when he was appointed C-in-C, Portsmouth. At the end of April 1920 he was relieved on medical grounds at his own request. He was promoted to admiral of the fleet on 20 November 1920 and was made a baronet in January 1921. Sir Cecil Burney retired in 1925. He died at his home, Upton House, near Poole, Dorset, on 5 June 1929 and was succeeded in his baronetcy by his son.

CALLAGHAN
Sir GEORGE ASTLEY, GCB, GCVO (1852–1920) [67]

George Callaghan, the third son of a magistrate of Lotabeg, County Cork, was born in London on 21 December 1852 and entered the Navy as a cadet in the training ship *Britannia* in January 1866. He became a midshipman on 15 October 1867, in the paddle despatch vessel *Liffey*, then under construction at Liverpool. In October 1870 he was appointed to the corvette *Wolverene* on the East Indies station, where he was promoted to acting sub-lieutenant on April 1872. After leaving this ship in 1874, he remained ashore with promotion to lieutenant on 15 April 1875. Callaghan married in 1876 Edith Grosvenor, daughter of the Rector of Dunkerton, Somerset, and later had with her a family of a son and three daughters. He returned to the East Indies in June 1877 in the corvette *Ruby*, where he earned a commendation from the Admiralty for saving the lives of seamen whose boat had capsized in the Irrawaddy River, Burma (Myanmar). From 1880 to 1885 he was at the gunnery school *Excellent*, first as a student and then, after qualifying as a gunnery officer, on the staff.

Callaghan was again appointed to *Ruby* in 1885 and served in her, as first lieutenant, on the South East Coast of America until his promotion to commander on 31 December 1887. In 1888 he became commander of the battleship *Bellerophon*, flagship on the North America station, where he remained until the ship returned to the United Kingdom in 1892. He was then given command of the despatch vessel *Alacrity*, yacht of the C-in-C, China station, in which he served until promoted to captain on 1 January 1894.

Between 1894 and 1897 Callaghan was naval adviser to the Inspector-General of fortifications at the War Office. He then became captain of the cruiser *Hermione* in the Channel before going in this ship to the China station, where in 1899 he was given command of the cruiser *Endymion*. During the Boxer Rebellion of 1900 he was mentioned in despatches and decorated for his command of a naval brigade in the Allied force that relieved the diplomatic legations at Peking (Beijing). After his return to the United Kingdom Callaghan commanded the cruiser *Edgar* in the exercises of 1901 before going to the Mediterranean, where he commanded the battleship *Caesar* from December 1901 to March 1903. During 1904 he was the captain of Portsmouth Dockyard. Between 1904 and 1905 he was again in the Mediterranean, in command of the battleship *Prince of Wales*. He was promoted to rear-admiral on 1 July 1905 and in 1906 was appointed to the Channel Fleet, with his flag in the battleship *Illustrious*. In 1907 he was given command of the Fifth Cruiser Squadron, with his flag successively in the cruisers *Leviathan* and *Shannon*. Callaghan became second-in-command of the Mediterranean Fleet, with his flag in the battleship *Duncan*, in 1908. He was awarded the KCVO in 1909 and was made a grand officer of the order of the Crown of Italy for his part in the fleet's aid to the survivors of an earthquake disaster at Messina, Sicily.

Sir George Callaghan was promoted to vice-admiral on 27 April 1910 and became second-in-command of the Home Fleet, with his flag in the battleship *King Edward VII*. In November 1911 he was appointed C-in-C, Home Fleet, with acting rank as admiral (confirmed on 17 May 1913). He held this post, with his flag successively in the battleships *Neptune*, *Hercules* and *Iron Duke*, during a period of increasing international tension and growing British concern at the emergence of the German Navy as a threat to British naval supremacy. In December 1913 he was notified that his tenure of command would be extended to October 1914.

On the outbreak of the First World War in August 1914 Callaghan sailed with his fleet to its war station at Scapa Flow, Orkney. His newly-appointed second-in-command, Sir John Jellicoe [68], joined him there with sealed orders requiring Callaghan to hand over command to him. Jellicoe had already been designated to succeed Callaghan when his tenure expired, but this abrupt change (arranged by the First Lord of the Admiralty, Winston Churchill, and his confidant, Prince Louis of Battenberg [74], the First Sea Lord) shocked the fleet and caused Jellicoe himself to protest. Callaghan himself accepted with great dignity the decision that he was not to command his fleet in the war for which he had trained it. He joined the Admiralty as an adviser and, together with Sir Hedworth Meux [66], conducted the enquiry into the failure of Rear-Admiral Troubridge to engage the German battle-cruiser *Goeben* before she escaped into Turkish waters in August 1914. They found Troubridge's decision "deplorable and contrary to the tradition of the British Navy", though a court-martial later found (to the chagrin of Churchill and Battenberg) that he had acted in accordance with the orders he had been given by the Admiralty. Callaghan became C-in-C, Nore, in January 1915. He remained there, with promotion to admiral of the fleet on 2 April 1917, until March 1918. Sir George Callaghan died in London on 23 November 1920 and was buried in Westminster Abbey.

CALTHORPE
SOMERSET ARTHUR GOUGH, see **GOUGH-CALTHORPE [76]**

CHATFIELD
Sir ALFRED ERNLE MONTACUTE, 1st Baron Chatfield,
GCB, OM, KCMG, CVO (1873–1967) **[83]**

Alfred Chatfield, the fourth child and only son of a naval captain (later admiral), was born in Southsea, Hampshire, on 27 September 1873. He was educated at St Andrew's School, Tenby, where his father had become superintendent of the nearby Pembroke Dockyard, and in 1886 joined the Navy as a cadet in the training ship *Britannia* at Portsmouth. After a brief period in the battleship *Iron Duke* he joined the corvette *Cleopatra* as a midshipman in November 1888. On Christmas Eve 1888, off Ushant, the square-rigged ship was taken aback by a heavy squall and only saved from total loss when cliphooks of an unauthorized pattern (fitted so that the ship would be able to carry out sail drill faster than her consorts) gave way under the strain. After reaching the South America station Chatfield was transferred to the cruiser *Warspite*, flagship of the C-in-C, Pacific, who was an old friend of his father and a distant cousin of his mother. The flag captain, the Honourable Hedworth Lambton, later Sir Hedworth Meux **[66]**, encouraged him in his promotion studies and he became a sub-lieutenant on 27 September 1892. After returning home at the end of 1892 (when his mother, who had not seen him for four years, embraced his travelling companion by mistake), Chatfield passed his promotion courses and became a lieutenant on 27 March 1894. He was appointed in May 1894 to the battleship *Royal Sovereign*, flagship of the Channel Fleet. In September 1895 he joined the gunnery school *Excellent* at Portsmouth, from where, after qualifying, he joined the staff of gunnery school *Cambridge* at Devonport in August 1897.

Chatfield became gunnery lieutenant of the battleship *Caesar* in the Mediterranean Fleet in January 1899, where he became a firm friend of her commander, Charles Madden **[75]**. He was one of the young officers consulted by the C-in-C, Sir John Fisher **[58]**, and liked his realistic approach to training, but was uncomfortable with Fisher's habit of criticizing their superiors, and regretted the way in which he split the Royal Navy into opposing factions. In January 1900 he joined the staff of the gunnery school *Wildfire* at Sheerness, where he incurred the displeasure of the Admiralty for taking the destroyer *Spitfire* along the Thames to Greenwich at a speed of twenty-seven knots. Chatfield returned to sea in November 1902 as gunnery lieutenant of the armoured cruiser *Good Hope*, flagship of the First Cruiser Squadron, with Madden as flag captain. After cruises to South Africa and the West Indies he was promoted to commander on 31 December 1903 and in January 1904 became commander of the battleship *Venerable*, flagship of the second-in-command of the Mediterranean Fleet.

Chatfield returned to *Excellent* as commander in March 1906 and remained there until promoted to captain on 30 June 1909. While at Portsmouth he met the eighteen-year-old Lillian Matthews, the sister of one of his sub-lieutenant students. They were married in July 1909 and later had two daughters and a son. While on honeymoon in Switzerland, he was invited to become flag captain in the battleship *Albemarle*, flagship of Sir Colin Keppel as second-in-command of the Atlantic Fleet. Chatfield held this appointment from September 1909 to February 1910, when the ship was paid off and her flag and crew transferred to the battleship *London*. He spent the first part of 1911 as a student on the War Course at the Royal Naval College, Portsmouth, after which he was selected by Sir Colin Keppel to be his flag captain in the converted liner *Medina*, carrying George V [64] to India for his coronation Durbar. On returning to the United Kingdom early in 1912 Chatfield went on half-pay, until given command of the cruiser *Aboukir* from the reserve fleet in the summer manoeuvres, as flag captain to Rear-Admiral David Beatty [69]. In September 1912 he was appointed to the cruiser *Southampton*, under construction in the Clyde, from where he was selected by Beatty to become his flag captain in the battle-cruiser *Lion* in March 1913.

After the outbreak of the First World War in August 1914 Chatfield remained in *Lion* and was Beatty's flag captain at the battles of Heligoland Bight (28 August 1914), the Dogger Bank (24 January 1915), where his ship was badly damaged and put out of action for four months, and Jutland (31 May 1916), where *Lion* narrowly escaped destruction. In November 1916, when Beatty succeeded Sir John Jellicoe [68] as C-in-C of the Grand Fleet, Chatfield went with him as flag captain and chief of staff, first in the battleship *Iron Duke* and then, after February 1917, the battleship *Queen Elizabeth*. Chatfield remained in this appointment throughout the rest of the war. He was succeeded in April 1919 and was awarded the KCMG. Sir Alfred Chatfield was also offered command of the royal yachts, in a gesture intended by George V to give him a break from combatant duties. He declined, and was instead appointed to the Admiralty in July 1919 as Fourth Sea Lord. Beatty, who became First Sea Lord in November 1919, appointed Chatfield as Assistant Chief of the Naval Staff in February 1920.

Chatfield was promoted to rear-admiral on 31 July 1920. He attended the Washington Naval Conference of 1920–21, as a technical adviser to Beatty, and became the senior British naval delegate in the closing stages of the negotiations. He left the Admiralty in September 1922 to assume command of the Third Cruiser Squadron in the Mediterranean Fleet, with his flag in the cruiser *Cardiff*. He spent eight months in the Dardanelles, at the time of the Chanak crisis, when there was a risk of hostilities with a renascent Turkey, before the fleet returned to its base at Malta on the conclusion of the Treaty of Lausanne. In 1925 Chatfield returned to the Admiralty as Third Sea Lord and Controller of the Navy, responsible for ship-building, dockyards and armaments. He found this a difficult time, as the Ten-year Rule instituted in 1923 was beginning to take effect, while the Treasury maintained its constant pressure for economies. He was promoted to vice-admiral on 1 March 1926. After the departure of Beatty from the Admiralty in July 1927, Sir Ernle Chatfield, as he became known about this time, remained there until September 1928. He became C-in-C, Atlantic Fleet, with his flag successively in the battleships *Nelson* and *Rodney*, on 1 March 1929.

Chatfield was promoted to admiral on 1 April 1930 and was appointed C-in-C, Mediterranean Fleet, with his flag in the battleship *Queen Elizabeth*, on 27 May 1930. He introduced a policy of realistic training, including night exercises, but set his face against detailed operations orders produced in what he referred to as the "Germanic" staff manner. He ended this command in September 1932 and became First Sea Lord on 12 January 1933, in the Board headed by Sir Bolton Eyres-Monsell in Ramsay MacDonald's second National Cabinet. Almost his first act was to countermand the First Lord's scheme for introducing sail training for potential petty officers as a means of improving their leadership skills. Chatfield, who remembered the hazards and unpopularity of such training from his days in *Cleopatra*, considered that the Royal Navy no longer had the expertise safely to operate full-rigged ships and saw little benefit in sending modern-minded ratings to sail in them. He nevertheless maintained good relations with Eyres-Monsell, himself a former naval officer, and found him a valuable ally and supporter. As part of his policy of restoring morale in the Fleet, he introduced the practice of Sea Lords wearing uniform when visiting ships or dockyards. Previously they had worn civilian clothing, indicating their constitutional position as members of a ministerial body rather than officers of the Navy, and thereby had come to be regarded as unsympathetic to the Service. Not to be outdone, the Civil Lords adopted a blue suit and yachting cap, for which a special badge was designed, for wear on official visits.

Chatfield proved himself adept at dealing with Cabinet reluctance to make adequate provision for naval expenditure. He was able to persuade Ramsay MacDonald that, despite opposition from the Foreign Office and the Treasury, the Navy should have seventy cruisers, rather than the fifty agreed at the Naval Conference of 1930, and that large battleships should continue to form the main force of the Fleet. In June 1935 Stanley Baldwin succeeded MacDonald at the head of a National government and, in June 1936, appointed Sir Samuel Hoare as First Lord of the Admiralty. In June 1936 a new office was created, Minister for the Co-ordination of Defence, filled by Sir Thomas Inskip. Chatfield, who had become chairman of the Chiefs of Staff Committee, was initially opposed to this move, seeing it as a threat to the unanimity that the three Chiefs had previously felt bound to reach in their deliberations. Nevertheless, with Hoare's full support, he was able to use Inskip as an arbitrator to meet two of his main targets. The first was to overcome the arguments of those who argued that the battleship was outmoded and vulnerable to air attack, and that bombers were both cheaper and more effective. The second was to obtain the removal of the Fleet Air Arm from the Royal Air Force to the Royal Navy, a cause he considered so important that he threatened to resign if the Air Ministry did not yield. A compromise was agreed in July 1937, whereby all aircraft and crews intended to operate from carriers became part of the Royal Navy, but maritime aircraft operating from coastal bases remained part of the Royal Air Force.

Chatfield played an important part in the 1935 Naval Agreement with Germany, arguing that Hitler had already denounced the naval clauses of the Versailles Treaty, but was at least ready to accept permanent inferiority to the British at sea. He took a similarly practical approach to the Ethiopian crisis of 1935–36, where he thought that the establishment of an Italian empire in East Africa would have the effect of making Italy more dependent on British goodwill. He was concerned to avoid any hostilities that would result in losses of ships before his rearmament programme was under way, and was initially sympathetic to the Nationalist side in the Spanish Civil War that began in 1936. Nevertheless, after Italian submarines (secretly operating in support of the Nationalists) began to attack merchant ships, he became a hero of the Left for his part in co-ordinating international plans against them. He remained at the Admiralty, being twice extended in office, until 10 August 1938, with promotion to admiral of the fleet on 3 May 1935 and the grant of a peerage as Baron Chatfield of Ditchling in the coronation honours of May 1937.

During the winter of 1938–39 Chatfield chaired a committee on the rearmament of the Army in India, taking account of the increasing cost of modern weapons and the limited finances of the Indian government. His tour was boycotted by Indian politicians, who argued that the British troops in India were an army of occupation and should be withdrawn. The dominant Congress party pressed for a national army, under the control of Indian ministers, and open to recruits from all classes rather than only those designated "martial" by the British. Chatfield judged that British troops were an important part of India's defences, not only against invasion, but also the increasing inter-communal tension. An army under the control of local politicians would, he thought, give unlimited power to "a sectional oligarchy". He had to admit that the Navy could no longer defend India's coasts and seaborne traffic, and proposed that external security should be achieved by one Indian division being kept available for deployment anywhere between Suez and Singapore. Recognizing that Indian politicians would not vote the necessary supplies from their own budget, he recommended that the army in India should be modernized at British expense.

On his return to London in February 1939 Chatfield accepted the post of Minister for Co-ordination of Defence, in succession to Inskip, in the National Cabinet under Neville Chamberlain, Prime Minister since May 1937. Having endured years of Treasury parsimony, he ranged himself alongside the Service ministers against the Chancellor of the Exchequer, Sir John Simon, who maintained his department's view that the growing defence estimates would ruin the country. He felt that Chamberlain had been right not to go to war for the sake of Czechoslovakia and saw that the British would be even less able to help Poland, but joined with the Cabinet decision to offer her a guarantee, in the hope this would deter a German attack on the Western democracies. On the outbreak of the Second World War in September 1939 Chatfield was invited to become a member of Chamberlain's War Cabinet, together with the three Service ministers. He soon found that, whereas previously, as deputy chairman of the Committee of Imperial Defence, he had been the Cabinet's main adviser on defence matters, he was now the "fifth wheel on the coach". Likewise, he had no place in the Chiefs of Staff Committee that he had dominated as First Sea Lord. Although adept at operating the machinery of government in Whitehall, he was less happy as a minister than he had been as an administrator, especially as he did not have an actual ministry to support him. In October 1939 he asked Chamberlain to abolish the title of Minister for Co-ordination for Defence and offered to remain in office as Minister without Portfolio. In April 1940 Chamberlain accepted the first part of this proposal and decided that the First Lord of the Admiralty, Winston Churchill, should become chairman of the Military Co-ordination Committee in Chatfield's place. Chatfield himself was persuaded to resign, with the offer of an unspecified important appointment overseas, but declined to leave the country in time of war. When Churchill became Prime Minister on the fall of the Chamberlain government in May 1940 he took the title Minister of Defence for himself. His relations with Chatfield during his years in the wilderness had been cordial, but the two were never close allies and Chatfield was not offered a place in the new administration. He busied himself in other ways, including chairing a committee on the evacuation of London's hospitals, and speaking from time to time in the House of Lords on defence questions. His memoirs, *The Navy and Defence* and *It Might Happen Again*, published in 1943 and 1947, pressed the case for adequate and timely provision for national defence. He retired to Farnham Common, Buckinghamshire, where he died on 15 November 1967, and was succeeded in the peerage by his son Ernle.

CLANWILLIAM
EARL OF, see **MEADE,** RICHARD JAMES, **[50]**

CLINTON
The Honourable GEORGE (1686–1761) **[4]**

The Honourable George Clinton, third son of the sixth Earl of Lincoln, was born in 1686. He joined the Navy in 1707, during the War of the Spanish Succession, after which he was appointed captain of the 5th-rate *Speedwell* on 16 June 1716. In 1720 he commanded the 4th-rate *Moncke* in the Baltic fleet under Sir John Norris [1]. The ship was lost in a storm on the return to England, but Clinton was able to save all his crew and most of his stores and was honourably acquitted at the subsequent court-martial. He returned to the Baltic in command of the 4th-rate *Nottingham,* where he served under Norris's command in 1721 and 1722. During 1727, in a brief war with Spain, Clinton was captain of the 4th-rate *Colchester,* blockading the Spanish coast and escorting home the annual convoy of Levant merchantmen from Smyrna (Izmir). Between July 1727 and May 1728 he commanded the 4th-rate *Sutherland.* In 1732 he was given command of the squadron sent annually to Newfoundland, with the associated function of civil governor. In 1734, at a time of tension between the United Kingdom and Spain, he was given command of the 3rd-rate *Berwick* in Norris's fleet in the Channel. Clinton served during 1736–37 as commodore and C-in-C in the Mediterranean and, on the outbreak of the War of Jenkins's Ear in 1739, was given command of the 3rd-rate *Prince Frederick.* In 1740, in the War of the Austrian Succession, he commanded the 2nd-rate *Marlborough.*

Clinton was appointed governor of the colony of New York in 1741, though he did not arrive to take up office until September 1743. Inexperienced as an administrator, he found himself opposed in council by a party led by the Chief Justice of the colony, James De Lancey, and failed to defend the crown prerogative against attacks in the New York Assembly. He was recalled in 1753 and became Member of Parliament for Saltash, Cornwall, in 1754. He became rear-admiral of the Red on 7 December 1743, vice-admiral of the White on 19 June 1744, vice-admiral of the Red on 3 April 1745, admiral of the White on 15 July 1747 and admiral of the fleet in March 1757. His naval and civil appointments probably reflected the patronage of his eldest brother, a faithful supporter of the eminent Whig politician, the Duke of Newcastle, who became Prime Minister in 1754. Clinton died on 10 July 1761. He was married to Anne Carle, the daughter of a major general. They had six children, of whom only two survived infancy. Their son, Lieutenant General Sir Henry Clinton (born in Newfoundland when his father was governor there) served as C-in-C, North America, during the American War of Independence. Their daughter, Mary, married a future admiral.

COCHRANE
Sir THOMAS JOHN, GCB (1789–1872) [28]

Thomas Cochrane was born in 1789, the eldest son of the Captain the Honourable (later Admiral Sir) Alexander Cochrane (a younger son of the eighth Earl of Dundonald), and his wife Maria, the widow of another naval captain. His cousin and namesake, Thomas, Lord Cochrane, later 10th Earl of Dundonald, was one of the boldest and most colourful frigate captains of the Napoleonic wars. Dismissed from the Royal Navy and imprisoned for fraud in 1814, Lord Cochrane went on to serve as an admiral in the Chilean, Brazilian and Greek Navies before being re-instated in 1832 and subsequently becoming an Admiral of the Red.

Thomas Cochrane joined the Royal Navy on 15 June 1796, during the French Revolutionary War, as a first class volunteer in his father's ship, the 5th-rate *Thetis*, in which he served for the next two years on the North American station. Early in 1800 he became one of his father's midshipmen in the 3rd-rate *Ajax* in the Channel fleet. They were soon deployed to Quiberon, to support the Chouans, the French Royalists fighting in Brittany. In May 1800 *Ajax* escorted a convoy of British troopships to Belle-Ile, only to find the place too heavily defended for a landing to be attempted. In August 1800 he was in the squadron covering a British landing to seize the Spanish naval base of Ferrol. This was found to be impregnable and the soldiers re-embarked to the indignation of their naval colleagues, who had expected handsome prize money. In a more successful operation in March 1801, his ship was at the landing of a British army in Egypt, leading to the defeat of the French at the battle of Alexandria (21 March 1801).

On the renewal of war with France in May 1803 Cochrane was in his father's flagship, the 3rd-rate *Northumberland*, where he served first on the Irish station and then the northern coast of Spain. He was appointed lieutenant in the 5th-rate *Jason* on 14 June 1805, in the West Indies, where his father was C-in-C, Leeward Islands, from 1805 to 1808. He became commander of the sloop *Nimrod* on 24 September 1805 and, after serving in the sloop *Melville*, was made acting captain of *Jason* on 23 January 1806, with his rank confirmed on 23 April 1806. On 27 January 1807, off the coast of Dutch Guiana (Surinam), he captured the French sloop *Favorite* and gained his first mention in despatches. In late December 1807, after Denmark had become a French ally, he took part in the capture of the Danish islands of St Thomas, St John and St Croix, off Puerto Rico.

Cochrane was given command of the 5th-rate *Ethalion* in October 1808, and was again mentioned in despatches for his part in the British recapture of the French West Indian islands of Martinique in February 1809 and The Saints (Iles des Saintes) in April 1809. He returned to the United Kingdom when his father's command in the West Indies came to an end and, in January 1812, married Matilda, the daughter of Lieutenant General Sir Charles Ross. They later had a family of two sons and two daughters. On 31 August 1812 Cochrane was appointed to the 5th-rate *Surprise*, which he commanded on the North American station during the American War of 1812. In this war he captured the United States privateer *Decatur* on 16 January 1813, served in the Chesapeake Bay area in support of Sir George Cockburn [20] in the British attacks on Washington and Baltimore, and took part in operations along the coast of Georgia. In 1815, with the end of the Napoleonic wars, he was placed on the half-pay list.

After the death of his wife in 1819 Cochrane returned to active duty in June 1820, commanding the 5th-rate *Forte*. He served on the North America and West Indies station until 1824 and was Governor of Newfoundland from 1825 to 1834. He then became Member of Parliament for Ipswich. In July 1841, during the First China War, he was appointed second-in-command to Sir William Parker [26] on the East India station, followed by promotion to rear-admiral of the Blue on 23

November 1841. Between 1845 and 1847 Cochrane was C-in-C, East Indies. He took personal command of operations against Borneo pirates and, in the summer of 1846, transferred his flag from the 3rd-rate *Agincourt* to the paddle-steamer *Spiteful* to lead an expedition up the Cherimon River in pursuit of the Sultan of Brunei. He was mentioned in despatches in 1845 and 1846 and was awarded the KCB in November 1847. Sir Thomas Cochrane became a vice-admiral of the Blue on 14 January 1850. From 1852 to 1855 he was C-in-C, Portsmouth, and in January 1853 married Rosetta Wheeler-Cuffe, the daughter of a baronet, with whom he went on to have a second family of two sons and two daughters. During 1854 he was responsible for fitting out ships for the Crimean War and offered to command the fleet sent to the Baltic. When Sir Charles Napier, to whom the command had been given, was recalled, Cochrane realized that whoever was appointed would be made the scapegoat for the shortcomings of Cabinet policy and did not put his name forward a second time. He was promoted to admiral of the Blue on 31 January 1856 and became an admiral of the fleet on 12 September 1865. Sir Thomas Cochrane died on 19 October 1872.

COCKBURN
Sir George, 2nd Baronet, GCB (1772–1853) [20]

George Cockburn, born in 1772, was the second son of James Cockburn (later an MP who was made a baronet for his parliamentary support to the Tories), and his wife Augusta, daughter of the Dean of Bristol. Of their children, one son became a major general, another a diplomat, and a third, the Dean of York. Cockburn entered the Navy on 12 March 1781, as captain's servant in a frigate commanded by Captain Samuel Rowley, grandson of Sir William Rowley [6]. His first sea service was between 1786 and 1787 in the sloop *Termagant,* prior to sailing for the East Indies station in 1788 in the sloop *Ariel.* He returned to the United Kingdom in 1791 and became midshipman and master's mate, first in the 5th-rate *Hebe* in the Channel and then in the 4th-rate *Romney,* in the Mediterranean. In 1792 he became acting lieutenant in the 5th-rate *Pearl* and on 21 January 1793 was appointed lieutenant in the sloop *Orestes.*

Following the outbreak of war with Revolutionary France in February 1793 Cockburn became ninth lieutenant of the 1st-rate *Britannia* (flagship of the second-in-command of the Mediterranean Fleet, Vice-Admiral William Hotham). He was then appointed tenth lieutenant of the 1st-rate *Victory,* (flagship of his patron, Lord Hood, as C-in-C of the Mediterranean Fleet), serving off Toulon in support of the French Royalists. With his seniors rapidly selected by the C-in-C to command other ships (one of the advantages of serving in a flagship), he rose to be first lieutenant before being made commander of the sloop *Speedy* on 11 October 1793. Having demonstrated his seamanship in the winter blockade of Genoa, he became acting captain of the 5th-rate *Inconstant* on 20 January 1794, with his promotion confirmed on appointment to the 5th-rate *Meleager* on 10 February 1794. He commanded this ship under Hood at the British landings in Corsica in February 1795 and, under Hood's successor, Hotham, in the battles of Leghorn (Livorno) (14 March 1795) and Toulon (13 July 1795).

Cockburn remained in the Mediterranean Fleet under Hotham's successors, Sir Hyde Parker and Sir John Jervis [12], and served during 1796 off the coasts of Piedmont and Genoa. His immediate superior was Commodore Horatio Nelson, with whom he harried the French Army's seaborne lines of communication in its North Italian campaign. He was mentioned in despatches for his part in cutting out transports carrying a French siege train, despite the fire of shore batteries (31 May 1796). Still penurious, but sprightly and fashionable, he became captain of the 5th-rate *Minerve* in August 1796 and remained in the same area, co-operating with the Austrians until their defeat by Bonaparte drove the Mediterranean Fleet from its Italian bases. Between 15 December 1796 and February 1797 *Minerve* wore the broad pendant of Commodore Nelson, whose own ship, the 3rd-rate *Captain*, was too slow for the allotted task of evacuating naval stores from Elba. On the way *Minerve* and her consort *Blanche* encountered two Spanish frigates and made a prize of one, the *Santa Sabina*. Nelson acknowledged Cockburn's part in the action by presenting him with a captured gold sword. He established a firm friendship both with Cockburn and his first lieutenant, Thomas Masterman Hardy, and at one point risked the ship to prevent Hardy (who had gone in a boat to search for a man overboard) from being captured.

Proceeding to join Jervis at Lisbon *Minerve* found herself sailing through the Spanish fleet from Cartagena, but weather conditions allowed her to escape. At the battle of St Vincent (14 February 1797) Cockburn was the first to report the presence of the Spanish fleet. He was present throughout the subsequent engagement, where Nelson, after *Captain* had been crippled by his use of her as a "patent bridge for boarding first-rates" ordered *Minerve* to carry him to the nearest ship of the line, *Irresistible*, where he rehoisted his flag. On 5 November 1797, when *Minerve* was unable to move from the mole at Gibraltar, Cockburn put out with three gunboats (pulled by oars) and rescued a becalmed convoy from a large flotilla of Spanish gunboats. Between December 1796 and the armistice with France on 22 October 1801 Cockburn's ship captured or destroyed the French frigates *Succes* and *Bravoure*, the corvette *Etonnant*, five privateers and a Danish sloop of war.

With the renewal of the war in May 1803, Cockburn was given command of the 5th-rate *Phaeton*. He served in the Channel, took the British Minister to the USA, carried treasure from there to British India and took part in the blockade of the Ile de France (Mauritius) in the Indian Ocean. In 1805 he returned to the United Kingdom in command of the store-ship *Howe*, a former East Indiaman, carrying the Governor-

General of Bengal, Marquis Wellesley. Between 1806 and 1809 he commanded in succession the 3rd-rates *Captain*, *Aboukir* and *Pompée*, taking the last to the West Indies in 1808 where he commanded the naval operations at the British capture of Martinique in February 1809. Cockburn returned to the United Kingdom in command of the 3rd-rate *Belleisle*, bringing the surrendered governor, garrison and ships from Martinique, and received the thanks of Parliament. In July 1809, in the sloop *Plover*, he led a division of small warships in the British landings at Walcheren, where he played a significant part in negotiating the capitulation of Flushing (Vlissingen) and covered the subsequent British withdrawal at the end of August 1809. In the same year he married his cousin, Mary Cockburn. They later had one child, a daughter, who married a naval commander. During 1810 Cockburn served off the Peninsular coast in the 3rd-rate *Implacable*, and carried treasure to Spain from Mexico. He became a commodore, with his broad pendant in the 4th-rate *Grampus*, on 26 November 1811.

Cockburn was promoted to rear-admiral of the Blue on 12 August 1812 and, following the outbreak of war with the United States of America, was sent to the North American station. He arrived in Chesapeake Bay early in 1813 and immediately began a series of descents along the coasts and rivers of the surrounding area, destroying shipping, burning stores and towns, and routing their defenders. In July 1813 he shifted his flag to the 3rd-rate *Sceptre* and descended on the coast of North Carolina, capturing the US sloops *Anaconda* and *Atlas*. He became a rear-admiral of the White on 4 December 1813 and rear-admiral of the Red on 4 June 1814. Sir John Warren, C-in-C, North America, from early 1813 to the spring of 1814, had some sympathy for non-combatants caught up in a pointless war. Like many British officers of the time, he regarded English-speaking Americans as kith and kin, and deplored Cockburn's incendiary activities. Warren's replacement, Sir Alexander Cochrane, took a different view and gave orders to lay waste and destroy all United States public property that could be reached. Cockburn, with his flag in the 3rd-rate *Albion*, returned from Bermuda in 1814 and was given command of the Chesapeake Bay area. His continual raids brought terror to the inhabitants of Maryland and Virginia up to ten miles inland of every coast and navigable river, with atrocity stories of arson, theft and rape making him an American hate-figure.

At the end of August 1814 Cochrane led his squadron's boats up the Patuxent River to achieve the destruction of a flotilla of US gunboats at Pig Point, after which he joined Major General Robert Ross in the British advance to Washington. There, in revenge for the burning of York (later Toronto), Ontario, by undisciplined US troops, and irritated by vulgar American puns on his name, he played a major part in the British decision to burn the public buildings of the new capital of the USA. This led to protests from the US government that, although most of the capitals of Europe had fallen to an enemy in the previous twenty years, none had been

49

put to the torch after occupation. The presidential residence subsequently became known as "the White House" from the wash applied to conceal the fire-damage sustained on this occasion. When the news reached London, this act of deliberate arson was condemned by the Prince Regent and others, who compared it with the burning of Ancient Rome by the Goths. By then Ross himself had fallen in the unsuccessful British attack on Baltimore, Maryland. This, the home port of numerous American privateers, withstood Cockburn's bombardment of Fort McHenry on the night of 12 September 1814, when his "rockets' red glare" inspired a spectator to write "The Star-Spangled Banner", later adopted as the national anthem of the USA. Cockburn was awarded the KCB in January 1815 and was preparing for a descent on Savannah, Georgia, when the War of 1812 came to an end. Between 1796 and 1814 he was eleven times mentioned in despatches.

Sir George Cockburn returned to Portsmouth in May 1815 to find Napoleon returned from Elba and a renewal of the war with France. On 8 August 1815 he sailed with his flag in the 3rd-rate *Northumberland*, as C-in-C and governor of St Helena, carrying the defeated emperor into exile, and remained there until June 1816. He sat as a Tory Member of Parliament successively for Portsmouth from 1818 to 1820, for Weobley, Herefordshire, from 1820 to May 1828, and for Plymouth from June 1828 until the reform of the House of Commons in 1832. Between April 1818 and May 1827 he was a Lord Commissioner of the Admiralty in the Board headed by Viscount Melville in Lord Liverpool's Cabinet. The Duke of Clarence [11] then became Lord High Admiral, with the Board of Admiralty reconstituted as his Council. As the senior member, Cockburn was the leading figure in the struggle to prevent Clarence from acting without his Council's advice, culminating in Clarence's removal from office in September 1828.

Cockburn became a vice-admiral of the Blue on 12 August 1819, vice-admiral of the White on 27 May 1825 and vice-admiral of the Red on 22 July 1830. As the senior naval lord of the Admiralty from the re-establishment of the Board in 1828, he encouraged efforts to improve the standard of gunnery in the fleet and approved the establishment of an experimental gunnery school at Portsmouth in the hulk *Excellent*. From December 1832 to February 1836 he was C-in-C, North America and West Indies, with his flag successively in the 4th-rates *Vernon* and *President*. Cockburn became admiral of the White on 10 January 1837. He returned to Parliament as MP for Ripley, Yorkshire, in September 1841 and was immediately re-appointed to the Admiralty as first naval lord, followed by promotion to admiral of the Red on 23 November 1841. He remained at the Admiralty, in the Board headed first by the Earl of Haddington and later by the Earl of Ellenborough, until the fall of Sir Robert Peel's second ministry in July 1846. (Cockburn's brother William, the Dean of York, was married to Peel's sister Elizabeth). Cockburn then gave up public office. He became admiral of the fleet on 1 July 1851 and inherited a baronetcy from his elder brother in February 1852. He died on 19 August 1853 and was succeeded in the baronetcy by his younger brother, the Dean of York. It was Sir George Cockburn who declared that, after the introduction of steam vessels into the Navy, he never saw a clean deck nor was waited on by a captain who did not look like a sweep.

CODRINGTON
Sir Henry John, KCB (1808–1877) [35]

Henry Codrington, born on 17 October 1808, was the youngest son of the then Captain (later Admiral Sir) Edward Codrington, a veteran of Trafalgar. The oldest son, Midshipman Edward Codrington, drowned in the Mediterranean when a cutter was upset. Henry Codrington joined the Navy on 21 February 1823 as a first class volunteer in the 5th-rate *Apollo* at Portsmouth, from which he transferred in July 1824 to the 5th-rate *Sybille* at Deptford. On 24 August 1824 he was appointed midshipman in the 5th-rate *Naiad*, in which he served in operations against pirates off the North African coast and the blockade of their base at Algiers in the same year. From then until 1826 he served off the coast of Greece, where the Greek War of Independence from Turkish rule was in progress. After returning to the United Kingdom he was appointed in October 1826 to the 2nd-rate *Asia*, his father's flagship as the newly-appointed C-in-C, Mediterranean.

In July 1827 the British, French and Russian governments agreed to use force to achieve Turkish recognition of Greek autonomy. Mehemet Ali, the Albanian ruler of Egypt, sent his own fleet to aid that of his nominal over-lord, the Sultan of Turkey. They met at Navarino (Neocastro or Pilos) on the south-west coast of the Morea (Peloponnisos), and were followed there by a combined British, French and Russian fleet under Admiral Codrington's command. In the battle of Navarino (20 October 1827), the last fleet action between wooden sailing ships, Codrington's fleet sank sixty ships without loss, though suffering 167 killed and many wounded. Among these was Henry Codrington, who was badly wounded in the leg by a piece of iron stern rail, driven into the cabin where he was acting as signal midshipman. The Lord High Admiral, the Duke of Clarence [11] sent Admiral Codrington his congratulations, but a new Tory government, led by the Duke of Wellington, described the battle as "an untoward event" and Codrington was recalled in the summer of 1828. Clarence made haste to distribute honours after the battle, for which more were awarded than in any previous encounter in the history of the Navy. Henry Codrington received nothing from his own sovereign, but was awarded the Russian Order of St Vladimir, the French Legion of Honour and (later) the Greek Order of the Redeemer.

Codrington then served successively in the 3rd-rate *Warspite* and the 5th-rate *Madagascar*, before becoming a lieutenant on 12 June 1829. In

August 1829 he joined the 1st-rate *Prince Regent*, flagship at the Nore, after which he was appointed to the 5th-rate *Briton* in April 1830. He became signal lieutenant in the 1st-rate *Caledonia*, his father's flagship in the Channel, in June 1831. Codrington was promoted to commander on 20 October 1831 and given command of the sloop *Orestes* on 6 June 1834, in which he served in the Mediterranean until his promotion to captain on 20 January 1836. In March 1838 he was appointed captain of the 6th-rate *Talbot* and joined the Mediterranean Fleet at Palermo, Sicily. During 1840, Mehemet Ali, encouraged by the French, seemed likely to seize control of the whole of Asia Minor from the Sultan of Turkey. The British, Russian and Austrian governments determined to oppose him by force and the Mediterranean Fleet was sent to the coast of Syria. Its arrival off Beirut, Lebanon, as part of a combined British, Austrian and Turkish naval force, led to a general rising throughout Syria against Mehemet Ali's oppressive rule. Acre, Palestine (Akko, Israel) was bombarded and captured on 4 October 1840, with Codrington taking part in a survey of the seaward approaches to the city during the previous night. Between March 1841 and December 1842 he was his father's flag captain as C-in-C Portsmouth, carried successively in the 1st-rates *Queen* and *St Vincent*. In October 1846 Codrington was appointed to the 5th-rate *Thetis* in which he returned to the Mediterranean in 1846. There, the despotic Grand Duke of Tuscany, regarded by Italian patriots as a puppet of the Austrians, was driven from his capital by a revolutionary uprising. He took refuge with his wife, children and attendants on board *Thetis* before agreeing to rule as a constitutional monarch. Codrington returned home with his ship in May 1850. He had married in 1849 Helen Webb Smith, with whom he later had two daughters.

In October 1853, at a time of increasing international tension with Russia, Codrington was appointed to the 1st-rate *Royal George*. After the outbreak of the Crimean War in March 1854 he was ordered to join the fleet sent to the Baltic under Admiral Sir Charles Napier. As senior officer in Napier's fleet, he put forward ideas on which he had worked for new tactics, but was disregarded. Napier pushed his fleet hard to improve its readiness for combat, but only gained the cordial dislike of his captains. *Royal George*, badly rigged and poorly crewed, failed to reach the required standard and Codrington was summoned to the flagship for a reprimand. Napier's complaints against Codrington and Captain Ryder [43] of the frigate *Dauntless* got as far as the Admiralty. Both officers were sufficiently well-connected to prevent any action being taken against them and eventually it was Napier himself who was recalled. Codrington took part in the Baltic operations and in February 1856 was given command of the 2nd-rate *Algiers*, leading a flotilla of gunboats and shallow-draught vessels intended for the capture of the Russian naval base at Kronshtadt. Russia made peace on terms favourable to the Allies in March 1856, after which Codrington saw no more active service. He was promoted to rear-admiral on 19 March 1857 and was Admiral Superintendent of Malta Dockyard from 1858 to 1863. He became vice-admiral on 24 September 1864. In 1865 he divorced his wife, but, as the innocent party, continued to be received in polite society and was awarded the KCB in March 1867. Sir Henry Codrington was promoted to admiral on 18 October 1867 and was C-in-C, Plymouth, from 1869 to 1872. In 1869 he married Catherine Aitchison, the widow of another admiral, and later had with her a daughter. He was promoted to admiral of the fleet on 22 January 1877 and died on 4 August 1877.

COMMERELL
Sir JOHN EDMUND, VC, GCB (1829–1901) [48]

John Commerell, the second son of John Commerell, Esquire, of Strood Park, Horsham, Surrey, was born in Grosvenor Square, London, on 13 January 1829. After attending Clifton College he entered the Navy on 8 March 1842 and was serving on the China station in the 3rd-rate *Cornwallis* at the end of the First China War in August 1842. He was subsequently appointed midshipman in the paddle frigate *Firebrand* under Captain James Hope [39] on the South America station. He took part in the battle of Punto Obligado (20 November 1845), where the local British and French admirals combined their forces to break the blockade of Montevideo, Uruguay, by an Argentine fleet. Commerell was in one of the boats from *Firebrand* that, under heavy fire, cut the cables of hulks supporting a chain across the River Parana. He became an acting mate in the sloop *Comus* on 16 May 1848, soon after his ship had returned to Woolwich, and was promoted to lieutenant on 13 December 1848. In April 1849 he was appointed to the paddle frigate *Dragon*, in which he served in the Mediterranean until August 1850, when he joined the screw frigate *Dauntless* at Devonport. He left this ship late in 1852 and in the following year married Mathilda, daughter of Joseph Bushby, Esquire, of Belgrave Square. They later had a family of three daughters.

Commerell returned to sea in February 1854, when, with the approach of the Crimean War, he was appointed lieutenant in the paddle frigate *Vulture*. He served in the Baltic campaign of 1854, prior to appointment on 20 February 1855 as lieutenant and commander of another paddle-steamer, the shallow-draught gun vessel *Weser*, in which he sailed for the Black Sea. The ship caught fire near Constantinople (Istanbul), struck a rock and had to be beached, but was eventually towed off and joined in the bombardment of Sevastopol on 16 June 1855. Commerell then took part in operations in the Sea of Azov, with promotion to the rank of commander on 29 September 1855. After hauling his boat across the Arabat spit, he landed with a party of his seamen on 11 October 1855 and went inland where he burnt stores of grain and forage intended for the Russian army in the Crimea. He then made a difficult return to his boat, pursued by Cossacks, in an action for which he was awarded the recently-instituted

Victoria Cross. During 1856–57 he commanded the steam vessel *Snake* in the Mediterranean Fleet.

In October 1858 Commerell was given command of the paddle sloop *Fury* on the East Indies and China station, where he took part in the Second China War. In the unsuccessful attack launched by Rear-Admiral James Hope (his old captain in *Firebrand*) against the Taku Forts at the mouth of the Peiho River (25 June 1859), he was second-in-command of the landing force. When this was repulsed with heavy casualties, he took over from his wounded senior officer and conducted a skilful withdrawal to the boats. Commerell was promoted to captain on 18 July 1859 and was appointed to the paddle frigate *Magicienne* in September 1859. After returning home with his ship late in 1861, he remained ashore until appointed to command the turret ship *Scorpion* at Portsmouth in May 1865. Between May 1866 and May 1868 he commanded the elderly paddle frigate *Terrible* in which he was employed in laying the trans-Atlantic telegraph cable, and from May 1869 to October 1870 commanded the turret ship *Monarch* in the Channel Squadron. In February 1871 Commerell was given command of the corvette *Rattlesnake*, as commodore 2nd Class and senior officer on the West Coast of Africa. In August 1873, while conducting a reconnaissance up the Pra River, Gold Coast (Ghana), in the preliminary phase of the Second Ashanti War, he was wounded in the lung by a musket ball and invalided home. He was awarded the KCB in 1874. From 1874 to 1879 Sir John Commerell was at Court as groom-in-waiting to Queen Victoria.

Commerell was promoted to rear-admiral on 12 November 1876. In July 1877 he was appointed second-in-command in the Mediterranean Fleet, with his flag in the battleship *Agincourt*. This was a time of growing international tension, with the despatch of the fleet to Constantinople (Istanbul) in February 1878 being countered by the arrival of a Russian army at the city gates. He hauled down his flag late in 1878, after the crisis had been resolved at the Congress of Berlin, and in 1879 became third naval lord in the Board of Admiralty under W H Smith in Disraeli's second Cabinet. He left the Admiralty in April 1880, when Gladstone and the Liberals returned to office. Commerell was promoted to vice-admiral on 19 January 1881 and served as C-in-C on the North America station from November 1882 to the autumn of 1885. He was then elected to Parliament as Conservative member for Southampton. Commerell left Parliament in July 1888 when he was appointed C-in-C, Portsmouth. Sir John Commerell was promoted to admiral of the fleet on 13 February 1892. He retired in January 1899 and returned to Court as groom-in-waiting. He died at his residence in Rutland Gate, London on 21 May 1901 and was buried in Folkestone Cemetery, where one of his daughters had been interred.

CORK AND ORRERY
EARL OF, see BOYLE, WILLIAM, [87]

CREASY
Sir GEORGE ELVEY, GCB, CBE, DSO, MVO (1895–1972)
[101]

George Creasy, the second son of a civil engineer, was born on 13 October 1895 at Badulla, Ceylon (Sri Lanka). He was a cadet at the Royal Naval Colleges, Osborne and Dartmouth, from September 1908 to 15 May 1913, when he was promoted to midshipman on appointment to the battleship *Conqueror*. After the outbreak of the First World War in August 1914 he remained in this ship in the Grand Fleet until 15 May 1915 when he was promoted to sub-lieutenant and appointed to the torpedo-boat destroyer *Lively* in the Harwich Force. Between February 1916 and May 1917 Creasy served in the destroyer *Milne*. He was promoted to lieutenant on 15 May 1917 and appointed first lieutenant of the destroyer *Nonsuch*, where he remained until January 1918. In May 1918 he joined the mining school at Portsmouth, and in November 1918, a few days before the end of hostilities, entered the torpedo school *Vernon*.

After qualifying, Creasy served between July 1920 and July 1922 as torpedo lieutenant of the destroyer *Malcolm*, leader of the Fifth Destroyer Flotilla in the Atlantic Fleet. He then returned to *Vernon* as a member of the permanent staff, and while there met and, in 1924, married Monica Ullathorne, the daughter of an Australian businessman. They later had a daughter, who died in infancy, and a son. After attending the Royal Naval Staff College, Creasy was promoted to lieutenant-commander on 15 December 1924 and appointed squadron torpedo officer in the cruiser *Frobisher*, flagship of the First Cruiser Squadron in the Mediterranean Fleet, in April 1926. From October 1926 to November 1927 he served in the battleship *Warspite*, flagship of the C-in-C Mediterranean Fleet, and from June 1928 to August 1929 was torpedo officer in the battleship *Rodney* in the Atlantic Fleet.

Creasy was promoted to commander on 30 June 1930. Between July 1930 and July 1932 he was on the permanent staff of the Tactical Training School at Portsmouth and from then until December 1933 was Staff Officer (Operations) to the C-in-C, Atlantic Fleet, with the flag in the battleship *Queen Elizabeth*. In July 1934 he was appointed commander of the cruiser *Sussex*, attached to the Royal Australian Navy. He was promoted to captain on 31 December 1935 and became an Assistant Director of Plans at the Admiralty in June 1936. From there he was appointed in May 1938 as Captain (Destroyers) of the First Destroyer Flotilla in the Mediterranean Fleet, in command of the flotilla leader *Grenville*. On the outbreak of the Second World War in September 1939 *Grenville* returned to home waters, where she was mined off Kentish Knock on 19 January 1940 and sank with heavy loss of life. Creasy was immediately appointed to her replacement, the flotilla leader *Codrington*, in which he carried Crown Princess Juliana of the Netherlands and her family to the United Kingdom to escape the invading Germans in May 1940. He took part in the evacuation of the

British Expeditionary Force from Dunkirk (26 May–4 June 1940) and was awarded the DSO.

Creasy then returned to the Admiralty, where he served from June to September 1940 as chief staff officer to the First Sea Lord, Sir Dudley Pound [89] and from then until August 1942 as Director of Anti-submarine Warfare, where he played an important part in the battle of the Atlantic. In September 1942 he became flag captain to Admiral Sir John Tovey [92], C-in-C Home Fleet, in the battleship *Duke of York*, in which he served until promoted to rear-admiral on 8 July 1943. In December 1943 he became chief of staff to Admiral Sir Bertram Ramsay, the newly appointed Naval C-in-C, Allied Expeditionary Force, and commenced planning for the Normandy landings of June 1944. The success of this operation, involving 5,000 ships in the greatest seaborne invasion in history, and the subsequent tasks of protecting Allied transports from mine and surface attacks, and clearing ports blocked by the defending Germans, all owed much to Creasy's grasp of staff duties. In October 1944 he was appointed Flag Officer (Submarines) and as such later went to the Far East to oversee the build-up of the Royal Navy's submarine strength in that theatre. He returned home in March 1945 and, with the surrender of Germany in May and Japan in August 1945, became responsible for the reception of enemy submarines ordered into British ports.

In February 1947 Creasy became Rear-Admiral (Air), commanding the aircraft carriers and naval air stations of the British Pacific Fleet and East Indies station, until promoted to vice-admiral on 4 January 1948. He joined the Admiralty as Fifth Sea Lord and Deputy Chief of the Naval Staff (Air) in September 1948, and was awarded the KCB in 1949. From November 1949 to the autumn of 1951 Sir George Creasy was Vice-Chief of the Naval Staff, with promotion to admiral on 15 January 1951. He served from January 1952 to January 1954 as C-in-C, Home Fleet, with his flag successively in the aircraft carrier *Indomitable* and the battleship *Vanguard*. From September 1954 to January 1956 he was C-in-C, Portsmouth, with promotion to admiral of the fleet on 22 April 1955. He then went onto half-pay and retired to Great Horkesley, Essex, where he died on 31 October 1972 and was buried in the churchyard of Saints Peter and Paul, Little Horkesley.

CUNNINGHAM
Sir ANDREW BROWNE, Viscount Cunningham of Hyndhope, 1st Baronet, KT, GCB, OM, DSO (1883–1963) [91]

Andrew Cunningham was born on 7 January 1883 at Dublin, where his father was at that time professor of anatomy. He was the second of three sons in a family of five and, with both parents coming from Scotland, was from 1892 to 1894 educated at Edinburgh Academy. He then attended Stubbington House, Fareham, Hampshire, prior to joining the Navy as a cadet in the training ship *Britannia* in January 1897. He was appointed a midshipman on 15 June 1898, in the cruiser *Fox* on the Cape of Good Hope and West Africa station. He initially joined the cruiser *Doris* at the Simon's Town naval base, Cape Town, before going with *Fox* to the east coast of Africa. Cunningham rejoined *Doris* as a supernumerary and from February to September 1900 served in a naval brigade during the Anglo-Boer South African War, where he was mentioned in despatches. He then returned to the United Kingdom, where in December 1900 he joined the battleship *Hannibal* in the Channel Squadron. Between July and October 1901 he was based at Portsmouth in the brig *Matilda*, a training ship for boys. He was then appointed to the cruiser *Diadem* until being promoted to acting sub-lieutenant on 7 January 1902 to begin his promotion courses. With his promotion confirmed on 14 March 1903, he was appointed to the battle-ship *Implacable* in the Mediterranean. In September 1907 he became first lieutenant of the torpedo-boat destroyer *Locust* and, when she returned home, was turned over with the rest of her complement to the torpedo-boat destroyer *Orwell*.

Cunningham was promoted to lieutenant on 31 March 1904 and appointed to the boys' training ship *Northampton*. In November 1904 he was transferred to the cruiser *Hawke*, a training ship for young seamen in which he served until May 1906, with cruises to North America and the West Indies. During the naval manoeuvres of 1906 he joined the protected cruiser *Scylla*, before serving from July 1906 to April 1908 in the armoured cruiser *Suffolk* in the Mediterranean Fleet. Between May 1908 and January 1910 he commanded Torpedo-boat 14 at Portsmouth. Cunningham then became lieutenant and commander of the torpedo-boat destroyer *Vulture* in the Home Fleet. He exchanged to the destroyer *Roebuck* in August 1910, but after she was put out of commission by problems with her boilers, was in January 1911 given command of the destroyer *Scorpion*. He proved a keen and zealous commanding officer, but incurred the displeasure of the Admiralty for using improper and exasperating language to a subordinate. After being exonerated from blame when *Scorpion* collided with and sank a sailing vessel, he was promoted to lieutenant-commander on 31 April 1912. In the autumn of 1913 he went with *Scorpion* to join the Mediterranean Fleet and was there in August 1914 on the outbreak of the First World War.

Cunningham spent most the war in this theatre, beginning with the blockade of the Dardanelles in September and October 1914. *Scorpion* was the first ship to go into action against the Turks, on 1 November 1914, four days before Turkey officially entered the war. She took part in the bombard-ment of the Dardanelles in February 1915 and was converted to a fast minesweeper in the following month. On 25 April 1915, as a minesweeper, she was at the landings on "V" beach, Gallipoli, and later was engaged in picking up survivors from the battleships *Triumph* and *Majestic*, torpedoed off the beachhead on 25 and 27 May 1915 respectively. When the remaining battleships were withdrawn, *Scorpion* and the other destroyers took their place giving gunfire support to the troops ashore until new monitors and cruisers arrived.

Cunningham was promoted to commander on 30 June 1915 and was awarded the DSO. He gained a reputation as a severe disciplinarian and dismissed a total of thirteen first lieutenants from *Scorpion* for failing to reach his exacting standards. On the other hand, he was a kind man in personal matters and throughout his career demonstrated concern for anyone sick or wounded, including those of the enemy as well as his own fleet. After taking his ship to Devonport to refit in July 1916 Cunningham returned to the Mediterranean to take command of the destroyer *Rattlesnake* and took part in the occupation of Greek-held island of Salamis and Piraeus, the port of Athens, in September 1916. He rejoined *Scorpion* at the Allied base on Mudros in October 1916. She was rammed and badly damaged on 30 November 1916 by her next astern, the destroyer *Wolverine*, and had to be repaired at Malta. After a year escorting convoys in the Mediterranean, *Scorpion* returned home in January 1918.

Cunningham was appointed to the destroyer *Ophelia* in the Grand Fleet on 28 February 1918, from where he transferred on 28 March 1918 to the destroyer *Termagant* in the Dover Patrol. At the end of May 1918 he engaged a numerically superior force of German destroyers and was reproved by his Captain (Destroyers) for having six times ignored the recall signal. He replied that he had six times signalled "enemy in sight" without receiving an acknowledgement. Cunningham continued to serve in the Channel until the Armistice of November 1918 and was awarded a bar to his DSO in February 1919. He remained in *Termagant* until March 1919, when he was appointed to the destroyer *Seafire* and sent to the Baltic. After maintaining a British naval presence during the tension associated with the creation of the new republic of Latvia as part of the post-war international settlement, he returned home in November 1919 and was awarded a second bar to his DSO.

Cunningham was promoted to captain on 31 December 1919. During 1920 and 1921 he played a leading part in arranging the demilitarization of the German island of Heligoland. In 1922 he was appointed Captain (Destroyers) of the Sixth Destroyer Flotilla in the Reserve fleet, in the flotilla leader *Shakespeare*, followed by appointment as Captain (Destroyers) of the First Destroyer Flotilla in the Atlantic Fleet, in the flotilla leader *Wallace*. During the Chanak crisis of September 1922, when there was a risk of war with Turkey, Cunningham was detached to the Mediterranean. From October 1924 to May 1926 he was captain of the destroyer base at Port Edgar. He then became flag captain to the C-in-C, North America and West Indies, in the light cruiser *Calcutta*, whose complement in November 1927 was turned over to the light cruiser *Despatch*. He returned home in September 1928 to attend the Army Senior Officers' course at Sheerness and then spent a year at the Imperial Defence College, London. In December 1929, after a three months' engagement, he married Nona Byatt, whom he had met in the West Indies while her brother was governor of

Trinidad. A week before his wedding he was appointed captain of the battleship *Rodney* in the Atlantic Fleet, in which he served until December 1930.

Known to his officers as ABC and to the lower deck as "Cutts", Cunningham was respected rather than popular. He displayed an intense will to win in every competition, disliked administration and staff work and was contemptuous of big ships and their routine. In July 1931 he became commodore of the Royal Naval barracks at Chatham, where he took a sympathetic interest in the welfare problems arising from the pay cuts that drove the Atlantic Fleet to mutiny in September 1931. He was promoted to rear-admiral on 24 September 1932 and left Chatham in February 1933. Cunningham became Rear-Admiral (Destroyers) in the Mediterranean Fleet in December 1933, with his flag in the light cruiser *Coventry*, and became a keen supporter of training for night action. In 1935 he hoisted his flag in *Despatch* but found her too slow to lead four flotillas totalling thirty-eight ships, and soon shifted his flag to the light cruiser *Galatea*. He remained in this appointment until March 1936, during the international crisis of 1935–36, when it seemed that the opposition of the British and French governments to the Italian invasion of Abyssinia (Ethiopia) would lead them into war with Italy . The Italian government saw little difference between its own designs for Abyssinia and the position already held by the British in Egypt or the French in Algeria, and resented the unfriendly attitude of these two countries, its former allies in the First World War.

Cunningham was promoted to vice-admiral on 22 July 1936 and became second-in-command of the Mediterranean Fleet, with his flag in the battlecruiser *Hood*, in July 1937. He was deployed to the coast of Spain to protect neutral shipping during the Spanish Civil War and returned to the United Kingdom on appointment as Deputy Chief of the Naval Staff at the Admiralty in September 1938. This was a period of intense activity following the Cabinet's agreement to a rearmament programme, and Cunningham's own work-load was increased by the ailing health of the First Sea Lord, Sir Roger Backhouse [88]. He was awarded the KCB in January 1939. On the appointment of Sir Dudley Pound [89] to succeed Backhouse in June 1939, Sir Andrew Cunningham took Pound's place as C-in-C, Mediterranean, with acting promotion to admiral and was there, with his flag in the battleship *Warspite*, on the outbreak of the Second World War in September 1939.

In June 1940, when Italy entered the war shortly before the fall of France, the new British Prime Minister, Winston Churchill, determined that French warships should not fall into Axis hands. Cunningham negotiated an agreement whereby the French squadron at Alexandria was detained without bloodshed. He then had to face a fast and powerful Italian surface fleet, which he first encountered at the battle of Calabria (9 July 1940). The Italians withdrew at speed, outrunning Cunningham, who broke off the pursuit when he came within range of Italian aircraft and torpedo craft. At Taranto (11 November 1940) he used torpedo bombers, flying by night from the aircraft carrier *Illustrious*, to disable three Italian battleships at their moorings, in the first carrier-based major victory in the history of naval warfare. His promotion to admiral was confirmed on 3 January 1941. At the battle of Matapan (28 March 1941), the first important fleet action since Jutland, Cunningham achieved another victory over the Italians. Against a numerically superior enemy, he sank five major surface combatants, while suffering the loss of only two aircraft.

In May 1941 the British army sent to support Greece against a German invasion was defeated and evacuated to Crete. From there, with the German Air Force having gained control of the sky, the survivors were withdrawn to Egypt, at heavy cost to Cunningham's fleet. Unlike his predecessors at the Dardanelles, he was prepared to accept the losses, declaring "It takes the Navy three years to build a ship but three hundred years to build a tradition . . . We must not let the Army down". In September 1941, with *Warspite* badly damaged, he hoisted his flag in the battleship *Queen Elizabeth*, though from time to time he exercised his command ashore (with great reluctance) from his base in Alexandria. His resources continued to dwindle under attack from the air, from mines and from Italian frogmen. In December 1941 his heaviest remaining ships were three light cruisers and an anti-aircraft cruiser at Alexandria and two light cruisers at Malta, but he nevertheless succeeded in maintaining the convoy routes to Malta and North Africa while his fleet strength was rebuilt.

In June 1942 Cunningham was summoned to Washington for discussions with the combined Chiefs of Staff committee. He was subsequently selected as Allied Naval Commander, Expeditionary Force, commanding the western basin of the Mediterranean and the fleet supporting the Anglo-American landings in French North Africa in November 1942. He resumed the appointment of C-in-C, Mediterranean, in February 1943, with responsibility for the western basin and much of the former North Atlantic Command area, while that for the eastern basin remained with the Levant Command established in November 1942. Cunningham was promoted to admiral of the fleet on 21 January 1943. He planned the Allied invasion of Sicily and in July 1943 was able to signal that the Italian fleet lay at anchor under the guns of the fortress of Malta. In September 1943 his ships covered the Allied landings at Salerno, on the Italian mainland.

Cunningham was called home to succeed Pound as First Sea Lord at the beginning of October 1943. His appointment was recommended by the First Lord, A V Alexander, but was resisted by Churchill on the grounds that Cunningham was too old and would not be able to cope with the pressure of work in the Chiefs of Staff Committee. It is more likely that Churchill believed (correctly) that the abrupt and forceful Cunningham would be not be easy for him to influence. He accordingly first offered the post to Sir Bruce Fraser [95] who replied that he believed he had the confidence of his own fleet, but Cunningham had that of the whole Navy. Cunningham proved well able to deal with Churchill and got on well with the other wartime Chiefs of Staff. He left the details of policy-making to his own subordinates, and allowed Fraser, as C-in-C Home Fleet, to conduct the operations leading to the destruction of the German capital ships *Scharnhorst* and *Tirpitz*. After the Normandy landings in June 1944, the greatest seaborne invasion in history, he complained at the slowness of the Army in clearing the mouths of the Scheldt and advocated a vigorous coastal campaign to occupy Hamburg and the Danish seaboard. The revival of the threat from German U-boats in early 1945 posed a serious problem, resolved only by heavy air attacks on their bases and their eventual occupation by advancing troops on the ground.

With victory in sight in Europe, attention turned to the war against Japan. Churchill, supported by his protégé Lord Louis Mountbatten [102] (Supreme Allied Commander, South East Asia), was in favour of using British naval resources for the re-conquest of Burma, Malaya and Singapore. Cunningham pressed for the employment of a powerful fleet in the Central Pacific, joining the United States in an offensive against the Japanese home islands and so ending the war more quickly, with the saving of many lives. Churchill, who saw political benefits in the plan, was persuaded to agree, but the idea was resisted by Admiral of the Fleet Ernest J King, US Chief of Naval Operations. King saw no need for a British presence in a theatre where the US Navy was achieving a string of victories and argued that the Royal Navy, weak in naval aircraft and logistic ships, and unused to the immense distances of the Pacific, would prove a drain on American resources. He was over-ruled by the Combined Chiefs of Staff. Cunningham, whose relations with his American opposite numbers (apart from King) were always cordial, then assembled a fleet and fleet train and despatched them to form the British Pacific Fleet, commanded by Sir Bruce Fraser. Based on Sydney, New South Wales, this took part in several major operations before the war ended with the Japanese offer to surrender on 10 August 1945. In September 1945 Sir Andrew Cunningham was raised to the peerage as Baron Cunningham of Hyndhope.

In the immediate post-war period Lord Cunningham had to cope with the effects of demobilization and of reductions in defence expenditure to help the rebuilding of the national economy. He broadened the base of officer recruitment, retained the Women's Royal Naval Service as a permanent part of the Royal Navy and urged the amalgamation of the Army's commandos with those of the Royal Marines. He retired from the Admiralty in May 1946 and was succeeded by his namesake Sir John Cunningham [94]. Lord Cunningham became a viscount in 1946 and a Lord High Commissioner of the Church of Scotland in 1950. In his later life he suffered from cardio-vascular illness, thought to have been brought on by the stress of high command in war. He died of a heart attack in a London taxi on 16 June 1963 and was buried at sea, off Portsmouth, from the guided missile destroyer *Hampshire*. He had no children and his peerage became extinct. Viscount Cunningham, with his record of victories in the Mediterranean unequalled since the days of Nelson, was admired not only by the Navy, but also by the British Army (in which his younger brother was a general) and by the Royal Air Force. To the other Services, he became known as "the Old Man of the Sea". To his own, he was a "salt-horse" (an officer who had never followed the intellectually demanding route of qualifying as a specialist). It has been suggested that this, and his lack of formal staff training, may have hindered him in fighting the Whitehall battles required of a First Sea Lord, but nothing can detract from his achievements as the Navy's foremost combat admiral of his day.

CUNNINGHAM
Sir JOHN HENRY DACRES, GCB, MVO (1885–1962) [94]

John Cunningham, the son of a barrister-at-law, was born at Demurrer, British Guiana (Guyana) on 18 April 1885. He entered the Navy in 1900 as a cadet in the training ship *Britannia* and on 1 June 1901 became a midshipman in the cruiser *Gibraltar*, flagship of the Cape of Good Hope and West Coast of Africa station. He was promoted to acting sub-lieutenant on 30 July 1904 at the beginning of his promotion courses and became a lieutenant on 30 October 1905. He served as a supernumerary in the battleship *Illustrious* in the Channel fleet from May to September 1906, when he was given command of the torpedo gun-boat *Hebe* at Haulbowline, Devonport, while he began his studies to qualify as a navigating officer. In January 1907 Cunningham was appointed to the navigation school *Dryad* at Portsmouth for instructional duties. From there he joined the protected cruiser *Indefatigable* on the North America and West Indies station, in which he served from January 1908 to January 1909. Between April 1909 to January 1910 he was in the protected cruiser *Iphigenia* in the Home Fleet. In 1910 he returned to *Dryad* and married Dorothy Hannay, of Ulverston, Lancashire. They later had two sons, one of whom was lost at sea in 1941 while serving in a submarine.

Cunningham was appointed navigating lieutenant of the armoured cruiser *Berwick* in May 1911 on the West Indies station. He was promoted to lieutenant-commander on 30 October 1913 and was still in the West Indies on the outbreak of the First World War in August 1914. He became navigating officer of the battleship *Russell* in the Mediterranean Fleet in July 1915 and survived when she was sunk by a mine off Malta on 27 June 1916. He was then appointed to the battle-cruiser *Renown* in the Battle-cruiser Fleet of the Grand Fleet. Cunningham was promoted to commander on 30 June 1917, and was transferred to the battle-cruiser *Lion*, flagship of the Battle-cruiser Fleet, in July 1918. He remained there following the end of hostilities in November 1918, under the flag of Sir Roger Keyes [80]. He followed Keyes to the battle-cruiser *Hood* in December 1919 and became the squadron navigating officer of the Battle-cruiser Squadron (reduced from a fleet on the dispersal of the Grand Fleet). In April 1921 he was appointed commander of *Dryad*.

Cunningham left *Dryad* in August 1923, when he was appointed Master of the Fleet (senior navigating officer) of the Atlantic Fleet, with the flag in the battleship *Queen Elizabeth*. He was promoted to captain on 30 June 1924 and, between February 1925 and January 1928, was on the staff of the Naval War College, Greenwich. He then returned to the Atlantic Fleet to command the minelayer *Adventure*, in which he served until November 1929. He became Deputy Director in the Plans Division at the Admiralty in December 1929 and was Director of Plans from December 1930 to December 1932. Between September 1933 and July 1934 Cunningham commanded the battleship *Resolution* in the Mediterranean Fleet. After attending the Senior Officers' War Course, he was promoted to rear-admiral on 1 January 1936 and joined the Board of Admiralty as Assistant Chief of the Naval Staff in October 1936. When the Fleet Air Arm was transferred from the Royal Air Force to the Royal Navy in August 1937 he became ACNS (Air). Cunningham left the Admiralty in July 1938. He was given acting promotion to vice-admiral on 19 August 1938, on appointment to the Mediterranean Fleet, with his flag in the cruiser *Devonshire* in the First Cruiser Squadron and his promotion confirmed on 30 June 1939.

On the outbreak of the Second World War in September 1939 Cunningham's squadron joined the Home Fleet. He took part in the Norwegian campaign of April–June 1940, evacuated the Allied troops from Namsos in May 1940 and, when Norway fell to the Germans, carried the King and his government into exile in the United Kingdom. With his flag still in *Devonshire*, Cunningham commanded the naval forces in the unsuccessful Allied attempt to capture the strategically important French West African base of Dakar, Senegal, (23–25 September 1940). He was present at the Free French capture of Douala, French Cameroons, in November 1940, where he remained for a time with his flag in the cruiser *Neptune*. Some years later he was made an honorary corporal in the French Foreign Legion, for having served with its members from the Arctic to the Equator. He returned to the Board of Admiralty early in 1941 as Fourth Sea Lord and Chief of Naval Supplies and Transport, and was awarded the KCB. Sir John Cunningham became an acting admiral on appointment as C-in-C, Levant, (the eastern Mediterranean basin) in June 1943. His promotion was confirmed on 4 August 1943 and, when Levant Command was abolished in December 1943, he succeeded Sir Andrew Cunningham **[91]** as C-in-C, Mediterranean Fleet and Allied Naval Commander, Mediterranean. As such he was responsible for conducting the naval operations in support of the Allied landings on the Anzio beachhead (24 January–24 May 1944) and the French Mediterranean coast (August 1944). He remained in the Mediterranean in the period following the end of the war in Europe in May 1945, at a time of continued tension in the Balkans.

In May 1946 Sir John Cunningham succeeded Lord Cunningham as First Sea Lord and became the first navigating officer to reach the head of his Service. The time was a difficult one for all three services, with the

Labour government, elected in 1945, giving priority to establishing a Welfare State and rebuilding an economy shattered by six years of war. The Treasury, as at the conclusion of every victorious war, argued that as there was no longer an enemy threat, expenditure on defence was hardly necessary. Cunningham hoped for support from A V Alexander, who had been First Lord of the Admiralty in Churchill's wartime coalition government and had retained this office in the new government, headed by his old friend and political ally, Clement Attlee. Alexander (later created Viscount Alexander of Hillsborough) became Minister of Defence in December 1946 and was succeeded by another former trade union leader, the newly created Viscount Hall. The new First Lord was not disposed to challenge the Cabinet's plans for rapid disarmament, hastened by a worsening economic situation and Cunningham was forced to scrap large numbers of serviceable ships and reduce the number of vessels on foreign stations.

Cunningham was promoted to admiral of the fleet on 21 January 1948. His formidable intellectual ability and high level of self-confidence had enabled him to argue convincingly, if unsuccessfully, against the reductions imposed on the Royal Navy, but his austere personality and sharp tongue left him without political allies in Whitehall. Despite his sound practical judgement, he was respected rather than popular, and was noted as a stern disciplinarian who rarely bestowed praise. It was said of him that he did not suffer fools gladly and that he placed 95% of those with whom he had to deal in this category. He left the Admiralty in September 1948 and became chairman of the Iraq Petroleum Company. He retired from this post in 1958 and died in the Middlesex Hospital, London, on 13 December 1962.

CURTIS
Sir LUCIUS, 2nd Baronet, KCB (1786–1869) [27]

Lucius Curtis was born on 3 June 1786, the second son of Commander Roger Curtis, who later became a baronet and admiral of the Red. He entered the Navy during the French Revolutionary War on 2 June 1795 as captain's servant in his father's flagship, the 1st-rate *Queen Charlotte*, in the Channel. In August 1798 he was appointed midshipman in his father's flagship, the 2nd-rate *Prince*, and subsequently served in the Channel and Mediterranean Fleets. He followed his father when the latter became C-in-C, Cape of Good Hope in 1799, and was promoted to lieutenant in his flagship, the 3rd-rate *Lancaster*, on 11 August 1801. Sir Roger Curtis remained at the Cape until 1808. Lucius Curtis moved to the 3rd-rate *Excellent* in September 1803 and returned to the Mediterranean, where he became commander of the sloop *Jalouse* on 16 November 1804. He was given command of the sloop *Rose* in June 1805 and was made captain of the 5th-rate *Magicienne* on 22 January 1806.

During 1808 he took part in operations against the French in the Indian Ocean and was in support of the capture of the Ile de Bourbon (Reunion) in July 1810. At the end of August 1810 *Magicienne*, in company with three other frigates, attacked Port Sud-Est (Grand Port), on the Ile de France (Mauritius). This attack, which military officers suspected was undertaken by their naval colleagues in the hope of making prize-money before the troops arrived, proved a disaster. *Magicienne* and her consort *Sirius* went aground and were burnt to prevent them falling into French hands. Their companies were taken off, but were subsequently captured when the two remaining frigates, *Nereid* and *Iphigenia*, encountered a superior French squadron. The civilized convention of the time was that prisoners of war were exchanged with those of equal rank on the other side as soon as possible, but on this occasion the local French authorities imposed delays. It was therefore not until Mauritius fell to a combined military and naval expedition in December 1810 that Curtis and his men were released.

After returning to the United Kingdom Curtis married Mary Greetham, daughter of the Deputy Judge Advocate of the Fleet, in June 1811. He was given command of the recaptured 5th-rate *Iphigenia* in January 1812, and became captain of the 5th-rate *Madagascar* in February 1813. He served at sea until September 1814, six months after the end of hostilities following Napoleon's first abdication. In 1816 Curtis inherited his father's baronetcy, as his elder brother, who was also a captain in the Navy, had died in 1801. Sir Lucius Curtis became a rear-admiral of the Blue on 28 June 1838 and a rear-admiral of the White on 23 November 1841. From March 1843 to March 1848 he was admiral superintendent of Malta Dockyard, where, on 12 February 1847 he became rear-admiral of the Red. He was promoted to vice-admiral of the Blue on 12 September 1849, vice-admiral of the White on 1 July 1851 and vice-admiral of the Red on 5 November 1853. Curtis then rose to be admiral of the Blue on 9 July 1855, admiral of the White on 30 July 1857, and admiral of the Red on 1 November 1864. He was promoted to admiral of the fleet on 11 January 1864 and died on 14 January 1869. He had a family of three daughters and four sons, of whom the two eldest became officers in the Navy. Lady Curtis and all his sons predeceased him, so that his baronetcy was inherited by his only surviving grandson.

DE ROBECK
Sir JOHN MICHAEL, 1st Baronet, GCB, GCMG, GCVO (1862–1928) [77]

John De Robeck, the second son of an Irish landholder, was born at Gowran Grange, Naas, County Kildare, on 10 June 1862. His father was Baron de Robeck in the nobility of Sweden, but both parents came from families forming part of the Anglo-Irish Protestant Ascendancy, with its long-established tradition of military service. John De Robeck was the first to join the Navy and was a cadet in the training ship *Britannia* from 1875 to 1877. He served as a midshipman in the frigate *Shannon* in the Channel Squadron between July 1878 and March 1881 and was appointed to the boys' training ship *St Vincent* at Portsmouth in April 1882. He became a sub-lieutenant on 27 July 1882 and joined the gunnery training school *Excellent* in 1883. In August 1883 he was appointed to the gunboat *Espoir* on the China station, where he was promoted to lieutenant on 30 September 1885. During 1886 De Robeck was in the battleship *Audacious*, flagship of the C-in-C, China station. In 1887 he was first lieutenant of the brig *Seaflower*, tender to the boys' training ship *Boscawen* at Portland, before being appointed to the battleship *Agincourt*, flagship of the Channel Squadron, in which he served from November 1887 to September 1888. From then until December 1890 he was on the staff of *Britannia*. De Robeck returned to the China station to serve in the flagship, the armoured cruiser *Impérieuse*, between January 1891 and February 1893. From August 1883 to March 1895 he was the senior lieutenant in *Britannia*.

De Robeck served as gunnery lieutenant in the corvette *Cordelia* on the North America and West Indies station from November 1895 until his promotion to commander on 22 June 1897. Between 1897 and 1899 he commanded in succession the torpedo-boat destroyers *Desperate*, *Angler* and *Mermaid*, based at Chatham, and from June 1900 to August 1901 was the commander of the cruiser *Pyramus* in the Mediterranean Fleet. He was promoted to captain on 1 January 1902. De Robeck then went on half-pay until August 1906, when he returned to the Mediterranean Fleet in command of the armoured cruiser *Carnarvon*. Between January 1908 and January 1910 he was captain of the battleship *Dominion* in the Channel fleet. He spent most of 1911 as Inspecting Captain of boys' training establishments, based at Devonport, until promoted to rear-admiral on 1 December 1911. De Robeck was appointed in April 1912 to the newly created post of Admiral of Patrols, commanding four flotillas of destroyers, each led by a cruiser, and was additionally responsible for organizing a reserve of motor-boats for inshore duties. He completed his tenure of command in May 1914, but on the approach of the First World War in August 1914 was appointed to command the Ninth Cruiser Squadron, formed from the Reserve, with his flag in the cruiser *Amphitrite*. Based at Finisterre, his ships were employed on trade protection and interdiction duties in the mid-Atlantic, where he captured the German liners *Schleisen* and *Graecia*.

At the beginning of 1915 De Robeck was appointed second-in-command of the naval force assembled to force a passage through the Dardanelles and attack Constantinople (Istanbul), with his flag in the battleship *Vengeance*. An initial bombardment carried out during February 1915 was judged unsuccessful. Vice-Admiral Sackville Carden, the Allied naval commander, was invalided home in March 1915. The senior naval officer on the station was Sir Rosslyn Wemyss [71], but the command was given to De Robeck, who had worked closely with Carden, and who accordingly took his place in the battleship *Queen Elizabeth*. A renewed attack on 18 March 1915, with De Robeck's flag in the battle-cruiser

Inflexible, cost one French and two British battleships. *Inflexible* was damaged by a mine, to the fury of the First Sea Lord, Lord Fisher **[58]**, who was expecting her return to the Grand Fleet. Shocked by the loss of the battleships, De Robeck decided that it was impossible to proceed without support from the Army and broke off the attack. He was present at the subsequent landings in Suvla Bay on 25 April 1915, with his flag in the cruiser *Chatham*. With *Queen Elizabeth* recalled to the Grand Fleet in May 1915 and two more battleships sunk by a German submarine, he withdrew his capital ships and gave the task of naval gunfire support to his destroyers, pending the arrival of new monitors and cruisers. The troops ashore could make no headway against the strengthened Turkish defences and were taken off by De Robeck's fleet in January 1916. He was awarded the KCB in the campaign honours.

Sir John De Robeck was appointed Vice-Admiral commanding the Second Battle Squadron in the Grand Fleet, with his flag in the battleship *King George V*, on 3 December 1916. He remained there, with substantive promotion on 17 May 1917, until the fleet was dispersed in May 1919 after the end of hostilities. Late in 1919 he was appointed British High Commissioner to Turkey and C-in-C, Mediterranean Fleet, with his flag in the battleship *Iron Duke*. De Robeck was promoted to admiral on 24 March 1920 and hauled down his flag in the Mediterranean in April 1922. He married in 1922 the widowed Hilda, Lady Lockhart, and from August 1922 to August 1924 was C-in-C, Atlantic Fleet. He was promoted to admiral of the fleet on 24 November 1925 and held no further naval commands. De Robeck continued his lifelong interest in sports and games, and in 1925 became President of the Marylebone Cricket Club. He died suddenly at his home in London on 20 January 1928. There were no children of his marriage and his baronetcy became extinct.

EDWARD VII
ALBERT EDWARD, HM King of Great Britain and Ireland, Emperor of India (1841–1910) **[44]**

Prince Albert Edward, eldest son and second child of Queen Victoria and her consort Prince Albert, was born on 9 November 1841. Created Prince of Wales and Earl of Chester soon after his birth, he was known as the Prince of Wales for most of his long life. Fearing that her son might copy the dissolute and improvident ways of her father and uncles, Victoria provided him with strict tuition and rules of behaviour and kept him under close control until he reached the age of 21. The Prince of Wales attended Christ Church, Oxford, from 1859 to 1860 and Trinity College, Cambridge, from January to December 1861. The Queen denied him any part in her political duties and he instead became the leader of fashionable society, especially after Victoria herself withdrew into secluded widowhood. In March 1863 he married Princess Alexandra of Denmark. As Princess of

Wales, she provided him with heirs and, accepting the conventions of her time, tolerated with resignation her husband's various mistresses and adulterous *affaires*. On 18 July 1887 he was made an honorary admiral of the fleet, a rank that the Navy had always denied his father, though the Army made no difficulty about either the Prince Consort or the Prince of Wales being made field marshals on the Active List.

In 1891 the Prince of Wales was a witness in a libel case, having been present at a game of baccarat when one player was accused of cheating. His playboy lifestyle then became a matter of public comment, so that he was obliged to issue a statement condemning intemperance and gambling. He kept up a keen interest in his racing stables and maintained his habit of attending lavish social events at home and abroad. He succeeded to the throne as Edward VII on 22 January 1901, though a serious illness led to the postponement of his coronation until August 1902. In domestic politics King Edward reigned as a constitutional sovereign and urged caution on the extreme Conservatives in the House of Lords when they sought to defy the Liberal majority in the Commons in 1909. In foreign affairs, as "the uncle of Europe", his visits to other heads of state gained him a reputation as a diplomat and peacemaker, though he had little real influence on events. Edward's personal relations with his nephew, the German Emperor William II [47], were outwardly cordial, but privately cool. This was partly because of the differences between William and his mother, (Edward's elder sister Victoria, widowed on the early death of her husband the Emperor Frederick) and partly because of William's open disapproval of his uncle's hedonistic ways. Edward VII was the first non-seafaring British monarch to be an admiral of the fleet and the only one to be appointed while Prince of Wales. On his accession, he dispensed with the honorary element of his rank. His reign, though marked by turbulence in both domestic and foreign politics, came to be seen by its survivors as a golden twilight age before the cataclysm of the First World War. He died at Buckingham Palace, London, on 6 May 1910 and was buried in St George's Chapel, Windsor.

EDWARD VIII
EDWARD ALBERT CHRISTIAN GEORGE ANDREW
PATRICK DAVID, HM King of Great Britain and Ireland,
Emperor of India, later HRH Duke of Windsor, KG, KT, KP,
GCB, GCSI, GCMG, GCIE, GCVO, GBE, ISO, MC
(1894–1972) [84]

Prince Edward (known in his family as David) was born on 23 June 1894 at White Lodge, Richmond Park, Surrey, the first in a family of five sons and one daughter of the then Duke and Duchess of York, later George V [44] and Queen Mary. Although in direct line of succession from his birth, Edward was initially given a naval education and from May 1907 was trained as a cadet at the Royal Naval Colleges, Osborne and Dartmouth. On the death of Edward VII [44] in May 1910, Prince Edward became heir apparent and was created Duke of Cornwall and Earl of Chester. On his sixteenth birthday he was created Prince of Wales, in a ceremony specially devised to appeal to Welsh national sentiment. The Prince found the event and the regalia rather fanciful and was glad to go to sea for three months later in 1911, as a midshipman in the battleship *Hindostan*. He went up to Magdalen College, Oxford, in 1912 and studied there for two years. At the outbreak of the First World War he was commissioned as a second lieutenant in the 1st Battalion, the Grenadier Guards on 6 August 1914. When this unit embarked for France on 8 September 1914, George V refused to allow him to go with it, or to perform any military duties on active service.

This prohibition remained a cause of dissatisfaction to the Prince of Wales who, like most young men of the time, wished to share the dangers of his friends and contemporaries. Instead, he was employed on the staff, where he was too junior in rank to be given important duties and too high in status to be used as an ADC. The Prince came under shell-fire on a number of occasions, on one of which his staff car was hit and his driver was killed. He was promoted to captain on 10 March 1916 and was awarded the Military Cross shortly afterwards, despite his representations that many more deserving officers had been overlooked. George V had previously had to order him to wear the decorations that he had been given by the French and Russian governments. The Prince himself, feeling he had done nothing to earn them, did so with reluctance. When it became clear that he would not be allowed into the line with the Guards Division, he asked to be allowed to leave the Western Front. In March 1916 he went to Egypt, ostensibly to report on the defences of the Suez Canal, but in practice to boost the morale of the British troops. He then returned to France, from where in November 1917 he went to Italy with the Allied reinforcements sent there after the victory of the Central Powers at Caporetto. He remained there until June 1918, when he returned to France until the end of hostilities in November 1918.

With the war over, the Prince of Wales began a series of tours of the British Empire, the Far East and the United States. Everywhere he was greeted with acclaim. During the next eighteen years, he remained popular at home and abroad, a leader of fashion, and the world's most eligible bachelor. On the death of his father on 20 January 1936 he succeeded to the throne as Edward VIII and, following the precedent set by George V, became an admiral of the fleet, a field marshal, and a marshal of the Royal Air Force the next day. It soon became clear that the new King wished to bring an element of freshness and informality into the monarchy. Influenced partly by his experience of military service in the First World War, he had developed vague humanitarian views on social matters and several times expressed sympathy for those whose lives were blighted by the consequences of mass unemployment. In November 1936, he gave hope to the distressed miners of South Wales and alarm to his Conservative ministers, by saying that "something must be done".

By this time, however, Edward's reign was nearly over. He had fallen in love with an American lady of strong character and considerable charm, Mrs Wallis Simpson, whom he became determined to marry. Stanley Baldwin, the Conservative Prime Minister of the day, supported by the Labour Opposition and by the Prime Ministers of the self-governing Dominions, advised him that the King's marriage was not one of personal choice alone, but a matter of state. An insurmountable objection to Mrs Simpson becoming Queen was that the Church of England taught that marriage was for life. It was therefore unacceptable for Edward, as Supreme Governor of that Church, to marry a lady with not merely one, but two divorced husbands still living. Despite all the urging of his friends, family and ministers, Edward decided that, if he must choose between his crown and Mrs Simpson, he would give up the former. He abdicated on 11 December 1936, telling his people that he could not carry out his duties in the way that *he* would wish to do, without the support and companionship of the woman he loved. He was succeeded by his younger brother, the Duke of York, who came to the throne as George VI [86]. Public opinion turned against Edward, who was seen by all classes as having put his personal feelings before his duty. Working class people in particular felt he had given Baldwin a way of removing someone who they imagined could have been the "people's king" and could not understand why he simply did not keep Mrs Simpson as a mistress, in the way that they expected kings to behave.

George VI granted his brother the title of HRH the Duke of Windsor. When the Duke married Mrs Simpson in France on 3 June 1937, she became Duchess of Windsor, but neither then nor later would George VI allow her the status of a Royal Highness. On the outbreak of the Second World War Windsor sought employment in the public service. After agreeing to waive his military rank as field marshal, he was made a major general and was attached to the British Military Mission in Paris. With the fall of France in June 1940, Windsor decided that the safety of his Duchess must be his first concern and fled with her first to Spain and then to Portugal. He refused orders to return to the United Kingdom and, in August 1940, accepted the post of governor of the Bahamas. This enabled him to support the war effort by promoting cordial relations with his American friends, including unauthorized private meetings with President Franklin D Roosevelt. At the end of the war Windsor was offered another West Indian post, as governor of Bermuda. He declined this and eventually returned to exile in France, where he died of cancer of the throat at his home in the Bois de Boulogne, Paris, on 28 May 1972. He was buried at the Royal Mausoleum, Frogmore, Windsor. He relinquished all service appointments at the time of his abdication, but retained the ranks of admiral of the fleet, field marshal and marshal of the Royal Air Force on the active list until his death.

ELLIOT
The Honourable Sir CHARLES GILBERT JOHN BRYDONE, KCB (1818–1895) [42]

Charles Elliot was born on 12 December 1818, the third son of the future second Earl of Minto, a Whig politician who from September 1835 to September 1841 sat in Lord Melbourne's second Cabinet as First Lord of the Admiralty. Charles Elliot's uncle, Captain (later Admiral) the Honourable Sir George Elliot, became First Secretary of the Admiralty and played an important part in both the politics and practicalities of warship design during the late 1830s and 1840s. Sir George's son, George Augustus Elliot, later became an admiral, and his father, Sir Charles Elliot, had been an admiral before him. The prominent Whig politician Lord John Russell, later Prime Minister, married in 1841 Lady Frances Elliot, who was Sir George's youngest sister and Charles Elliot's aunt. Charles Elliot entered the Navy on 6 May 1832 and became a lieutenant on 27 June 1838. He was appointed to the 2nd-rate *Rodney* in August 1838 and to the 6th-rate *Talbot* in October 1838, on the Mediterranean station, where on 16 July 1840 he became commander of the sloop *Hazard*. Elliot took part in the Allied bombardment of Acre, Palestine (Akko, Israel) on 2 November 1840, in support of the Sultan of Turkey against his rebellious subject Mehemet Ali, the Albanian ruler of Egypt and Syria. He was awarded the Navy silver medal and promoted to captain on 16 August 1841, in command of the frigate *Spartan* on the West Indies and North America station, where he remained until 1845.

Elliot returned to sea in May 1853 as captain of the 5th-rate *Sybille* and on 26 January 1855 became commodore on the East Indies and China station. During the Second China War he took part in several boat actions and landing parties in the estuary below Canton (Guangzhou) and was in a major action against Chinese war-junks at Fat-shan Creek (1 June 1857), with his broad pendant in the screw gunboat *Haughty*. He returned with *Sybille* to Devonport in March 1858 and was given command of the 3rd-rate *Cressy* in the Mediterranean in April 1859. He was promoted to rear-admiral on 5 August 1861. In 1863 he married Louisa Blackett, the daughter of a baronet. They later had four children, of whom three died in infancy before her own death in 1870.

Elliot served as C-in-C, South America, from April 1864 to May 1866, when he was succeeded in post after being promoted to vice-admiral on 6 April 1866. He flew his flag in the screw ship *Bombay* until she was burnt by accident at Montevideo, Uruguay, in August 1864, after which he moved to the frigate *Narcissus*. Elliot was C-in-C at the Nore (based in the block ship *Pembroke* at Chatham) from July 1871 until his promotion to admiral on 8 February 1873. In 1874 he married Lady Harriet Liddell, daughter of the first Earl of Ravensworth, with whom he later had a family of three daughters and a son. His final command was as C-in-C, Devonport, from January 1880 to December 1881, with the award of the

KCB in 1881. Sir Charles Elliot was promoted to admiral of the fleet on 1 December 1881 and exercised his right to remain on the active list as a supernumerary on half-pay until his death in the spring of 1895.

ERSKINE
Sir JAMES ELPHINSTONE, KCB (1838–1911) [54]

James Elphinstone Erskine was born on 2 December 1838 and became a mate in the Navy on 1 January 1858. One of his grandfathers was a landed proprietor of Cardross, married to the daughter of the eleventh Baron Elphinstone, and the other was a lieutenant general. With several senior naval officers in his family, Erskine joined the Navy in 1852 and was appointed third mate in the paddle frigate *Valorous*, on the North America and West Indies station, on 1 January 1858. He left the ship on promotion to lieutenant on 28 June 1858 and between July 1859 and December 1860 was flag lieutenant to his uncle, Rear-Admiral John Elphinstone Erskine, with his flag in the 2nd-rate *Edgar* in the Channel Squadron. He was then appointed to the 2nd-rate *Aboukir* on the North America and West Indies station, where the outbreak of the American Civil War in April 1861 had led to tension between the United States and the United Kingdom. This arose largely from maritime issues, including the detention by a United States cruiser of Confederate envoys on passage in the British ship *Trent* and the provocative conduct of British blockade-runners. Erskine left *Aboukir* on his promotion to commander on 4 August 1862. He commanded the gunboat *Speedwell* on the West Coast of Africa from 1865 to 1867 and was promoted to captain on 4 November 1868.

From November 1873 to the end of 1877 Erskine commanded the corvette *Eclipse* on the North America and West Indies station. Between April and October 1878 he was captain of the corvette *Boadicea*, based at Portsmouth, and then went to the South-East Coast of America station in command of the corvette *Garnet*. He returned home to become private secretary to the First Lord of the Admiralty, Lord Northbrook, in May 1880, and was appointed to the armoured ship *Nelson* in June 1881. From January 1882 to November 1884 he was commodore on the Australia station. After returning home in 1885, he married Margaret Constable, fourth daughter of the rector of Marston Bigot, Somerset. They later had one son, who became an officer the Navy. In May 1885 Erskine became fourth naval lord in the Board of Admiralty headed by Lord Ripon in Gladstone's third administration. He left office when the Liberal government fell in July 1885 and was promoted to rear-admiral on 18 January 1887. From June 1891 to January 1892 he was senior officer on the West Coast of Ireland, based at Queenstown, with his flag in the battleship *Triumph*. He was promoted to vice-admiral on 14 February 1892 and served between May 1895 and September 1897 as C-in-C, North America and West Indies station, with his flag in the cruiser *Crescent* and promotion to admiral on 23 August 1897. During 1898 Erskine was a member of a Commission set up to address claims to valuable fishing rights based on the French islands of St Pierre and Miquelon in the mouth of the St Lawrence, the sole remnants of France's empire in North America. He was awarded the KCB in January 1899 and was promoted to admiral of the fleet on 3 October 1902. Sir James Erskine retired in December 1908 and died at Venlaw, Peeblesshire, Scottish Borders, on 25 July 1911.

FANSHAWE
Sir ARTHUR DALRYMPLE, GCB, GCVO (1847–1936) [63]

Arthur Fanshawe was born on 2 April 1847, the third of four sons of Admiral Sir Edward Gennys Fanshawe and his wife Jane, sister of the leading Liberal politician, Edward (later Viscount) Cardwell. His grandfather was General Edward Fanshawe, who had one brother who became an admiral and three sisters who married future admirals. Their father, Rear-Admiral Robert Fanshawe, had commanded at sea in the American War of Independence before becoming commissioner of the Navy at Portsmouth. Arthur Fanshawe joined the Navy in September 1860 and became an acting sub-lieutenant on 6 June 1867, appointed to the frigate *Constance* on the North America and West Indies station. He was promoted to lieutenant on 21 September 1868 and from July 1869 to September 1870 was a supernumerary in the armoured ship *Ocean*. He then became flag lieutenant to his father on the North America and West Indies station in the armoured ship *Royal Alfred*. He was promoted to commander on 5 January 1874, when he was given one of the nominations at that period allotted to a C-in-C (in this case, his father) on hauling down his flag. In 1874 he married Sarah Fox, daughter of the proprietor of Adbury Park, Hampshire, They later had two daughters and two sons, of whom the elder became an officer in Foot Guards and the younger a captain in the Navy.

Fanshawe became commander of the frigate *Undaunted*, flagship of the C-in-C, East Indies, in March 1875 and returned home with the ship at the end of 1878. He then commanded the boys' training ship *Ganges* at Falmouth from July 1879, until his promotion to captain, to 31 December 1881. He returned to sea as captain successively of the Indian troopships *Jumna* from December 1886 to August 1887 and *Malabar* from then until early 1890. These ships were unpopular commands, as they were transports rather than combatants, and questions over the control of troops on board was frequently a cause of friction between the naval and military officers. From 1890 to 1892 he commanded the armoured cruiser *Aurora* in the Channel Squadron, and from September 1892 to January 1897 the battleship *Alexandra*, in the Coast Guard at Portland, flagship of the Admiral Superintendent of Naval Reserves. Fanshawe was promoted to rear-admiral on 23 February 1897 and went ashore until June 1899, when he became second-in-command of the Channel Squadron in the battleship

Magnificent. He completed his tenure of this appointment in June 1900 and was promoted to vice-admiral on 25 January 1902. From November 1902 to December 1905 he served as C-in-C on the Australia station, with his flag in the cruiser *Royal Arthur.* During this period the Admiralty concluded a naval agreement with the new Dominions of Australia and New Zealand, and the Royal Australian and New Zealand Navies were established as separate Services. Fanshawe made a valuable contribution to these new arrangements and in 1904 was awarded the KCB. Sir Arthur Fanshawe was promoted to admiral on 22 July 1905 and was appointed President of the Royal Naval College at Greenwich in 1906. He became C-in-C, Portsmouth in March 1908, with promotion to admiral of the fleet on 30 April 1910, when he hauled down his flag. He remained on the active list during the early years of the First World War, but was not employed, and retired in April 1917. He died in London on 21 January 1936, and his funeral was held at Burghclere parish church, Newbury, Berkshire.

FIELD
Sir FREDERICK LAWRENCE, GCB, KCMG (1871–1945) [81]

"Tam" Field was born in Killarney, County Kerry, on 19 April 1871, the second son and fifth child in a family of ten. His father became a colonel in the Royal Warwickshire Regiment and his maternal grandfather was a colonel in the 97th Foot (The Earl of Ulster's). Field joined the Navy in 1884 as a cadet in the training ship *Britannia* and was promoted to midshipman in the armoured ship *Minotaur,* flagship of the Channel Squadron, on 15 November 1886. In March 1888 he was appointed to the armoured cruiser *Impérieuse* on the China station, from which he returned with the cruiser *Constance* early in 1889. He became an acting sub-lieutenant on 14 November 1890, at the beginning of his promotion courses, and was appointed to the battleship *Dreadnought* in the Mediterranean Fleet in April 1892. Field was promoted to lieutenant on 1 April 1893 and joined the cruiser *Volage* in the Training Squadron in October 1894. He went to the torpedo school *Vernon* at Portsmouth in November 1895 and, after qualifying, joined the staff of the torpedo school *Defiance* at Devonport. He was appointed torpedo lieutenant of the battleship *Barfleur* on the China station in July 1898. During the Boxer Rebellion of 1900 he took part with a multi-national naval brigade in the first, unsuccessful, attempt to relieve the diplomatic legations besieged by the Boxers at Peking (Beijing). Field was mentioned in despatches for carrying out repairs to damaged armoured trains while under heavy fire and was wounded on 14 July 1900. After his promotion to commander on 30 June 1902 he married Mrs Annie Jackson, the widow of a Plymouth barrister. In August 1902 he was appointed commander of the battleship *Albion,* flagship of the second-in-command on the China station. Field returned home to join the staff in *Vernon,* where he served from 1904 to

74

1907. He was promoted to captain on 31 December 1907 and was then appointed to command the torpedo school *Defiance* at Devonport.

Between 1910 and 1912 Field was flag captain in the battleship *Duncan* in the Mediterranean Fleet. He was appointed in 1912 to be Superintendent of Naval Signal Schools, where he remained until September 1914 when, shortly after the outbreak of the First World War, he became captain of *Vernon*. He subsequently became flag captain to Vice-Admiral Sir Martyn Jerram (under whom he had previously served in *Duncan*) in the battleship *King George V* in the Second Battle Squadron of the Grand Fleet. He served in this ship at the battle of Jutland (31 May–1 June 1916) and was again mentioned in despatches. Field was appointed chief of staff to Sir Charles Madden [75], when the latter became second-in-command of the Grand Fleet in December 1916, and remained with him successively in the battleships *Marlborough* and *Revenge* until June 1918. He then moved to the Admiralty as Director of Torpedoes and Mines.

Field was promoted to rear-admiral on 11 February 1919, and appointed to the Board of Admiralty as Third Sea Lord and Controller of the Navy in March 1920. He was awarded the KCB in January 1923 and was subsequently given command of the Battle-cruiser Squadron, with his flag in the battle-cruiser *Hood*. From November 1923 to September 1924 Sir Frederick Field took *Hood*, with the battle-cruiser *Repulse* and a squadron of light cruisers, in a well-publicized cruise around the world. *Hood*, the largest warship then afloat, became the best-known ship in the Fleet and achieved almost legendary status as the symbol of British sea power. He was promoted to vice-admiral on 26 September 1924. In 1925 he rejoined the Board of Admiralty as Deputy Chief of the Naval Staff. During the abortive Geneva naval limitation conference he argued strongly, though unsuccessfully, the Navy's case that it needed seventy cruisers for the protection of British trade. He became C-in-C, Mediterranean Fleet, in June 1928, with promotion to admiral on 8 April 1928.

In July 1930 Field was appointed First Sea Lord in the Board headed by A V Alexander in Ramsay MacDonald's second Labour Cabinet. During the summer of 1931 a financial collapse in central Europe threw a strain on banks in London, and led to a run on the pound. International bankers agreed to help only if the British government produced large-scale cuts in government spending. MacDonald formed a National government (so incurring the lasting obloquy of his own party for "selling out to the Tories"), in which Alexander's place as First Lord of the Admiralty was taken by Austen Chamberlain. When the Cabinet ordered reductions in the wages of public employees, the Admiralty decided that naval pay should be reduced by a flat rate of one shilling per day. This meant that the lower the pay, the greater was the effect of the reduction (twenty-five per cent, for an able seaman). On 15 September 1931, in protest at the injustice of this decision, men of the Atlantic Fleet at Invergordon refused orders to put to sea. This caused another run on the pound, so forcing the United Kingdom off the gold standard, to which it was destined never to return, six days later.

Field, who had for some years been suffering from an internal ulcer, was on sick leave at the beginning of this crisis. The junior Sea Lords and some members of the Cabinet were at first disposed to use coercion against what was technically a mutiny, though most of the men involved saw their action as a strike. Chamberlain accepted Field's advice that the Admiralty should announce a review of its decision. At the same time, Field shrewdly ordered the fleet to disperse to its home ports, where the married men could be with their families. For many, their very homes, largely furnished by hire-purchase agreements, had been put at risk by the extent of the pay cuts, with some men fearing that their wives would be driven onto the streets to feed their children. At the suggestion of George V [64], the popular Admiral Sir John Kelly [85] was given command of the Atlantic Fleet in place of the unfortunate Rear-Admiral Wilfred Tomkinson, much as Lord Howe [9] had been sent to settle the Spithead mutiny of 1797. Chamberlain persuaded the Cabinet that the unfair flat-rate cuts should be replaced by a general ten percent reduction, as was the case with most other public sector employees. While the fleet returned to duty, Field, who had offered to resign, remained at the Admiralty. Despite promises of no victimization, twenty-four men were dismissed, at a time of high unemployment. Among their seniors, Sir Frederick Dreyer (Deputy Chief of the Naval Staff) was denied his expected command of the Atlantic Fleet, and Sir Cyril Fuller (Second Sea Lord, and as such in charge of personnel matters) was not employed again.

In 1932, with Sir Bolton Eyres-Monsell as First Lord in MacDonald's second National Cabinet, Field played an important part in the decision to abandon the infamous "Ten Year Rule" (a Treasury invention requiring the Armed Services to base their annual estimates on the assumption that no major war was to be anticipated within ten years) and urged the building of a fleet large enough to undertake operations against Japan while still remaining effective in European waters. Field was an officer of considerable intellectual and practical ability and, as a hobby, was a keen conjurer and member of the Magic Circle. In his final appointment he incurred criticism from other senior officers whose careers he failed to advance. Sir Roger Keyes [80] thought he was a schemer, and Kelly wrote that he was "as crooked as a dog's hind leg". He left office in January 1933. After retiring into private life he died, without offspring, on 24 October 1945, and was buried at Escrick, Yorkshire.

FIELDHOUSE
Sir JOHN DAVID ELLIOTT, Baron Fieldhouse, GCB, GBE
(1928–1992) [112]

John Fieldhouse, the son of a Civil Servant who rose from a junior grade to be awarded a knighthood as Secretary of the National Assistance Board, was born on 12 February 1928. He joined the Navy in 1944 as a cadet at the Royal Naval College, Dartmouth, and became a midshipman on 1 September 1945. He was appointed in November 1945 to the cruiser *Norfolk*, flagship of the Fifth Cruiser Squadron in the East Indies Fleet, where he served until returning home in 1946. He was promoted to sub-lieutenant on 1 May 1947, at the beginning his promotion courses. During 1948 he volunteered for the Submarine Service and in March 1949, with his promotion confirmed, was appointed to the submarine *Thule*. Fieldhouse became a lieutenant on 1 October 1949 and joined the submarine *Astute*, in which he served from November 1949 to 1951. From 1951 to 1952 he was in the submarine *Aeneas* and in 1953 married Margaret Cull, with whom he later had two daughters and a son. Between November 1954 and 1955 Fieldhouse served in the submarine *Totem*, followed by command of the submarines *Subtle* from January to March 1956 and *Acheron* from March 1956 to 1957. He was promoted to lieutenant-commander on 1 October 1957 and became commanding officer of the submarine *Tiptoe* in June 1958. He then joined the newly established department of nuclear science and engineering at the Royal Naval College, Greenwich.

After serving at the submarine base *Dolphin*, Gosport, Fieldhouse was in January 1961 appointed to the submarine *Walrus*, which he commanded until returning to *Dolphin* in September 1962, where he was promoted to commander on 31 December 1962. From July 1964 to April 1966 he commanded the nuclear-powered fleet submarine *Dreadnought* and from 1966 to 1967 was commander (executive officer) of the aircraft carrier *Hermes*. After promotion to captain on 31 December 1967 he became Captain (Submarines) of the Third Submarine Squadron, equipped with the Polaris strategic ballistic nuclear missile system. This operated from the submarine base *Neptune* on the Clyde, where Fieldhouse was also Queen's Harbourmaster. Between October 1970 and December 1971 he commanded the frigate *Diomede*, and during 1972, as commodore, was the NATO Allied Commander, Standing Naval Force, Atlantic (STANAV-FORLANT). He became Director of Naval Warfare at the Ministry of Defence in February 1973 and was promoted to rear-admiral on 7 January 1975, on appointment as Flag Officer commanding the First Flotilla. From November 1976 to 1978 he was Flag Officer, Submarines (FOSM), and NATO Allied Commander, Submarine Force, Eastern Atlantic Area (COMSUBEASTLANT) and was promoted to vice-admiral on 1 April 1978. Between January 1979 and March 1981 he was a member of the Admiralty Board as Controller of the Navy. At a time of economic difficulty, high inflation and rapidly-escalating costs, Fieldhouse supported the construction of modern surface combatants, including a new class referred to as "through-deck cruisers" to conceal their true nature (light aircraft carriers) from the Treasury. He also played an important part in the Cabinet decision to adopt the Trident missile system, in place of the ageing Polaris, as the British submarine nuclear deterrent, and was awarded the KCB in 1980.

In April 1981 Sir John Fieldhouse was appointed C-in-C, Fleet, and NATO Allied C-in-C, Channel (CINCHAN), and Eastern Atlantic Area (CINCEASTLANT), with promotion to admiral on 23 July 1981. Following the invasion of the Falkland Islands by Argentina (1–2 April 1982), he was selected as C-in-C of the British task force sent to the South Atlantic to recover them. With the advantage of late twentieth century communications, he was able to control the conduct of the campaign from his headquarters at Northwood, Middlesex, ending with the surrender of the Argentine troops in the Falklands within ten weeks of their landing. Fieldhouse's success in conducting an improvised campaign over 8,000 miles from his home base, and his skill in acting as an intermediary between the operational commanders and the Ministry of Defence, gained him well-deserved praise. The Falklands victory saved the Prime Minister of the day, Margaret Thatcher, and ministerial gratitude, together with Fieldhouse's ability to deal with politicians, helped in his appointment as First Sea Lord in December 1982.

Fieldhouse's main task was then to analyse and apply the lessons of the Falklands War. Thatcher's Defence Minister, John Nott, continued to maintain that the conflict was of little relevance to his policy of providing only for operations in the NATO area, but the Treasury agreed to fund the replacement of ships lost during the campaign. By convention, the post of Chief of the Defence Staff had previously been filled by the senior officer of each Service in rotation. The vacancy created by the retirement of Field Marshal Sir Edwin Bramall in 1985 would normally have been filled by the Royal Air Force, but it was instead allotted to the Royal Navy, so that Fieldhouse, with the advantage of his Falklands War experience, could be appointed. At the completion of his time as First Sea Lord he was promoted to admiral of the fleet on 2 August 1985 and was immediately appointed Chief of the Defence Staff, where he maintained his reputation as a formidable Whitehall in-fighter. He left office in May 1989 and was made a life peer as Baron Fieldhouse, of Gosport, in 1990. Lord Fieldhouse died on 17 February 1992.

FISHER
Sir JOHN ARBUTHNOT, 1st Baron Fisher of Kilverstone, GCB, OM, GCVO (1841–1920) [58]

"Jackie" Fisher was born on 25 January 1841 in the British colony of Ceylon (Sri Lanka), the eldest of the eleven children of Captain William Fisher of the 95th (Derbyshire) Regiment, then ADC to the governor of Ceylon, and his wife Sophia, daughter of a New Bond Street wine merchant. Captain Fisher left his regiment and settled in Ceylon as a coffee planter. Three of his sons served in the Navy, two reaching senior flag rank and one being lost at sea as a lieutenant. John Fisher's godmother, Lady Horton, settled at Catton Hall, Derbyshire, where she prevailed on her neighbour, Sir

William Parker [26], to give him a nomination as a naval cadet. Fisher joined the Navy in July 1854 in the 2nd-rate *Calcutta*, in which he took part in the Baltic campaign during the Crimean War. Between May and July 1856 he served in the Mediterranean Fleet in the 2nd-rate *Agamemnon*.

Fisher was appointed midshipman on 13 July 1856, in the frigate *Highflyer* in which he served in the Second China War and took part in the attack on Chinese war-junks at Fat-shan Creek (1 June 1857) and the storming of Canton (Guangzhou) (29 December 1857). In the unsuccessful attack on the Taku Forts by Rear-Admiral James Hope [39] (20 May 1859), he was in the gunboat *Banterer*, employed in rescuing the wounded, with his own commanding officer among them. He was promoted acting mate on 25 January 1860 and was appointed by Hope, as C-in-C, China station, to be his flag mate in the frigate *Chesapeake*. His first command was for four days in Hope's yacht, *Coromandel*. On 21 March 1860 he was appointed acting lieutenant (confirmed on 4 November 1860) in the paddle frigate *Furious*, in which he took part in the capture of the Taku Forts (1 August 1860). He returned home in August 1861 and was confirmed as a lieutenant with seniority from 4 November 1860. In January 1862 he joined the gunnery school *Excellent* at Portsmouth, from which in 1863 he became gunnery lieutenant of the new frigate *Warrior*, the Navy's first armoured ship. He returned to *Excellent* in June 1864. Fisher married in April 1866 the daughter of a clergyman, the twenty-five-year-old Frances Delves-Broughton, whom he had first met at Portsmouth in 1861. They later had a family of three daughters, all of whom married officers in the Royal Navy, and one son.

Fisher was promoted to commander on 2 August 1869. He was appointed in November 1869 commander of the 1st-rate *Donegal* on the China station, where he later transferred to the flagship, the armoured ship *Ocean*. Between September 1872 and November 1876 he was again in *Excellent*, training as a torpedo warfare specialist, with promotion to captain on 30 October 1874, followed by temporary command of the corvette-ram *Pallas* in the Mediterranean Fleet. He served as a flag captain of the battleship *Bellerophon* on the North America and West Indies station from April 1877 to June 1878, and of the battleship *Hercules* in the Channel from June to August 1878. He then held a brief command of the frigate *Valorous* until going on half-pay in September 1878. In January 1879, on the recommendation of Sir Geoffrey Hornby [45], C-in-C, Mediterranean Fleet under whom he had previously served, Fisher was re-appointed to *Pallas*. He then joined the fleet at Constantinople (Istanbul) as the strained relations between the United Kingdom and Russia mellowed in the aftermath of the Congress of Berlin. Between September 1879 and January 1881 he was flag captain of the battleship *Northampton* on the North American and West Indies station and, while there, was involved in the search for his brother's ship, the training frigate *Atalanta*, lost without trace in May 1880.

Fisher returned home to command the new battleship *Inflexible*, commissioned in October 1881. After joining the Mediterranean Fleet, *Inflexible* took part in the British bombardment of Alexandria (11 July 1882), in response to an Egyptian nationalist uprising led by Colonel Arabi ('Urbi) Pasha. During the subsequent landings, Fisher commanded the naval brigade and, in conjunction with Captain Arthur Wilson [59] of the torpedo depot ship *Hecla*, devised an armoured train fitted with naval ordnance. He was awarded the CB, but contracted a severe form of dysentery which made him unfit for duty for the following nine months. In April 1883 he became captain of *Excellent*, where, with his characteristic contempt of traditions that had outlived their time, he reformed the system of gunnery training. During 1885, when there was a threat of war between the United Kingdom and Russia over the disputed control of Penjdeh on the borders of Afghanistan and Turkmenistan, a fleet was assembled in the Channel under Hornby's command. Fisher was appointed captain of the fleet (chief of staff) in Hornby's flagship, the armoured ship *Minotaur*, but the international crisis was resolved by diplomacy and the fleet was then dispersed. Between 1886 and 1890 Fisher was Director of Ordnance and Torpedoes at the Admiralty, and hastened the introduction of breech-loaders and quick-firing guns. He considered leaving the Navy at this time to take up a lucrative offer of employment with the arms manufacturer, Whitworth, but then decided to stay in the Service. He was promoted to rear-admiral on 2 August 1890 and spent 1891 as admiral-superintendent of Portsmouth Dockyard.

From February 1891 to August 1897 Fisher was third naval lord on the Board of Admiralty and Controller of the Navy. As the member responsible for the design and construction of ships, he played an important part in implementing new developments in artillery and armour. He brought the first destroyers into service and, in "the Battle of the Boilers", approved the adoption of water-tube boilers for large ships. He was also the leading spokesman for the first naval lord, Sir Frederick Richards [52], in the struggle for funds for naval rearmament that culminated in the resignation of William Gladstone, the Prime Minister of the day, in 1894. He was awarded the KCB in 1894.

Sir John Fisher was promoted to vice-admiral on 8 May 1896. From August 1897 to March 1899 he was C-in-C, North America and West Indies, with his flag in the battleship *Renown*. During the Spanish-American War (April-August 1898), in order to avoid any incidents with British merchantmen in the area, he made a point of establishing good relations with Rear-Admiral William T Sampson, United States Navy, commanding the squadron blockading Cuba. At the time of the Fashoda incident late in 1898, when war between the United Kingdom and France seemed likely, Fisher prepared a plan to release the unfortunate Captain Dreyfus from the French West Indian prison on Devil's Island. The intention was to restore him to his homeland, where it was thought his presence would spread dissension, though it is doubtful whether Dreyfus, a French patriot, would have assisted his country's enemies in this way.

During May and June 1899 Fisher was the British naval delegate at the first Hague conference, where, apart from the establishment of an international Court of Arbitration, nothing of importance was agreed. Fisher himself saw no place for moderation in the conduct of warfare, and later argued privately that war was best deterred by the thought that it would be waged without mercy, including the slaughter of non-combatants. He thought that the Japanese attack on the Russian fleet at Port Arthur (Lushun) in February 1904, without a declaration of war, was a sound decision, as the attack itself was a declaration of war. He went on to advocate a similar policy in respect of the growing German fleet, which he envisaged sinking at anchor in Kiel, just as Nelson had destroyed the Danish fleet at Copenhagen.

In September 1899 Fisher was appointed C-in-C, Mediterranean, with his flag once more in *Renown*. He set about improving the training and efficiency of his fleet, and encouraged his junior officers to study naval warfare and to give him their own ideas. His relations with his senior officers were less agreeable, as he openly criticized them to their juniors, and made offensive signals, in clear, to his successive seconds-in-command, Sir Gerard Noel [61] and Lord Charles Beresford. In the summer of 1901 he took the chance of a visit to Malta by Lord Selborne, then First Lord of the Admiralty in Salisbury's Cabinet, to press his ideas for comprehensive naval reform. He was promoted to admiral on 2 November 1901.

Fisher became second naval lord at the Admiralty in February 1902. His first major reform was to lower the age of entry of cadets from fifteen to twelve and to train all future officers in a common syllabus before they joined either the executive or engineering branches, or the Royal Marines. A new college was set up at Osborne House, Isle of Wight, to be attended by cadets in their first three years, after which they would transfer to the new Royal Naval College then being built at Dartmouth to replace the old training ship *Britannia*. This provoked much opposition from traditionalists, and some aspects of it, particularly the inclusion of Royal Marine cadets, and the concept that executive and engineer officers should be interchangeable, eventually proved unworkable. Fisher himself came to admit that the College's fees, unless subsidized, would bear hardly on less affluent families from whom most engineer officers had previously come. True to his nickname of "Radical Jack", he argued that all cadets should be selected by merit rather than nomination and that fees should be abolished, so as to allow the Navy to draw its officers from all classes of society. The new college opened in September 1903, at the same time that Fisher was appointed C-in-C, Portsmouth. He served there, working on various schemes for further reforms, until October 1904, when, to the alarm of many senior admirals, he was appointed to the Admiralty with the new title First Sea Lord (replacing that of first naval lord) in the Board under the Earl of Selborne in A J Balfour's Cabinet.

In April 1905 Selborne was succeeded at the Admiralty by Earl Cawdor, who continued to support Fisher until leaving office on the fall of the Conservative ministry in December 1905. Fisher was promoted to admiral of the fleet on 4 December 1905, by a special Order in Council, so that he could remain in office after reaching the retirement age for his previous rank. He remained as First Sea Lord under Lord Tweedmouth, who came into office with Sir Henry Campbell-Bannerman's Cabinet. Under pressure to produce efficiency savings, Fisher reduced costs by abolishing the Pacific, North America and South East Coast of America stations and closing long-established naval bases in Canada, the West Indies and Ceylon. Some hundred and fifty older ships, scorned by Fisher as too weak to fight and too slow to run, were taken out of commission (though half of them were subsequently brought back again). This allowed him to re-deploy their crews to previously unmanned ships of the reserve fleet, which could be brought up to full strength by reservists on mobilization.

Meanwhile, in the vanguard of developments in ship design, he introduced the concept of a new kind of battleship, faster and more heavily armed than any then in service, with a main armament consisting entirely of heavy guns of the same calibre. The first of this class, *Dreadnought*, was completed in December 1906. He also brought into service a new type of ship, the battle-cruiser, of which the first, *Invincible*, was completed in 1908. Originally intended to outmatch enemy heavy cruisers, a role in which it proved extremely successful, the battle-cruiser was classified by Fisher as a capital ship. With the guns of a battleship, but with limited armour, it was seen by him as powerful enough to operate in advance of the main battle-fleet, but fast enough to disengage when necessary. Speed, he said, was their armour. Improved engine design, with turbines replacing triple expansion, gave higher speed to both types of ship. Looking to the future, he gave thought to the evolving importance of underwater warfare and envisaged large submarines equipped with heavy guns and surfacing to give battle. Demands for further savings at the end of 1907 led the Second Sea Lord, Sir Henry May [65], and his two juniors to threaten resignation if Fisher agreed to unacceptable cuts in the rebuilding programme.

These reforms, following those Fisher had forced through as second naval lord, attracted the opposition of several other senior admirals, who questioned both the wisdom and speed of his actions. In response, he adopted an attitude of personal hostility to any naval officer who challenged his views, and of favouritism to those who agreed with him, who were said to be "in the Fishpond". The Navy was split into two camps, with the popular, well-connected and outspoken Lord Charles Beresford, by this time C-in-C, Channel Fleet, becoming one of Fisher's leading opponents. Fisher's sallow complexion and distinctive facial appearance had given rise to a legend that he was the son of a Chinese or Siamese mother, and Beresford freely referred to him as "the Oriental". Anyone who questioned his reforms was perceived by Fisher as a Beresford sympathizer, and treated as an enemy, irrespective of earlier friendships. Among these were Sir Gerard Noel [61], Sir Henry May [65], Sir Hedworth Lambton (later Meux) [66] and Sir Doveton Sturdee [73]. One of his favourites was Prince Louis of Battenberg [74], who in turn admired Fisher, though not always

1.Sir Edmund Hawke, Lord Hawke. [7]

2. Sir Richard "Black Dick" Howe, Earl Howe. [9]

3. William IV, formerly Duke of Clarence, "The Sailor King". [11]

4. Sir John Jervis, Earl of St Vincent. [12]

5. Sir Fairfax Moresby. [33]

6. Sir Edward Seymour. [57]

7. Sir John Fisher, 1st Baron Fisher of Kilverstone. [58]

8. The Hon. Hedworth Lambton (later Sir Hedworth Meux) with canine friend. [66]

9. Sir John Jellicoe, Earl Jellicoe. [68]

10. *Left to right:* Sir David Beatty, Earl Beatty [69]; Rear-Admiral Hugh Rodman, USN; HM King George V [64]; Vice-Admiral W.S. Sims, USN; HRH the Prince of Wales [84] (later HM King Edward VIII and Duke of Windsor).

uncritically. A particular issue was the formation of an Atlantic Fleet, based at Gibraltar, and the addition of active ships to the Reserve fleet to form a Home Fleet, in both cases at the expense of the Channel Fleet. Beresford, a Member of Parliament, forced an enquiry into allegations of favouritism at the Admiralty. Fisher was supported by King Edward VII [44] and by Reginald McKenna, who had become First Lord of the Admiralty in Asquith's Liberal Cabinet in April 1908. He also gained the eventual support of the enigmatic and influential Lord Esher, an intimate of the King. Early in 1909 Fisher abolished the Channel Fleet and absorbed most of its ships into an enlarged Home Fleet in which both active and reserve elements were combined. Beresford was obliged to haul his flag down earlier than expected and come ashore. Fisher himself entered the Lords at the end of 1909, when he was raised to the peerage as Baron Fisher of Kilverstone, and left the Admiralty in January 1910.

Lord Fisher then became chairman of a commission whose recommendations led to the replacement of coal by oil as the fuel for marine engines. He maintained contact with McKenna and with Winston Churchill, who became First Lord in McKenna's place in October 1911. He continued on good terms with Battenberg, who became First Sea Lord at the end of 1912. When Battenberg resigned his appointment on 29 October 1914, two months after the outbreak of the First World War, Fisher was re-appointed First Sea Lord. He arrived too late to have an immediate effect on the position in the South Atlantic, where a British squadron was defeated by the Germans at Coronel (1 November 1914), but immediately despatched two battle-cruisers that avenged Coronel at the battle of the Falkland Islands (8 December 1914).

With the British Expeditionary Force engaged in a stalemate in the Western Front, Fisher urged a return to the traditional British way in warfare, using the Army as the sword of the fleet in landings upon the enemy coast. Indeed, he had little use for soldiers other than as marines and, in the pre-war battle for funds, had made enemies among the military by belittling the usefulness of the Army. His favoured scheme was a descent on the Baltic shores of Prussia, from where a Russian army could march to Berlin, and he devoted much time to planning a force of light craft for use in this theatre. He remained convinced that the Navy should control the Baltic as it had in former wars, but even Churchill would not support him. The small ships intended by Fisher for inshore operations in the Baltic eventually found a valuable role as anti-submarine vessels when the German U-boat offensive became a major threat to British survival later in the war. Churchill was more interested in using the Navy to force a passage through the Dardanelles, a plan that Fisher agreed to only with reluctance, foreseeing that it would become a combined operation with the Army.

The expedition to the Dardanelles became just as much a stalemate as the Western Front. Churchill called for more ships, but Fisher was not prepared to weaken the Grand Fleet he had created as the keystone of his naval strategy. Nor was he prepared to tolerate Churchill's continual interference in the details of naval operations. He told Asquith that he would only remain in office on six conditions, which were to be published to the Fleet. These included the removal of Churchill from the Cabinet, and of Sir Arthur Wilson (his old comrade in the Egyptian campaign, who had formerly been "in the Fishpond", and was at this time Churchill's special adviser) from the Admiralty; the appointment of an entirely new Board of Admiralty; and the transfer of all naval affairs, operational and administrative, into his own hands. When this was refused, he resigned on 15 May 1915, despite attempts to dissuade him by Esher, McKenna, the other Sea Lords, and Wilson himself.

After resigning, Fisher left his office at the Admiralty building and for several days was nowhere to be found. Churchill considered this as tantamount to desertion, a view shared by George V [64], who had never been a Fisher enthusiast. A former naval officer himself, the King later declared that Fisher should have been dismissed in disgrace, or preferably hanged at the yardarm for abandoning his post in the face of the enemy. Fisher never again returned to high office, though he was found employment as chairman of the Admiralty's Inventions Board. After the war he published his memoirs and defended the record of his ships at the battle of Jutland, pointing out that no British battleship was sunk and claiming that the battle-cruisers had suffered losses only because they had not taken advantage of the speed he had given them. He died on 10 July 1920 and was buried at Kilverstone, being succeeded in the peerage by his son.

FORBES
Sir CHARLES MORTON, GCB, DSO (1880–1960) [90]

Charles Forbes, the son of a Scottish broker, was born at Colombo, Ceylon (Sri Lanka) on 22 November 1880. He was educated at Dollar Academy, Clackmannanshire, before attending Eastman's Naval Academy at Southsea, Hampshire, and entering the Navy as a cadet in the training ship *Britannia* in 1894. He passed out in 1896 with first class certificates in all five subjects, so gaining twelve months' seniority and obtaining promotion to midshipman on 15 July 1896. Forbes served in the battleship *Magnificent*, flagship of the second-in-command of the Channel Squadron, from September 1896 to July 1897, when he was appointed to the armoured cruiser *Impérieuse*, flagship of the C-in-C on the Pacific station. He returned to the United Kingdom to become an acting sub-lieutenant on 15 January 1900, at the beginning of his promotion courses.

Forbes was promoted to lieutenant on 15 January 1901 and appointed to the battleship *Royal Oak* in the Mediterranean Fleet. During 1903 he attended the gunnery school *Excellent* from which, after qualifying, he was in June 1904 appointed to the staff of the gunnery school *Cambridge* at Devonport. Between May 1905 and February 1908 he was gunnery lieutenant in the armoured cruiser *Carnarvon* in which he served successively in the Mediterranean and Atlantic Fleets. He was appointed in May 1908 to the battleship *Dominion*, under Captain J M De Robeck [77] in the Channel. In 1909 he married Agnes Ewen, the younger daughter of a Hertfordshire magistrate, and later had with her a family of a son and a daughter. From October 1910 to February 1911 he was attached to the staff of the Inspectorate of Target Practice, based in London, and then became gunnery lieutenant of the battleship *Superb* in the Home Fleet. After being promoted to commander on 31 December 1912 he returned to *Excellent* for experimental duties and was still there on the outbreak of the First World War in August 1914.

In November 1914 Forbes was appointed commander of the battleship *Queen Elizabeth*, De Robeck's flagship in the Mediterranean Fleet, in which he took part in the initial naval attack on the Dardanelles (18 March 1915). He joined the Grand Fleet in October 1915 as flag commander to Sir John Jellicoe [68] in the battleship *Iron Duke* and was present at the battle of Jutland (31 May–1 June 1916), for which he was awarded the DSO. Jellicoe was succeeded by Sir David Beatty [69] in December 1916 and Forbes moved in February 1917 to become flag commander to the second-in-command, Sir Charles Madden [75] in the battleship *Revenge*. He was promoted to captain on 30 June 1917 and given command of the light cruiser *Galatea*, in which he served with the Grand Fleet for the rest of the war. He was succeeded in command in August 1919 and then became a naval member of the Ordnance Committee. During 1920 he attended the Senior Officers' War Course at the Royal Naval War College, Greenwich, and from August 1921 to May 1923 was Deputy Director of the Royal Naval Staff College. Forbes's wife had died in 1915. He was remarried in 1921, to a Swedish lady, with whom he later had a second daughter.

Forbes returned to sea in June 1923 as flag captain to Sir John De Robeck, C-in-C, Atlantic Fleet, in *Queen Elizabeth*. In October 1924 he became flag captain of *Iron Duke* and chief staff officer to the Rear-Admiral commanding the Third Battle Squadron and second-in-command of the Mediterranean station. From June 1925 until 5 October 1928, when he was promoted to rear-admiral, he was at the Admiralty as Director of Naval Ordnance. He then went on half-pay until August 1930, when he was appointed Rear-Admiral (Destroyers), commanding the destroyers (four flotillas each of eight ships) of the Mediterranean Fleet, with his flag in the cruiser *Coventry*. After a year in this command Forbes again went on half-pay before joining the Admiralty as Third Sea Lord and Controller of the Navy in March 1932, with promotion to vice-admiral on 21 January 1933. He remained there until May 1934,when he was appointed Vice-Admiral commanding the Third Battle Squadron and second-in-command of the Mediterranean Fleet, with his flag in *Revenge*. He was awarded the KCB in 1935 and was with the fleet when it moved from Malta to Alexandria to avoid the threat of a surprise attack from Italy during the Abyssinian (Ethiopian) crisis of 1935–36. Sir Charles Forbes left the Mediterranean with promotion to admiral on 19 August 1936.

In April 1938 Forbes was appointed C-in-C, Home Fleet, with his flag in the battleship *Nelson*, at a time of increasing international tension culminating in the outbreak of the Second World War in September 1939. *Nelson* was damaged by a mine in Loch Ewe in December 1939, causing Forbes to transfer his flag to the battleship *Rodney*. He was promoted to admiral of the fleet on 8 May 1940. The Home Fleet suffered serious losses in the Norwegian campaign of April-June 1940 and *Rodney*, with Forbes on board, was damaged by air attack. The German losses included three cruisers and ten destroyers sunk. This led Forbes to appreciate, after the fall of France in June 1940, that a seaborne invasion of the United Kingdom was unlikely, and to dispose his ships accordingly. He did not get on well with either Winston Churchill (appointed First Lord of the Admiralty in Neville Chamberlain's War Cabinet on the outbreak of the war), or the First Sea Lord, Sir Dudley Pound [89], both of whom he felt exercised too close a control over his operations. Churchill, who became Prime Minister in June 1940, disagreed with Forbes over the invasion threat, at least until the victory of Fighter Command in the Battle of Britain in late 1940. Pound was aware that there was some criticism of Forbes within the fleet and decided that he should be replaced by Sir John Tovey [92] in December 1940.

In May 1941 Forbes was appointed C-in-C, Plymouth, in peace-time a largely ceremonial post, but carrying operational responsibilities in war, including naval defence against heavy air raids. He hauled down his flag on 24 August 1943 and retired to his home, Cawsand Place, Wentworth, Surrey, where he was able to indulge his hobby as a keen golfer, and to devote himself to charitable causes. He died in London on 28 August 1960.

FORBES
The Honourable JOHN (1714–1796) [8]

The Honourable John Forbes, second son of an Irish peer, the third Earl of Granard, was born on 17 July 1714 in Minorca, where his father was then in command of a naval squadron. He joined the Navy in May 1726 in the 3rd-rate *Burford*, commanded by his maternal uncle, the Honourable Charles Stewart. In 1729 Stewart was appointed to command the 3rd-rate *Lion* and, taking his nephew with him, sailed for the West Indies, where Forbes became a lieutenant in *Lion* on 16 March 1731. After a period ashore, he became a lieutenant in the 1st-rate *Britannia*, flagship of Sir John Norris [1] in the fleet sent to Lisbon in 1737 to deter the Spanish from invading Portugal. On 7 March 1737 he was given command of the 5th-rate *Poole*. He was promoted to captain on 24 October 1737 and commanded the 6th-rate *Port Mahon* off the coast of Ireland during 1738. Forbes's subsequent commands were the 4th-rate *Severn* in the Channel in 1739, at the beginning of the War of Jenkins's Ear; the 5th-rate *Tiger* in 1740, when this conflict was overtaken by the outbreak of the War of the Austrian

Succession; the 4th-rate *Guernsey* in 1741 and finally the 3rd-rate *Norfolk*, in which he was one of the few British captains to serve with credit at the battle of Hyeres, Toulon (11 February 1743). He gave up his command on medical grounds in September 1745.

Forbes became a rear-admiral of the Blue on 15 July 1747 and rejoined the fleet in the Mediterranean. He was promoted to rear-admiral of the White on 12 May 1748 and, with the war over, was given command of the Mediterranean Fleet in 1749. He was elected to the Irish Parliament as MP for St. Johnstown, County Donegal, in 1751. Poor health led him to take the waters at the health resort of Spa, from where in 1754 he declined offers of the command of a squadron in the Indian Ocean and appointment as resident governor of the colony of New York. He became a vice-admiral of the Blue on 6 January 1755. In 1755, on the outbreak of hostilities with France in advance of the Seven Years War, Forbes was still medically unfit for service at sea. In December 1756 he was appointed a Lord Commissioner of Admiralty in the Board headed by Earl Temple in the Duke of Newcastle's administration. Forbes, who had become a vice-admiral of the Red in February 1757, left the Admiralty at the same time as Temple in April 1757, after refusing to sign the warrant for the execution of Vice-Admiral John Byng (shot for having failed to relieve Minorca the previous year). Although the legality of the sentence had been upheld by a bench of twelve senior judges, Forbes declared that in so grave a matter, "a man must be guided by his own opinion". His was that the court-martial had tried Byng under the wrong Article of War, so that he was charged with "failing to do his utmost" (for which death was the only possible sentence) rather than for cowardice, disaffection or negligence, of which he was cleared.

In July 1757, when the Cabinet was formed, led by Newcastle and William Pitt, with Lord Anson [5] as First Lord of the Admiralty, Forbes rejoined the Board and remained there successively under Anson, the Earl of Halifax and George Grenville, until the end of the Seven Years War in 1763. Forbes was promoted to admiral of the Blue on 5 February 1758. In the same year he married Lady Mary Capel, daughter of the third Earl of Essex. They had no son, but were fortunate in their twin daughters, who both made advantageous marriages. The elder, Catherine, became Countess of Mornington, and the younger, Maria, became Countess of Clarendon. Forbes was returned to the Irish Parliament as Member for Mullingar, County Meath, in 1761. When Grenville succeeded the Earl of Bute as Prime Minister in April 1763 Forbes left the Admiralty and retired from active employment with a sinecure appointment as general of marines. He was promoted to admiral of the White on 18 October 1770 and became admiral of the fleet on 24 October 1781. He continued to be consulted by the Cabinet on naval matters, but played no part in the American War of Independence (1775–83). He died on 10 March 1796, having for the previous twenty years been a complete invalid.

FRASER
Sir BRUCE AUSTIN, Baron Fraser of North Cape, GCB, KBE (1888–1981) [95]

Bruce Fraser, the younger in a family of two sons of a retired general of Engineers, was born at Acton, Middlesex, on 5 February 1888. He attended Bradfield College, Berkshire, before joining the Navy as a cadet in the training ship *Britannia* in September 1902 and became a midshipman in the battleship *Hannibal* in the Channel fleet on 15 January 1904. From February 1905 to March 1907 he served in the Channel in the battleship *Prince George*. After serving briefly in the battleship *Goliath*, Fraser was promoted to acting sub-lieutenant on 15 March 1907 at the beginning of his promotion courses. From May to September 1907 he served in the battleship *Triumph*, followed by a period in the destroyer *Gipsy* and promotion to lieutenant on 15 March 1908. After serving in the cruiser *Lancaster* in the Mediterranean Fleet, he was appointed in 1910 to the light cruiser *Boadicea*, flagship of the destroyer flotillas at Harwich, from where he joined the gunnery school *Excellent* in 1911 to qualify as a gunnery specialist. After passing out first in his course, he was lent to the staff at Greenwich for the Advanced Gunnery Course of October 1912. In 1913 Fraser was appointed to the instructional staff at *Excellent*, and in July 1914 received the thanks of the Admiralty for compiling the handbook of director-controlled firing. He was then appointed gunnery lieutenant of the cruiser *Minerva*, mobilized from the Third (Reserve) fleet for annual manoeuvres.

After the outbreak of the First World War in August 1914 *Minerva* was deployed to the west coast of Ireland, prior to joining the Mediterranean Fleet late in September 1914. Fraser served in this ship in the Red Sea, bombarding the Turkish positions at Aqaba and occasionally landing on the Arabian coast with small parties of Marines. *Minerva* was recalled to Suez in February 1915, when a Turkish force threatened the Canal. At the end of February 1915 she joined the force preparing for the Allied expedition to the Dardanelles. Fraser took part in this campaign, giving naval gunfire support to the troops ashore until August 1915, when his ship was recalled to carry troops for the defence of Egypt's western frontier against Senussi tribesmen from Libya. Early in 1916 he returned to the staff of *Excellent*, where he remained until appointed to the new battleship *Resolution*. After spending the autumn of 1916 with the ship under completion, Fraser took over as gunnery lieutenant when she was commissioned in December 1916. He spent the rest of the war with the Grand Fleet at Scapa Flow and was present when the German High Seas Fleet arrived for internment in November 1918.

Fraser was promoted to commander on 30 June 1919 and went back to the Mediterranean as commander of *Resolution*. He did not get on with his new captain, so in April 1920 responded to a call for volunteers to serve with the White Russian Caspian flotilla. On arrival at Baku, Azerbaijan, he and the rest of his party were arrested by the Bolsheviks and remained in uncomfortable internment until released in November 1920. He returned to *Excellent* until 1922, when he joined the Naval Ordnance Department at the Admiralty to work on development of a new fire control system. During 1925 Fraser became fleet gunnery officer of the Mediterranean Fleet, where he served successively in the battleships *Queen Elizabeth* and *Warspite* until promoted to captain on 30 June 1926. He was then appointed to the Tactical Division of the Admiralty, after which he commanded the cruiser *Effingham* on the East Indies station between 1929 and 1932. Following a brief command of the cruiser *Leander*, he was employed at the Admiralty from 1933 to 1935 as Director of Naval Ordnance. In 1936 he was given command of the aircraft carrier *Glorious*, in the Mediterranean Fleet, where he served until late in 1937. He was promoted to rear-admiral on 11 January 1938 and was appointed chief of staff to Sir Dudley Pound [89], C-in-C, Mediterranean Fleet.

In March 1939 Fraser joined the Board of Admiralty as Third Sea Lord and Controller of the Navy, where he remained in post on the outbreak of the Second World War in September 1939. As such, he was responsible for ship design and construction, and introduced a new class of convoy escort vessel, for which the name "corvette" was revived. He also played an important part in the reconstruction of fast merchantmen as escort carriers, and the adoption of catapult ships, able to launch (though not recover) fighters for the defence of convoys against long-range bombers. Equally important in the battle of the Atlantic were the new anti-submarine warfare electronic systems brought into service in his time as Controller. He was promoted to vice-admiral on 8 May 1940 and awarded the KCB in June 1941.

In June 1942 Sir Bruce Fraser was appointed second-in-command of the Home Fleet, with his flag at various times in the battleship *Anson* and the aircraft carrier *Victorious*. During August 1942, as an observer in the battleship *Rodney* in the Mediterranean Fleet, he accompanied a major convoy to reinforce Malta, and came under enemy air attack. A legend arose that he personally shot down a German dive-bomber, though he always disclaimed this. He became C-in-C, Home Fleet, on 8 May 1943. In October 1943, the Prime Minister, Winston Churchill, offered him the post of First Sea Lord in succession to Pound. Fraser declined, with the reply "I believe I have the confidence of my own Fleet. Cunningham has that of the whole Navy". Fraser continued the task of protecting Atlantic and Arctic convoys and, with his flag in the battleship *Duke of York*, sank the battle-cruiser *Scharnhorst*, the last effective major German unit in northern waters, in the battle of the North Cape (26 December 1943).

Fraser was promoted to admiral on 7 February 1944. He left the Home Fleet in June 1944, prior to appointment as C-in-C of the Eastern Fleet, with his flag initially in the battle-cruiser *Renown*. He established cordial relations with the Allied Supreme Commander, South-East Asia, Lord

Louis Mountbatten [102], with the result that Mountbatten recorded that relations between the two Commands had improved "beyond recognition". In December 1944 Fraser became C-in-C, British Pacific Fleet, to which the most powerful units of the Eastern Fleet (with reinforcements expected from Europe) were assigned, while the remainder remustered as the East Indies Fleet. The formation of a British Pacific Fleet (accepted by President Franklin D Roosevelt at Churchill's behest) was greeted without enthusiasm by the United States admirals. Making impressive advances against the Japanese without the need for British assistance, they doubted the ability of Fraser's ships to sustain prolonged operations over the vast distances of the Pacific without draining resources from the United States Navy, and had well-founded reservations about the efficiency of British naval aviation. Fraser made every effort to achieve acceptance, including the abandonment of the Navy's own system of signal communication and the adoption of that used by the United States.

Fraser commanded his fleet from his shore HQ at Sydney, New South Wales, but, while on a liaison visit, narrowly escaped death at the bombardment of Luzon, when the United States battleship *New Mexico* was hit by a Japanese kamikaze suicide bomber on 6 January 1945. Hostilities were ended by the use of atomic weapons against Japan in August 1945. Fraser, with his flag in *Duke of York*, joined the British contingent in the Inland Sea and, at the ceremony on board the USS *Missouri* in Tokyo Bay (2 September 1945), was the United Kingdom signatory to the Japanese instrument of surrender. He returned home in 1946 and was raised to the peerage as Baron Fraser of North Cape. Lord Fraser was C-in-C, Portsmouth, from September 1947 to September 1948. He then became First Sea Lord in the Board headed by Viscount Hall in Clement Attlee's first Labour administration and was promoted to admiral of the fleet on 7 February 1948. Fraser got on well with Attlee, a fellow veteran of the Dardanelles campaign, and was able to slow the rate of post-war reductions in the strength of the Navy. He was helped in this by the deteriorating international situation in Europe and by the outbreak of the Korean War, which led the Cabinet to introduce rearmament despite a difficult economic situation.

Fraser appreciated the need to work closely with the United States and Dominion Navies for the protection of British interests in the Pacific and Indian Oceans. In the West he was involved in the establishment of the North Atlantic Treaty Organization naval command structure and accepted that the Supreme Allied Commander, Atlantic (SACLANT), should be a United States admiral, an arrangement much resented by British public opinion of the time. For this he was severely criticized by Winston Churchill, who was then in opposition, but later returned to office on the fall of Attlee's second administration in October 1951. Fraser's period as First Sea Lord saw the demise of the battleship, with only one left in commission. Accepting that aircraft had become the Navy's most powerful weapon, he defended expenditure on aircraft carriers and successfully resisted a proposal by the Chief of Air Staff to set up a Joint Maritime Air Force.

Fraser left office in April 1952 and thereafter lived in retirement, emerging occasionally to speak in the Lords on naval matters. He was not an intellectual (he claimed never to have read a novel in his life) and some have seen this as a weakness in his battles in Whitehall. Nevertheless, his straightforward character allowed him to get on well with most of those with whom he had to deal and he was widely respected as an old sea-dog. He was popular with the Fleet as a whole and during the Korean War took pains to ensure that there would be no repetition of ships on that station becoming "the Forgotten Fleet" as his British Pacific Fleet had been dubbed. On the escape of the frigate *Amethyst* down the Yangtse River past Chinese Communist shore batteries, he personally directed the local flag officer to make additional recommendations for honours and awards to the ship's company. He died in London on 12 February 1981. Lord Fraser never married and his barony became extinct.

FREEMAN
WILLIAM PEERE WILLIAMS (1742–1832) [13]

William Williams was born on 6 January 1742 at Peterborough, where his father, Dr Frederick Williams, rector of Peakirk, Northamptonshire, was prebendary and his maternal grandfather, Dr Robert Clavering, was the bishop. A maternal great-uncle, John Freeman, was the owner of Fawley Court, near Henley, Oxfordshire. William Williams' paternal grandfather, also called William Peere Williams, was a wealthy barrister and MP, whose estates included one at Hoddesdon, Hertfordshire. Williams entered the Navy during the Seven Years War in June 1757. He did not go to sea until August 1759, when he sailed in the 3rd-rate *Magnanime*, commanded by Lord Howe [9], in which he served at the battle of Quiberon Bay (20 November 1759). He followed Howe when the latter became flag captain in the 3rd-rate *Princess Amelia* in August 1762 and, after Howe joined the Board of Admiralty early in 1763, was appointed to the 4th-rate *Romney*, stationed at Halifax, Nova Scotia. Williams became a lieutenant on 18 September 1764, in the 5th-rate *Rainbow*, based in Virginia until returning home in October 1766. He was promoted to commander on 26 May 1768, possibly through the influence of his patron Howe at the Admiralty, and became a captain on 10 January 1771. On 20 June 1771 he married the twenty-five-year old Henrietta Wills, daughter of a country gentleman. In December 1771 he was given command of the 6th-rate *Active* and sailed for the West Indies. There he contracted a tropical fever and was in July 1773 re-deployed with his ship to Newfoundland. In November 1773 he exchanged into the 6th-rate *Lively* and returned home.

During 1777 and 1778, in the American War of Independence, Williams commanded the 5th-rate *Venus*, part of Howe's fleet on the North America station and was at the occupation of Rhode Island in August 1778. After again returning home, he was appointed in April 1780 to the 5th-rate *Flora* in which he captured the French frigate *Nymphe* (10 August 1780) and took part in the relief of Gibraltar in March 1781. When escorting a convoy in company with the 28-gun frigate *Crescent*, he defeated two Dutch frigates off Gibraltar, capturing one and driving off the other in a hard fight (30 May 1781). Going on with the convoy, he was intercepted off Finisterre on 19 June 1781 by two French frigates. As both *Crescent* and the Dutch prize had been dismasted and could only sail under jury rig, Williams declined action and left them to be captured while he convoyed the merchantmen, his primary concern, to safety. He was judged to have acted correctly but, after going onto half-pay in April 1782, was not again employed at sea.

In 1784, on the death of his childless cousin Sir Booth Williams, he inherited the family estate at Hoddesdon. Thereafter, Williams was promoted to rear-admiral of the White on 12 April 1794, rear-admiral of the Red on 4 July 1794, vice-admiral of the White on 11 February 1775, admiral of the Blue on 25 October 1809, admiral of the White on 9 November 1805 and admiral of the Red on 25 October 1809. He took no part in the Napoleonic wars and lived as a country gentleman, at his home (renamed Yew House in 1800) in Hoddesdon. In 1804 the local clergyman noted in his diary that the admiral was insufferably proud and rude, and that Mrs Williams was extremely rude and unfeeling, and that he, the writer, had never during his previous twenty-two years in the parish received the most trifling favour from either of them. Henrietta Williams died in 1811, leaving two sons, both of whom predeceased their father, though the second left an heir. In November 1821 Williams succeeded to the Fawley estate, and assumed the additional surname Freeman in acknowledgement of his benefactor. As the senior admiral of the Red, Williams Freeman was the first to be promoted when three new admirals of the fleet were created to mark the accession of William IV [11]. His promotion, on 28 June 1830, was marked by the presentation of the same naval baton (designed by George IV) that the new monarch himself had held as admiral of the fleet. Williams Freeman died at Hoddesdon on 11 February 1832 and was buried in his family's vault in the nearby parish church of St Augustine, Broxbourne.

GAGE
Sir WILLIAM HALL, GCB, GCH (1777–1864) [23]

William Gage was the sixth and youngest son of General the Honourable Thomas Gage, who had been governor of Massachusetts at the beginning of the American War of Independence. Born on 2 October 1777, he joined the Navy in November 1789 as a first class volunteer in the 3rd-rate *Bellona* at Portsmouth and became a midshipman in the 3rd-rate *Captain* on

1 September 1790. In subsequent years, with the outbreak of the French Revolutionary War in 1793, he served in the Channel, the West Indies and the Mediterranean, successively in the 3rd-rate *Colossus*; the 6th-rate *Proserpine*; the 3rd-rates *America* and *Egmont*; the 2nd-rate *Princess Royal*, in which he took part in the battles of Leghorn (Livorno) (14 March 1795) and Toulon (13 July 1795); the 3rd-rate *Bedford*, in which he was in action off Cadiz; and the 1st-rate *Victory*, flagship of Sir John Jervis [12] as C-in-C of the Mediterranean Fleet. On 19 January 1796 Gage was appointed acting lieutenant (confirmed on 11 March 1796) in the 5th-rate *Minerve*. He was present under the command of Captain George Cockburn [20] at the capture of the French corvette *Etonnant*, and, with Commodore Horatio Nelson on board, was at the capture of the Spanish frigate *Santa Sabina* (20 December 1796) for which he was mentioned in despatches. He served in *Minerve* at the battle of St Vincent (14 February 1797) and was again mentioned for his part in a boat action cutting out the French corvette *Mutine* (28 May 1797).

Gage was made a commander on 13 June 1797, followed by promotion to captain of the 5th-rate *Terpsichore* on 26 July 1797. He returned to the Mediterranean with the British fleet in the summer of 1797, where he seized several French vessels harboured at Tunis and took part in the blockade of the French-held island of Malta. In February 1799 he carried the King of Piedmont (forced by the French to abdicate) to safety in Sardinia and in June 1799 captured the Spanish brig *San Antonio*. After returning home, Gage was with a group of frigates in the Channel that met a Danish convoy heading for France in July 1800. The Danes held that, as neutrals, they were exempt from the British blockade. When the convoy refused to stop and be searched, its escort, the frigate *Freija*, was fired upon and brought into the Downs. The incident increased international tension and played a part in the establishment of the Armed Neutrality of December 1800, whereby the Baltic states declared they would use naval action against any belligerent (in practice, the United Kingdom) interfering with the free passage of their ships. Gage was appointed to the 5th-rate *Uranie* in March 1801 and remained in the Channel, where on 21 July 1801 he gained his sixth mention in despatches for leading a flotilla of ships' boats to cut out the corvette *Chevrette* from Camaret Bay, Finisterre. After the formal declaration of peace with France in March 1802, he was placed on half-pay.

The war with France was renewed in May 1803. Gage returned to sea in July 1805 on appointment to the 5th-rate *Thetis*, which he commanded in the North Sea and the Mediterranean until 1808. In February 1813 he was given command of the 3rd-rate *Indus* in the Mediterranean Fleet and, off Toulon, took part in the last significant naval combat of the war (13 February 1814). In September 1814, with Napoleon exiled to Elba and the fleet subjected to the usual post-war reductions, Gage returned to half-pay. He was promoted to rear-admiral of the Blue on 19 July 1821, rear-admiral of the White on 27 May 1825 and rear-admiral of the Red on

22 July 1830. Between December 1825 and January 1830 he was C-in-C, East Indies. During the summer of 1833, when a British fleet blockaded the Dutch coasts and the mouths of the Scheldt in support of the newly created Kingdom of the Belgians, he commanded a squadron in the Downs and was awarded the KCB in 1834. Sir William Gage was promoted to vice-admiral of the White on 10 January 1837. From April to December 1837 he was C-in-C of a British fleet sent to Lisbon to support the young Queen Maria II of Portugal at a time of continuing civil strife. He became a vice-admiral of the Red on 23 November 1841, followed in February 1842 by appointment as a Lord Commissioner of the Admiralty, where he served in the Board headed by the Earl of Haddington until the fall of Sir Robert Peel's administration in 1846. Gage was promoted to admiral of the Blue on 9 November 1846, admiral of the White on 27 December 1847. From 1848 to 1851 he was C-in-C, Plymouth, where he became an admiral of the Red on 1 July 1851. He was awarded the GCB in 1860 and was promoted to admiral of the fleet on 20 May 1862. He retired to Thurston, near Bury St Edmund's, Suffolk, where he died on 4 January 1864 and was buried in St Peter's churchyard.

GAMBIER
JAMES, Baron Gambier, GCB (1756–1833) **[14]**

James ("Jimmy") Gambier, of Huguenot descent, was born on 13 October 1756 in New Providence, Bahamas, where his father was then lieutenant governor. His aunt became the wife of Sir Charles Middleton (later Lord Barham), a future Comptroller of the Navy and First Lord of the Admiralty. Middleton himself was related to Henry Dundas, a prominent Tory politician and a close political ally of William Pitt the Younger, Prime Minister during most of the period between December 1783 and January 1806. Gambier was in 1767 entered on the books of the 3rd-rate *Yarmouth*, commanded by his uncle, a future vice-admiral, and may have sailed with him when he was appointed C-in-C on the North America station in 1770. During the American War of Independence Gambier was promoted to lieutenant on 12 February 1777 and became commander of the bomb vessel *Thunder* on 9 March 1778. He was captured off the American coast by the French fleet later that year, but was soon exchanged for another officer of equal rank. On 9 October 1778 he became captain of the 5th-rate *Raleigh*, in which he served at the capture of Charleston, South Carolina, in May 1780.

Gambier did not again serve at sea until April 1793, when, at the beginning of the French Revolutionary War, he was appointed to command the 3rd-rate *Defence* in the Channel. He became noted for his evangelical or Methodist views and required his crew to join him in divine worship at frequent intervals. From his prohibition of profane language and intemperance, he gained the nickname "Dismal Jimmy". His ruling that all

94

women on board should produce their marriage certificates caused much ill-feeling on the lower deck and made a fortune for forgers in the Portsmouth taverns. At the battle of the Glorious First of June (1 June 1794), *Defence* was the first ship to break the French line and suffered heavy damage. The captain of his sister ship *Invincible* hailed him with the text "Whom the Lord loveth, He chasteneth", but, despite this derision of his piety, he was praised by Lord Howe [9] and awarded a gold medal for his conduct. At the end of the year Gambier became captain of the 2nd-rate *Prince George* but did not put to sea before being appointed, in March 1795, to the Board of Admiralty headed by Earl Spencer in Pitt's Cabinet. He was promoted to rear-admiral of the White on 1 June 1795, vice-admiral of the Blue on 14 February 1799 and vice-admiral of the White on 1 January 1799.

Gambier became a close friend of Pitt's wealthy supporter, the anti-slavery campaigner William Wilberforce, and was parodied by the poet Thomas Hood in a verse beginning "Oh Admiral Gam, I dare not mention *bier*, in such a temperate ear". After the fall of Pitt's first administration in February 1801, Gambier was appointed third in command of the Channel fleet, with his flag in the 2nd-rate *Neptune*. The Treaty of Amiens, signed on 27 March 1802, brought peace with France and hasty reductions in the fleet. Gambier was given the post of governor of Newfoundland. Hostilities were renewed in May 1803 and, following Pitt's return to office early in 1804, Gambier was re-appointed to the Admiralty, serving in the Board headed by Henry Dundas, Viscount Melville. After Melville's fall in April 1805 Gambier continued to serve under the new First Lord of the Admiralty, Lord Barham, until the "Ministry of all the Talents" was formed in February 1806. When this ministry was replaced by one led by the Duke of Portland Gambier was re-appointed to the Admiralty on 6 April 1807, where he served in the Board headed by Lord Mulgrave. While at the Admiralty, in 1807 he raised the pay of naval chaplains from £11 per annum (less than that of an ordinary seaman) to £150. He also commanded the naval element of the expedition suddenly sent to Copenhagen to prevent the Danish fleet from falling into French hands. After a three-day bombardment of their capital (2–5 September 1807), the Danes surrendered their fleet and Gambier was rewarded with a peerage.

After leaving the Admiralty in May 1807 Lord Gambier was given command of the fleet in the Channel. In March 1809 the French fleet in Brest slipped past his blockade. After a few days, they were discovered in the Basque Roads, covering the approaches to Rochefort. Gambier followed them and re-established the blockade, but the Cabinet feared they might escape again and make for the West Indies. Captain Lord Cochrane, one of the most daring and imaginative frigate captains of his day, was sent with a flotilla of fire-ships to attack the French in their anchorage. Cochrane warned the Admiralty that placing him in charge of the attack over the heads of the many officers senior to him already on station would cause problems, but the Cabinet was determined to act without delay and his reservations were disregarded. He arrived on board Gambier's flagship to find the admiral being subjected to a furious complaint by his own second-in-command, Rear-Admiral Sir Eliab Harvey, a Trafalgar veteran, who had already volunteered to perform the task allotted by the Cabinet to Cochrane. Gambier, whose religious feelings had been shocked by the burning of Copenhagen, seems to have considered a night attack by infernal machines upon an anchored fleet almost as a war crime. He also regarded the idea of sending heavy ships into shoal water in support of the attack as unacceptably hazardous.

Harvey made no secret of his view that Gambier's excessive caution made him unfit to command a fleet, and that he himself had been passed over because "I am no canting Methodist, no hypocrite nor a psalm singer". It was indeed widely believed that captains under Gambier's command were more likely to be favoured if they shared his religious views, but Harvey had gone too far and was subsequently dismissed from his command for using grossly insubordinate language. Cochrane's own flamboyant manner did nothing to reduce Gambier's own indignation at being ordered to give his full support to a junior officer in an operation of which he disapproved. When the attack was made, on the night of 11–12 April 1809, it proved an initial success, but Gambier refused to send any of his ships of the line to Cochrane's support, so that seven out of eleven French ships stranded in trying to avoid the fireships eventually escaped up-river.

The affair was presented as a great victory by the Cabinet, whose political position it saved, and a vote of thanks was passed by its supporters in Parliament. Cochrane, sitting as a Radical MP, opposed the motion, in protest at Gambier's inaction. Gambier then demanded a court-martial. This took place under the presidency of Gambier's close friend, Admiral Sir Roger Curtis. Gambier was exonerated, though Cochrane's supporters claimed that the trial had been rigged by a Cabinet unwilling to lose the political benefit of an acclaimed victory, especially as Gambier had family connections with some its members. Most sea officers seem to have felt that, despite his psalm-singing, he did not deserve humiliation at the instance of a young Scottish nobleman on the make, for whom he had obtained the KB as reward for the action in question.

Gambier remained in command of the Channel fleet with his flag in the 1st-rate *Caledonia* until 1811, with promotion to admiral of the White on 31 July 1810. Thereafter he carried no further public duties apart from acting in 1814 as one of the British peace commissioners negotiating with the United States at the end of the War of 1812. He was promoted to admiral of the Red on 4 June 1814 and admiral of the fleet on 22 July 1830, when he was one of the three senior officers in the Navy promoted to this rank to mark the accession of William IV [11]. He had married in 1788, but had no children and his peerage became extinct. He was buried in St Peter's churchyard, Iver, Buckinghamshire.

GEORGE V
GEORGE FREDERICK ERNEST ALBERT, HM King of Great Britain and Ireland, Emperor of India (1866–1936) **[64]**

Prince George of Wales, the second son of the Prince and Princess of Wales (later Edward VII **[44]** and Queen Alexandra) was born at Marlborough House, London, on 3 June 1865. He was intended for a career in the Navy and joined the training ship *Britannia* at Dartmouth in September 1877. Together with his elder brother, Prince Albert Victor, later Duke of Clarence, George was appointed to the corvette *Bacchante* in 1879 and went round the world in the Flying Squadron between 1880 and 1882. Cabinet reservations at the idea of risking at sea the two princes in direct line of succession to the throne were over-ruled by the Queen. The fears of her Ministers were borne out when *Bacchante* lost contact with the squadron for some days in a violent storm in the Indian Ocean in May 1881 and was saved from broaching-to only by her commander, an experienced seaman, using the crew as a human sail. Some on this cruise, including George himself, reported sighting the phantom "Flying Dutchman". Neither prince was spared the rigorous duty and bullying that went with a naval education of the times, and George later felt he had been treated the more harshly because of his royal blood. He was promoted to midshipman on 8 January 1880 and appointed to the corvette *Canada*, on the North America and West Indies station, in 1883. He became an acting sub-lieutenant on 3 June 1884, at the beginning of his promotion courses, and a lieutenant on 8 October 1885. He then served in the Mediterranean Fleet from 1886 to 1888, successively in the battleships *Thunderer*, *Dreadnought* and *Alexandra*, before returning home to serve in the battleship *Northumberland* in the Channel in 1889. Always close to his parents, and especially to his mother, George did not relish these long absences from his family and was much afflicted by home-sickness. Ashore, he consoled himself in the usual manner of princes.

George was given command of a torpedo-boat in 1889 and proved himself a capable ship handler when going to the rescue of a consort that had broken down in heavy weather. His next command was the gunboat *Thrush* on the North America and West Indies station in 1890, followed by promotion to commander on 24 August 1891. On the death of the Duke of Clarence in January 1892 George became the Prince of Wales's direct heir and was created Duke of York soon afterwards. He inherited not only his brother's place in the succession but also his fiancée, Princess May (only daughter of the Duke of Teck, a minor German principality), whom he married in July 1893. York was promoted to captain on 2 January 1893 and commanded the cruiser *Melampus* off the Irish coast in the manoeuvres of 1893. His royal duties brought his time at sea to an end and his last command was of the cruiser *Crescent* in the manoeuvres of 1898. He was promoted to rear-admiral on 1 January 1901. After the accession of his father as Edward VII on 22 January 1901 he became Duke of Cornwall and

York and was known by this title until 9 November 1901, when he was created Prince of Wales. He was promoted to vice-admiral on 26 June 1903 and to admiral on 1 March 1907. On 6 May 1910 he succeeded his father as King George V and became an admiral of the fleet.

During the First World War George V became a figure of national unity. He held numerous investitures and toured military establishments, hospitals and factories, including five visits to the Grand Fleet at Scapa Flow. In May 1917, bowing to ministerial pressure for all British subjects possessing German titles to disclaim them, he changed the name of his own family from Saxe-Coburg to Windsor. He declined to offer refuge to his friend and cousin, the Emperor Nicholas II of Russia [60], after the latter's abdication in March 1917, on the grounds that the arrival in England of an unpopular autocrat with a German-born wife could place his own throne in jeopardy. In the post-war period George V emerged as the model of a modern constitutional monarch and was widely respected by his subjects as a symbol of stability in an uncertain world. He died at Sandringham, Norfolk, on 20 January 1936, and was buried at St George's Chapel, Windsor. He had a family of one daughter and five sons, the eldest of whom succeeded him as Edward VIII [84].

GEORGE VI
ALBERT FREDERICK ARTHUR GEORGE, HM King of
Great Britain and Ireland, Emperor of India (1895–1952) [86]

Prince Albert of York was born on 14 December 1895 at York Cottage, Sandringham, the second of five sons of the then Duke and Duchess of York, later George V [64] and Queen Mary. He was a shy and nervous child, greatly in awe (like the rest of their children) of his royal parents, whose life-style inhibited any outward expression of affection. In early childhood, Prince Albert ("Bertie" to his family) developed a speech impediment, which he strove to overcome with great determination and eventual success. Like his father, he was originally intended for a naval career and followed his example by attending the Royal Naval College at Osborne in 1909 and Dartmouth in 1911. Albert joined the cruiser *Cumberland* as a cadet in January 1913 and was gazetted as a midshipman on 15 September 1913. He was appointed to the battleship *Collingwood* in October 1913 and served in the Mediterranean. Shortly after the outbreak of the First World War in August 1914 Albert was sent ashore with the first of the several gastric problems that affected his naval career. In November 1914 he was posted to the War Staff at the Admiralty. He rejoined *Collingwood* at Portsmouth as her senior midshipman in February 1915, and became an acting sub-lieutenant on 15 September 1915 but was then again sent ashore for medical treatment.

George V, who refused to allow the more robust Prince of Wales [84] to serve in combat, was far less concerned about the health of his second son and, despite medical advice, supported him in his wish to rejoin the fleet. Albert was therefore able to go back to *Collingwood* on 5 May 1916 and to serve in her at the battle of Jutland (31 May–1 June 1916). He was promoted to lieutenant on 15 June 1916, but at the end of August was once more sent ashore, suffering from a duodenal ulcer. After a period on the staff at Portsmouth, Albert joined the battleship *Malaya* in May 1917 and remained in this ship until August 1917, when a recurrence of gastric illness ended his time as a sea-going officer. On 1 January 1918, at his own suggestion, he was posted to the Royal Naval Air Station at Cranwell, Lincolnshire. He served there as the officer commanding No 4 Squadron, Boy Wing. When the Royal Air Force was formed on 1 April 1918 Albert, with the encouragement of the King, transferred to the new Service as a flight lieutenant.

In October 1919, Albert went up to Trinity College, Cambridge, where he spent the next three terms. He was created Duke of York and Earl of Inverness in June 1920. He then met and fell in love with Lady Elizabeth Bowes-Lyon, ninth of the ten children of the fourteenth Earl of Strathmore. York proposed to her the following year, but was refused, as Lady Elizabeth, brought up in a happy domestic life, had little desire to enter the restrictive circles of the Royal Family. York persevered in his suit and the couple married on 26 April 1923. Their marriage proved a happy one, with the Duke of York's health improving as his Duchess gave him a calm and loving home, with two daughters born in 1926 and 1930 respectively. He undertook his share of public duties and rose steadily through the ranks of the Royal Navy and Royal Air Force, to become a rear-admiral on 3 June 1932 and an air chief marshal on 21 January 1936.

The Abdication crisis of late 1936 was greeted by the Yorks with horror. Neither wished for the throne that Edward VIII chose to vacate in order to marry the woman he loved. Nevertheless, with a characteristic regard for duty, York accepted the crown and took the regnal name of King George VI, to emphasize both that the monarchy continued and that his model would be his late father. Following the precedents set by George V and Edward VIII, he became an admiral of the fleet, field marshal and marshal of the Royal Air Force on 11 December 1936, the date of his accession. He set himself to restore the prestige of the British Crown and succeeded in gaining the respect and sympathy of his subjects. When the Second World War began in September 1939 George VI assumed a natural role as the symbol of his country. His modest and self-disciplined manner made it easier for ordinary people to identify with their King than with the extrovert war-time Prime Minister, Winston Churchill, who was regarded by many working people as a war-monger and strike-breaker.

During the war, in addition to his normal duties of state, George VI made frequent visits to ships and units at home and abroad. He went to France before the German offensive in 1940, to North Africa after the Allied victories in 1943 and to Normandy ten days after the Allied landings in June

1944. In 1940, when invasion was expected, George VI refused the advice of his ministers to send the Queen and the princesses to safety in Canada. He installed a small-arms range in the grounds of Buckingham Palace where he practised with revolvers and sub-machine guns, for personal defence in case of a German assault. Accompanied by Queen Elizabeth, he made visits to the East End of London, Coventry and other cities devastated by German air raids. He continued to work from Buckingham Palace during both the Blitz of 1940–1941 and the attacks by V-weapons in 1944–1945 and was at the palace when it was hit by a bomb on 11 September 1940. To mark courageous acts by civilians or service personnel when not in the physical presence of the enemy, he instituted two new decorations, the George Cross and the George Medal.

Victory in Europe on 8 May 1945 was followed by a general election that gave the Labour party a landslide victory and a mandate to introduce far-reaching domestic reforms. The King, reigning as a constitutional monarch, retained his popularity, while his new ministers introduced an ambitious programme laying the foundations of a Welfare State. On 22 June 1947, when British rule in South Asia ended, George VI disclaimed his title as Emperor of India. He continued with his public duties, but his health, never robust, began to decline. He was found to be suffering from cancer and, in September 1951, underwent an operation for the removal of his left lung. His medical advisers doubted his ability to survive further surgery. Not long after saying farewell to his heiress, Princess Elizabeth, on her departure for a visit to Kenya, George VI died in his sleep at Sandringham, on 6 February 1952. He was buried at St George's Chapel, Windsor.

GILLFORD
VISCOUNT, see **MEADE,** RICHARD JAMES, 4th Earl of Clanwilliam **[50]**

GORDON
Sir JAMES ALEXANDER , GCB (1782–1869) **[30]**

James Gordon was born on 6 October 1782, the eldest son of a Highland gentleman of modest means. His aunt, married to a Scottish nobleman, Lord Glenbervie, was a friend of Captain James Hawkins Whitshed **[17]**. With the French Revolutionary War having begun nine months earlier, Whitshed was given command of the 3rd-rate *Arrogant* and took Gordon on board as a captain's servant on 25 November 1793. Gordon served in *Arrogant* in the Channel fleet during 1794, employed in escorting convoys or on blockade duty of Brest. After a short time in harbour, successively in the 3rd-rates *Invincible, Ramillies* and *Defence,* he joined the 6th-rate *Eurydice,* under Whitshed's friend Captain Francis Cole. In 1795 he followed Cole to the 5th-rate *Revolutionnaire*, newly captured from the French, and served in the Channel under Sir Alexander Hood (Lord Bridport). They were present at "Bridport's Action" when three French ships of the line were captured off the Ile de Groix, Lorient (23 June 1795). In 1796 Cole explained to Gordon that, although he had spent three years at sea, he could not be considered for appointment as a midshipman as he was still semi-literate.

Whitshed, at this time commanding the 2nd-rate *Namur*, agreed to take him back as a first class volunteer. Gordon took part in the battle of the Glorious First of June (1 June 1794) and subsequently transferred to the 2nd-rate *Goliath*, commanded by another of Whitshed's friends, Captain Thomas Foley. He served in this ship at the battle of St Vincent (14 February 1797) and received sufficient education from the ship's schoolmaster to be appointed a midshipman and mate. Gordon was in *Goliath* at the battle of the Nile (1 August 1798) and took part in the blockade of French-occupied Malta until returning home late in 1798.

Gordon was appointed second lieutenant of the 6th-rate *Bourdelois* on 27 January 1800 and served in the West Indies, where he was mentioned in despatches for his part in the capture of the French brig *Curieuse* (29 January 1801). In the autumn of 1801, while in command of a small vessel, taken as a prize by *Bourdelois*, he was captured by a French privateer. He spent four months on parole in the French colony of St Domingue (Haiti), western Hispaniola, before being exchanged and returning to his ship just as news arrived that peace had been proclaimed by the Treaty of Amiens (27 March 1802). *Bourdelois* was paid off as part of the rapid post-war reduction of the Navy, but Gordon was able to find an appointment as lieutenant in the brig *Racoon* in which he returned to the West Indies late in 1802. After the renewal of hostilities in May 1803, *Racoon* was involved in numerous engagements against French vessels, including the capture of the corvette *Lodi* off Leogane, Haiti, on 11 July 1803, for which Gordon was mentioned in despatches a second time. He was given command of *Racoon* on 23 October 1803, with confirmation of the rank of commander on 2 March 1804. Gordon was deployed off the coast of Haiti, where his prizes included three privateers, a troop transport and several schooners.

On 16 May 1805 Gordon was promoted to captain, with command of the captured Spanish frigate *Diligentia* (taken into the Navy as a 6th-rate and renamed *Ligaera*) in which he returned home, but, suffering from the effects of yellow fever, he was forced to give up his command on medical grounds. While convalescent, he stayed with his father (at that time serving as a military paymaster) and his younger sisters at Marlborough. There he met Lydia Ward, the nineteen-year-old daughter of a local solicitor. Each was attracted to the other, but her father's view was that no engagement should be entered into at that time, as Gordon was wholly dependent on his naval pay and could be expected to return to active service. In the event, Gordon remained on half-pay until 18 June 1807, when he was given command of the 6th-rate *Mercury*. Following a period on trade protection duties in the North Atlantic and the Channel, he joined the squadron blockading Cadiz after the battle of Trafalgar (21 October 1805). He was again mentioned in despatches for his part in intercepting a Spanish convoy off Rota (4 April 1808).

Between June 1808 and June 1812 Gordon commanded the 5th-rate *Active*, in which he served in the Mediterranean Fleet, mostly in the Adriatic, where he was frequently engaged in coastal and boat actions. He took or destroyed a large number of minor vessels and was again mentioned in despatches for his part in a raid on Ortano (Ortona), off the east coast of French-occupied Naples (12 February 1811). Gordon was at the battle of Lissa (Vis) on 13 March 1811, off the French-occupied principality of Dalmatia (Croatia), in an action between two frigate squadrons for which he was awarded a gold medal. In another frigate action in the same area, off Pelagosa (Palagruza), he sank the French *Pomone*, but was badly wounded by cannon-shot, losing his left leg at the knee (29 November 1811). After treatment at Malta, he returned home with *Active* in June 1812. He had by this time gained sufficient funds from prize-money, together with a pension for the loss of his leg, to make him an acceptable suitor for the hand of Miss Ward. She, by this time aged twenty-six, had remained faithful to him and had given a lock of her hair to his sisters to send him. They were married at Marlborough on 28 August 1812 and later had eleven children, of whom seven daughters and a son survived to adulthood.

On 14 September 1812 Gordon was appointed to the 5th-rate *Seahorse*. After a brief deployment to the West Indies, he returned to Portsmouth and, during August 1813, patrolled the Western Atlantic in a fruitless search for American privateers in the War of 1812. He then joined the blockade of Cherbourg and, on 13 November 1813, sank the French privateer *Subtile*. Gordon was a humane commanding officer, who disliked having to order floggings as part of his duty, and on one occasion wrote to his wife that he hoped that some of his men who had deserted would not be found, so that he would not have to punish them. After the fall of Napoleon in April 1814 *Seahorse* was among the reinforcements sent to the British forces in North America. In August 1814 Gordon led a diversionary raid up the Potomac, where he captured Alexandria, Virginia, and seized twenty-one vessels. This feat, carried out in shallow river-waters protected by shore defences, brought him another mention in despatches. He was present at the bombardment of Fort McHenry, in the unsuccessful British attack on Baltimore, Maryland (commemorated in the United States national anthem "The Star-Spangled Banner"). His last active service was in providing logistic support for the British descent on New Orleans in December 1814 and in supplying arms to the Creek Indians of Appalachicola, West Florida, notionally subjects of Spain, but prepared to be allies of the British. In 1815 he was awarded the KCB and received the last of his nine mentions in despatches.

After the end of the Napoleonic wars Sir James Gordon was appointed to the 5th-rate *Madagascar*, in which he served on the Home station from November 1815 to October 1816. He then moved to the 6th-rate *Maeander* and in December 1816, by good seamanship, saved her from being wrecked in a storm off Orford Ness. After a period ashore, he commanded his old ship *Active* successively in the North Atlantic, the Mediterranean and the Irish Sea from 1819 to 1822. In 1828 he was appointed Superintendent of the Naval Hospital, Plymouth. From July 1832 to 10 January 1837, when he was promoted to rear-admiral of the Blue, Gordon was Superintendent of Chatham Dockyard. In July 1840 he became Lieutenant-Governor of the Royal Naval Hospital, Greenwich, with promotion to rear-admiral of the White on 23 November 1841, rear-admiral of the Red on 9 November 1847, vice-admiral of the Blue on 8 January 1848, and vice-admiral of the Red on 26 October 1853. During 1853 he was appointed Governor of the Royal Naval Hospital. Gordon, a well-built man over six feet tall, coped well with his false leg for many years, frequently walking from Greenwich to London, but a bad fall in 1848 reduced his mobility. He was promoted to admiral of the Blue on 21 January 1854 and admiral of the fleet on the retired list on 30 January 1868. He died at the Royal Naval Hospital on 8 January 1869 and was buried in the Hospital grounds.

GOUGH-CALTHORPE
The Honourable Sir SOMERSET ARTHUR, GCB, GCMG, CVO (1864–1937) **[76]**

Somerset Gough Calthorpe, born in London on 23 December 1865, was the younger son of the seventh Baron Calthorpe and his wife Eliza, who was herself the only child of one naval captain, the widow of another and the granddaughter of an admiral. The young Calthorpe spent part of his boyhood in France, where he acquired a knowledge of French language and culture that proved useful later in his career. After joining the Navy in 1878 as a cadet in the training ship *Britannia*, he became a midshipman on 19 March 1880 and served from 1880 to 1883 in the armoured ship *Northampton*, flagship of the North America and West Indies station. He was promoted to acting sub-lieutenant on 19 March 1884, at the beginning of his promotion courses, and was appointed to the corvette *Rover* in the Training Squadron in September 1885. He became a lieutenant on 19 March 1886 and joined the armoured turret ship *Colossus* in June 1886. Between 1887 and 1889 Calthorpe was at the torpedo school *Vernon* where, after qualifying as a torpedo specialist, he joined the instructional staff in 1890. From August 1891 to August 1893 he was based at Hong Kong for torpedo duties and from January to October 1894 he was again in *Vernon*. He then became torpedo lieutenant of the cruiser *St George* on the Cape of Good Hope and West Coast of Africa station, where he served from October 1894 to the end of 1895.

Calthorpe was promoted to commander on 1 January 1896 in recognition of his services at the beginning of the Fourth Ashanti War (December 1895-January 1896). He was then appointed commander of the armoured cruiser *Impérieuse*, flagship of the Pacific station, and returned home in the summer of 1899. In 1900 he married Effie Dunsmuir, of Victoria, British Columbia. He spent most of this year as a supernumerary at *Vernon* before being given command of the torpedo gunboat *Halcyon* in the Mediterranean in September 1900. Calthorpe was promoted to captain on 1 January 1902. He spent the next three years as naval attaché to Russia, Sweden and the newly-independent Norway, and then commanded successively the cruiser *Roxburgh* and the battleship *Hindostan*. In December 1909 he was appointed commodore 1st Class and captain of the fleet to Sir Henry May [65], C-in-C, Home Fleet, in the battleship *Dreadnought* until promoted to rear-admiral on 27 August 1911. During 1910 he adopted the surname Gough-Calthorpe.

Between 1912 and 1913 Gough-Calthorpe was second-in-command of the First Battle Squadron, with his flag in the battleship *St Vincent*, and from 1914 to 1916, in the early years of the First World War, commanded the Second Cruiser Squadron, with his flag in the cruiser *Shannon*. He was promoted to acting vice-admiral on 11 March 1915 and was awarded the KCB. Sir Somerset Gough-Calthorpe served during 1916 as Second Sea Lord at the Admiralty and became Admiral commanding the Coastguard and Reserves at the end of that year. He was confirmed as vice-admiral on 26 April 1917 and was appointed C-in-C, Mediterranean Fleet, in July 1917, with his flag successively in the battleships *Superb* and *Iron Duke*. As president of a committee of British, French, Italian and Japanese admirals, he was at the head of Allied naval operations in the Mediterranean, and by the end of the war also had ships of the United States and Royal Greek Navies under his control.

In October 1918 Gough-Calthorpe was authorized to act as sole Allied negotiator in response to Turkish proposals for an Armistice. He sent a cruiser from his base at Mudros to collect the Turkish representatives and concluded an agreement with them on 30 October 1918. The French premier, Clemenceau, protested that the Allied supreme commander in the Mediterranean, Admiral Gauchet, had not been fully informed of the negotiations, nor been present when the armistice was signed, but the Admiralty gave Gough-Calthorpe its full backing and sent him additional battleships to match the numbers of the French. It also insisted that any Allied warships entering the Black Sea should be under Gough-Calthorpe's command and that when the Allied fleets steamed into Constantinople (Istanbul) on 13 November 1918 the British C-in-C should be at their head.

Gough-Calthorpe was given the additional appointment of British High Commissioner in Turkey pending the establishment of a peace treaty. He was promoted to admiral on 31 July 1919. After a period of intense post-war diplomatic activity, with Anglo-French rivalry over former Turkish territory compounded by the continuation of civil war in Russia, he returned home late in 1919. Sir Somerset Gough-Calthorpe served from 1920 to 1923 as C-in-C, Portsmouth, followed by promotion to admiral of the fleet on 8 May 1925. He retired in 1930 and died at Ryde, Isle of Wight, on 27 July 1937.

HAMOND
Sir GRAHAM EDEN, 2nd Baronet, GCB (1779–1862) [24]

Graham Hamond, born in London on 30 December 1779, was the only son of Captain Sir Andrew Snape Hamond, who had served the Navy during in the Seven Years War and the American War of Independence, and was later awarded a baronetcy. In September 1785 Graham Hamond was entered as captain's servant on the books of the 3rd-rate *Irresistible*, commanded by his father as commodore and C-in-C in the Medway. In 1790 he became a midshipman and subsequently served under his father successively in the 3rd-rates *Vanguard* and *Bedford* and the 2nd-rate *Duke* until the outbreak of the French Revolutionary War in 1793. He then joined the 5th-rate *Phaeton*, commanded by his cousin, Sir Andrew Snape Douglas, in the Channel fleet, shortly before Sir Andrew Hamond became Comptroller of the Navy. In the first year of the war *Phaeton* was present at the capture of the French brig *General Dumouriez* and her prize the Spanish *St Iago* (both carrying valuable cargoes), the French frigate *Pompée*, the corvette *Blonde* and a privateersman. Hamond followed his cousin in April 1794 when the latter was given command of the 1st-rate *Queen Charlotte*, flagship of Earl Howe [9] as C-in-C of the Channel Fleet, and served with him at the battle of the Glorious First of June (1 June 1794). After serving as acting lieutenant in the 5th-rate *Aquilon* and the 3rd-rate *Zealous*, he joined the 1st-rate *Britannia*, flagship of Admiral Sir William Hotham, C-in-C of the Mediterranean Fleet, in June 1795, and was at the battle of Toulon (13 July 1795). He was confirmed as lieutenant on 19 October 1795 and, after serving in the 5th-rate *Aigle* in the Mediterranean in 1796, returned home from Lisbon in the 5th-rate *Niger* during 1797.

On 20 October 1798 Hamond became commander of the sloop *Echo*, deployed in the Channel and North Sea on blockade and convoy escort duties. He was promoted to be captain of the 6th-rate *Champion* on 30 November 1798 and served during 1799 in the Baltic, the North Sea, and the Arctic, capturing the French privateer *Anacreon* and escorting a convoy from Archangel (Arkhangelsk). Early in 1800 he took part in the blockade of the French in Malta and served ashore in the siege of Valetta, before exchanging to the 3rd-rate *Lion* on medical grounds and returning home. He was then appointed to the 5th-rate *Blanche*, in which he served in the Baltic under Sir Hyde Parker at the battle of Copenhagen (2 April 1801). In the fleet reductions that followed the Treaty of Amiens (27 March 1802), *Blanche* was paid off in September 1802.

Late in February 1803, shortly before the renewal of the war with France, Hamond was given command of the 3rd-rate *Plantagenet*. He captured the French brig *Courier de Terre Neuve* and the corvette *Atalanta* before giving up his command on medical grounds in November 1803. On July 1804 he was appointed to the 5th-rate *Lively*. By the autumn of 1804 it became clear that the Spanish government, under pressure from Napoleon, was prepared to place its fleet at the disposal of the French. The British protested at Spanish breaches of neutrality and moved to intercept the flow of silver from Mexico to Spain. On 5 October 1804 Hamond was involved in the capture of three Spanish frigates carrying treasure, and the destruction of a fourth, for which he was mentioned in despatches. On 7 December 1804 he was at the capture of the Spanish treasure ships *San Miguel* and *Santa Gertruyda* off Cape St Vincent. As the outraged Spaniards did not declare war until 12 December 1804, the Admiralty ruled that only one quarter of the proceeds was allowable as prize money. Hamond was even less fortunate when he brought the treasure (totalling five million Spanish dollars) home in the following March, as the payment of freight-money for the conveyance of treasure was suspended after the outbreak of hostilities. Returning to his station, he engaged the Spanish 74-gun ship *Glorioso* in an indecisive single-ship duel off Cadiz on 29 May 1805. In November 1805 he carried troops to Naples, where a combined British and Russian force landed to threaten Napoleon's southern flank. In June 1806 he returned home, where on 30 December 1806 he married Elizabeth Kimber, the daughter of a country gentleman of Fowey, Cornwall. They later had a family of three daughters and two sons, both of whom became officers in the Navy.

Between December 1808 and September 1809 Hamond commanded the 3rd-rate *Victorious* on the Home station and was in the fleet covering the British expedition to Walcheren (July-August 1809). From May 1813 to March 1814, when Napoleon abdicated, he commanded the 3rd-rate *Rivoli* in the Mediterranean. In March 1824 Hamond was appointed to the 3rd-rate *Wellesley* in which he went to Brazil with a British diplomatic mission. On promotion to rear-admiral of the Blue on 27 May 1825, he returned home in the 3rd-rate *Spartiate* and later succeeded to his father's baronetcy on 12 September 1828. Sir Graham Hamond became a rear-admiral of the White on 22 July 1830 and returned to the South American station as C-in-C in September 1834, where he remained, with his flag successively in *Spartiate* and the 5th-rate *Dublin* until May 1838. He became a vice-admiral of the Blue on 10 January 1837, vice-admiral of the Red on 23 November 1841, admiral of the Blue on 22 January 1847, admiral of the White on 15 September 1849 and admiral of the Red on 5 July 1855. Hamond was promoted to admiral of the fleet on 10 November 1862. He died at Freshwater, Isle of Wight, on 20 December 1862 and was succeeded in his baronetcy by his son, Vice-Admiral Andrew Snape Hamond.

HAWKE
Sir EDWARD 1st Baron Hawke, KB (1705–1781) **[7]**

Edward Hawke, the only son of a barrister-at-law, was born in London in 1705. On his father's death in 1718 he became the ward of his mother's brother, Colonel Martin Bladen, a wealthy Yorkshire landowner, then Commissioner of Trade and Plantations. Hawke joined the Navy on 20 February 1720 as a volunteer in the 6th-rate *Seahorse*, in which he served on the North America and West Indies station until June 1725. He then passed for promotion to lieutenant and joined the 5th-rate *Kingsale* in which he served off West Africa and in the West Indies until July 1727 as a supernumerary officer (held on the books as an able seaman). He was appointed third lieutenant of the 4th-rate *Portland*, in the Channel, on 11 April 1729. From November to December 1729 he served in the 4th-rate *Leopard*, and in May 1731 became fourth lieutenant of the 4th-rate *Edinburgh* in the Mediterranean. Between January and November 1732 Hawke was on the North America and West Indies station in the 6th-rate *Scarborough*, commanded by Sir Peter Warren, under whom he had served in *Leopard*. He was appointed first lieutenant of the 4th-rate *Kingston* at Jamaica in 24 December 1732, and commander of the sloop *Wolf* on 13 April 1733. He was promoted on 20 March 1734 to be captain of the 6th-rate *Flamborough*, in which he returned home in September 1735.

In 1737 Hawke married the seventeen-year-old Catherine Brook, the heiress to several estates in Yorkshire, to whose family his own was already connected by marriage. They later had seven children, three of whom died in infancy. On the approach of war between Spain and the United Kingdom (the War of Jenkins's Ear) Hawke returned to sea on 30 July 1739 as captain of *Portland* on the North America and West Indies station. In November 1741 the ill-found *Portland* was dismasted in a gale off Boston, Massachusetts, and was fortunate to reach her base in Barbados. Catherine Hawke joined her husband there and the two returned together to England in January 1742. The war had by this time been overtaken by a wider European conflict, the War of the Austrian Succession. In June 1743 Hawke was given command of the new 3rd-rate *Berwick*, with which he joined the Mediterranean Fleet in January 1744 at Hyeres, Toulon. In the subsequent engagement with the combined French and Spanish fleets (11 February 1744) Hawke was one of the few officers to emerge with credit. On his own initiative, he engaged and captured the French ship *Polder* only for this prize to be looted and burned at a later stage in the battle by the pusillanimous Captain Richard Norris, elder son of Sir John Norris **[1]**. On 3 August 1745 Hawke became captain of the 2nd-rate *Neptune* in which he returned home six weeks later.

Following the British victory off Cape Finisterre (3 May 1747) Lord Anson **[5]** had handed over his command of the Western Squadron (in effect, the Channel fleet) to Hawke's old patron, Sir Peter Warren. Hawke became rear-admiral of the White on 15 July 1747 and second-in-command of the squadron, with his flag in the new 4th-rate *Gloucester*, three weeks later. Shortly afterwards, with Warren suffering from scurvy, Hawke succeeded to his command. On 12 October 1747, with his flag in the 3rd-rate *Devonshire*, he encountered a large convoy of French West Indiamen off La Rochelle. The convoy escaped, but seven of its nine major escorts were captured and most of the merchantmen were taken later by British warships (forewarned by Hawke's despatches) in the West Indies. Hawke was awarded the KB on 15 November 1747 and spent most of the remaining months of the war in the Bay of Biscay with Warren again in command. Sir Edward Hawke entered Parliament in December 1747 as Member for Portsmouth, a seat in the gift of the Duke of Bedford, (at that time First Lord of the Admiralty) and continued to represent that borough until he was elevated to the peerage. He was promoted to vice-admiral of the Blue on 26 May 1748 and succeeded Warren in command of the fleet in home waters from 26 July 1748 to November 1752.

Hostilities with France in North America were resumed in May 1754. Although the two nations were not formally at war until after the outbreak of the Seven Years War in 1756, the British Cabinet decided to prevent French reinforcements reaching Canada. In February 1755 Hawke was appointed to the 1st-rate *St George*. The Duke of Newcastle, Prime Minister of the day, originally considered giving him no definite instructions, so that Hawke, rather than the ministers, would be blamed if anything went wrong. In July 1755 he was sent to cruise off Brest, with orders to attack any French ships he met, but there was no contact, and sickness among his crews and the poor state of his ships forced him back to Portsmouth at the end of September. During the early part of 1756 Hawke was again in the Bay of Biscay, blockading the French naval base at Rochefort. In June 1756, in the 4th-rate *Antelope*, he sailed for the Mediterranean, where Admiral John Byng had been removed from command after failing to relieve Minorca. Hawke hoisted his flag in the 2nd-rate *Ramillies* at Gibraltar on 4 July 1756, but found that the British garrison of Minorca, after holding out for seventy days, had surrendered on 28 June. The French fleet returned to Toulon and at the end of 1756 Hawke, saddened by the death of his wife in October that year, was recalled to England with most of his ships. He was promoted to admiral of the Blue on 24 February 1757.

In June 1757 William Pitt the Elder became the dominant figure in the Cabinet. As part of his policy of waging war from the sea, Pitt planned a descent on Rochefort in September 1757. Hawke, with his flag in *Ramillies*, commanded the naval element and covered the initial landings, as well as the subsequent re-embarkation when the military commanders decided that a further advance was impracticable. He was given command in the Channel on 5 March 1758 and made another raid on the approaches to Rochefort in April 1758, destroying coastal fortifications and preventing the departure of French reinforcements for Canada. After returning to Portsmouth, Hawke was waited upon on 10 May 1758 by Captain Richard Howe [9], who had been selected to command the naval element of a new

108

raid. Hawke assumed that this was another attack on Rochefort, where he had twice been in charge of the naval operations, and took Howe's appointment as a personal affront. In protest, he struck his flag without orders, only to discover, after being summoned to the Admiralty to explain his conduct, that Howe was going not to Rochefort but to St Malo. His previous services saved him from public censure for this grave breach of discipline, but he was not allowed to resume command of his fleet. Instead, Lord Anson [5], then First Lord of the Admiralty, felt obliged to take command in person. Hawke rehoisted his flag as second-in-command, but after two weeks at sea, covering the raid on St Malo, returned to Portsmouth on medical grounds.

Hawke was restored to command of the Western Squadron on 9 May 1759. He resumed the blockade of Brest, where the French had collected a fleet of twenty-one ships under an experienced admiral and marshal of France, the Comte de Conflans. Further south, in Quiberon Bay, a French army was assembled for the invasion of England. In the middle of November 1759, with Hawke driven to Torbay by bad weather, Conflans sailed for Quiberon Bay to join the troop transports. Hawke, with his flag in the 1st-rate *Royal George*, caught up with him on 20 November 1759. Accepting the risks of combat in heavy swell and gale-force winds, in confined waters on a short winter day, Hawke destroyed seven French ships for the loss of two British. With the rest of the French fleet forced to take refuge in nearby estuaries, the battle of Quiberon Bay was one of the most important British victories of the war. Hawke remained with his blockading ships until early January 1760 when, with his flag in the 2nd-rate *Torbay*, he returned home.

In August 1760 Hawke sailed in *Royal George* to resume command of the blockade. In October he was asked by Anson to report on the best place for a landing on Belle-Ile. He replied with an alternative plan, for a landing in the Quiberon area, but was overruled by Pitt, who had selected Belle-Ile. Hawke remained on blockade for another winter and then returned to Portsmouth in March 1761. Belle-Ile, where General Studholme Hodgson (a veteran of the unsuccessful expedition against Rochefort in 1757) landed early in April 1761, surrendered to the British eight weeks later. In April 1762 he was appointed C-in-C in the Channel, the Soundings, the coast of Ireland and in the Bay of Biscay. Despite the vast extent of this command, with detached squadrons at sea in the Downs and off Le Havre and Rochefort, he was ordered to sea with another squadron in June 1762, to ensure the Spanish fleet remained in Ferrol during the closing months of the war. He was promoted to admiral of the White on 21 October 1762.

In December 1766 Hawke became First Lord of the Admiralty in the Duke of Grafton's Cabinet, with promotion to admiral of the fleet on 15 January 1768. As First Lord, Hawke had to deal with the usual problems experienced by Service ministers in a period of peace gained by a victorious war and his name featured in a jingle of the lower deck:

'Ere Hawke did bang Mounseer Conflang
You sent us beef and beer.
Now Mounseer's beat, we've nought to eat
Since you have nought to fear"

As would happen some two centuries later, it was only a crisis over possession of the Falkland Islands that induced an unpopular prime minister (in this case, Lord North in 1770) to restore, at least in the short term, cuts that the Treasury had imposed on the fleet. Hawke remained in North's Cabinet until January 1771. As First Lord he authorized the voyages of exploration by Captain James Cook, who named Hawke's Bay, New Zealand, in his honour. Hawke was in poor health in his later years, and suffered great pain from gout and urinary calculi, or "gravel", an illness deriving from a deficiency of Vitamin A and an inadequate intake of fresh water, both of which were common features of seafaring life in his time. His closing years were saddened by the continued mental instability of his daughter Kitty and by the deaths of his second son, Lieutenant Colonel Edward Hawke, in the hunting field, in October 1773, and of his third, the prodigal Cornet Chaloner Hawke, in a road accident in September 1777. He was granted a peerage as Baron Hawke, of Towton (one of his wife's estates), on 20 May 1776. Lord Hawke died at his house in Sunbury-on-Thames, on 17 October 1781, and was buried near his wife and their four-day old son William in the parish church of St Nicholas, North Stoneham, Swaythling, near Southampton. He was succeeded by his eldest son, Martin Bladen Hawke.

HAWKINS
JAMES, see **WHITSHED,** Sir JAMES HAWKINS, [17]

HAY
The Right Honourable Lord JOHN, GCB (1827–1916) **[46]**

Lord John Hay, the fourth son of the eighth Marquess of Tweeddale, a veteran of the Napoleonic wars and the American War of 1812, was born in Geneva, Switzerland, on 23 August 1827. Lord John's uncle and name-sake, Rear-Admiral the Right Honourable Lord John Hay (third son of the seventh marquess) also served in the Napoleonic wars, in which he lost an arm at the age of fifteen. He later served from 1846 to 1848 as a lord commissioner of the Admiralty. Lord John joined the Navy in 1840 and served in the First China War (1841–42) and subsequently in operations against pirates in Borneo. After passing for promotion to lieutenant and spending the required six years on the books of a naval ship, he was appointed mate on 2 December 1846 in the paddle sloop *Spiteful*, at Woolwich. He was promoted to lieutenant on 19 December 1846 and from

April 1848 to 1850 was in the 2nd-rate *Powerful* in the Mediterranean. He then served for a few months as flag lieutenant to his uncle and namesake in the 1st-rate *St George*.

Hay was promoted to commander on 28 April 1851 and returned to sea in August 1852 in command of the steam sloop *Wasp*. He joined the Mediterranean Fleet and, in 1853, as tension with Russia increased, was senior officer in a small flotilla sent to Constantinople (Istanbul) to show support for the Turkish government. During the Crimean War, he served in 1854 with the fleet in the Black Sea, where he was the first naval commanding officer to permit his ship's company to wear beards and moustaches. He was promoted to captain on 27 November 1854 in recognition of his services with the naval brigade in the siege of Sevastopol. He was briefly appointed to the corvette *Tribune* and went onto half-pay during 1855, though continuing to serve with the naval brigade before Sevastopol and being commended for his zeal and gallantry. From December 1855 to the end of hostilities in 1856 he was in command of the steam mortar frigate *Forth*. He entered Parliament in 1857 as Liberal Member for Wick, Caithness, which he represented until 1859.

Between 1859 and the end of 1862 Hay was in command of the paddle frigate *Odin* on the East Indies station. During the Second China War he led a flotilla of gunboats in operations against the Taku Forts at the mouth of the Pei-ho River, and was promoted to commodore during 1861. He returned to Parliament in 1866 as Member for Ripon, Yorkshire, which he continued to represent until 1871. From June to September 1866 he was fourth naval lord in the Board of Admiralty and returned there as third naval lord from 1868 to November 1871, when he was given command of the turret ship *Hotspur*. He was promoted to rear-admiral on 7 May 1872.

Hay was appointed second-in-command of the Channel Squadron on 2 January 1875, with his flag successively in the armoured ships *Northumberland* and *Black Prince*. In 1876 he married Anne, youngest daughter of Nathaniel Lambert, MP, of Denham Court, Buckinghamshire. They later had two sons and two daughters, of whom one died in infancy. Their elder son became an officer in the Navy and their surviving daughter married Lord Aberdour, eldest son of 21st Earl of Morton. Between November 1877 and December 1879 Hay was senior officer in command of the Channel Squadron, with his flag in the armoured ship *Minotaur*, and promoted to vice-admiral on 31 December 1877. During the summer of 1878, while negotiations at the Congress of Berlin settled international tension over the Turkish Question, he was sent to the eastern Mediterranean without any clear orders as to his movements on arrival. He eventually learned that his mission was to occupy Cyprus, previously under Turkish rule, but about to be transferred to British control as part of the Berlin agreement. Hay took over the government of the island from its last Turkish governor-general and covered the landing of the British garrison in July 1878.

After the return to power of the Liberals in April 1880 Hay became second naval lord and remained on the Board of Admiralty until appointed C-in-C, Mediterranean, with his flag in the battleship *Alexandra*, in February 1883. He was promoted to admiral on 8 July 1884 and received the thanks of Parliament for his fleet's support to the Gordon Relief Expedition in the Sudan during 1884. After completing his tenure of the Mediterranean command, he became first naval lord in the Board of Admiralty headed by the Marquess of Ripon in Gladstone's third Cabinet, in March 1886. He left the Admiralty when the Liberal ministry fell in August 1886, and was C-in-C, Plymouth, from May 1887 to 15 December 1888, when he was promoted to admiral of the fleet. He retired in August 1892 and died at Fulmer, Buckinghamshire, on 4 May 1916.

HENRY (HEINRICH)
ALBERT WILLIAM HENRY, HRH Prince Henry of Prussia, KG (1862–1929) [62]

Prince Henry of Prussia, the second son of Frederick, Crown Prince of Prussia, and his wife Princess Victoria, eldest daughter of Queen Victoria, was born on 14 August 1862. Frederick died of cancer of the throat in June 1888, having reigned as German Emperor for nineteen days. The imperial crown then passed to Prince Henry's elder brother Frederick William Victor Albert [47] who, as William II, became the third and last of the Hohenzollern German Emperors. While Crown Princess, Victoria encouraged her two elder sons to develop their interest in the sea, the element on which her native country (which she always preferred to Germany) was supreme. In 1874 the two princes went to school at Cassels, Hesse, where Queen Victoria sent her grandson Henry (who had determined on a naval career) numerous books about the sea, all of which were also eagerly read by his elder brother. In 1877 the two went to Kiel for Henry's first night aboard ship as a naval cadet. Henry had difficulty with his hammock, lost his blanket and in the morning ate his captain's breakfast by mistake. The Crown Princess always considered her second son rather plain-looking and not very bright. It was commonly believed that the decision to send him to the Modern School at Cassels, rather than the more academic Gymnasium attended by his brother, was because he lacked the necessary intellectual ability. It was officially given out that the more technical syllabus of the Modern School was better suited to a future naval officer. Henry always shared his elder brother's enthusiasm for the Imperial German Navy, a new force founded with the German Empire in 1871 and officered largely by sons of the wealthy bourgeoisie that flourished with the economic growth of the new empire.

In May 1888 Henry married Princess Irene Louise Maria Anna, the twenty-one year-old third daughter of Ludwig IV, Grand Duke of Hesse and bei-Rhine, and later had three sons, of whom the youngest died in infancy in 1904. In 1889, in the ship *Valkyrie*, Henry led a German naval squadron escorting his brother the Kaiser on an official visit to the Royal Regatta at Cowes, IOW. This was the first of several such visits, which served as useful occasions for informal diplomatic exchanges. In 1897 the Kaiser, in one of the public telegrams that played so large a part in his conduct of affairs, sent Prince Henry a message regretting that he had no better ship than the old *Koenig Wilhelm* in which to send him to Queen Victoria's Diamond Jubilee Review. He alarmed British opinion by adding that he would not rest until the German Navy was brought to the same high level as the German Army. Later that year Henry was given command of a squadron sent to occupy the territory of Kiao-Chow (Jiaozhou) ostensibly in retaliation for the murder of German missionaries by Chinese extremists, but actually to establish a German coaling station in the Far East

Henry had become a rear-admiral in 1895. In 1899 he was promoted to vice-admiral commanding the East Asiatic cruiser squadron. On passage, he encountered a British fishery protection vessel and, when he did not receive the proper gun salute, sent a cruiser to investigate. The British commander's explanation that he did not have a saluting cannon on board was deemed inadequate and a complaint was lodged through diplomatic channels. In 1901, with promotion to admiral, he was given command of a squadron of eight battleships, with which he paid a courtesy visit to the United Kingdom. From 1903 to 1906 he was chief of the Baltic station and from 1906 to 1909 commanded the new High Seas Fleet, with his flag in the battleship *Deutschland*. In an echo of a similar controversy over status in the Royal Navy at the same time, he decided that engineer officers should wear the sash of executive officers, in recognition of their increasingly important role and rising social position. At the same time he was horrified at the thought of engineer officers' wives being allowed to call on those of executive officers and ruled that they could only meet at social events held on board ship. During his command of the High Seas Fleet, he pressed for the enlargement of the Kiel canal and emphasized the importance of Wilhelmshaven and Heligoland as locations from which his fleet could make sorties against the British fleet or threaten the east coast of England.

In 1909 Henry was promoted to grand admiral, the German equivalent to admiral of the fleet, and on 27 January 1910 was made an honorary admiral of the fleet in the Royal Navy. In 1910 he was appointed Inspector General of the Imperial German Navy. He took an interest in naval aviation and became the first German naval officer to qualify as an aviator. By 1912 he had come to the conclusion that Germany could no longer afford to build large capital ships and recommended that fast "torpedo-battleships" should be designed instead. On the approach of the First World War in 1914 Prince Henry was at Cowes Regatta, which he regularly attended. He waited upon his cousin, George V [64], whose vague expression of hope that the United Kingdom would be able to keep out of the conflict he interpreted as a statement of policy, which he relayed to his brother the

Kaiser. This played a part in the latter's feeling of betrayal by "Georgie" when the British subsequently entered the war.

When hostilities began, Henry was given command of the Baltic Naval Forces. He remained there until December 1917, with little real action, but preparing plans for the occupation of the Danish and Norwegian coasts in the event of either country joining the war on the side of the Entente Powers. During 1917 calls for peace by socialist deputies in the Reichstag and increasing war-weariness among his men led him to encourage membership of the patriotic Fatherland Party, and to order his officers to eat the same food as their crews. A more successful morale-boosting operation was the capture of islands in the Gulf of Riga from a disaffected Russian fleet in October 1917. In January 1918 he again became Inspector General of the Navy. In October 1918, as the will of the German people to continue the war began to wane, Henry proposed another sortie, this time by the High Seas Fleet, with the Kaiser and himself sailing with it. This triggered a naval mutiny that began the collapse of the German Empire. On 5 November 1918, driving a lorry flying the red flag, he escaped from Kiel, complaining that the mutiny was the result of British "silver bullets" (secret payments to the mutineers). With the end of the war, Henry retired into private life. As inflation began to destroy the value of his savings, he supplemented his income by book-binding, a traditional craft of Hohenzollern princes, which he had long practised as a hobby. He died at his home, Herrenhaus Hemmelmark, near Eckenforde, on the Baltic coast of Schleswig, on 20 April 1929.

HILL-NORTON
Sir PETER JOHN, Baron Hill-Norton, GCB (1915-) [107]

Peter John Hill-Norton was born on 8 February 1915 and, after attending the Royal Naval College, Dartmouth, was appointed to the cruiser *London*, with promotion to midshipman on 1 May 1932. After joining the battleship *Rodney* in the Home Fleet in September 1934 for a brief tour in which he studied for his seamanship examinations, he became an acting sub-lieutenant on 1 May 1935 (confirmed on 1 September 1935 on the completion of his promotion courses). He then returned to the Home Fleet where he served in the battleship *Ramillies* from August 1936 to August 1938. In 1936 he married Margaret Eileen Linstow, with whom he later had a son (who became a vice-admiral) and a daughter. After qualifying at the gunnery school *Excellent* in 1939 Hill-Norton served during the Second World War successively as a gunnery officer with convoy escorts in the Arctic and the North-Western Approaches, a staff officer at the Admiralty and gunnery officer of the battleship *Howe* in the Far East. With the end of the war in 1945 he was appointed gunnery officer of the cruiser *Nigeria* in the South Atlantic Squadron. He was promoted to commander on 31 December 1947 and to captain on 31 December 1952. From 1953 to

11. Prince Louis of Battenberg [74]
    (later Marquess of Milford Haven)
    with his sons Dicky (left) (later
    Lord Louis Mountbatten) [102]
    and Georgie (later Earl of Medina).

12. Sir Roger Keyes, Lord Keyes. [80]

13. Sir William Boyle, Earl of Cork and Orrery. [87]

14. Sir Dudley Pound. [89]

15. Sir Andrew Cunningham, Viscount Cunningham of Hyndhope. [91]

16. Sir James Somerville. [93]

17. Lord Louis Mountbatten [102], 1st Earl Mountbatten of Burma, with his Countess, Edwina, and their daughter Patricia, later 2nd Countess Mountbatten of Burma, a third officer, WRNS.

18. Sir Julian Oswald [114] with Sub-Lieutenant (SSC) Victoria Heathcote RNR, the author's daughter, and staff of TS *Diadem*, the Camberley and Farnborough Sea Cadet unit. *(Barry Mitchell)*

1955 he was naval attaché in the British embassies to Uruguay, Paraguay and the Argentine Republic. He commanded the destroyer *Decoy* from 1956 to 1957 and then became head of the Weapon Equipment Section at the Admiralty and chairman of the Defence Policy Staff committee. In 1958 he suggested that the Weapon Equipment Section should be merged with the Tactical and Staff Duties Division and subsequently became Director of the new Tactical and Weapons Policy Division. He returned to sea to command the aircraft carrier *Ark Royal* from October 1959 to January 1962.

Hill-Norton was promoted to rear-admiral on 8 January 1962 and became Assistant Chief of the Naval Staff at the Admiralty in February 1962. He was appointed Flag Officer, second-in-command, Far East Fleet, in June 1964, with his flag in the guided-missile destroyer *Kent*. He was promoted to vice-admiral on 7 August 1965. In 1966 he returned home to become Deputy Chief of the Defence Staff (Personnel and Logistics) in the Ministry of Defence. In this appointment he originated a new system of pay for all the Armed Services, the Military Salary. Under this system, the costs of quantifiable emoluments previously provided free of charge, such as rations and accommodation, were deducted from pay, but the actual rates of pay were increased to compensate for this, so allowing a direct comparison with wage rates in civil employment, where individuals paid for their food and housing as a matter of course. He was awarded the KCB in 1967 and was from January to August 1967 a member of the Admiralty Board as Second Sea Lord and Chief of Naval Personnel. From then until 1968 Sir Peter Hill-Norton was Vice-Chief of the Naval Staff, where he sought economies in the fleet support organization, leading to many civilian redundancies and large-scale reductions in the Royal Dockyards. He also proposed that the long-standing custom of the daily issue of rum and "grog" should be abolished, a reform eventually carried through in 1968. While VCNS, Hill-Norton devised the concept of a new class of light aircraft carriers designated as "through-deck cruisers" in order to evade the decision of Defence Secretary of the day, Denis Healey, that no more carriers were to be built. These ships were eventually commissioned as the Navy's new carrier force and played a vital part in its subsequent operations. He was promoted to admiral on 1 October 1968.

In March 1969 Hill-Norton became Joint Service C-in-C, Far East, before returning to the Ministry of Defence in July 1970 to become First Sea Lord in succession to Sir Michael Le Fanu [106]. Le Fanu, who had just discovered that he was suffering from leukaemia and had not long to live, warned Lord Carrington, Secretary of State for Defence in Edward Heath's Cabinet, that he would not be able to become Chief of the Defence Staff as had been planned. Hill-Norton therefore accepted a shorter period than usual as First Sea Lord so as to become CDS in April 1971. He was promoted to admiral of the fleet on 12 March 1971 and served as CDS until April 1974. Between then and 1977 he was the Chairman of the Military Committee of NATO. In 1978 he was granted a life peerage as

Baron Hill-Norton, of South Nutfield, Surrey. From 1977 to 1984 Lord Hill-Norton was President of the Sea Cadet Association. He continued to play a part in various maritime and City organizations and published several influential works on NATO and defence policy. He settled at Hyde, Fordingbridge, Hampshire, and remained an active member of the House of Lords until his sight was badly affected in 1998.

HOPE
Sir JAMES, GCB (1808–1881) [39]

James Hope was born on 3 March 1808, the son of a Trafalgar veteran, Captain (later Admiral) Sir George Hope, and his wife Lady Jemima Johnstone Hope, a daughter of the third Earl of Hopetoun. Between 1820 and 1822 he attended the Royal Naval College, Portsmouth, after which he served in the 5th-rate *Forte* in the West Indies and the 4th-rate *Cambrian* in the Mediterranean. He became a lieutenant on 9 March 1827 and was appointed to the 5th-rate *Maidstone*, under orders for the East Indies station, in September 1827. On his return home Hope became the flag lieutenant of the Earl of Northesk, C-in-C Portsmouth, in August 1829, and was promoted to commander on 26 February 1830. From July 1833 to 28 June 1838, when he was promoted to captain, he commanded the sloop *Racer* on the North America and West Indies station. In 1838 he married the Honourable Frederica Kinnaird, daughter of the eighth Lord Kinnaird, and settled in Linlithgow, where his mother's family held extensive estates.

Hope returned to sea in December 1844, in command of a paddle steamer, the frigate *Firebrand*, on the South America station. There, at a time of civil war in Uruguay, he took part in the battle of Punto Obligado (20 November 1845) where the local British and French admirals combined their forces to break the blockade of Montevideo by an Argentine fleet. Hope went forward under heavy fire in his gig to supervise the cutting of a chain across the Parana River, for which he was mentioned in despatches. After returning home he remained ashore until the outbreak of the Crimean War in 1854, in which he commanded the 2nd-rate *Majestic* in the Baltic campaign.

Hope became a rear-admiral on 19 November 1857 and was appointed C-in-C, China, in March 1859, with his flag in the frigate *Chesapeake*. Hostilities in the Second China War had been suspended following the treaty of Tientsin (Tienjin) in June 1858, but the Chinese refused to allow the British and French ministers to proceed to the capital at Peking (Beijing). The Allies determined to clear a way up the Peiho River by force and Hope led an attack on the Taku Forts at the mouth of the river (25 June 1859). After having had the gunboats *Plover* and *Cormorant* sunk under him, suffering heavy casualties among his landing parties and being badly wounded in the thigh, he was forced to abandon the operation.

116

Commodore Josiah Tattnall, United States Navy, although his squadron was officially neutral in this encounter, sent a steamer to help the British escape, famously remarking "Blood is thicker than water". A few years later he placed his sword at the disposal of his native state, Georgia, and became one of the Confederacy's senior naval officers during the American Civil War. Lord Elgin, the British minister, wrote that Hope had behaved like a madman in launching this attack, but would escape blame as he was an admiral. Nevertheless, Hope, a tall and imposing figure, was much respected in his own Service and in August 1860 covered the disembarkation of the Allied troops who took the Taku Forts from the landward side. In November 1860, after the war had ended with the Allied occupation of Peking (Beijing), he was awarded the KCB.

Sir James Hope remained in China and in February 1862 was wounded by a musket ball while co-operating with the Imperial Chinese army against the Taiping rebels. After returning home at the end of 1862, he served as C-in-C, North America and the West Indies, from late 1863 to early 1867, with promotion to vice-admiral on 16 September 1864, at a period of international tension between the United Kingdom and United States during the American Civil War. Between 1869 and 1872 he was C-in-C, Portsmouth, with promotion to admiral on 21 January 1870. He retired in March 1878 and became an admiral of the fleet on the retired list on 15 June 1879. Hope married again after the death of his wife in 1856, but had no children. He died at his home, Carriden House, Linlithgow, on 9 June 1881.

HORNBY
Sir GEOFFREY THOMAS PHIPPS, GCB (1825–1895) [45]

Geoffrey Hornby, second son of Captain (later Admiral Sir) Phipps Hornby and grandson of the rector of Winwick, Cheshire, was born at Winwick on 20 February 1825. This living was in the gift of the Stanleys, the Earls of Derby, and had previously been held by Geoffrey Hornby's great-grandfather, a brother-in-law of the twelfth Earl of Derby. Geoffrey Hornby's mother Maria, a daughter of General John Burgoyne (the "Gentleman Johnny" who had been defeated in the American War of Independence) lived with the Stanley family from her father's death in 1792 until her marriage to Captain Phipps Hornby. In 1832, a year after Edward Stanley (later fourteenth Earl of Derby) had become a minister in Earl Grey's Cabinet, Captain Hornby was appointed superintendent of the naval hospital and victualling yard, Plymouth. Geoffrey Hornby attended Southwood's School, Plymouth, and developed an interest in ships and the sea. He entered the Navy on 8 March 1837 as a first class volunteer in the 1st-rate *Princess Charlotte*, flagship of his father's friend Sir Robert Stopford in the Mediterranean Fleet.

Hornby served in the Mediterranean until the summer of 1841. This period included the international crisis of 1839–40, when there was a threat of war between France (supporting the Albanian ruler of Egypt and Syria, Mehemet Ali) and an alliance of the United Kingdom, Russia, Prussia and Austria (supporting his nominal overlord, the Sultan of Turkey). The appearance of a combined British, Austrian and Turkish fleet off Beirut, Syria, in August 1840 led to a successful rising against Mehemet Ali's rule. Hornby was present at the naval bombardment and capture of Acre, Palestine (Akko, Israel) (2 November 1840). In the spring of August 1842 he was appointed a midshipman in the 4th-rate *Winchester*, flagship of the C-in-C, Cape of Good Hope.

Hornby became mate (from 15 June 1845, lieutenant) in the frigate *Cleopatra*, in which he served on anti-slaving operations on the coast of East Africa. These activities included boat actions in creeks and shallows, and the capture of two slave-ships, with Hornby being sent back to the Cape in charge of one of them. He returned home in the sloop *Wolverine* in 1847 and, on the death of his elder brother in 1848, added the name Phipps to his own in acknowledgement of having become the heir to Littlegreen, a Hampshire estate left to his father by the latter's godfather, Thomas Phipps, Esquire.

From 1848 to 1850 Hornby was flag lieutenant to his father as C-in-C, Pacific, in the 2nd-rate *Asia*, based at Valparaiso, Chile. On 19 February 1850, when the commander of *Asia* was promoted out of the ship, Hornby was given the consequential vacancy. In 1851 he returned home and joined his contemporary Lord Stanley (later fifteenth Earl of Derby) for a tour of India, only to be invalided home after reaching Ceylon (Sri Lanka). In February 1852 Admiral Hornby, with a view to improving his son's prospects, accepted a seat on the Board of Admiralty under the Duke of Northumberland in the Cabinet headed by the fourteenth Earl of Derby. When Derby's first administration fell in December 1852 Northumberland allotted to Hornby one of the two promotions customarily at the disposal of First Lords on leaving office. Hornby accordingly became a captain on 18 December 1852. Admiral Sir Thomas Hornby had resigned from the Board with the other Derby partisans, so that, without a patron, his son was not given a ship during the Crimean War of 1854–56. When the admiral inherited the family home at Winwick, Hornby took over the Littlegreen estate and lived as a country gentleman at Lordington. In 1853 he married Emily, daughter of the Reverend J J Coles, of Ditcham Park, Hampshire. They later had four children, of whom their second son won the Victoria Cross as a major in the Royal Artillery in the Anglo-Boer South African War.

When the Earl of Derby returned to office as Prime Minister in February 1858 Hornby asked Lord Stanley (at this time in his father's Cabinet as Colonial Secretary) to use his influence to find him a ship. He was given command of the corvette *Tribune* on the China station, where he arrived in October 1858 to find the ship overcrowded with marines and stores intended for the Second China War, but with rotten masts, bad rigging, and a crew untrained in the use of sails. *Tribune* played no part in the war and sailed for the Pacific station to meet the possibility of a landing by United States troops on the disputed San Juan Islands, between Vancouver and the northern Oregon (the modern state of Washington). Given full responsibility by the colonial governor of Victoria (British Columbia), Hornby avoided coming into conflict with the Americans (whose claim to the islands was later agreed) and was praised for his diplomatic conduct. He returned home at the end of June 1860. Derby's government had fallen in February 1859, but Hornby's reputation was by this time high enough for him to be appointed in February 1861 to the converted 1st-rate *Neptune* in the Mediterranean, where he served until the end of 1862. He was then appointed flag captain to the C-in-C, Channel Squadron, in the 2nd-rate *Edgar*. In January 1864 the squadron shadowed the Austro-Hungarian fleet on its way to assist Prussia in the war with Denmark over the Schleswig-Holstein question. Lord Palmerston, Derby's successor as Prime Minister, had encouraged the Danes to count on British support, but, without a Continental ally, the most that he could give was a promise to sink the Austro-Hungarian ships if they bombarded Copenhagen. The Prussian Chancellor, Otto von Bismarck, indicated his opinion of the British Army by stating that, if it landed on his coast, he would send the police to arrest it. Meanwhile, Hornby remained close to Derby's party and primed Stanley with awkward questions about warship design to put to the ministers in the House of Commons.

In the spring of 1865 Hornby was appointed commodore and C-in-C on the West Coast of Africa, with his broad pendant successively in the 2nd-rate *Formidable* and the frigate *Bristol*. He argued against continuing the close blockade of the coast against slavers, on the grounds that the cost of keeping fourteen ships in an area where crews suffered many losses from fever was no longer justified. He condemned the independent rulers of West Africa for continuing to supply slaves as, since the American Civil War, the only civilized country not to have abolished the institution of slavery was Brazil. He shifted his broad pendant to the sloop *Greyhound* while *Bristol* was sent back to the United Kingdom for engine repairs in 1866–67, and was relieved at his own request in November 1867. Hornby was promoted to rear-admiral on 1 January 1869 and given command of the Flying Squadron, consisting of four frigates and two corvettes, with his flag in the frigate *Liverpool*. This circumnavigated the globe between 1869 and 1870 (losing 200 men on the way by desertion to the Australian gold-fields) with the aim of training its officers and ratings in seamanship under sail and demonstrating the Navy's capacity to send a force into any waters. On returning home, Hornby was presented with the last surviving sheep of the fresh rations. It had become a pet of his crew, who begged for its life, so that it went with him to live in retirement at Lordington. From August 1871 to April 1874 he was C-in-C, Channel fleet, with his flag in the battle-ship *Minotaur*, where his duties included the entertainment at Gibraltar of General Ulysses S Grant, making his famous world tour after serving as President of the United States.

Hornby became second naval lord at the Admiralty, with promotion to vice-admiral, on 1 January 1875. He pressed for the funds to replace obsolete ships, only to find that the Ministers preferred economy to efficiency. At a time of increasing tension between the United Kingdom and Russia over the Turkish Question, he left the Admiralty in January 1877 to become C-in-C, Mediterranean Fleet, with his flag in the battleship *Alexandra*. The despatch of the Mediterranean Fleet to Constantinople (Istanbul) in February 1878 was matched by the arrival of a Russian army at the gates of the city. Hornby played his part in crisis management by sending only four of his battleships all the way to Constantinople and anchoring there short of the city limits. He had a personal audience with the Sultan, explaining to him the limits of British policy and, in the process, formed the view that it would be better for everyone if the British took over the Ottoman Empire as they had the Mughal Empire in India.

In June 1878 he was joined by Lord John Hay [46] who had been sent to the Mediterranean by the Cabinet to take the Turkish-ruled island of Cyprus under British control. Hornby privately deplored the British occupation of Cyprus, on the grounds that it would look like sharing with other robbers the spoils of Russia's recent campaign. He also felt that the arrangements for the future of the Turkish province of Rumelia (southern Bulgaria) would only inflict on its Muslim inhabitants the mass murders, rapes and looting that they themselves had inflicted on the Bulgarians, and saw nothing to choose between either side. He was nevertheless awarded the KCB in appreciation of the close discipline he had exercised over his fleet during the crisis and for his diplomacy in dealing with the Russians.

Sir Geoffrey Hornby ("Uncle Geoff" to his fleet) returned to his base at Malta in April 1879 and was promoted to admiral on 15 June 1879. He was much respected for his seamanship and for his operational skill in fleet exercises, and Captain John Fisher [58], who served under him at this time, later described him as the finest admiral afloat since Nelson. After leaving the Mediterranean in March 1880 Hornby served as president of the Royal Naval College, Greenwich, from March 1881 to November 1882, when he became C-in-C, Portsmouth. During 1885, when the United Kingdom and Russia were on the verge of war over the disputed control of Penjdeh on the borders of Afghanistan and Turkmenistan, a large fleet was assembled at Portsmouth. Hornby hoisted his flag in the armoured ship *Minotaur*, but once more the crisis passed and he saw no more operational service before he finally hauled down his flag in November 1885. He then returned to his plough at Lordington, living as "Yeoman Hornby" and taking part in the usual activities of a country gentleman of his day. He remained influential in naval politics and was consulted both by Fisher [58] and by Fisher's future opponent, Lord Charles Beresford, each of whom sought his aid in their plans for naval reform.

Hornby was promoted to admiral of the fleet on 1 May 1888 and became the senior serving officer of the Navy on the death of the aged Sir Provo Wallis on 13 February 1895, before retiring on his seventieth birthday a week later. He died of influenza at Lordington on 3 March 1895 and his ashes were scattered at Compton, Sussex.

HOTHAM
Sir CHARLES FREDERICK, GCB, GCVO (1843–1924) [55]

Charles Hotham, the eldest son of a captain in the Bengal Horse Artillery, and a distant relative of several senior naval officers, was born on 10 March 1843. He joined the Navy in 1856 and became a lieutenant on 17 February 1863, when he was appointed to the frigate *Curacoa*, pendant-ship of the commodore on the Australia station. *Curacoa* contributed to a naval brigade in New Zealand during the Second Maori War and Hotham took part in the attack on Rangariri (20 November 1863), where he was wounded, and the Gate Pa (29 April 1864), where he earned a recommendation for promotion to commander. He completed the necessary length of service on 19 April 1865, when he was promoted to this rank accordingly. He then returned home and was appointed to the gunboat *Jaseur* in August 1867. Hotham served in this ship on the West Coast of Africa until the summer of 1869 and thereafter in the Mediterranean Fleet. After being promoted to captain on 29 December 1871 he went on half-pay and married Margaret Milne-Horne, the daughter of a Berwickshire gentleman, and a niece of Sir Alexander Milne [41]. They later had a daughter and two sons, of whom the elder, a Clerk to the House of Lords, predeceased him in 1924, and the younger became an admiral.

Hotham commanded the corvette *Charybdis* on the China station from February 1877 to 1880. In November 1881 he became flag captain to Sir Beauchamp Seymour (Lord Alcester), C-in-C, Mediterranean, in the battleship *Alexandra*. He took part in the British bombardment of Alexandria (11 July 1882) in response to an Egyptian nationalist uprising led by Colonel Arabi ('Urbi') Pasha, and served as Seymour's chief of staff in the subsequent operations ashore. After leaving *Alexandra* in 1884 Hotham served from April to December 1885 as senior officer on the South East Coast of America, in command of the corvette *Ruby* and a flotilla of three gunboats. During 1886–7 he was at the Admiralty as assistant to the Admiral Superintendent of Naval Reserves, followed by promotion to rear-admiral on 6 January 1888. In the same month he was appointed to the Board of Admiralty as fourth naval lord. Hotham left the Admiralty at the end of 1888 and served from February 1890 to May 1893 as C-in-C, Pacific, with his flag in the cruiser *Warspite*. In February 1891, during a revolution in Chile, he was shot at while going ashore in his gig to arrange an armistice. The fighting continued until 28 August 1892, when a multi-national naval brigade from British, French, German and United States warships was landed to restore order. He was promoted to vice-admiral on 1 September 1893 and awarded the KCB in 1895. Sir Charles Hotham was C-in-C, Nore, from December 1897 to July 1899, with promotion to

121

admiral on 1 January 1899. Between October 1900 and August 1903 he was C-in-C, Portsmouth. He was promoted to admiral of the fleet on 30 August 1903 and retired in March 1913. He died on 23 May 1925.

HOWE
RICHARD, Earl Howe, KG (1726–1799) [9]

Richard Howe, the second son of an Irish viscount and his wife, the daughter of George I and his Hanoverian mistress, the Countess of Dartmouth, was born in London on 8 March 1726. This royal connection proved of value to the family and Viscount Howe held the post of governor of Barbados from 1732 until his death there in 1735. Richard Howe entered Eton College in 1735. With the outbreak of the War of Jenkins's Ear, he was appointed on 16 July 1739 to the 4th-rate *Pearl*, commanded by his cousin, the Honourable Edward Legge, though he probably remained at school for another year until joining Legge in the 4th-rate *Severn*. This ship formed part of the squadron under Anson [5] intended for operations against the Spanish in the Pacific. It sailed with him, but after rounding Cape Horn was driven back by storms and eventually returned to England in June 1742. In the meantime, the war between the United Kingdom and Spain had been overtaken in 1740 by the outbreak of a wider conflict, the War of the Austrian Succession. Howe was appointed in August 1742 to the 3rd-rate *Burford*, in which he served in the West Indies, and took part in the British attack on La Guiaria, Caracas, Venezuela (18 February 1743). On 10 March 1743 he moved to the 3rd-rate *Suffolk*, flagship of Sir Charles Knowles, second-in-command in the West Indies station. He was appointed an acting lieutenant in the 5th-rate *Eltham* on 10 July 1743, before returning to *Suffolk* as a midshipman on 8 October 1743.

Howe was appointed lieutenant on 25 May 1744 at Antigua, in the bomb vessel *Comet*, with which he returned home in August 1745. With his commission confirmed, he became lieutenant in the 1st-rate *Royal George* on 12 August 1745, prior to being made commander of the sloop *Baltimore*, deployed in the North Sea and Scottish waters at the time of the 1745 Jacobite Rising. On 1 May 1746 he was wounded when *Baltimore*, together with another sloop and a light frigate, was engaged with two heavily-armed French privateers off the west coast of Scotland. After returning to Portsmouth Howe was appointed captain of the 6th-rate *Tryton*, with seniority from 10 April 1745. In 1747 he sailed on convoy protection duty to Lisbon, where he exchanged to take command of the 4th-rate *Ripon*. He took this ship to the West Indies, where he rejoined Knowles (by this time C-in-C, Jamaica) in October 1748 and became his flag captain in the 2nd-rate *Cornwall*. With the War of the Austrian Succession over, he returned home and remained ashore until March 1751, when he was given command of the 5th-rate *Glory*, in which he served for a year off the coast of West Africa and in the West Indies. Between June 1752 and August 1754 he commanded the 6th-rate *Dolphin* in the Mediterranean, engaged in trade protection duties against North African pirates.

In January 1755, at a time of increasing tension between France and the United Kingdom in North America, Howe was appointed to command the 4th-rate *Dunkirk*. He sailed in April 1755 in a squadron under Admiral Edward Boscawen, ordered to intercept French ships carrying reinforcements to Canada. Although war had not been declared, two unsuspecting French stragglers were captured off the St Lawrence on 8 June 1755. Howe's ship fired the first shot of the maritime war, after he had gallantly allowed time for ladies on the deck of the French 60-gun *Alcide* to be escorted below. Formal hostilities began with the Seven Years War in 1756. Howe, in *Dunkirk*, spent the summer of 1756 in command of a flotilla defending the Channel Islands. In May 1757 he entered Parliament as Member for Dartmouth and continued to represent that borough until his elevation to the House of Lords in 1782. On 2 July 1757 he went with his entire crew to the 3rd-rate *Magnanime* in which he served under Sir Edward Hawke [7] in the unsuccessful British expedition against Rochefort (September 1757).

In 1758 Howe was selected to command the naval element of another descent on the French coast. Hawke, under the mistaken impression that this expedition was intended for Rochefort, temporarily resigned his command of the Channel fleet in protest at what he took as a slight. In fact, the raid was destined for St Malo. Howe, as commodore with his broad pendant in the 3rd-rate *Essex,* covered the landings on 5 June 1757 and the subsequent re-embarkation a few days later. Another brief landing, at Cherbourg in August 1757, was followed by a return to St Malo at the beginning of September. There the British rearguard was forced to re-embark under fire across an open beach. Howe was among the captains who went in their boats to rescue the troops and was widely commended for his efforts and his personal encouragement of the seamen. In 1758, on the death of his elder brother, who fell in the British attack on the French fort of Ticonderoga, New York (5 July 1758), he succeeded to the family estates and peerage, as the third Viscount Howe. In the same year he married Mary Hartopp, the daughter of a neighbouring landowner in Nottinghamshire.

During 1759, once more in *Magnanime*, Lord Howe served under Hawke in the fleet blockading Brest and was in the lead in the successful attack on the French fleet in Quiberon Bay (20 November 1759). He remained on this station for the rest of the Seven Years War and became a colonel of the Marines on 4 February 1760. In 1762 he was appointed flag captain of the 3rd-rate *Princess Amelia*, flagship of the newly promoted Rear-Admiral the Duke of York (younger brother of George III), who had begun his naval career as a midshipman under Howe in *Essex* in 1758. Between 20 April 1763 and 31 July 1765 Howe was a lord commissioner of the Admiralty. He then served as Treasurer of the Navy until 18 October 1770, when he was promoted to rear-admiral of the Blue. Earlier in 1770 an invasion force from the Spanish colony of Argentina had expelled the British garrison of the Falkland Islands. After the news reached London, the unpopular Prime Minister of the day, Lord North, (whose survival in office would otherwise have been in doubt) agreed to a show of force. Howe was nominated in November 1770 as C-in-C of a hastily assembled fleet, but hostilities were averted by a settlement in which Spain disavowed the action of the local governor, while both sides secretly agreed to evacuate the islands. Howe was promoted to rear-admiral of the White on 31 March 1775 and vice-admiral of the Blue on 7 December 1775.

In the opening phase of the American War of Independence Howe's younger brother, Lieutenant General Sir William Howe, commanded the British forces at the battle of Bunker Hill, Massachusetts (17 June 1775). As the war continued, Lord Howe was appointed C-in-C on the North America station in February 1776. The two brothers, who had some sympathy with the colonials, were authorized by North to offer conciliatory terms, but these proved unacceptable. During the next two years the Howes undertook a number of combined operations, occupying New York and Long Island in August and September 1776, and establishing control of the coast from Rhode Island to Chesapeake Bay and the Delaware. The entry of France into the war in 1778 brought a French fleet to North America, where Howe, promoted to vice-admiral of the Red, was considerably outnumbered and at first declined to give battle. After a severe gale off Rhode Island damaged many of the French ships in August 1778, Howe pursued them to the colonial-held port of Boston, Massachusetts. With no immediate sign that they intended to put to sea, and his own fleet strengthened by the arrival of long-delayed reinforcements, Howe took the opportunity to resign his command. He returned to London, where he told the ministers that the American colonies could not be held. Believing that they intended to make him a scapegoat for their own failures, he refused to serve again while they remained in power.

Howe accepted command of the fleet in the Channel on 2 April 1782, five days after the fall of North's ministry. He became admiral of the Blue on 8 April 1782 and was raised to the peerage of Great Britain as Viscount Howe of Langar on 20 April 1782. With his flag in the 1st-rate *Victory*, he spent May 1782 watching the Dutch fleet in the Texel. In September 1782 he sailed with a large convoy and escort, totalling 183 ships, to relieve Gibraltar, under siege by the Spanish. He achieved this, a task that he considered the most difficult he ever attempted, between 11 and 16 October 1782, despite the presence of a larger Franco-Spanish fleet and the usual difficulties of controlling merchantmen. Nevertheless, one of his officers, Lord Hervey, publicly questioned Howe's valour, for failing to close with the enemy. Howe challenged him to a duel, but, at their meeting, Hervey gave satisfaction by retracting his criticism.

Howe became First Lord of the Admiralty in the Earl of Shelburne's administration on 30 January 1783, shortly before the end of the war. He left the Board in April 1783, when the Fox-North coalition came into office, but was re-appointed on 31 December 1783, as a member of the new Cabinet under William Pitt the Younger. He was promoted to admiral of the White on 24 September 1787. Howe became very unpopular as he implemented the usual post-war cuts in defence expenditure and, finding himself unsupported by Pitt, resigned in July 1788. His efforts were acknowledged in August 1788 by advancement in the peerage to an Earldom together with a new barony that, as he had no son, was granted a remainder in the female line. In May 1790 Earl Howe was appointed to command the fleet formed to meet the threat of a new war with Spain, over the possession of Nootka Sound (Vancouver, British Columbia). During August 1790 he cruised in the Channel, performing fleet evolutions and introducing a new code of flag signals on which he had been working for several years. As a mark of distinction, he was ordered to fly the Union flag at the maintopmast (so making him acting admiral of the fleet) in his flagship, the 1st-rate *Queen Charlotte*. After the crisis was resolved without bloodshed he hauled down his flag in December 1790.

With the outbreak of war with Revolutionary France on 1 February 1793 Howe, at the express request of George III, again accepted command of the fleet in the Channel, and the flag of an acting admiral of the fleet. Described as "undaunted as a rock and as silent", he maintained a blockade of the French Atlantic naval bases from May to December 1793, when, reluctant to expose his precious ships to winter gales, he returned to port, a decision strongly supported by the Treasury. Howe again put to sea with his fleet in May 1794. After detaching one division to escort the outgoing British convoys, he searched the Atlantic for the American grain convoy on which the French were relying to avert a threatened famine. On 1 June 1794, with twenty-two battleships under command, he encountered a French fleet of twenty-five, sent out to protect the convoy. In a major fleet action he captured seven of them and two weeks later returned to Portsmouth in triumph. Although "The Glorious First of June" was hailed by the British as a great victory, the grain fleet reached Brest in safety and thus allowed the French to continue the war. Howe was again at sea in 1795, remaining in command of the fleet only in deference to the King's wishes, and thereafter spending most of his time at Bath. On 12 March 1796 he became admiral of the fleet.

Early in 1797 Howe received a number of petitions from seamen at Portsmouth, seeking his support for redress of grievances over pay and conditions of service. About to hand over the fleet to his second-in-command, Lord Bridport (Sir Alexander Hood), Howe took no action beyond forwarding them to the Admiralty. On 16 April 1797, when Bridport gave orders to make sail, the crews of sixteen ships refused to obey. Concessions were eventually offered, but the seamen placed little faith in the Admiralty. It was only when Howe himself, aged and infirm, but a favourite with the lower deck, was sent with full powers to grant whatever was required that confidence was restored. On 15 May 1797, after twelve hours of being rowed round the fleet, where he spoke to every ship and was received with cheers, "Black Dick" was carried on the shoulders of his men to the port governor's house, where he and his countess entertained the ships' delegates to dinner.

His part in resolving this crisis must count as the greatest of all Howe's services to his country. On 2 June 1797 he became the first officer to be awarded the Garter solely in recognition of naval duties. He suffered increasingly severe pain from gout, and in 1799 agreed to the latest form of medical treatment, electric shock therapy. He died, probably of a stroke, on 5 August 1799 and was buried in the family vault at St Andrew's parish church, Langar, Nottinghamshire. He was devoted to his wife and their three daughters, of whom the eldest, Sophie, who married the heir to the first Viscount Curzon, inherited his barony. The Irish peerages passed to his brother, Sir William Howe, and his earldom became extinct. His name was given to a number of geographical features in the South Seas.

JACKSON
Sir HENRY BRADWARDINE, GCB, KCVO (1855–1929) **[70]**

Henry Jackson, the eldest son of a farmer in Cudworth, Yorkshire, was born at his mother's family home in Barnsley, Yorkshire, on 21 January 1855. After attending school at Chester and a naval tutorial establishment at Fareham, Hampshire, he entered the Navy as a cadet in the training ship *Britannia* in December 1868. He became a midshipman on 20 April 1870, in the armoured ship *Hector*, a ship of the Reserve at Southampton Water, from which he joined the corvette *Cadmus* as a supernumerary in December 1871. He remained there until promoted to acting sub-lieutenant on 18 October 1874 at the beginning of his promotion courses. Jackson was appointed a sub-lieutenant in the corvette *Rover* on the North American and West Indies station in August 1876 and was promoted to lieutenant on 27 October 1877. In March 1878 he was appointed to the corvette *Active*, from which he served ashore during 1879 in the Zulu War. From 1881 to 1884 he was at Portsmouth in the torpedo school *Vernon* and qualified as a torpedo lieutenant, a specialization that included responsibility for ships' electrical systems. Jackson was promoted to commander on 1 January 1890. In the same year he married Alice Burbury, the daughter of a distinguished scientist. On 30 June 1896 he was promoted to captain and was appointed to command the torpedo school *Defiance*. From 1897 to 1899 he was naval attaché in the British Embassy at Paris, followed by appointment to command the torpedo depot ship *Vulcan*. Jackson's pioneering achievements in the field of radio (with the Marconi wireless system having been adopted for the fleet a year earlier) were acknowledged in 1901 by his election as a Fellow of the Royal Society. In 1902 he became Assistant Director of Torpedoes at the Admiralty, from where he became captain of *Vernon* in 1904.

Jackson returned to the Admiralty in February 1905 as Third Sea Lord and Controller of the Navy, responsible for the design and building of ships during a period of increasing tempo in the naval race with Germany. He was promoted to rear-admiral on 18 October 1906 and awarded the KCVO. On leaving the Board of Admiralty in 1908 Sir Henry Jackson was given command of the Sixth Cruiser Squadron in the Mediterranean, with his flag in the cruiser *Bacchante*. He became a vice-admiral on 15 March 1911, with appointment as Director of the Naval War College at Portsmouth. In February 1913 he became Chief of the War Staff at the Admiralty. He was promoted admiral on 10 February 1914. It was intended that Jackson should move in August 1914 to be C-in-C, Mediterranean Fleet, but uncertainty over his health meant that on the outbreak of the First World War in that month he was retained at the Admiralty and employed as an adviser on overseas expeditions. As such, he supported the seizure by Australia and New Zealand respectively of the German colonies of New Guinea and Samoa. In May 1915, when Lord Fisher [58] resigned office as First Sea Lord, Jackson was appointed in his place and also became Chief of the Naval Staff. Thereafter, the posts of First Sea Lord and Chief of the Naval Staff were combined into a single appointment.

Jackson, a dour Yorkshireman, approached his duties in a spirit of scientific caution, said little and declined to delegate decisions to his subordinates. He was a capable administrator and established a good relationship with the new First Lord, Arthur Balfour, who succeeded Winston Churchill in Asquith's Cabinet in May 1915. Jackson's first task was to co-operate with the military in closing down the Gallipoli campaign, after which he turned to deal with the growing menace of submarine warfare. He left the operations of the Grand Fleet in the hands of its C-in-C, Sir John Jellicoe [68], and played little part in the Admiralty's contribution to the battle of Jutland (31 May–1 June 1916), which he entrusted to Sir Henry Oliver [78], Chief of the War Staff. As a radio specialist, he was irritated by Jellicoe's subsequent criticisms of the fleet's inadequate communications, and also by his complaints that the Admiralty had not provided him with enough destroyers. With his Yorkshire habit of plain speaking, Jackson told Jellicoe that the Grand Fleet had been given everything that the Admiralty had at its disposal. Nevertheless, the feeling spread that Jackson and Balfour had failed to obtain for the Navy its proper share of the national defence effort. Their prestige suffered when German destroyers appeared in the Channel and German submarines continued to sink British merchantmen. Their calm steady approach, at first welcomed after the hyperactivity of Fisher and Churchill, came to be seen as ineffectual and uninspiring, and they became the targets of a Press campaign for their removal. Jackson himself came to feel that he had been too long away from a seagoing command and resigned in favour of Jellicoe on 4 December 1916.

Jackson was then appointed President of the Royal Naval College,

Greenwich, where he remained until promoted to admiral of the fleet on 31 July 1919. In 1920 he became the first chairman of the Radio Research Board of the Department of Scientific and Industrial Research, where he continued his enthusiastic support for developments in this field, carrying out his own research, visiting laboratories and discussing experiments with their staff. He went onto the retired list in December 1924 and was awarded the Hughes medal of the Royal Society in 1926. Sir Henry Jackson died without offspring at his home, Salterns House, Hayling Island, Hampshire, on 14 December 1929 and was buried in the island cemetery.

JELLICOE
Sir JOHN RUSHWORTH, 1st Earl Jellicoe, GCB, OM, GCVO (1859–1935) [68]

John Jellicoe was born at Southampton on 5 December 1859, the second son of a merchant captain and marine superintendent in the service of the Royal Mail Steam Packet Company. He included several officers of the Royal Navy among his ancestors and his mother's grandfather had been an admiral during the Napoleonic wars. He was educated at Southampton and Rottingdean, before entering the Navy in 1872 as a cadet in the training ship *Britannia*. He passed out top of his term and was appointed midshipman in the autumn of 1874, in the frigate *Newcastle*, in which he served in the South Atlantic, Indian and Pacific oceans before returning home early in 1877. Jellicoe joined the battleship *Agincourt* in July 1877 and served in the Mediterranean Fleet during the international crisis of 1878 when there was a risk of war between the United Kingdom and Russia over the Turkish Question. He became a sub-lieutenant on 5 December 1878, and remained in *Agincourt*, which became the flagship of Sir Beauchamp Seymour as C-in-C, Mediterranean Fleet. During 1880 Jellicoe completed his promotion courses before returning to sea as signal sub-lieutenant in the battleship *Alexandra*, flagship of the C-in-C, Mediterranean. He was promoted to lieutenant on 23 September 1880 and, after returning home, was re-appointed to *Agincourt* in the Mediterranean in February 1881. In May 1882, when *Agincourt* carried troops from Malta to reinforce the British operations against a nationalist insurgency in Egypt, he commanded a rifle company in the naval brigade at Ismailia. From there, disguised as a refugee, he was sent with despatches to the fleet at Port Said.

Jellicoe qualified as a gunnery officer in 1883. He was appointed to the staff of *Excellent* in May 1884 and supported its captain, John Fisher [58], in the reforms he was at that time introducing there. During 1885, when the United Kingdom and Russia were on the verge of war over the disputed control of Penjdeh on the borders of Afghanistan and Turkmenistan, a fleet was briefly mobilized in the Channel, under Sir Geoffrey Hornby [45], C-in-C, Portsmouth, with his flag in the armoured ship *Minotaur*. Fisher was appointed captain of the fleet and selected Jellicoe as one of his staff officers. Jellicoe became gunnery officer successively of the turret ship *Monarch* in September 1885 and the battleship *Colossus* in April 1886. Later in 1886 he returned to the staff of *Excellent* as an experimental officer and remained there until September 1889, when Fisher, as Director of Naval Ordnance at the Admiralty, arranged for Jellicoe to join his staff. Jellicoe was promoted to commander on 30 June 1891. In March 1892 he again joined the Mediterranean Fleet as commander of the battleship *Sans Pareil*. Early in 1893 he was selected by Sir George Tryon, C-in-C, Mediterranean, to be commander of his flagship, the battleship *Victoria*. On 22 June 1893, when this ship was rammed and sunk by the battleship *Camperdown* during fleet evolutions off the coast of Lebanon, Jellicoe was in sick bay with dysentery. He survived by clinging to wreckage and, after sick leave, was appointed commander of the new flagship, the battleship *Ramillies*, in which he served in the Mediterranean from October 1893 to December 1896. He was promoted to captain on 1 January 1897 and spent the following year as a member of the Admiralty's Ordnance Committee.

In December 1897 Jellicoe became flag captain to Vice-Admiral Sir Edward Seymour [57], C-in-C on the China station, in the battleship *Centurion*. In May 1898, in response to the German occupation of Kiao-Chow (Jiaozhou), Seymour was ordered to occupy Wei-hai-wei, subsequently leased to the British by the Government of China. At the end of May 1900, when the diplomatic legations in Peking (Beijing) were besieged by anti-western rebels known as the Boxers, a multi-national naval brigade commanded by Seymour, with Jellicoe acting as chief of staff, set out to their relief. The force left the mouth of the Pei-ho River on 10 June 1900, but met serious opposition when Chinese Imperial troops joined the Boxers, and was driven back to Tientsin (Tienjin). On 21 June 1900 Jellicoe was badly wounded in the lung by a bullet that stayed there for the rest of his life. He was not expected to survive, but did so and was evacuated to Wei-hai-wei, from where he returned home in September 1901.

Jellicoe was appointed in March 1902 to the newly created post of Naval Assistant to the Controller of the Navy and third naval lord of the Admiralty, whose primary responsibilty was for ship design and construction. He had not previously married, though he had become engaged in every rank that he held. Now he renewed an earlier friendship with the twenty-four year-old Gwendoline, the second daughter of a self-made Scottish millionaire and shipping-line owner, Sir Charles Cayzer. They married in July 1902 and later had a son and five daughters. A young woman with a mind and money of her own, Gwendoline Jellicoe proved an excellent Navy wife. Her care for her own appearance led her husband later to comment that he could get the Grand Fleet to sea in a shorter time than she took to get ready to go out. Between August 1903 and November 1904 he commanded the armoured cruiser *Drake* on the North America and

West Indies station. Fisher, who had become First Sea Lord in October 1904, recalled Jellicoe to the Admiralty where in February 1908 he was appointed Director of Naval Ordnance. With Fisher's other supporters, he played an important part in the development of fast battleships armed entirely with heavy guns, and a new type of capital ship, the battle-cruiser (built as the *Dreadnought* and *Invincible* classes respectively). Jellicoe was promoted to rear-admiral on 8 February 1907 and became second-in-command of the Atlantic Fleet, with his flag in the battleship *Albemarle*, in August 1907, followed by the award of the KCVO.

Sir John Jellicoe returned to the Admiralty as Third Sea Lord and Controller of the Navy in October 1908, where he implemented a major building programme to maintain British superiority at sea. He became acting vice-admiral in command of the Atlantic Fleet in December 1910 (confirmed on 18 September 1911), with his flag in the battleship *Prince of Wales*, and in December 1911 was appointed second-in-command of the Home Fleet, with his flag in the battleship *Hercules*. Jellicoe was appointed Second Sea Lord in December 1912, in the Board led by Winston Churchill in Asquith's Cabinet, with Prince Louis of Battenberg [74] as First Sea Lord. Both Churchill and Battenberg came to share Fisher's assessment that, in the event of war with Germany, Jellicoe would prove another Nelson. In August 1914, on the outbreak of the First World War, he was sent to join the Grand Fleet at Scapa Flow, ostensibly as second-in-command to its existing C-in-C, Sir George Callaghan [67], but with sealed orders instructing him to take command. Jellicoe protested, but, in obedience to orders, succeeded Callaghan, with his flag in the battleship *Iron Duke*, and was promoted to admiral on 4 August 1914. He appointed Rear-Admiral Charles Madden [75] (who had married a younger sister of Lady Jellicoe) as his Chief of Staff and introduced a set of detailed War Orders, to ensure that his captains conformed exactly to his carefully planned tactics.

Famously described by Churchill as "the only man who could lose the war in an afternoon", Jellicoe was determined not to take needless risks. The fact that his opponent in command of the German High Seas Fleet was subject to similar constraints meant that the two only met once, at the battle of Jutland (31 May–1 June 1916), the greatest encounter between ironclad fleets in the history of naval warfare. Although the High Seas Fleet turned for home, it was not destroyed and lost fewer ships and men than did the larger Grand Fleet. British dominance of the North Sea, and with it the naval blockade of Germany, remained in place, but British public opinion was disappointed that Jutland was not another Trafalgar. Controversy between the supporters of Jellicoe and those of Vice-Admiral David Beatty [69], who commanded the Battle-cruiser Fleet in this action, continued for many years, with the former's prudence (or excessive caution) being contrasted with the latter's daring (or rashness).

In December 1916 Jellicoe handed over command of the Grand Fleet to Beatty and became First Sea Lord and Chief of the Naval Staff, shortly before Sir Edward Carson took office as First Lord of the Admiralty on the formation of David Lloyd George's first Cabinet. The most urgent task was to deal with the growing menace of attacks on Allied merchant shipping by German submarines. Jellicoe took a gloomy view and declared that nothing more could be done to defeat the U-boats. He was initially opposed to introducing a convoy system, on the grounds that the Grand Fleet needed all the available escorts, that merchant captains could not keep station and that the ports could not deal with large numbers of ships arriving at the same time. Nevertheless, under political pressure, he began to investigate the idea and, after Lloyd George's personal intervention, put it into successful operation in June 1917. He withstood Lloyd George's proposals for attacks on enemy-held coasts, or any other plans that would divert resources from the Grand Fleet and the protection of trade. His outright refusal to countenance any such imaginative schemes brought him the appellation "the granite sailor" or "Silent Jack".

In July 1917, Lloyd George appointed Sir Eric Geddes, an eminent railwayman (previously appointed a temporary major general and vice-admiral to give the Army and Navy the supposed benefit of a businessman's approach to planning large-scale supply and transport operations) as First Lord in Carson's place. When Jellicoe maintained his opposition to any change in naval strategy, Geddes attempted to outflank him by creating a new post of Deputy First Sea Lord, filled by Admiral Wemyss [71] from the Mediterranean theatre.

Jellicoe's calm, analytical approach to any question led to clashes with Geddes (nicknamed "Goddes" from his imperious style), who was steeped in the frenetic ways of the commercial world. Geddes disliked being reminded by Jellicoe that, constitutionally, the First Lord was the colleague rather than the master of the other lords commissioners of the Admiralty. Their final disagreement was over the future of Vice-Admiral Reginald Bacon, commanding the Dover Patrol and, as such, held responsible for failing to close the Channel to German ships and submarines. When Jellicoe refused to dismiss Bacon, he was himself abruptly dismissed on Christmas Eve 1917, a date chosen by Geddes to ensure that, as there were no newspapers on Christmas Day, there would be immediate opportunity for adverse publicity.

Jellicoe was raised to the peerage as Viscount Jellicoe of Scapa Flow in January 1918 and promoted admiral of the fleet on 3 April 1919. He was Governor-General of New Zealand from 1920 to 1924 and was created Earl Jellicoe in June 1925. From 1928 to 1932 he was president of the British Legion, in succession to Field Marshal Earl Haig. He died of pneumonia at his home in Kensington, London, on 20 November 1935 and was buried in St Paul's Cathedral. His peerage was inherited by his son, who served with distinction during the Second World War in the 1st Special Air Service and Special Boat Service Regiments and later held high political office, including that of Minister of Defence for the Navy.

JERVIS
Sir JOHN, 1st Earl of St Vincent, GCB (1735–1823) [12]

John Jervis, the second son of an impoverished barrister-at-law, was born in his family home at Meaford, Staffordshire, on 9 January 1735. His mother, Elizabeth, was the sister of Sir Thomas Parker, a prominent Whig politician and a distant relation of Lord Anson [5]. Jervis attended a grammar school at Burton-on-Trent until 1747, when his father was appointed solicitor to the Admiralty and treasurer of Greenwich Hospital, and moved to Greenwich with his family. On 4 January 1749 Jervis was entered as an able seaman in the 4th-rate *Gloucester*, in which he served in the West Indies until 25 June 1752. He was then appointed a midshipman in the 4th-rate *Severn*, from which he transferred to the 6th-rate *Sphinx* in June 1754 before returning home. He became lieutenant in the 1st-rate *Royal George* on 19 February 1755. A month later, at a time of growing international tension, he moved to the 4th-rate *Nottingham* in the fleet under Admiral Edward Boscawen sent to prevent French reinforcements reaching Canada. At the beginning of the Seven Years War Jervis served from March to June 1756 in the 3rd-rate *Devonshire* and from June to October 1756 in the 2nd-rate *Prince* in the Mediterranean. He transferred to Rear-Admiral Charles Saunders' flagship, the 3rd-rate *Culloden*, in November 1756. While in temporary command of the 6th-rate *Experiment* he was in combat with a French privateer off Cape Gata, south-eastern Spain (17 March 1757). He followed Saunders to the 1st-rate *St George* in June 1757 and returned home in May 1758 as prize captain of *Foudroyant*, captured from the French.

In January 1759 Jervis joined the 2nd-rate *Neptune*, Saunders' flagship as C-in-C on the North America station. He was appointed commander of the sloop *Scorpion* on 15 May 1759, but did not join the ship until September 1759. During the operations against Quebec he became on 4 July 1759 acting commander of the sloop *Porcupine*, in which he carried Major General James Wolfe up the St Lawrence to outflank the French defences. As a mark of distinction, he was sent home with the despatches. Jervis was ordered back to North America with official messages, but *Scorpion* sprang a leak and Jervis was forced to leave her and take passage in another ship. He joined the fleet in the Channel in May 1760 and became captain of the 5th-rate *Gosport* on 13 October 1760. During 1761 his ship was deployed in the North Sea and during 1762 in the North Atlantic, including the successful defence of a convoy (11 May 1762). He took part in the recapture of St John's, Newfoundland, in 1762 and returned home at the end of hostilities in 1763.

In February 1769 Jervis was appointed to the 5th-rate *Alarm* and sent with treasure to the British trading community in Genoa. There two escaping galley slaves were picked up by one of his ship's boats. The local harbour guard forced the boat's crew to hand them over, whereupon Jervis threatened to bombard the city unless they were returned and a full apology made for the insult to the British flag. The slaves were accordingly released and the overzealous members of the guard were thrown into their own prison. *Alarm* returned home in May 1771, after nearly being wrecked off Marseilles (with Jervis being commended for his seamanship in saving her from disaster). From 1772 to 1775 he toured extensively in France and around the Baltic, enjoying the social aspects of his travels, but also gathering intelligence about the various coastlines and naval installations along his way.

Jervis returned to sea in June 1775, at the beginning of the American War of Independence, in command of the 3rd-rate *Kent*. In September 1775 he was appointed to *Foudroyant*, which had been taken into the Navy as a 3rd-rate. He was at the battle of Ushant (27 July 1778), the relief of Gibraltar (January 1780 and March 1781) and in an action off Brest, where he captured the French 74-gun *Pégase* in a single-ship duel (19 April 1782). He was slightly wounded in this engagement and awarded the KB in recognition of his victory. Sir John Jervis took part in a further relief of Gibraltar in October 1782 and was in a minor action off Cape Spartel (20 October 1782). He then returned with the fleet to England, where he married his cousin Martha, daughter of the influential Sir Thomas Parker. With the end of the war in sight, he entered Parliament in January 1783 as Member for Launceston. In the elections of 1784 he became Member for Yarmouth. He continued to represent this borough until 1790, when he became Member for Chipping Wycombe, and retained his seat, supporting the Whigs, until 1794.

Jervis was promoted to rear-admiral of the Blue on 24 September 1787 and briefly flew his flag in the 3rd-rate *Carnatic*. In 1790, when a fleet was mobilized at the time of a threatened war with Spain over the possession of Nootka Sound (Vancouver, British Columbia), he again briefly commanded a squadron, with his flag in *Prince*. He became a rear-admiral of the White on 21 September 1790 and vice-admiral of the Blue on 1 February 1793 (the same day that the French Republic declared war on the United Kingdom). Jervis was appointed C-in-C, West Indies, in the autumn of 1793. With his flag in the 2nd-rate *Boyne*, he took part in combined operations in the capture of the French islands of Martinique, St Lucia and Guadeloupe during the spring of 1794. By the end of the year a French force succeeded in recovering Guadeloupe, where the British garrison had been reduced by yellow fever. Jervis attempted to support the surviving troops, but was driven off by French coastal artillery. He gave up his command on medical grounds in November 1794 and returned home to be promoted to admiral of the Blue on 1 June 1795.

Jervis was nominated as C-in-C, Mediterranean, but his appointment was delayed by a vote of censure moved by the West India interest in the House of Commons for having levied a contribution on merchandise from Martinique. It was therefore not until November 1795 that he sailed in the 6th-rate *Lively* to join the fleet off Corsica, at that time a British possession. His arrival, noted Captain Horatio Nelson, was "to the joy of some, and the sorrow of others". He continued the blockade of Toulon, while at the same time tightening the lax discipline he found in the fleet. In the spring of 1796 Bonaparte began his conquest of Italy and, in October, Spain declared war on the United Kingdom. By November 1796, with the loss of his bases in Italy and Corsica, Jervis was forced to leave the Mediterranean and establish himself at Lisbon. After putting heart into the Portuguese government and refitting his ships, he put to sea again in mid-January 1797, declaring that "inaction in the Tagus will make us all cowards". On 14 February 1797, off Cape St Vincent, south-west Portugal, with his flag in the 1st-rate *Victory*, he encountered a Spanish fleet. As the mist lifted and his captain of the fleet counted the increasing odds from "There are eighteen sail of the line, Sir John" up to "There are twenty-seven sail of the line, Sir John, near double our own", he merely acknowledged each report with "Very well, Sir" until finally declaring, "Enough, Sir! No more of that! The die is cast and if there are fifty sail of the line, I will go through them." In the ensuing battle, where Captain Horatio Nelson was praised by Jervis for his initiative in disregarding the Admiralty's standard Fighting Instructions, four Spanish ships were taken. Although the rest escaped to Cadiz, the immediate threat of their joining the French fleet to cover an invasion of Ireland was removed. Jervis's victory not only saved the country but also the government, which showed its gratitude by raising him to the peerage as Earl of St Vincent on 23 June 1797.

St Vincent maintained his blockade of Cadiz throughout the next two years. During the summer of 1797, as news of the mutinies at Portsmouth and the Nore reached his fleet, he enforced the sternest discipline. He was asked to pardon one offender on the grounds of previous good character, but responded that he was glad to demonstrate that good characters as well as bad would be hung for sedition. He grew unpopular with many of his subordinates and his second-in-command, Rear-Admiral Sir John Orde (whom he had superseded in favour of his junior, Rear-Admiral Horatio Nelson) asked for St Vincent to be tried by court-martial for cruelty and oppression. In May 1798 St Vincent ordered Nelson to report on French activity at Toulon and, a fortnight later, when the Cabinet decided that a significant force should return to the Mediterranean, sent his ten finest ships to join him. These made up the squadron with which Nelson subsequently won the battle of the Nile (1–2 August 1798). Afterwards St Vincent refused to allow damaged ships to return home and insisted that they refit at Gibraltar. Nevertheless, he could display a human side. One young English lady, the seventeen-year-old Miss Elizabeth Wynne, evacuated with her family from Italy by the Navy, wrote of him as a gallant, friendly old man, for whom she sang duets with her sister after dinner in *Victory*. She noted in her correspondence "The old gentleman is very partial to kisses . . . and always obliges all the gentlemen that are present to kiss us". (Betsey Wynne, with her £8,000 a year, was soon snapped up by one of Jervis' captains, the future Vice-Admiral Sir Thomas Fremantle, and became the ancestress of a line of admirals).

St Vincent was promoted to admiral of the White on 14 February 1799. He resigned the Mediterranean command on medical grounds in June 1799 and set up home at Rochetts, near South Weald, Brentwood, Essex, where he gave his name to St Vincent's Hamlet. In October he was challenged to a duel by Sir John Orde, who had been denied a court-martial, though the Admiralty had sent St Vincent a rebuke. The King forbade St Vincent to accept the challenge and both parties were bound over to keep the peace. At the end of the year St Vincent was given command of the fleet in the Channel in place of the tired and ailing Lord Bridport (Sir Alexander Hood). St Vincent himself was old and sick, suffering from the dropsy, but accepted the command declaring it mattered little whether he died on shore or at sea. The Hood family had long been enemies of St Vincent and encouraged the second-in-command, Sir Alan Gardner, to lodge a strong protest at being superseded. St Vincent's reputation as a disciplinarian had preceded him, and his appointment was greeted by his new subordinates with horror. Standing orders, previously ignored, were thereafter fully enforced. No officer on blockade duty was allowed to sleep ashore, even when driven by storms to shelter off the English coast. No captain could take his ship to a dockyard without permission. St Vincent, who claimed in every other respect, including dress, to pattern himself on Earl Howe [9] differed from him by maintaining a close blockade of the French bases even in bad weather. Despite the subterfuges of his captains and the indignation of his officers' wives, he kept his fleet at sea, with his flag in the 1st-rate *Royal George*, throughout the summer of 1800 and the winter of 1800-01. On 19 February 1801, after Pitt's ministry had fallen over the question of Catholic emancipation, St Vincent left his exhausted but efficient fleet to become First Lord of the Admiralty in a new Cabinet led by Henry Addington.

The Treaty of Amiens (27 March 1802) brought a short-lived peace with France and allowed St Vincent to turn his attention to the Navy's administration. He condemned the abuse of patronage in the promotion of officers, attacked the corrupt practices of officials and defence contractors and, in December 1802, organized a royal commission to investigate further the large-scale frauds he had uncovered. Nevertheless, in his enthusiasm for achieving the peace dividend sought by the new Cabinet, he more than halved the number of ships in commission, reduced the number of seamen from 130,000 to 70,000 and placed hundreds of officers on half-pay. Highly skilled workmen were discharged from the dockyards. Surplus stores were sold to the French Navy, which was taking advantage of the peace to obtain the supplies that years of blockade had denied them.

The renewal of war with France in May 1803 was soon followed by the threat of invasion. St Vincent, like almost every other British admiral, saw little need for the large-scale home defence measures that the government then put in hand. He regarded the Sea Fencibles (raised to guard dockyards and shore installations) and coastal gunboats (built to protect estuaries and harbours) as a useless diversion of manpower and resources from the main fleet. With the blockade of French coasts once more in force, he declared that he did not say the French could not invade, only that they could not do so by sea. Although events justified this confidence, his political opponents (especially those who had suffered from his purge of the dockyards) attacked him both for neglecting coast defence and for failing to build new ships of the line. Sea officers criticized him for enforcing, as a Cabinet minister, the same penny-pinching economies that he had condemned as an admiral. When Addington's ministry fell in May 1804 St Vincent was replaced at the Admiralty by Henry Dundas, Viscount Melville, the close friend and ally of Pitt, who had returned to office as Prime Minister.

St Vincent was offered command of the fleet in the Channel, but refused to serve while Pitt was Prime Minister, so that it was not until after the latter's death in January 1806 that he again returned to sea. He was promoted to the newly created rank of admiral of the Red on 9 November 1805 and in March 1806, as acting admiral of the fleet, resumed his old command. With his flag in the 1st-rate *Hibernia*, he joined the blockade of Brest, where he remained (with a brief diversion to Lisbon to counter the threat of a French invasion) until the fleet withdrew to home waters for the winter. There, in deference to his age and health, he was allowed to live on shore until April 1807, when, with the fall of Grenville's "Ministry of all the Talents", he gave up the command he had only accepted under ministerial pressure.

St Vincent took little further part in public affairs. In January 1815, when the Order of the Bath was reorganized in the post-war honours, he became a GCB. To mark the accession of George IV, he was made admiral of the fleet on 19 July 1821, the first occasion that more than one officer at a time held that rank. St Vincent died on 14 March 1823 and was buried in his family mausoleum in the churchyard of St Michael's, Stone, Staffordshire. His countess predeceased him in 1816, leaving no children, and his earldom became extinct. His name was given to Jervis Bay, New South Wales, Australia.

JOHN
Sir CASPAR, GCB (1903–1984) [104]

Caspar John, the second of the five sons of the famous artist Augustus John and his wife Ida, was born at their home in Fitzroy Street, London, on 22 March 1903. Ida John died in 1907, and her husband's bohemian life-style meant that his many children had little conventional education until 1909, when her sons went to Dane Court Preparatory School, Parkstone, Dorset. There Caspar John won a school prize, for which the award was a copy of *Jane's Fighting Ships*, and this, together with a desire for a more structured and conventional way of life, led him to seek a career in the Navy. From September 1916 to December 1920 he was a cadet at the Royal Naval Colleges at Osborne and Dartmouth, from which he was promoted to midshipman on 15 January 1921, and appointed to the battleship *Centurion* in the Mediterranean Fleet in February 1921. He transferred to the battleship *Iron Duke*, flagship of the Mediterranean Fleet, in April 1921, and to the destroyer *Spear* in August 1922. During the Chanak crisis of 1922 he served with the fleet in the Dardanelles. John became an acting sublieutenant on 15 May 1923 at the beginning of his promotion courses and returned to the Mediterranean to join the aircraft carrier *Hermes* in December 1924. He then decided to specialize as a naval aviator, at that time an unconventional choice. Most senior naval officers of the day believed in the supremacy of the battleship, although opposing the arrangement whereby the Fleet Air Arm was part of the Royal Air Force.

In August 1925 John joined the RAF Flying Training School, Netheravon, where he was promoted to lieutenant on 30 August 1925 and qualified as a pilot in 1926. From April to December 1926 he served at RAF Leuchars, Fife, and, like all naval officers at that time on flying duties, was granted a RAF commission of equivalent rank to his naval one. He then joined *Hermes* on the China station, based at Hong Kong. He remained in *Hermes* until 1929, including a brief return home to refit at the end of 1927. Despite a number of accidents, he remained an enthusiastic aviator and in 1930 bought his own civil aeroplane, an Avro Avian, in which he took part in three successive Royal Aero Club annual King's Cup races. In April 1930 he joined No.450 Flight in the aircraft carrier *Furious* in the Atlantic Fleet. He also flew from the aircraft carriers *Argus* and *Courageous* and irritated the authorities by landing his Avian on the flight deck of the latter.

In January 1931 John reverted to general service and relinquished his RAF commission on being appointed to the battleship *Malaya* in the Atlantic Fleet. He returned to flying duties in December 1931 as a seaplane pilot in the cruiser *Exeter* in the Home Fleet (the renamed Atlantic Fleet). He remained there, with a deployment to the West Indies in February 1932 and a parachute course in August 1932, until promoted to lieutenant-commander on 30 August 1933. From October 1933 to the summer of 1934 he was employed in the battle-cruiser *Renown*, testing the Supermarine Walrus flying-boat and assessing different types of ship-borne aircraft.

In August 1934 John was appointed to the aircraft carrier *Courageous* as Staff Officer (Operations) to the Rear-Admiral commanding aircraft carriers in the Home Fleet. In the summer of 1935 as international tension increased over the question of British and French opposition to the Italian invasion of Ethiopia, *Courageous* was sent to the Mediterranean. When she returned home at the end of 1935, John remained in Egypt, appointed to the aircraft carrier *Glorious* but based ashore with 825 (Naval Air) Squadron. He was promoted to commander on 31 December 1936. In January 1937 he was appointed to the Air Materiel division of the Admiralty and was involved in the discussions leading to Inskip Award of July 1937, by which control of the carrier-borne Fleet Air Arm was transferred from the RAF to the Navy. In the spring of 1938 he sailed to the United States as part of a procurement mission to the US aircraft industry and in June 1939 became commander of the cruiser *York* on the America and West Indies station.

After the outbreak of the Second World War in September 1939 John served in *York* in Atlantic convoys and in the Norwegian campaign of early 1940; as a convoy escort around the Cape of Good Hope to Egypt; and in the Aegean and eastern Mediterranean campaigns of late 1940 and early 1941. He was then ordered home, where he was promoted to captain on 30 June 1941 and appointed to the Ministry of Aircraft Production, Millbank, as Director-General of Naval Aircraft Development and Production. After spending November 1942 on another procurement mission to the United States, he was appointed in March 1943 naval air attaché at the British Embassy, Washington, and naval air representative in the Admiralty delegation to the Joint Chiefs of Staff. As such he played an important part in obtaining naval aircraft and spares from American manufacturers and in arranging the training of British naval aircrews and maintenance personnel at United States and Canadian air stations.

John returned home in August 1944 to command the aircraft carrier *Pretoria Castle*, a converted liner used for aircraft evaluation trials. He renewed his friendship with, and then married, the New Zealand-born Mary Vanderpump, who had spent the war first as an ambulance driver in the London Blitz and then in the crew of a canal narrowboat. They later had two daughters and a son. In June 1945 he was given command of the new light aircraft carrier *Ocean*, intended to serve as a nightfighter carrier with the British Pacific Fleet. The end of hostilities with Japan in August 1945 meant that the ship was instead deployed to the Mediterranean, where John, a strict disciplinarian, continued to train his war-weary crews at full intensity. He spent 1947 at the Imperial Defence College, London and in January 1948 was given command of the Naval Air Station, Lossiemouth. He subsequently returned to the Admiralty, first as Deputy Chief of Naval Air Equipment and then as Director of Air Organization and Training, until his promotion to rear-admiral on 8 January 1951. John was then appointed to command the Third Aircraft Carrier Squadron in the Home Fleet, with his flag in the aircraft carrier *Vengeance*. Later in 1951 his command became the Heavy Squadron. From 1952 to 1954 he served in the Ministry of Supply, Holborn, as Chief of Naval Air Equipment. In 1955 he became Flag Officer (Air), Home, based at the Naval Air Station, Lee-on-Solent. He was promoted to vice-admiral on 22 June 1954 and awarded the KCB in 1956.

Sir Caspar John was promoted to admiral on 10 January 1957 and became Vice-Chief of the Naval Staff in the Board of Admiralty in May 1957. His main task was to implement the large-scale reorganization and reductions in the British defence establishment that followed the Suez Canal campaign of October 1956. These included the closure of the naval base at Scapa Flow and four out of the ten naval air stations, the scrapping of every battleship save one, and the reduction of the naval reserves from 30,000 to 5,000. In April 1959 he left the Admiralty, after being nominated

C-in-C, Home Fleet. Instead, in May 1959, he was appointed to succeed the ailing Sir Charles Lambe [103] as First Sea Lord in the Board headed by Lord Carrington in Harold Macmillan's Cabinet. In response to budgetary considerations, he decided that the Mediterranean Fleet should be sacrificed and urged that as many as possible of the next generation of aircraft should be designed to meet the needs of both the Royal Air Force and the Fleet Air Arm. He was unable to secure agreement with the Air Ministry, but at the end of his time at the Admiralty he had obtained Cabinet approval for a new fleet carrier and its complement of Blackburn Buccaneer aircraft.

John had also to deal with the moves, led by Lord Mountbatten [102] as Chief of the Defence Staff, towards a unified Ministry of Defence. A man of outspoken ways and fiery temperament, John disliked Mountbatten's personal flamboyance and his cavalier attitude towards honesty in the conduct of official business, but generally shared his views on naval policy. John was promoted to admiral of the fleet on 23 May 1962 and left office in August 1963. After going on half-pay he declined a peerage, but accepted office in a number of public bodies and charitable organizations. He later became seriously affected by vascular illness which led to the loss of his legs in 1978 and confined him, still in pain, to a wheelchair. He retired to Mousehole, Cornwall, where he died of pneumonia at Hayle, Cornwall, on 11 July 1984.

KELLY
Sir JOHN DONALD GCB, GCVO (1871–1936) [85]

John Kelly, the second son of an officer in the Royal Marine Artillery, was born on 13 July 1871 at Southsea, Hampshire, and became a cadet in the training ship *Britannia* in 1884. He was promoted to midshipman on 15 November 1886, with appointment to the corvette *Calliope* in January 1887. He joined the battleship *Agincourt*, flagship of the second-in-command of the Channel Squadron, in August 1888, before being turned over, with the rest of her complement, to the battleship *Anson*. In September 1889 he was appointed to the cruiser *Volage* in the Training Squadron, where he served until becoming an acting sub-lieutenant on 14 February 1891 at the beginning of his promotion courses. Kelly was promoted to lieutenant on 31 December 1893 and appointed in February 1894 to the cruiser *Katoomba*, for trade protection duties in Australasian waters. In November 1897 he joined the cruiser *Royal Arthur*, the new flagship of the Australia station. He returned home at the end of 1901 to qualify at the gunnery training school *Excellent*, from which in January 1902 he was appointed gunnery lieutenant in the cruiser *Forte* on the Cape of Good Hope and West Coast of Africa station.

Kelly was promoted to commander on 30 June 1904 and became commander of the armoured cruiser *Sutlej* on the China station in

November 1904. After returning home in 1906 he was appointed commander of the protected cruiser *Hawke* in the Reserve fleet at Chatham, from where he became commander of the battleship *Cornwallis* in the Atlantic Fleet in January 1907. Between July 1908 and February 1911 he was commander of the Royal Naval College, Dartmouth. After being promoted to captain on 22 June 1911, he went to the Royal Naval War College in October 1912 and became captain of the school of physical training and superintendent of PT at the naval barracks, Portsmouth, in January 1913. Kelly was given command of the light cruiser *Hermione* in the Home Fleet in April 1914, from where he was appointed to the light cruiser *Dublin* in the Mediterranean Fleet in July 1914.

On the outbreak of the First World War in August 1914 Kelly, together with his younger brother Howard (then captain of the light cruiser *Gloucester*), sighted the German battle-cruiser *Goeben*, but was outpaced and lost contact. Later in the war he returned home to command successively the light cruiser *Weymouth* and the cruiser *Devonshire*. In 1915 he married Mary Kelly, of Glenyarrah, Sydney, New South Wales, and later had a daughter with her. In 1917 he was given command of the battle-cruiser *Princess Royal* in the Battle-cruiser Fleet, where he remained for the rest of the war. In July 1919 Kelly became Director of Operations at the Admiralty and was promoted to rear-admiral on 21 November 1921. During 1922–23, when there was a risk of war with Turkey at the time of the Chanak crisis, he commanded a naval force sent to strengthen the Mediterranean Fleet.

From 1924 to 1926 Kelly was at the Admiralty as Fourth Sea Lord and Chief of Supplies and Transport. He was promoted to vice-admiral on 25 October 1926 and from April 1927 to April 1929 was second-in-command of the Mediterranean Fleet, with his flag in the battleship *Warspite* and command of the First Battle Squadron. After being awarded the KCB, Sir John Kelly left the Mediterranean in April 1929 and became Admiral commanding Reserves in August 1929, with promotion to admiral on 12 December 1930. He saw no prospect of further employment and, on completing his tenure of command in August 1931, applied for transfer to the retired list, to improve the promotion prospects of younger officers.

In the summer of 1931, a financial collapse in central Europe was followed by a run on the pound. International bankers agreed to help only if the British government produced large-scale cuts in public expenditure. When the Cabinet split over the issue, the minority Labour government fell. The Prime Minister, Ramsay MacDonald, condemned by his own party for "selling out to the Tories", formed a National government that agreed on 8 September 1931 to reduce the wages of all public sector employees. The Treasury refused to release new pay scales before Parliament was informed. The Admiralty decided that the cuts in naval pay should be a flat rate of one shilling per day. This meant that, in the case of able seamen, there would be a reduction in their pay of one quarter, compared with a seventh in that of teachers, who were the next worse off.

Cuts of this scale were especially severe on married men, many of whom had furnished their homes under hire-purchase arrangements geared to existing rates of pay. Some even feared that their wives would be driven into prostitution to feed their children. On 15 September 1931 men of the Atlantic Fleet at Invergordon refused orders to put to sea. This caused another run on the pound, so forcing the United Kingdom off the gold standard (to which it was destined never to return) six days later.

George V [64], a former naval officer, in an echo of Lord Howe [9] and the Spithead mutiny of 1797, proposed that Kelly (who was known to be trusted by the lower deck) should be given command of the Atlantic Fleet. Austen Chamberlain, who had become First Lord of the Admiralty at the end of August 1931, persuaded the Cabinet that the unfair flat-rate cuts should be replaced by a general ten per-cent reduction, as was the case with most other public sector employees. The First Sea Lord, Sir Frederick Field, ordered the ships to disperse to their home ports. Kelly insisted that the leaders of the mutiny should be drafted out of their ships before he took command at the beginning of October 1931, with the new title of C-in-C, Home Fleet (the Atlantic Fleet renamed), with his flag in the battleship *Nelson*. He visited every ship and spoke in plain language to the men, promising that their grievances would be heard with sympathy, but that indiscipline or disrespect to officers would not be tolerated. Some senior officers condemned him as a "Popularity Jack", but he succeeded in re-establishing good order in the fleet and so calmed the mood of national anxiety. After listening to his men's complaints, he reported that confidence would not be restored as long as the existing Board of Admiralty remained in office. Kelly left the Home Fleet in September 1933 and served as C-in-C, Portsmouth, from January 1935 until July 1936. One day before leaving office on his sixty-fifth birthday, he was promoted to admiral of the fleet on 12 July 1936. He retired to his home at Greenham Hall, Taunton, Somerset, and died in London on 4 November 1936. He was buried at sea.

KEPPEL
The Honourable Sir HENRY, GCB (1809–1904) [36]

The Honourable Henry Keppel, sixth son of the fourth Earl of Albemarle, was born in Kensington, Middlesex, on 14 June 1809. He joined the Royal Naval College, Portsmouth, on 7 February 1822, from which he was appointed midshipman in the 5th-rate *Tweed* and served at the Cape of Good Hope. He was promoted to lieutenant on 29 January 1828 and joined the 5th-rate *Galatea* under Captain (later Admiral Sir) Charles Napier, on the West Indies station, in February 1830. He moved in July 1831 to the 5th-rate *Magicienne*, in which he went to the East Indies station and served in the Gulf of Tongking and the South China Sea. Keppel returned home after being promoted to commander on 30 June 1833. In 1834 he was appointed to command the brig *Childers*, in which he served first off the coast of Spain, in the British fleet supporting the constitutionalist Queen-Regent Christina against her absolutist brother-in-law Don Carlos, and subsequently on the West Coast of Africa. He left *Childers* after being promoted to captain on 3 December 1837 and returned home early in 1834. In 1839 he married Katherine Crosbie, the daughter of a general. Keppel was given command of the 5th-rate *Dido* in August 1841, in which he served in the First China War and was in the British advance up the Yangtse River to capture Shanghai in June 1842.

After the end of hostilities with China in August 1842 Keppel was ordered to Singapore, from where he co-operated with the East India Company's agent, James Brooke, in the suppression of Borneo pirates. In August 1844 they undertook a series of boat actions up the rivers and creeks of Sarawak, burnt five pirate strongholds and destroyed over two hundred war vessels. Keppel then returned to Portsmouth, where he found that his wife, whom he had not seen for four years, was a few miles away at Droxford. As *Dido* was ordered to pay off at Sheerness, he changed clothes with the ship's master and made that officer take the ship round to the Thames, while he himself collected his wife and drove across Southern England with her in a yellow post-chaise, to rejoin *Dido* three days later. He then went on half-pay until 1847, when he was appointed to the 5th-rate *Maeander* and rejoined Brooke in Borneo. Keppel returned home in 1851 and went back to sea in command of the 1st-rate *St Jean d'Acre* in 1853. During the Crimean War he commanded this ship first in the Baltic during 1854 and then in the Black Sea. In July 1855 he transferred to the 2nd-rate *Rodney* and commanded the naval brigade in the siege of Sevastopol. Towards the end of the war he was appointed to the 3rd-rate *Colossus* in command of a division of shallow draught ships intended for service in the Baltic. Hostilities ended before the flotilla sailed and *Colossus* made a brief trip to the Crimea to help in the re-embarkation of the army.

In September 1856 Keppel was given command of the frigate *Raleigh*. He selected a number of other well-connected officers to join him, and his ship's company included a young relative, Arthur Knyvet Wilson [59], and the future Earl Clanwilliam [50]. Hastening to join the Second China War, the ship struck an uncharted rock near Hong Kong and became a total loss, though all her crew was saved. Keppel subsequently served in boat actions in the estuary below Canton (Guangzhou), at Escape Creek (25 May 1857) and Fat-shan Creek (1 June 1857) and the capture of Canton (29 December 1857). He was awarded the KCB and returned home after being promoted to rear-admiral on 22 August 1857.

Between September 1858 and May 1860 Sir Henry Keppel was a member of the Royal Household as groom-in-waiting to the Queen. His first wife died childless in June 1859. During 1860 he served briefly as C-in-C, Cape of Good Hope, with his flag in the frigate *Forte*, before becoming C-in-C on the South-East Coast of America station. In 1861 he married Jane, the daughter of Martin West, Esquire. Their son became an admiral and their daughter married a captain who later achieved flag rank.

Keppel was promoted to vice-admiral on 11 January 1864 and was C-in-C on the China station, with his flag in *Rodney* (rebuilt in 1860 as a screw ship) from the beginning of 1867 to 11 January 1869, when he was promoted to admiral. Keppel was C-in-C, Plymouth, from 1872 to 1875 and was promoted to admiral of the fleet on 5 August 1877. He was an intimate of the Prince of Wales, later Edward VII [44] (one of whose mistresses was Alice Keppel, the wife of his elder brother George) and was a prominent figure in London society. He died in London on 17 January 1904 and was buried in the churchyard of St Mary the Virgin, Winkfield, Berkshire.

KERR
The Right Honourable Lord WALTER TALBOT, GCB
(1839–1927) [56]

Lord Walter Kerr, the fourth son of the seventh Marquess of Lothian, was born at Newbattle Abbey, Midlothian, on 28 September 1839. He attended Radley School, Abingdon, Oxfordshire, from 1851 until 1853 when he joined the Navy as a cadet in the 1st-rate *Prince Regent*. During the Crimean War he served in 1854 in the 1st-rate *Neptune* and in 1855 in the 3rd-rate *Cornwallis*, with promotion to midshipman in August 1855. Kerr sailed with the frigate *Shannon* for the China station at the beginning of the Second China War in 1856, but the ship was almost immediately redeployed to Calcutta following the outbreak of the Indian Mutiny in May 1857. Most of her company disembarked to form a naval brigade, in which Kerr commanded a division of two heavy guns throughout the campaign in Oude (Awadh) in Northern India. He was wounded at Cawnpore (Kanpur) in December 1857 but recovered and took part in the British recapture of Lucknow in February 1858. He was mentioned in despatches and promoted to mate, serving in *Shannon* until she paid off, and then, for a few months, in the royal yacht *Victoria and Albert*.

Kerr became a lieutenant on 5 September 1859 and was from 1860 to 1863 in the frigate *Emerald* in the Channel. Between 1864 and 1867 he was in the 2nd-rate *Princess Royal* at the Cape of Good Hope and in the East Indies. On 3 April 1868 he was promoted commander, and during the next three years was commander of the battleship *Hercules* in the Channel Squadron. At Lisbon he gained a medal from the Royal Humane Society for diving overboard from a height of thirty feet to rescue a seaman who had fallen from the rigging into the Tagus. Kerr was promoted to captain on 30 November 1872. In 1873 he married Lady Amabell Cowper, youngest daughter of the sixth Earl Cowper, and later had four sons and two daughters with her. He served as flag captain to Sir Beauchamp Seymour (Lord Alcester), commanding the Channel Squadron, with his flag in the battleship *Lord Warden*, from 1874 to 1877, and the Mediterranean Fleet, with his flag in the battleship *Alexandra*, from 1880 to 1881. In September 1880 he acted as special representative from the

143

multinational fleet, under Seymour's command, assembled to enforce the Balkan peace terms agreed at the 1878 Congress of Berlin. In a mission to the Turkish governor-general of Albania, he supervised the handover of the port of Dulcigno (Ulcinj) to allow the newly independent Montenegro an outlet to the sea.

Kerr then became captain of the Medway steam reserve until being appointed in 1885 naval private secretary to Lord George Hamilton, First Lord of the Admiralty in Lord Salisbury's first Cabinet. He was senior, as a captain, to some members of the Board and proved a valuable adviser to Hamilton in disputes that arose between Sir Arthur Hood and Lord Charles Beresford, the first and fourth naval lords respectively. Beresford, a hero of the recent Egyptian and Sudan campaigns and a close friend of the Prince of Wales [44], caused difficulties by criticizing various aspects of naval policy and challenging Hood's supremacy over the other naval lords. His resignation from the Board in 1888 came as a relief to his colleagues.

Kerr became a rear-admiral on 1 January 1889 and remained at the Admiralty until the end of the year, when he became second-in-command of the Mediterranean Fleet, with his flag in the battleship *Trafalgar*. In 1892 he returned to the Admiralty as fourth naval lord. The third naval lord at this time, John Fisher [58], was junior as a flag officer to Kerr, but this anomaly ended in November 1893 when Kerr was appointed second naval lord. He was promoted to vice-admiral on 20 February 1895 and remained in the Admiralty until May 1895, when he was given command of the Channel Squadron, with his flag in the battleship *Majestic*. He hauled down his flag in 1897 and returned to the Admiralty as second naval lord in May 1899. Kerr became first naval lord in August 1899, in the Board headed by G J Goschen in Salisbury's third Cabinet, and was promoted to admiral on 21 March 1900. He remained in this post when the Earl of Selborne succeeded Goschen in October 1900, during a period of continued rearmament arising from the emergence of Germany as a major naval power, and was promoted to admiral of the fleet on 16 June 1904. He left office in October 1904 and settled at Melbourne Hall, Derbyshire, an estate inherited by Lady Amabell Kerr in 1905 from her brother, the seventh Earl Cowper. Lord Walter Kerr retired in September 1909 and died at Melbourne Hall on 12 May 1927 where he was buried at the nearby parish church of St Michael.

KEYES
Sir ROGER JOHN BROWNLOW, 1st Baron Keyes, 1st Baronet, GCB, KCVO, DSO (1872–1945) [80]

Roger Keyes, the second in a family of nine children, was born on 4 October 1872, in the Punjab, then a province of British India. His father, a colonel (later major general) in the Madras Staff Corps and commandant of the Punjab Frontier Force, came from the Anglo-Irish Protestant Ascendancy, and his uncle, at that time military member of the Governor-General of India's Council, was the future Field Marshal Sir Henry Norman. His maternal grandfather, James Norman, had begun his career in the merchant marine. Keyes joined the Navy as a cadet in the training ship *Britannia* in July 1885. He was appointed to the frigate *Raleigh*, flagship at the Cape of Good Hope, in July 1887, with promotion to midshipman on 15 November 1887. He transferred to the cruiser *Turquoise* in 1889 and was subsequently employed in anti-slaving patrols on the east coast of Africa. He was promoted to acting sub-lieutenant on 14 November 1891, at the beginning of his promotion courses, and became a lieutenant on 28 August 1893, when he was appointed to the sloop *Beagle* on the South-East Coast of America station. He returned home early in 1897 and was appointed lieutenant and commander of the destroyer *Opossum*, at Plymouth, in January 1898. He became lieutenant and commander of the torpedo-boat destroyer *Hart* on the China station in September 1898, from which he transferred to the torpedo-boat destroyer *Fame* in January 1899.

During the Boxer Rebellion of 1900 Keyes took part in the multinational operations to relieve the diplomatic legations at Peking (Beijing) and served in a naval brigade under Captain George Callaghan [67]. He was given special promotion to commander on 19 November 1900, in recognition of his part in this campaign. In May 1901 he was given command of the torpedo-boat destroyer *Bat* at Devonport, where he transferred in May 1902 to command another destroyer, *Sprightly*, until early in 1903. He spent 1904 in the Naval Intelligence Department at the Admiralty and from 1905 to 1908 was naval attaché at the British Embassy, Rome, with promotion to captain on 30 June 1905. In 1906 he married Eva Bowlby, of Gilston Park, Hertfordshire, with whom he later had two sons and three daughters. In 1908 Keyes was given command of the cruiser *Venus*, from which, in November 1910, he became Inspecting Captain of Submarines. He developed an enthusiasm for this new branch and in 1912 was appointed commodore of the Submarine Service, based at Portsmouth. Among his achievements was the defeat of a proposal from the then First Lord of the Admiralty, Winston Churchill, that the official collective term for submarines should be "shoals", on the analogy of that for aircraft being "flights".

At the outbreak of the First World War in August 1914 Keyes commanded the Eighth Submarine Flotilla, based at Harwich. In response to German sorties into the southern North Sea, he proposed an attack on their patrols in the Heligoland Bight, with the aim of drawing out heavier ships to where his submarines would be waiting. This developed into the first naval battle of the war (28 August 1914), in which, with his broad pendant in the destroyer *Lurcher*, he took part in a joint operation with the First Battle-cruiser Squadron under Rear-Admiral Beatty and the Harwich Force under Commodore Reginald Tyrwhitt [82]. *Lurcher* went alongside the sinking German cruiser *Mainz* and picked up a total of 220 survivors. Keyes was mentioned in despatches, but told that he was not again to go to sea in a destroyer, as this was too risky for an officer in his appointment.

On 22 September 1914, when three British cruisers were torpedoed while patrolling the Dogger Bank, Keyes put to sea in the light cruiser *Fearless*, with the intention of picking up survivors and counter-attacking the U-boat involved. He continued to work closely with Tyrwhitt and, at the beginning of October 1914, went in *Lurcher* to Zeebrugge, to examine the facilities for the disembarkation of British troops. When most of the Belgian coast fell to the Germans, he pressed for his submarines to operate in the Baltic, despite initial Admiralty fears of infringing Danish neutrality. In February 1915 Keyes was made chief of staff in the squadron deployed to attack the Turkish positions in the Dardanelles, where he served first under Vice-Admiral Carden and then Rear-Admiral De Robeck [77]. He remained a keen supporter of the Dardanelles campaign and continued to press for another attack by the fleet, even though the associated land operations made no progress. He was twice mentioned in despatches and awarded the DSO and CMG, as well as earning the gratitude of the First Lord of the Admiralty, Winston Churchill, who had devised the Dardanelles strategy and was ultimately forced from office over its failure. After returning from the Mediterranean, Keyes was given command in June 1916 of the battleship *Centurion* in the Grand Fleet. He was promoted to rear-admiral on 10 April 1917, in command of the Fourth Battle Squadron, with his flag in the battleship *Colossus*.

In October 1917 Keyes joined the Admiralty as Director of Plans. He grew concerned at the way in which German U-boats, operating from Belgium, managed to pass the Dover Straits to take part in the increasingly serious submarine offensive against Allied shipping. At the end of December 1917 the new First Sea Lord, Sir Rosslyn Wemyss [71], gave Keyes command of the Dover Patrol, with the acting rank of vice-admiral and told him to put his plans for operations in the Channel into practice. Keyes proved an active and energetic leader of the light forces at his disposal, with his enthusiasm for the offensive culminating in his attacks on the U-boat bases at Zeebrugge and Ostend (22–23 April 1918). Although the landing parties suffered heavy casualties and the Germans were able to resume operations after a short interval, these raids gave a great boost to national morale and made Keyes a hero with the public. He was awarded the KCB on 24 April 1918 and made plans for a new attack, while continuing to bombard the German-held coast with his monitors and other shallow-draught ships. Sir Roger Keyes received a further mention in despatches and, in the post-war honours, was created a baronet. In March 1919 he was given command of the Battle-cruiser Fleet and reverted to the rank of rear-admiral when this fleet was reduced to a squadron. He was promoted to vice-admiral on 16 May 1921, and joined the Admiralty as Deputy Chief of the Naval Staff.

Like most naval officers Keyes was unhappy at the Cabinet decision that all maritime aircraft should be operated by the Royal Air Force. Sir Hugh Trenchard, Chief of the Air Staff and a determined advocate of the concept of the indivisibility of the air, had married in 1920 Lady Keyes's widowed younger sister Katherine, but the two brothers-in-law managed to keep their official and family relations separate. In 1925 Keyes became C-in-C, Mediterranean Fleet, with promotion to admiral on 1 March 1926. During 1925 he was involved in a forced landing after taking off from the aircraft carrier *Eagle* and nearly drowned. A problem of discipline in the battleship *Royal Oak* (where the rear-admiral, whose flagship she was, clashed both with his flag captain and the ship's commander) led Keyes to remove all the contending parties from the ship, but he was thought to have handled the affair badly. This episode, plus his expressed opinion that polo (a sport open only to rich men) was essential in developing the spirit he looked for in his officers, played a part in frustrating his expectation of succeeding Sir Charles Madden [75] as First Sea Lord. Keyes himself felt that he had been the victim of an intrigue, but Madden doubted his readiness to carry out the policy of the Labour government of the day in reducing naval expenditure. He was C-in-C, Portsmouth from April 1929 to May 1931, with promotion to admiral of the fleet on 8 May 1930. He settled at Tingewick, Buckinghamshire, in 1931 and went onto the retired list in May 1935.

In 1934 Keyes was elected to Parliament as the Conservative Member for North Portsmouth. He spoke in favour of rearmament, and against the Royal Air Force's continued control of the Fleet Air Arm. With his old friend Winston Churchill, he was among those Conservative MPs who abstained from voting in support of the Munich agreement in October 1938. After the outbreak of the Second World War in September 1939 he sought more active employment and criticized the Chiefs of Staff for lack of offensive spirit. In October 1939 he obtained an interview with Churchill, who had returned to office as First Lord of the Admiralty, and offered to lead an attack on Trondheim in obsolete heavy ships. After the Allied defeat in Norway in April 1940 he went down to the House of Commons in his uniform as an admiral of the fleet and made an impassioned speech in the adjournment debate of 7 May 1940, condemning the Cabinet and the Naval Staff for their conduct of the campaign.

This debate led to the fall of Neville Chamberlain's Conservative administration and the establishment of a Coalition government led by Churchill. On 10 May 1940, when Germany invaded the previously neutral Low Countries, Keyes was appointed Churchill's personal liaison officer to King Leopold III of the Belgians. That monarch's decision to surrender to the Germans on 28 May 1940, despite the wishes of his government and without informing his allies, brought him, and Keyes, much public criticism. Keyes continued to defend Leopold and instituted a libel action against the *Daily Mirror* newspaper, which had published a leader referring to Leopold as "The Rat King". In June 1940 Churchill proposed the formation of units (later given the title "Commandos") trained to launch seaborne attacks on enemy-held coasts. On 17 July 1940 he appointed Keyes as the head of a newly-formed Combined Operations Command, including responsibility for the Commandos and for planning descents upon hostile coasts.

Churchill justified this selection on the grounds of Keyes's high rank, which would emphasize the importance to be placed upon such operations, and on his proven offensive spirit and experience. Other officers felt that Churchill had acted out of misguided loyalty to an old friend and supporter, who had been constantly badgering him for a command. Some even thought it was to stop him advertising the shortcomings of the British Expeditionary Force in his defence of Leopold. Despite his success in organizing the Commando forces and developing many of the special craft required for amphibious operations, Keyes own aggressive personality, and his access to Churchill made him unpopular with the Chiefs of Staff (all junior in rank to him) and the senior commanders with whom he needed to work. The Admiralty resented his criticism of the Norwegian campaign, the Army disliked his having control over the Commandos and the Royal Air Force (having lost control over the Fleet Air Arm) was subjected to his constant complaints about the weakness of Coastal Command.

Churchill remained attracted by Keyes's bold and imaginative schemes (considered by the Chiefs of Staff and theatre commanders to be rash and impractical), but was eventually persuaded to remove him from office early in October 1941. His place was given to the politically more astute Captain Lord Louis Mountbatten [102], who had Churchill's ear, but whose relatively junior rank was not such as to alarm the Chiefs of Staff. Keyes, resentful of his betrayal, remained on the back-benches criticizing the Cabinet's conduct of the war. In July 1942, following the fall of Tobruk, he seconded a vote of no confidence in Churchill's administration. The motion was defeated and the tide of the war turned, but to prevent Keyes causing any more trouble in the Commons he was given a peerage as Baron Keyes, of Zeebrugge and of Dover, in January 1943. He himself was happy to accept, as Trenchard had already gone to the Lords, where he acted as an advocate of the RAF. Early in 1944 Keyes suffered a detached retina. A near miss by a bomb on the hospital where he was being treated affected his recovery from surgery and he lost the vision of his right eye.

During the summer of 1944, sponsored by the Ministry of Information, Lord Keyes made a lecture tour of Canada, the United States, Australia and New Zealand. He was invited to sea with United States Pacific Fleet and was present at the battle of the Philippine Sea (19–20 October 1944) in the USS *Appalachian*, flagship of Vice-Admiral Richard L Conolly, United States Navy. Covering the invasion of Leyte, *Appalachian* was attacked by Japanese aircraft and the ship's anti-aircraft smoke blanketed Keyes and others on the bridge. The damage to his lungs caused by smoke inhalation was made worse when he later had to fly without oxygen and he never fully recovered. Keyes died at Tingewick on 26 December 1945, from a heart condition aggravated by the injuries he had sustained in the Pacific. He was buried in the Zeebrugge corner of the cemetery of St James's, Dover. His elder son, Lieutenant Colonel G C T

Keyes, VC, had been killed leading a raid on General Erwin Rommel's headquarters in Libya in November 1941, and the peerage was inherited by Lord Keyes's younger son, at that time a lieutenant in the Navy.

LAMBE
Sir CHARLES EDWARD, GCB, CVO (1900–1960) [103]

Charles Lambe, the only son of Henry Lambe of Grove House, Stalbridge, was born at Stalbridge, Dorset, on 20 December 1900. Lambe became a cadet in the Royal Naval College, Osborne, in 1914 and after completing his education at Dartmouth during the First World War, joined the Fleet as a midshipman in the battleship *Emperor of India* on 15 August 1917. He remained there until the end of hostilities in November 1918 and subsequently served in the battleship *King George V* from June 1919 to January 1921. He qualified as a free balloon pilot and later obtained a private aircraft pilot's licence. He was promoted to sub-lieutenant on 15 January 1921 and was appointed to the light cruiser *Raleigh* in March 1921. He was promoted to lieutenant on 15 February 1922 and was one of the young naval officers (immortalized in Rudyard Kipling's poem *The Scholars*) sent to Cambridge University to fill the gaps in their education caused by their war service. In August 1923 he was appointed to the battleship *Benbow*, flagship of the Fourth Battle Squadron in the Mediterranean Fleet. During 1925–26 he attended the torpedo school *Vernon* at Portsmouth. After qualifying, he served from 1927 to 1929 as torpedo lieutenant in the destroyer *Stuart*, leader of the Second Destroyer Flotilla in the Mediterranean Fleet. He was promoted to lieutenant-commander on 15 February 1930 and then attended the Royal Naval Staff College, Greenwich. In 1932 he joined the cruiser *Hawkins*, flagship of the C-in-C, East Indies.

Lambe was promoted to commander on 30 June 1933 and joined the staff of Rear-Admiral A B Cunningham [91], then commanding the destroyer flotillas of the Mediterranean Fleet. Lambe returned home in 1935 to become commander of *Vernon* from which he was promoted to captain on 31 December 1937. In January 1939 he was given command of the cruiser *Dunedin*, a seagoing training ship for boys and target ship in the Reserve fleet at Portsmouth. On the outbreak of the Second World War in September 1939 she became an operational unit of the Home Fleet and spent ninety-two of the first hundred and twenty days of the war at sea, mostly in the Northern Patrol. In 1940 he married the daughter of a baronet, Sir Walter Corbet, and later had with her a son and a daughter. In October 1940 Lambe was appointed to the Plans Department of the Admiralty, where he spent most of the war successively as Assistant Director, Deputy Director and Director. Early in 1944 Lambe left the Admiralty to become captain of the aircraft carrier *Illustrious* in the British Pacific Fleet and took part in air operations against Japan. His ship was hit by a kamikaze suicide bomber on 6 April 1945 but cleared her flight deck

149

within twenty minutes and remained on station until ordered home a week later for a long-delayed refit.

After the end of the Second World War in August 1945 Lambe returned to the Admiralty as Assistant Chief of Staff (Air), with promotion to acting rear-admiral on 29 August 1945. With his promotion confirmed on 8 July 1947, he remained at the Admiralty as Flag Officer, Flying Training, from September 1947 to August 1949. He commanded the Third Aircraft Carrier Squadron in the Home Fleet, with his flag in the aircraft carrier *Vengeance* from September 1949 to January 1951, and was promoted to vice-admiral on 1 December 1950. Between March 1951 and January 1953 Lambe was Flag Officer (Air) Home, based at the Royal Naval Air Station, *Daedalus*, Lee-on-Solent. He served as C-in-C, Far East station, from March 1953 to April 1955, where he was awarded the KCB, and promoted to admiral on 30 March 1954. Sir Charles Lambe was Second Sea Lord and Chief of Naval Personnel at the Admiralty from 1954 to 1957. Between November 1957 and February 1959 he was C-in-C, Mediterranean Fleet and NATO C-in-C, Allied Forces, Mediterranean (CINCAFMED).

Lambe was then appointed First Sea Lord, on the recommendation of Earl Mountbatten, Chief of the Defence Staff [102]. Mountbatten's view was that Lambe would have the confidence of the Fleet because he was known to be well able to fight the Navy's battles in Whitehall. He had also played a valuable part in supporting Mountbatten and Sir Rhoderick McGrigor [100] in their earlier struggle with Duncan Sandys, Defence Minister in Harold Macmillan's first Cabinet, over the question of keeping aircraft carriers. Moreover, he sympathized with Mountbatten's policy of subordinating the separate Service Departments to a unified Ministry of Defence. Lambe served in the Boards of Admiralty headed successively by the Earl of Selkirk and by Lord Carrington in Macmillan's administration, but suffered a serious heart attack six months after his appointment. He left office, with promotion to admiral of the fleet on 10 May 1960 and died at his home in Newport, Fife, on 29 August 1960. He was a keen horseman and polo-player, a competent artist and a talented musician, who kept two pianos in his flagships so that he could play duets with his composer friends.

LAMBTON

HEDWORTH, see **MEUX,** the Honourable Sir HEDWORTH LAMBTON, **[66]**

LEACH

Sir HENRY CONYERS, GCB (1923-) **[111]**

Henry Leach, third son of the future Captain J C Leach, Royal Navy, was born on 18 November 1923. After preparatory schooling at St Peter's

Court, Broadstairs, Kent, he joined the Royal Naval College as a cadet in 1937. He remained there on the outbreak of the Second World War in September 1939 and was promoted to midshipman on 1 January 1941. He was then appointed successively to the cruiser *Mauritius* and battleship *Rodney*, prior to joining the cruiser *Edinburgh* in which he served in the South Atlantic and Indian Ocean. On the outbreak of war with Japan in December 1941 he was based at Singapore, where he had his last conversation with his father, captain of the battleship *Prince of Wales*, who was shortly afterwards lost with his ship off the coast of Malaya. After returning home, Henry Leach served in the destroyer *Sardonyx* before being promoted to sub-lieutenant on 1 October 1942. He was appointed to the battleship *Duke of York*, flagship of the Home Fleet, in January 1943 where he was promoted to lieutenant in October 1943, and elected to remain in the flagship, in charge of "A" turret. In *Duke of York*, he took part in escorting convoys to northern Russia and the sinking of the German battle-cruiser *Scharnhorst* at the battle of the North Cape (26 December 1943). In the autumn of 1944 he joined the destroyer *Javelin*, in which he served in the Home Fleet and the Mediterranean.

After the end of the Second World War in 1945 Leach served in *Javelin* in the 14th Destroyer Flotilla off Palestine (then a British mandate). When both the commanding officer and the first lieutenant were posted out following a refusal by a number of ratings to do duty, Leach was advanced to first lieutenant to fill the vacancy in this appointment. In 1946 he was appointed to the destroyer flotilla leader *Chequers*, from which he joined the gunnery school *Excellent*. He qualified as a gunnery officer in 1947 and was re-appointed to *Excellent* as an instructor. There, he declined an offer to train and command the Portsmouth team in the naval field gun race at the annual Royal Tournament. Leach was subsequently given (to his widowed mother's despair) what he perceived as a penal appointment for having declined this offer, the post of gunnery officer to the Second Minesweeping Flotilla in the Aegean, in the flotilla leader *Fierce*, which was armed only with light anti-aircraft guns. On this station he met his future wife, Mary, the seventeen-year-old daughter of Rear-Admiral (later Admiral Sir Henry) McCall.

Leach was promoted to lieutenant-commander on 1 February 1952 and then attended the Royal Naval Staff College, Greenwich. This was followed by eight months at the Admiralty as Staff Officer for the Naval Brigade in London for the coronation of HM Queen Elizabeth II. In July 1953 he became gunnery officer of the Fifth Cruiser Squadron on the Far East station in the cruiser *Newcastle* and served off the coast of Korea at the end of the Korean War. During 1955 he took part in the Malayan insurgency campaign, giving naval gunfire support to ground operations. He was promoted to commander on 30 June 1955 and served as Application Commander for Seaslug, the Navy's first Guided Weapons system. Between August 1957 to November 1959 Leach was again at the Admiralty, dealing with the officer structure of the Navy and the reductions

151

arising from the general reorganization of the Armed Services in the aftermath of the Suez expedition of October 1956. In 1958 Leach married Mary
McCall and later had with her a family of two daughters. Despite
temporarily suffering from double vision as the result of a serious car accident, he took command of the destroyer *Dunkirk* at the end of 1959 in
the Mediterranean, where he served until July 1961. He then returned
to the Admiralty in the Training Directorate, and then attended the Joint
Services Staff College at Latimer, Buckinghamshire, with promotion to
captain on 31 December 1961. In July 1962 he became Chief Staff Officer
(Plans and Operations) in Far East Fleet headquarters at Singapore. At the
end of 1962 a revolt against the British-protected Sultan of Brunei marked
the beginning of a prolonged period of confrontation with Indonesia, in
which Leach had the task of programming a variety of ships in support of
the British ground forces until returning home late in 1964.

Leach served as Captain (Destroyers) of the Twenty-Seventh Escort
Squadron in the Home Fleet and the Mediterranean, in the frigate *Galatea*,
from November 1965 to February 1967 and became Director of Naval
Plans at the Ministry of Defence in February 1968. From March 1970 to
January 1971 he commanded the commando carrier *Albion*, in which he
learnt to fly helicopters. He strongly supported the abolition in 1970 of the
tradition of a daily issue of rum, as being no longer appropriate in a modern
navy operating with highly technical equipment. He was promoted to rear-
admiral on 7 July 1971 and returned to the Ministry of Defence as Assistant
Chief of the Naval Staff (Policy). In May 1974 Leach became Flag Officer
commanding the First Flotilla, based at Portsmouth and comprising about
a third of the Navy's surface fleet, with his flag in a number of ships,
principally the cruiser *Blake*. He was promoted to vice-admiral on 6 July
1974 and became Vice-Chief of Defence Staff (which he considered a
"non-job") in January 1976, with the award of the KCB in 1977.

Sir Henry Leach was promoted to admiral on 30 March 1977 and served
as C-in-C, Fleet, and NATO Allied C-in-C, Channel (CINCHAN) and
Eastern Atlantic Area (CINCEASTLANT). Normally based ashore at
Northwood, Middlesex, he took the opportunity of Queen Elizabeth II's
Silver Jubilee Fleet Review at Spithead to fly his flag in the aircraft carrier
Ark Royal. In July 1979 he became First Sea Lord. He was happy with the
improvements to servicemen's pay introduced by the new Conservative
government led by Margaret Thatcher, but had reservations about the
readiness of her Secretary of State for Defence, Francis Pym, to protect
the Navy from reductions. These reservations were increased with the
arrival of Pym's successor, John Nott, in January 1981. Leach fought hard
to save the assault ships and anti-submarine aircraft carriers, but in many
cases his professional opinion was disregarded and Keith Speed, the
Minister for the Navy, was dismissed for supporting him.

The announcement that, as part of the reductions in the fleet, the survey
ship *Endurance* would be withdrawn from the Antarctic was followed by
the Argentine invasion of the Falkland Islands (1–2 April 1982). Leach

considered that, despite the risks, it was the Navy's duty to attempt the recovery of the islands, something he considered essential for national prestige. He is quoted as saying, "We must go" and, in the absence overseas of the Chief of the Defence Staff, Sir Terence Lewin [110], immediately prepared a naval task force for this purpose. He had to explain to the Conservative Prime Minister of the day, Margaret Thatcher, that the ships would take three weeks, not the three days that she envisaged, to reach the South Atlantic. When asked about the aircraft carrier *Ark Royal*, he pointed out that the old one was being scrapped and the new one would take two years to complete. Nevertheless, his advice was that, even with only two small carriers to provide air cover, the Falklands could be recaptured and that the operation should proceed. This was greeted by the Prime Minister with relief and approval. He came to admire her qualities of leadership and determination, and gave her his full support during what proved to be a rapid and successful campaign, though his opinion of Nott was less favourable.

In the post-Falklands period Leach remained in office for four months longer than the usual period in order to fight for the ships promised as replacements for those lost in the South Atlantic. Discovering the draft of a ministerial statement giving the misleading impression that the strength of the Navy had not been reduced, he leaked a rebuttal to the Press, to the irritation of his political masters. He was promoted to admiral of the fleet when he retired from active duty on 1 December 1982. Shortly afterwards, Nott was succeeded as Secretary of State for Defence by Michael Heseltine. In retirement Sir Henry Leach settled at his home in Wonston, Winchester, Hampshire. He published his memoirs and undertook many public and charitable offices. From 1983 to 1993 he was President of the Sea Cadet Association.

LE FANU
Sir MICHAEL, GCB DSC (1913–70) [106]

Michael Le Fanu, generally known as "Lef", (but also, on account of his red hair, as "Ginger"), the son of a naval commander (later captain) of Huguenot descent, was born at Lindfield, Sussex, on 2 August 1913. After attending Bedford School, Bedfordshire, he joined the Royal Naval College, Dartmouth, in 1926. From January 1931 to June 1933 he served in the cruiser *Dorsetshire* in the Atlantic Fleet, with promotion to midshipman on 1 September 1931. He was then appointed to the cruiser *York* before becoming an acting sub-lieutenant on 1 January 1934 at the beginning of his promotion courses. Le Fanu joined the destroyer *Whitshed* in the Mediterranean Fleet in March 1935 and was promoted to lieutenant on 1 June 1935. From September 1936 to the end of 1937 he was in the destroyer *Bulldog* in the Home Fleet, prior to training during 1938 as a gunnery specialist. After qualifying, he was appointed to the staff of the

C-in-C, Mediterranean Fleet, where he was serving on the outbreak of the Second World War in September 1939. In December 1939 he became gunnery officer of the light cruiser *Aurora*, in the Home Fleet. *Aurora* took part in North Atlantic patrols, the Norwegian campaign (9 April–9 June 1940) where Le Fanu was mentioned in despatches, and in the operations leading to the sinking of the German battleship *Bismarck* (24–27 May 1941). With his ship in the Mediterranean as part of Force K, he was awarded the DSC for his conduct during a night action in which a heavily-escorted Italian convoy was destroyed (8 November 1941). On 19 December 1941, escorting a convoy to Malta, *Aurora* was badly damaged by a mine.

In June 1942 Le Fanu joined the gunnery staff of the C-in-C, Home Fleet, with the flag in the battleship *Duke of York*. He was promoted to lieutenant-commander, and became responsible for the gunnery training of newly-commissioned ships. To his chagrin, he missed the sinking of the German battle-cruiser *Scharnhorst* (25–26 December 1943), the last surface engagement between capital ships in the history of the Navy, as he was on leave, marrying Prudence Morgan, the daughter of an admiral. They later had a family of two sons and a daughter. In March 1944 he became gunnery officer of the battleship *Howe* and sailed to join the Eastern Fleet in the Indian Ocean. Le Fanu was promoted to commander on 31 December 1944 and was appointed naval liaison officer between the British Pacific Fleet and the United States Pacific Fleets at the end of January 1945. He established good working relations with Admiral Raymond A Spruance and Vice-Admiral William F Halsey, United States Navy, and played a valuable part in arranging a British presence in the Allied force that sailed into the Inland Sea to receive the Japanese surrender. He was in the American flagship, USS *Missouri*, at the surrender ceremony on 2 September 1945.

After returning home Le Fanu served from 1946 to 1949 on the experimental staff at *Excellent* and during 1948 was commander of the cruiser *Superb*. He was promoted to captain on 30 June 1949 and was appointed a Naval Assistant at the Admiralty, where his old chief in the Home Fleet, Lord Fraser of North Cape [95], was First Sea Lord. From October 1951 to May 1952 he commanded the frigate *Relentless* as Captain (F) of the Third Training Squadron, based at Londonderry, specializing in anti-submarine warfare. He returned to the Admiralty in 1952 to the department of the Chief Scientist, to examine the naval consequences of the emergence of nuclear weapons. From there he spent most of 1953 at the Imperial Defence College, before commanding the boys' training establishment *Ganges* at Harwich from December 1954 to 1957. He was then appointed flag captain to the Flag Officer, Aircraft Carriers, in the aircraft carrier *Eagle*, from where he was promoted to rear-admiral on 7 July 1958.

Le Fanu became Director-General of the Weapons Department at the Admiralty in July 1958. He served as second-in-command, Far East station, with his flag in the aircraft carrier *Hermes* from July 1960 to 1961, when he was appointed Third Sea Lord and Controller of the Navy, with promotion to vice-admiral on 25 October 1961. As the member responsible for shipbuilding and design, he endorsed a new type of general-purpose frigate, the highly successful *Leander* class. He was awarded the KCB in 1963. On leaving the Admiralty Board of the Navy Department (as the Board of Admiralty had become in 1964), Sir Michael Le Fanu was promoted to admiral on 29 September 1965 and appointed Joint Service C-in-C, Middle East, based at Aden, in December 1965. In February 1966 the Labour government of the day, led by Harold Wilson, decided to withdraw British forces from the area east of Suez. Aden itself was the scene of increasingly violent nationalist demands for independence and was evacuated by the British under Le Fanu's command on 26 November 1967.

Le Fanu returned to the Admiralty Board as First Sea Lord in August 1968. In response to a worsening economic situation, Denis Healey, the Secretary of State for Defence, brought forward to 1971–72 the dates of closing the Far East station and scrapping the remaining aircraft carriers. Le Fanu was therefore faced with the task of reshaping the Navy as a force intended to operate primarily in an anti-submarine role in the North Atlantic. He did much to keep up the morale of his Service in a period of disillusion and diminishing strength, and toured extensively, including a visit to ships exercising off Malaysia. A flamboyant and extrovert character, he mixed freely and informally with all ranks and became one of the best-loved First Sea Lords of his time. Despite the opinion of the Minister for the Navy, David Owen, that the future of the Navy lay under the water, he laid the foundations of a fleet that, although including nuclear-powered ballistic missile submarines, would have a mix of escort vessels, amphibious warfare ships and light carriers with anti-submarine helicopters and Sea Harrier fighters to counter Soviet long-range maritime aircraft. A man of ready wit, who delighted in word-play, he dubbed himself "Dry Ginger" after presiding over the abolition of the Navy's time-honoured daily rum issue. When it became the Navy's turn to fill the office of Chief of Defence Staff in October 1970, Le Fanu was nominated, but he was already suffering from leukaemia and being given frequent blood transfusions. He retired on medical grounds with promotion to admiral of the fleet on 3 July 1970 and died in London on 28 November 1970.

LEWIN
Sir TERENCE THORNTON, Baron Lewin, KG, GCB, LVO, DSC (1920–1999) [110]

Terry Lewin, the younger son in a family of two children of an executive officer in the Office of Works, was born at Dover, Kent, on 19 November 1920 and was educated at The Judd School, Tonbridge. He joined the Navy in January 1939 by the recently enlarged Special Entry scheme and, after completing his initial cadet course in the training cruiser *Frobisher*, went to sea in May 1939 in the training cruiser *Vindictive*. On the outbreak of the Second World War in September 1939 he was appointed a midshipman in the cruiser *Belfast* in the Home Fleet. After *Belfast* was disabled by a German mine on 21 November 1939 he was transferred to the battleship *Valiant*. Lewin served as a midshipman in this ship successively in the Home Fleet during the Norwegian campaign in May 1940, in Force H in the bombardment of the French fleet at Mers-el-Kebir (3 July 1940) and in the Mediterranean Fleet, where he came under Italian air attack. He returned home to become an acting sub-lieutenant at the beginning of his promotion courses in April 1941 and joined the destroyer *Highlander* on 4 October 1941. He took part in the battle of the Atlantic on convoy escort duties, but in November 1941 was sent to hospital with diphtheria. After recovering, he was appointed as gunnery control officer in the destroyer *Ashanti* in January 1942. Between March and June 1942 *Ashanti* escorted three Arctic convoys to Northern Russia. Lewin was mentioned in despatches and was later promoted to lieutenant with seniority from 1 July 1942.

During August 1942 *Ashanti* took part in a major convoy action to reinforce Malta, in which Lewin was at his station in the gunnery control tower for a total of 60 hours. This operation, together with his experience in other convoys, left him with a lasting admiration of the Merchant Service. In September, again escorting Arctic convoys, *Ashanti* took in tow her torpedoed sister-ship *Somali* to which he led a boat-party in an attempt to re-establish electrical power. After working for several hours in bitterly cold water, he succeeded, but the weather deteriorated and *Somali* broke up and sank after a tow of 420 miles. Lewin was awarded the DSC for his part in rescuing survivors.

In January 1943 he became first lieutenant of *Ashanti*, in which he took part in the Allied landings in North Africa in November 1942, in further Arctic convoys in 1943, and in the seaward defence of the Allied landings in Normandy (6 June 1944). He was mentioned in despatches a second time for a night action in which his flotilla sank a German destroyer (9 June 1944) and a third time when it intercepted a German convoy off St Nazaire (5 August 1944). In February 1944 he married Jane Branch-Evans, a Leading Wren in the Women's Royal Naval Service and the daughter of the rector of St Lawrence's church, Sigglesthorne, East Yorkshire. They later had a family of two sons and a daughter.

At the end of 1944, with *Ashanti* in refit, Lewin decided to become a gunnery specialist and in January 1945 joined the gunnery school *Excellent* for the Long Gunnery Course. He was appointed to the permanent staff in May 1945, shortly before the end of the war in Europe, and in April 1946 joined the light cruiser *Bellona* as gunnery officer. During 1947 he qualified on the Advanced Gunnery Course at the Royal Naval College, Greenwich, and in December 1947 returned to the permanent staff at *Excellent*. He was promoted to lieutenant-commander on 1 July 1949 and was appointed gunnery officer of the First Destroyer Flotilla in the Mediterranean Fleet, in the flotilla leader *Chequers*. Lewin returned to the staff of *Excellent* in January 1952, with promotion to commander on 31 December 1952. In September 1953 he was appointed to the staff of the Second Sea Lord at the Admiralty and in October 1955 was given command of the destroyer *Corunna*, in which he served successively in the Home and Mediterranean Fleets.

From there Lewin became in April 1957 commander of the royal yacht *Britannia*, an appointment which he initially sought to decline, but from which he came to have a regard for the high standards applied in the ship. When significant reductions were made in the defence establishment in 1957 Lewin applied for voluntary redundancy, but there were more volunteers than were needed and his request was refused. He was promoted to captain on 30 June 1958, but continued to wear the rank of a commander until November 1958, when he was succeeded in *Britannia* and joined the Admiralty as Assistant Director in the Tactical Ship Requirements and Staff Duties Division. There he fully supported a proposal by the head of the Weapon Equipment Priority section, Captain Peter Hill-Norton [107], that this should be merged with the Tactical and Staff Duties Directorate, and became Assistant Director in the new Tactical and Weapons Policy Division when this was set up in 1960. During 1961 he attended the Imperial Defence College, London.

In December 1961 Lewin was appointed Captain (F) of the Seventeenth Frigate Squadron, the Dartmouth training squadron, successively in the frigates *Urchin* and *Tenby*. He returned to the Admiralty as Director of Tactical and Weapons Policy in December 1963 and was serving there when the Admiralty became the Navy Department on the establishment of a unified Ministry of Defence in 1964. In May 1966 he was given command of the aircraft carrier *Hermes*. He served in the North-Western Approaches, the Mediterranean and the Indian Ocean, before returning home in *Hermes* via the Cape of Good Hope in September 1967 and being promoted to rear-admiral on 7 January 1968.

In January 1968 Lewin became Assistant Chief of the Naval Staff (Policy). His appointment coincided with the decision of the Labour Cabinet of the day that, in a worsening economic situation, British defence policy would be based exclusively on the NATO alliance and that the date of withdrawal from the Far East and de-commissioning the Navy's aircraft carriers would be brought forward to 1971–72. In consequence, he was tasked with reducing the Navy's training and support structure. Following his recommendations, many shore establishments, including the Royal Dockyard at Chatham and the torpedo school *Vernon* were eventually closed, and others, including the Admiralty itself, were subjected to reform and rationalization. He returned to sea in August 1969 as second-in-command of the Far East Fleet, with his flag in the destroyer *London*. During 1970 he flew his flag in the cruiser *Blake* and, when she broke down, in the guided missile destroyer *Fife*, the assault ship *Fearless*, the frigate

Charybdis and the Royal Fleet Auxiliaries *Tarbat Ness* and *Olmeda*. He was promoted to vice-admiral on 7 October 1970.

In January 1971 Lewin was appointed Vice-Chief of the Naval Staff. Among his achievements in this post were an agreement with the Royal Air Force on the concept of a carrier-borne version of the Harrier Vertical Take-Off and Landing aircraft (the Sea Harrier); the introduction of annual Group Deployments of five or six warships out of the NATO area, in place of the single ships permanently on station; and increased provision for the maritime defence of British oil installations in the North Sea. In 1973 he was awarded the KCB.

Sir Terence Lewin was promoted to admiral on 1 December 1973, with appointment as C-in-C, Fleet, and NATO Allied C-in-C, Channel (CINCHAN), and Eastern Atlantic Area (CINCEASTLANT). In November 1975 he became C-in-C, Naval Home Command, responsible for the Navy's shore-based training and support systems in the United Kingdom. As such, he pressed on with the implementation of his previous recommendations for closures and rationalization. He also implemented proposals for a Naval Social Service, with trained social workers to replace the long-established Naval Family Welfare organization. With the abolition of the post of Admiral Commanding Reserves, Lewin became responsible for the Royal Naval Reserve, the Royal Naval Auxiliary Service and the Sea Cadet Corps. In a characteristic morale-boosting gesture, he wrote to the commanding officer of every Reserve, Auxiliary and Sea Cadet unit and to the chairmen of the Sea Cadet unit management committees, and took care to attend as many of their activities as he could. On his last day in this appointment he presented his wife with her medals for war service in the WRNS.

Lewin was appointed First Sea Lord in March 1977. He himself described his time in this office as "the dullest I ever had in the Navy". His problems included an exodus of trained personnel following the imposition of pay restraint on public sector employees, reflected in civil society by the "Winter of Discontent" that led to the fall of James Callaghan's Labour administration in May 1979. The new Conservative Cabinet, led by Margaret Thatcher, began by improving the pay of the Armed Services, but soon called for savings in other areas. Lewin became Chief of the Defence Staff in September 1979. He continued to argue that the British nuclear deterrent should be provided by the Navy, with Trident ballistic missiles carried in submarines. John Nott, appointed Secretary of State for Defence in January 1981, agreed, but ruled that the cost was to be borne exclusively by the Navy. This decision was followed by sweeping naval reductions ordered in June 1981 in response to Prime Ministerial demands for "value for money". Lewin's acceptance of these made him for a time unpopular with some in his own Service, though he felt that his duty as CDS required him to remain impartial. He also felt that he lacked the resources to provide the Cabinet with the best professional advice and introduced a new system whereby the CDS became the principal military adviser to the Government, rather than simply the chairman of the Chiefs of Staff Committee, bound to represent their collective view.

At the end of March 1982, when there were indications that Argentina might take action against British possessions in the South Atlantic, Lewin was on an official visit to New Zealand. Opinion in Whitehall was that to cut short his visit would be deemed a provocative act, so that it was only after Argentine forces landed in the Falkland Islands on 1–2 April 1982 that he began his return. He arrived home to find that the Chief of the Naval Staff, Sir Henry Leach [111], had assured the Prime Minister that the islands could be retaken and had already instructed the C-in-C, Fleet, Sir John Fieldhouse [112], to assemble a task force for this purpose. During the campaign Lewin played an important part in the War Cabinet, gaining the confidence of the Prime Minister and giving her his resolute support when losses began to be suffered. Followed the Argentine surrender on 14 June 1982, he was granted a life peerage as Baron Lewin, of Greenwich. Lord Lewin left office in October 1982. In April 1983 he was made a Knight of the Garter, the first officer to be so decorated solely for naval services since Lord Howe [9]. He retired to Ufford, Suffolk, and took part in many naval, charitable and historical activities and spoke widely on naval matters. He died at Ufford on 23 January 1999.

LYONS
Sir ALGERNON McLENNAN, GCB (1833–1908) [51]

Algernon Lyons, the second son of an officer in the East India Company's service, was born in western India at Bombay (Mumbai) on 30 August 1833 and went to school at Twickenham before entering the Navy in 1847. He was appointed to the frigate *Cambrian* in which he served on the East Indies and China station until late in 1850. His uncle, Sir Edmund (later Lord) Lyons, a veteran of the Napoleonic Wars, became second-in-command of the Mediterranean Fleet in 1853 and Algernon Lyons then joined his flagship, the 2nd-rate *Albion*. He was promoted to mate in October 1853 and became lieutenant in the paddle frigate *Firebrand* on 28 June 1854, in which he served at the beginning of the Crimean War in the blockade of the Russian-held Danube estuary. On 8 July 1854, when a landing party entered the river to destroy Russian signal stations, he took command of *Firebrand*'s boats after her commanding officer, Captain Hyde Parker, was killed.

Lyons was mentioned in despatches and given command of *Firebrand*, in which he served at the bombardment of Sevastopol on 17 October 1854, towing *Albion* into action and then out again after she was set on fire by Russian coastal artillery. In December 1854, when Sir Edmund Lyons became C-in-C of the Mediterranean Fleet, he appointed his nephew as his flag lieutenant in the flagship, the 1st-rate *Royal Albert*. During October 1855 Lyons took part in the operations at Kerch in the eastern Crimea in

May 1855, and Kinburn (Pokrovskiy), guarding the strategically important Russian port of Ochakov in the Dnepr estuary (Dneprovskiy Liman). He remained his uncle's flag lieutenant after the war ended in 1856 and was made a commander by Sir Edmund Lyons on 9 August 1858, in one of the "haul-down promotions" which, at that period, C-in-C's were authorized to make on completion of their appointment. Lyons served on the North America station from 1861 to 1862 in command of the sloop *Racer*. This included the opening period of the American Civil War, with Anglo-American relations strained by British merchantmen claiming the protection of the Royal Navy while they ran the United States Navy's blockade of Confederate ports. He was promoted to captain on 1 December 1862, and went onto half-pay until appointed to the corvette *Charybdis* on the Pacific station, where he served from January 1867 to 1871. In October 1872 he became captain of the frigate *Immortalité* and second-in-command of a detached squadron. Between 1875 and 1877 he was commodore and senior officer at Jamaica. In April 1878 Lyons was appointed to the armoured turret ship *Monarch* in the Mediterranean and was deployed with the fleet to Constantinople (Istanbul) when there was a risk of war with Russia over the Turkish question. He left his ship on promotion to rear-admiral on 26 September 1878. In 1879 he married Louisa, daughter and heiress of Thomas Penrice, Esquire, of Kilvrough Park, Glamorganshire, with whom he later had two sons and two daughters.

From December 1881 until his promotion to vice-admiral on 27 October 1884 Lyons was C-in-C, Pacific, with his flag in the armoured ship *Swiftsure*. He was C-in-C, North America and West Indies, with his flag in the armoured ship *Bellerophon*, from September 1886 until promoted to admiral on 15 December 1888. He was awarded the KCB in 1889. Sir Algernon Lyons was C-in-C, Plymouth, from June 1893 to 23 August 1897, when he became an admiral of the fleet. He retired on 30 August 1903 and died at his home in Glamorganshire on 9 February 1908.

McGRIGOR
Sir RHODERICK ROBERT, GCB, DSO (1893–1959) [100]

"The Wee McGrigor", as he was commonly known in allusion to his diminutive stature, was born in York on 12 April 1893, the only son of an officer (later a brigadier-general) in the King's Royal Rifle Corps. After spending his childhood in South Africa he attended the Royal Naval Colleges at Osborne and Dartmouth and passed out at the head of his intake. He was promoted to midshipman on 15 September 1910 and was appointed to the battleship *Formidable* in the Atlantic Fleet in April 1911. He joined the battleship *Africa* in the Home Fleet in May 1912, from which he became an acting sub-lieutenant on 15 January 1913, at the beginning of his promotion courses. In October 1913 McGrigor was appointed to the battleship *Agamemnon* in the Home Fleet and in March 1913 joined the destroyer *Foxhound* in the Mediterranean Fleet. After the outbreak of the First World War in August 1914 he was promoted to lieutenant on 15 October 1914 and served in the Dardanelles campaign of 1915. He was subsequently appointed to the battleship *Malaya* in the Grand Fleet, in which he took part in the battle of Jutland (31 May–1 June 1916).

After the conclusion of hostilities in November 1918 McGrigor served in the light cruiser *Highflyer* from June 1919 to 1921. He was promoted to lieutenant-commander on 15 October 1922 and in September 1923 went to the Royal Naval Staff College, Greenwich, for the War Staff Course. After qualifying as a torpedo specialist, he was appointed flotilla torpedo officer in *Montrose*, leader of the First Destroyer Flotilla in the Mediterranean Fleet, in February 1925. He was promoted to commander on 31 December 1927 and joined the staff of the Tactical School at Portsmouth. In August 1930 he became Staff Officer (Operations) to the C-in-C, Home Fleet, with his flag in the battleship *Nelson*. McGrigor married in 1931 the widow of a major in the Grenadier Guards. They later adopted twin boys. Between August 1932 and January 1933 he commanded the destroyer *Versatile* in the Home Fleet. He was promoted to captain on 31 December 1933 and joined the Training and Staff Duties Division at the Admiralty in August 1934. He returned to sea in September 1936 as Captain (Destroyers) of the Fourth Destroyer Flotilla in the Home Fleet, successively in the flotilla leaders *Campbell* and *Kempenfeldt*. McGrigor was promoted to commodore, second class, on 26 August 1938, and was appointed chief of staff to the C-in-C, China station, in the flagship *Kent*, where he was serving on the outbreak of the Second World War in September 1939.

McGrigor returned home late in 1940 to become flag captain of the battle-cruiser *Renown*, flagship of Vice-Admiral Sir James Somerville [93], commanding Force H, based at Gibraltar. He took part in several actions in the Eastern Atlantic and Western Mediterranean, including the bombardment of Genoa (9 February 1941) and the sinking of the German battleship *Bismarck* (26–27 May 1941) and was commended for his staff work and his ship-handling in combat. After being promoted to rear-admiral on 8 July 1941 he was appointed to the Admiralty as Assistant Chief of the Naval Staff (Weapons). Eighteen months later McGrigor was given command of an amphibious force in the Mediterranean, and took part in the capture of the island of Pantelleria (11–12 June 1943) and the invasion of Sicily (10 July 1943), for which he was awarded the DSO. After serving as Flag Officer, Sicily, he became Allied naval commander, Southern Italy, and chief Allied liaison officer to the Italian Navy, which had become a co-belligerent force.

In March 1944 McGrigor was given command of the First Cruiser Squadron in the Home Fleet, with his flag successively in the cruisers *Kent* and *Norfolk*. He remained there until the end of the war in 1945, taking part in several operations off the coast of Norway and escorting Arctic convoys to the Soviet Union. He was appointed second-in-command of the Home Fleet on 8 April 1945 and promoted to vice-admiral on 15 April 1945, with the award of the KCB. Sir Rhoderick McGrigor was appointed to the Board of Admiralty as Vice-Chief of the Naval Staff in October 1945, with the primary task of implementing the Navy's transition to post-war conditions. He was promoted to admiral on 2 September 1948 and served from January 1949 to January 1950 as C-in-C, Home Fleet, with his flag in the battleship *Duke of York*. Between March 1950 and October 1951 he was C-in-C, Plymouth.

In December 1951 McGrigor became First Sea Lord in the Board headed by J P L Thomas in Winston Churchill's second administration. In the face of demands for post-war defence economies, and an entirely new strategic situation arising from the emergence of nuclear weapons, McGrigor pressed strongly for a powerful, balanced fleet. He argued that the Navy would continue to play an essential part both in limited conventional conflicts and in the period of "broken-backed warfare" that was expected to follow any nuclear exchange. His major achievement was a successful defence of the fleet carrier against those who believed that this type of ship was no longer required. He revived the title Fleet Air Arm (renamed Naval Aviation in 1946) and gained Cabinet approval for the provision of new naval aircraft, but, as an economy measure, disbanded the Royal Naval Volunteer Reserve air squadrons.

A product of the long-established system of naval officers beginning their careers as thirteen-year-old cadets, McGrigor would have been happy to see this revived, but accepted that in the changed social and political circumstances of the day, it was no longer feasible. He therefore supported his colleagues in the decision to raise the age of cadet entry to eighteen, in line with the other two Armed Services. He was promoted to admiral of the fleet on 1 May 1953 and was succeeded as First Sea Lord by Lord Mountbatten [102] in April 1955. He had laid the foundations of much for which Mountbatten would subsequently claim credit and had begun to move the fleet towards the replacement of guns by guided missiles and the adoption of gas turbine engines for ship propulsion. McGrigor retired to his home in the Scottish Highlands, and died at Aberdeen, after surgery, on 3 December 1959.

MADDEN
Sir CHARLES EDWARD, 1st Baronet, GCB, OM, GCVO, KCMG (1862–1935) [75]

Charles Madden, the second son of an officer in the 4th Foot (The King's Own), was born at Brompton, Chatham, Kent, on 5 September 1862. His parents, both of whom came from the Anglo-Irish Protestant squirearchy, decided that he should embark on a career in the Navy, which he joined as a cadet in the training ship *Britannia* in 1875. He was appointed a midshipman on 22 October 1877 in the battleship *Alexandra*, flagship of the C-in-C, Mediterranean, and served in the fleet sent to Constantinople (Istanbul) during the international crisis of February 1878. In 1880 Madden was appointed to the corvette *Ruby* on the East Indies station. He returned home with promotion to sub-lieutenant at the beginning of his promotion courses on 27 October 1881. During the Egyptian campaign of 1882–83 he served at Suez and was mentioned in despatches, followed by appointment in September 1883 to the battleship *Minotaur*, flagship in the Channel Squadron. He was promoted to lieutenant on 27 July 1884 and served in the troopship *Assistance* from November 1884 to September 1895. Madden then decided to specialize in torpedo warfare and attended the torpedo school *Vernon* at Portsmouth, as a student from 1884 to 1885 and as member of the staff from 1885 to 1887. He then served as torpedo lieutenant successively in the cruiser *Raleigh* on the Cape of Good Hope and West Coast of Africa station between March 1888 and September 1891 and the battleship *Royal Sovereign*, flagship of the Channel Squadron between 1892 and 1893.

Madden returned to the staff of *Vernon*, where he was promoted to commander on 30 June 1896 and was subsequently the commander successively of the cruiser *Terrible* and the battleship *Caesar* in the Mediterranean. In 1899 he returned to *Vernon*, where he remained until promoted to captain on 30 June 1901. In 1902 he was appointed flag captain of the armoured cruiser *Good Hope* in a cruiser squadron on the North America and West Indies station. Late in 1903 the new wife of Captain John Jellicoe [68] of the armoured cruiser *Drake* in the same squadron visited her husband at Bermuda, with her youngest sister Constance as her travelling companion. These two ladies were the daughters of the self-made Scottish millionaire and shipping-line owner, Sir Charles Cayzer. A shy and gentle girl (unlike her more forceful two elder sisters), Constance found herself attracted to the flag captain of her brother-in-law's squadron and Madden returned her affection. They married in 1905 and later had two sons and four daughters.

Madden came to the notice of the First Sea Lord, Sir John Fisher [58], who appointed him in December 1904 to the Ship Design Committee, an influential body that recommended the construction of the new *Dreadnought* class of fast, all-big-gun battleships, and the *Invincible* class of battle-cruisers. In February 1905 he became Naval Assistant to Captain Henry Jackson [70] (himself a torpedo specialist), Third Sea Lord and Controller of the Navy. From December 1905 to August 1907 he was Naval Assistant to the First Sea Lord and was then given command of the new *Dreadnought* as flag captain and chief of staff to the C-in-C, Home Fleet. In December 1908 he became Naval Private Secretary to the First Lord of the Admiralty. Madden joined the Board as Fourth Sea Lord in January 1910 and remained there, with promotion to rear-admiral on

12 April 1911, until December 1911. During 1912 he commanded a division of the Home Fleet, with his flag in the battleship *St Vincent*. He commanded the Third Cruiser Squadron, with his flag in the cruiser *Antrim*, during 1913 and the Second Cruiser Squadron, with his flag in the cruiser *Shannon*, during 1914. He was then selected to become Third Sea Lord, but on the outbreak of the First World War in August 1914 his brother-in-law, Sir John Jellicoe, the newly appointed C-in-C, Grand Fleet, asked for him as his chief of staff.

Madden accordingly joined Jellicoe in the battleship *Iron Duke*, with acting promotion to vice-admiral in June 1915 and the award of the KCB in January 1916. He took part in the battle of Jutland (31 May–1 June 1916) and was confirmed as vice-admiral on 10 June 1916. When Jellicoe left the Grand Fleet in December 1916 Sir Charles Madden became second-in-command to his successor, Sir David Beatty [69], and served under him, with his flag successively in the battleships *Marlborough* and *Revenge*, until the Grand Fleet was dispersed in April 1919. He was promoted to admiral in February 1919 and was given command of the Atlantic Fleet that took the place of the Grand Fleet at Scapa Flow, with his flag in the battleship *Queen Elizabeth*. He retained this command until August 1922, with the award of a baronetcy in 1919, and was exonerated from any blame when the German High Seas Fleet, interned at Scapa Flow, scuttled itself on 21 June 1919.

Madden was promoted to admiral of the fleet on 31 July 1924. He was recalled to the Admiralty as First Sea Lord in succession to Beatty in July 1927. This appointment was greeted with mixed opinions in the Fleet, but had the merit of neutrality between the rival supporters of Beatty and Jellicoe in the controversy over their actions at Jutland, as Madden had served under both. In 1929 William (later Viscount) Bridgeman, First Lord of the Admiralty in Stanley Baldwin's second Cabinet, arranged a special Order in Council allowing Madden to remain on the active list as a supernumerary admiral of the fleet for as long as he was First Sea Lord. This was to avoid the turbulence of making a new appointment in the approach to a General Election. The new Labour Cabinet that came into office in 1929 was determined to avoid a naval arms race with the United States and Madden was therefore obliged to accept parity in cruisers with the United States Navy at a figure of fifty. He defended this outcome on the grounds that he only had forty-eight in any case, and also felt that, having given his best professional advice, it was his duty to implement the policy of the elected government of the day. He retired on 30 July 1930 and was succeeded by Sir Frederick Field [81], whom he recommended in preference to Sir Osmond Brock [79] and Sir Roger Keyes [80]. Sir Charles Madden died in London on 5 June 1935. His elder son, who followed him into the Royal Navy, succeeded him in his baronetcy. After creditable service during the Second World War, the second baronet ended his naval career in 1965 as C-in-C, Home Fleet and died in April 2001.

MARTIN
Sir GEORGE, GCB, GCMG (1764–1847) [18]

George Martin, born in 1764, was the third and youngest son of Captain William Martin, Royal Navy, and his wife Arabella, daughter of Sir William Rowley [6], the sister of one future rear-admiral and the aunt of two more. Captain Martin died in 1766 and his widow married Colonel Gibbs, the proprietor of Horsley Park, East Horsley, Surrey. George Martin was carried on the books of the yacht *Mary* from December 1771 to April 1774. After the beginning of the American War of Independence he became a captain's servant in the 3rd-rate *Monarch*, commanded by his uncle, the then Captain Joshua Rowley, on 20 November 1776. He served with his uncle at the battle of Ushant (27 July 1778) as a midshipman and subsequently went in the 3rd-rate *Suffolk* to the West Indies, where he took part in four fleet actions, one off Grenada (6 July 1779) and three off Martinique (April–May 1780). Martin then served in the sloops *Camelion, Rover* and *Alert,* prior to becoming lieutenant in the 3rd-rate *Russell* on 16 July 1780. He was next appointed to the 2nd-rate *Princess Royal* and then to the 5th-rate *Ulysses* and finally the 2nd-rate *Sandwich,* before being made commander of the sloop *Tobago* on 9 March 1782, through the patronage of his uncle, who was also on the West Indies station. On 17 March 1783 he became captain of the 4th-rate *Preston.* After the conclusion of the war Martin returned to the United Kingdom and went onto half-pay until given command of the 6th-rate *Porcupine,* on the coast of Ireland, from July 1789 to August 1792.

Following the outbreak of war with Revolutionary France in February 1793 Martin was appointed to command of the 5th-rate *Magicienne* and sent to the West Indies. In 1795, back in European waters, he commanded the 3rd-rate *Irresistible* at the battle of St Vincent (14 February 1795), to which Commodore Horatio Nelson shifted his broad pendant after his own ship *Captain* was disabled. Together with the captains of the other ships present, Martin was awarded a gold medal in appreciation of his part in the victory. On 26 April 1795, in company with the 5th-rate *Emerald,* he captured the Spanish frigates *Ninfa* and *Santa Elena* at Conil Bay, near Cape Trafalgar. From 1798 to 1802 he was in the Mediterranean as captain of the 3rd-rate *Northumberland* and took several prizes, included the French frigate *Diane* and 74-gun ship *Généraux.* In September 1800, as senior officer of the blockading squadron, he was the British signatory to the surrender of Malta, where the French garrison of Valetta, down to its last rat, had withstood a two-year siege. In March 1801 he was with the fleet at the landing of a British army in Egypt, leading to the French defeat at the battle of Alexandria (21 March 1801). After the Treaty of Amiens brought peace with France in March 1802 the usual post-war reductions in the fleet placed Martin on half-pay in September 1802.

With the renewal of hostilities in May 1803 (partly caused by the British refusal to give up Malta), Martin served in the Channel in command successively of the 3rd-rate *Colossus* during 1803 and the 2nd-rates *Glory* and *Barfleur* during 1804. In April 1804 he married the younger daughter of the well-connected Captain William Bentinck, Royal Navy. Her elder sister was married to Rear-Admiral James Whitshed [17]. In *Barfleur* Martin took part in the indecisive battle of Finisterre (22 July 1805) against Villeneuve's fleet on its return from the West Indies. Martin was promoted to be rear-admiral of the Blue on 9 November 1805. In 1806 he was second-in-command at Portsmouth. After the death of his young wife he returned to sea duty in 1807, blockading Cadiz, with his flag in the 3rd-rate *Cumberland*. From there he joined the Mediterranean Fleet with his flag successively in the 3rd-rate *Montagu*, the 2nd-rate *Queen* and the 3rd-rate *Canopus*. Martin became rear-admiral of the White on 28 April 1808. In June 1809 he carried Lieutenant General Sir John Stuart's army from Sicily to land on the islands of Ischia and Procida in the Bay of Naples. In October 1809, detached with the eight fastest ships of the line from the main fleet, he pursued a squadron of five French ships to Cette (Sete) in the Gulf of Lyons, driving two ashore and two into harbour. He was made rear-admiral of the Red on 25 October 1809 and vice-admiral of the Blue on 31 July 1810.

In the summer of 1810, having taken Stuart's army back to Sicily, Martin received his seventh mention in despatches and was awarded a knighthood from the King of Naples. On 12 August 1812 he became a vice-admiral of the White. From 1812 to 1814, during the last two years of the Peninsular War, he was C-in-C, Lisbon, with his flag successively in the 3rd-rate *Impétueux*, the 6th-rate *Sabrina* and the 3rd-rate *Rodney*. In June 1814, when the fleet had returned to Portsmouth after the fall of Napoleon, Martin was awarded a knighthood and became a vice-admiral of the Red. Sir George Martin married again in 1814, this time to the daughter of William Locke, of Norbury Park, Surrey. In January 1815, when the Order of the Bath was reorganized, he was made a KCB. He became an admiral of the Blue on 19 July 1821 and was C-in-C, Portsmouth, from March 1824 to April 1827. He became an admiral of the White on 22 July 1830, admiral of the Red on 10 January 1837 and admiral of the fleet on 9 November 1846. Martin died, without offspring, in his house at Berkeley Square, London, on 28 July 1847.

MARTIN
Sir THOMAS BYAM, GCB (1773–1854) [19]

Thomas Martin, the third son of Captain Sir Henry Martin, a future naval commissioner at Portsmouth and later Comptroller of the Navy and Member of Parliament for Southampton, was born on 25 July 1773. He was entered on the books of several warships between 1781 and 1784, including the *Foudroyant*, under Captain John Jervis [12], but did not actually report for duty until August 1785, when he joined the Royal Naval

Academy at Portsmouth. He first went to sea in April 1786, as captain's servant in the 6th-rate *Pegasus*, commanded by Prince William, the future William IV [11], on the North America and West Indies station. When the crew of *Pegasus* was turned over to the 5th-rate *Andromeda* in March 1788, Martin was appointed as midshipman and served under Prince William in the Channel and on the North America and West Indies station, until the prince was recalled home with his ship early in 1789. Martin subsequently served in the Channel in the 3rd-rate *Colossus*, the 5th-rate *Southampton*, the 2nd-rate *Barfleur* and the 1st-rate *Royal George*, prior to becoming a lieutenant in 3rd-rate *Canada* on 22 October 1790. During the next two years he remained in the Channel, successively in the 5th-rates *Inconstant* and *Juno*.

After the outbreak of war with Revolutionary France in February 1793 Martin was appointed commander of the 6th-rate *Tisiphone* and sent to the Mediterranean, where he took part in operations off Toulon. On 5 November 1793 he was appointed captain of the 5th-rate *Modeste*, followed by command of the 5th-rate *Artois*, in which he served at the taking of Bastia, Corsica, in 1794. His next command was the 5th-rate *Santa Margarita*, based on the coast of Ireland, from where he captured the French corvette *Jean Bart* and the privateers *Buonaparte*, *Vengeur* and *Tamise*. In December 1796, commanding the 5th-rate *Tamar*, he went to the West Indies. Martin was at the unsuccessful British attempt to seize the Spanish colony of Puerto Rico in early 1797, but spent the following five months more profitably by making prizes of a total of nine privateers. During 1798 he commanded the 3rd-rate *Dictator* and, after returning home, was appointed to the 5th-rate *Fisguard* in which, in a single-ship duel off Brest, he captured the French frigate *Immortalité* (20 October 1798). He remained in *Fisguard*, from which he commanded a night raid by boats of his squadron up the River Quimper, Finisterre, to destroy three coastal batteries (23 June 1800). His prizes included the French frigate *Vénus*, the corvette *Dragon*, two privateers and four smaller warships. When the Treaty of Amiens brought peace with France in March 1802 the fleet was rapidly reduced and Martin went on half-pay.

With the renewal of hostilities in May 1803 Martin was given command of the 3rd-rate *Impétueux* in the Channel, where he served until December 1805. During 1807 he returned to the Channel in command of the 2nd-rate *Prince of Wales*. In 1808, in the 3rd-rate *Implacable*, he was with the force sent to the Baltic to support Sweden against Russia, France's new ally in the north. In an encounter between the Russian and Swedish fleets (26 August 1808) he was credited with the destruction of the Russian 74-gun ship *Vsevolod* and awarded a Swedish knighthood. In 1809 he captured nine merchantmen in the Gulf of Narva and gained his fifth mention in despatches. On 1 August 1811 Martin was made a rear-admiral of the Blue. In 1812, with Russia once again a British ally, he returned to the Baltic, with his flag in the 3rd-rate *Aboukir* and supported the Russians in the defence of Riga against a French attack. From 1812 to 1814 he was second-in-command at Plymouth, with his flag at different times in the 3rd-rates *Prince Frederick* and *Ganges*, the 2nd-rate *Impregnable*, the 5th-rate *Creole* (off the Spanish coast) and the 4th-rate *Akbar* (off the Scheldt estuary). He was promoted to rear-admiral of the White on 12 August 1812, rear-admiral of the Red on 4 June 1814, with the award of a knighthood the same year, and the KCB in January 1815, when the Order of the Bath was reorganized.

Sir Thomas Martin was Deputy Comptroller of the Navy from January 1815 to February 1816 and Comptroller from then until November 1831, shortly before the duties of the Navy Board were taken over by a reformed Admiralty. At the Navy Board he had to deal with the reductions that followed the end of the Napoleonic Wars in 1815, but was also responsible for a new generation of large, fast warships that formed the nucleus of the Navy's last sailing fleet. He entered Parliament reluctantly, only because this was part of the Comptroller's duties as the officer responsible for shipbuilding and dockyards, and sat as a Member for Plymouth from 1818 until the reform of Parliament in 1832. He became vice-admiral of the Blue on 12 August 1819, of the White on 19 July 1821 and of the Red on 27 May 1825, followed by the award of the GCB in March 1830. He married Catherine Fanshawe, daughter of the Resident Commissioner of Plymouth Dockyard, sister of one future admiral and sister-in-law of three more. They had a family of three daughters and three sons, of whom two became captains in the Navy and the third became a lieutenant colonel in the Army.

Martin enjoyed the support of his old captain, William IV, both as Lord High Admiral and as sovereign, but was not always in accord with Sir George Cockburn [20], who was the senior naval member of the Board of Admiralty, but junior to Martin as a flag officer. Martin declined to give his parliamentary support to the new Whig administration that came into office in November 1830 and was dismissed from the Navy Board in October 1831. In the same year he was twice offered command of the Mediterranean Fleet, but declined on the grounds of his wife's ill-health. He became an admiral of the Blue on 22 July 1830, admiral of the White on 10 January 1837, admiral of the Red on 23 November 1837 and admiral of the fleet on 30 October 1849. On the outbreak of the Crimean War in March 1854 he contributed to the planning of the naval campaign in the Baltic. Sir Thomas Martin died at Portsmouth on 21 October 1854.

MAY
Sir WILLIAM HENRY, GCB, GCVO (1849–1930) [65]

Henry May, the third son in a family of ten children, was born in Liscard, Cheshire, on 31 July 1849. His ancestors had for many generations lived in the Netherlands and, at the end of the Napoleonic wars, his grandfather had been simultaneously a captain in the Royal Navy and an admiral in the Royal Netherlands Navy. May's father, a businessman, settled in Liverpool, where he served as the Netherlands consul. Henry May was educated at the Royal Institution School, Liverpool, and Eastman's Naval Academy, Southsea, Hampshire, from which he entered the training ship *Britannia* in 1863. From there he joined the 1st-rate *Victoria*, flagship of the Mediterranean Fleet, in 1864, and transferred as a midshipman to the frigate *Liffey* in 1867. He was promoted to sub-lieutenant on 29 March 1869. He then served for a short time in the battleship *Hercules* before being appointed in June 1871 to the royal yacht *Victoria and Albert*, where he remained until promoted lieutenant on 7 September 1871. In April 1872 he rejoined *Hercules* in the Channel Squadron from where he went to the gunnery school *Excellent* at Portsmouth. After qualifying as a gunnery officer he was appointed in September 1874 to the frigate *Newcastle* in a detached squadron at Sheerness. He subsequently volunteered to join the sloop *Alert*, in which he served as navigating officer during an Arctic exploration in 1875–76. In 1878 he married Kinbarra Marrow, the daughter of a merchant, and later had a family of two sons. From 1877 to 1880 he was at Portsmouth in the torpedo school *Vernon*, followed by a few months in the frigate *Inconstant*. May was promoted to commander on 9 March 1881 and from then until 1884 was commanding officer of the torpedo-ram *Polyphemus*. From 1884 until his promotion to captain on 9 May 1887 he was second-in-command of *Victoria and Albert*.

In March 1888 May became flag captain to Sir Nowell Salmon [53], C-in-C on the China station, in the armoured cruiser *Impérieuse*. On his voyage out, complying with secret orders from the Admiralty, he established British authority over Christmas Island (now an Australian dependency) in the Indian Ocean, and became known as Christmas May. After returning home in 1890 he spent the next two and a half years in a series of appointments as naval attaché in the British embassies at Berlin, Paris and St Petersburg. In 1893 he became Assistant Director of Torpedoes at the Admiralty, from where in January 1895 he was appointed flag captain to the C-in-C, Mediterranean Fleet, in the battleship *Ramillies*. In the first part of 1897 he was once more flag captain to Sir Nowell Salmon, as C-in-C, Portsmouth, and after the Diamond Jubilee Review, was appointed captain of *Excellent* in August 1897. May returned to the Admiralty in January 1901 as Director of Naval Ordnance and Torpedoes, and in April 1901 became Controller of the Navy and third naval lord of the Admiralty. He was promoted to rear-admiral on 28 March 1901 and remained at the Admiralty, with the award of the KCVO in January 1905. Sir Henry May assumed command of the new Atlantic Fleet, based at Gibraltar, in February 1905, with his flag in the battleship *King Edward VII*, and promotion to vice-admiral on 26 June 1905.

May returned to the Admiralty in 1907 as Second Sea Lord. At the end of 1907 the Liberal Chancellor of the Exchequer, Herbert Asquith, looking for resources to fund the old-age pensions that the government had promised to introduce, rejected the Navy Estimates. Fisher, as First Sea Lord, was prepared to accept a reduction in the rate of building, but May led the other two Sea Lords in offering to resign if this was taken too far. A compromise was reached early in 1908, but May was cast out of "the Fishpond" (as Fisher's favourites had become known). He nevertheless shared Fisher's view that all ships in home waters, including the Channel Fleet and the Home Fleet (formed in 1906 by adding a fully manned new squadron at the Nore to the partly-manned reserve fleet), should be under a single operational command. He was promoted to admiral on 5 November 1908 and he was appointed C-in-C of the newly-enlarged Home Fleet in March 1909, with his flag in the battleship *Dreadnought*.

May remained there until March 1911, after making it clear that he had no wish to succeed Fisher when the latter left the Admiralty in January 1910. Fisher, who had succeeded in installing Sir Arthur Wilson [59] as his successor, nevertheless remained suspicious of May's intentions and believed he was intriguing to become First Sea Lord in succession to Wilson. Winston Churchill, who had become First Lord of the Admiralty in Asquith's Cabinet in October 1911, considered May as a possible successor to Wilson, but was told by Fisher that he was unpopular in the Fleet. May's last command was as C-in-C, Devonport, from April 1911 to 20 March 1913, when he was promoted to admiral of the fleet. During the First World War he was a member of the Committee of Inquiry into the failure of the Dardanelles campaign and was also chairman of the Reconstruction committee, set up to consider likely post-war reductions. He also sat as a member of a sub-committee on fisheries. May retired in 1919 and settled at the Scottish Border town of Coldstream, Berwickshire, where he died on 7 October 1930.

MEADE
RICHARD JAMES, 4th Earl of Clanwilliam, GCB, KCMG (1832–1907) [50]

Richard Meade, by courtesy Lord Gillford, was born on 3 October 1832, the eldest son of the third Earl of Clanwilliam, an Irish peer who had spent some time as a diplomat and been made a baron in the United Kingdom peerage in 1828. Gillford's mother was the daughter of George Herbert, eleventh Earl of Pembroke, and a member of one of Victorian England's most influential families. Gillford was educated at Eton College and joined the Navy in November 1845. After becoming a lieutenant on 15 September 1852 he was appointed in December 1852 to the frigate *Impérieuse*, in which he served in the Baltic in 1854 and 1855 during the Crimean War. In September 1856, together with several other young noblemen, he joined the frigate *Raleigh* under the Honourable Henry Keppel [36]. Hastening to join the Second China War, the ship struck an uncharted rock near Hong Kong and became a total loss, though all the crew was saved. Gillford remained with Keppel and served with him in boat actions in the estuary below Canton (Guangzhou), at Escape Creek (25 May 1857) and Fat-shan

Creek (1 June 1857). In August 1857 he was appointed to the 2nd-rate *Calcutta*, flagship of the C-in-C, East Indies, Sir Michael Seymour, in personal command of the operations on the Chinese coast. Gillford landed with a naval brigade in December 1858, and at the storming of Canton (29 December 1857) was badly wounded in the arm by a heavy musket ball. He was mentioned in despatches and promoted on 26 February 1858 to be commander of the sloop *Hornet*, with which he returned to the United Kingdom.

Gillford was promoted to captain on 22 July 1859 and commanded the corvette *Tribune* in the Pacific from 1862 to 1866. He returned home and married Elizabeth Kennedy, daughter of the Governor of Queensland, and later had with her a family of four sons and four daughters. From 1868 to 1871 he commanded the battleship *Hercules* in the Channel, followed in 1872 by command of the steam reserve at Portsmouth. Gillford became third naval lord at the Admiralty in 1874, when Disraeli's second administration came into office, and remained until the Conservative ministry fell in April 1880. He was promoted to rear-admiral on 31 December 1876 and succeeded his father to become fourth Earl of Clanwilliam on 7 October 1879. Between 1880 and 1882 Lord Clanwilliam (promoted to vice-admiral on 26 July 1881) commanded the Flying Squadron, with his flag in the frigate *Inconstant*, and took his ships around the world under sail. Among them was the corvette *Bacchante*, carrying the future King George V [64] and his elder brother, Prince Albert Victor. Clanwilliam was C-in-C, North America and the West Indies, with his flag in the battleship *Bellerophon* from August 1885 to September 1886, when he vacated the command after being promoted to admiral on 22 June 1886. Clanwilliam's last command was as C-in-C, Portsmouth, from June 1891 to June 1894. He became an admiral of the fleet on 20 February 1895 and retired on 3 October 1902. He died at Badgemore, Henley, Oxfordshire, on 4 August 1907 and was buried in the Herbert family vault at Wilton House, Wiltshire. His eldest son, a former naval officer, predeceased him in 1905 and the earldom passed to Clanwilliam's second son.

MEUX
The Honourable Sir HEDWORTH LAMBTON, GCB, KCVO (1856–1929) [66]

The Honourable Hedworth Lambton, third son of the second Earl of Durham, was born in London on 5 July 1856. He was educated at Cheam School and joined the Navy as a cadet in the training ship *Britannia* in 1870. From there he was appointed in December 1871 to the frigate *Endymion* in the Channel, in which he served until August 1874, when he transferred as a midshipman to the battleship *Agincourt*, flagship of Sir Beauchamp Seymour as C-in-C, Channel Squadron, with Lord Walter Kerr [56] as flag captain. In March 1875 he was appointed to the cruiser *Undaunted*, which was at that time fitting out at Sheerness to be the new flagship on the China station, but left her to begin his promotion courses, with promotion to acting sub-lieutenant on 20 September 1875. Late in 1876 he was appointed to the battleship *Alexandra*, flagship of the C-in-C, Mediterranean Fleet, where he served until promoted to lieutenant on 27 February 1879.

Lambton was re-appointed to *Alexandra* in February 1880 as flag lieutenant to Sir Beauchamp Seymour and was present in her at the British bombardment of Alexandria (11 July 1882) and subsequent operations in response to an Egyptian nationalist uprising led by Colonel Arabi ('Urbi) Pasha. When Seymour (Lord Alcester) left the Mediterranean to join the Admiralty he gave Lambton one of the nominations at that period allotted to a C-in-C on hauling down his flag, so that Lambton became a commander on 10 March 1883. During 1883 he was at the Royal Naval College, Greenwich, before becoming an aide-de-camp on the staff of Earl Spencer, Lord Lieutenant of Ireland. As a wealthy young nobleman, he played a full part in Court and social life, both in London and Dublin. He had a strong interest in the Turf and had already begun to breed his own bloodstock. Spencer left Dublin in 1885 and Lambton returned to sea in July 1886 in command of the sloop *Dolphin* in the Mediterranean. He was appointed to the royal yacht *Osborne* in February 1888, where he remained until promoted to captain on 30 June 1889. Between 1890 and 1894 he was flag captain to the C-in-C, Pacific, Rear-Admiral Charles Hotham [55], in the cruiser *Warspite*.

In August 1892 Spencer became First Lord of the Admiralty in Gladstone's fourth Liberal Cabinet and appointed Lambton as his Naval Private Secretary. When George (later Viscount) Goschen succeeded Spencer after Lord Salisbury took office as Conservative Prime Minister in June 1895 Lambton was retained in post until 1897. He exerted considerable influence on officer appointments and some naval lords of the Admiralty resented his high-handed approach to themselves, who were senior to him in age and rank. He was nevertheless on good terms with Rear-Admiral Sir John Fisher [58] and Lord Charles Beresford, Fisher's future opponent, with both of whom he had served in the Mediterranean Fleet under Seymour. Between 1897 and 1899 Lambton was on the China station in command of the cruiser *Powerful*. On his way home he was ordered to Durban, Natal, at the beginning of the Anglo-Boer South African War. Acting on his own initiative, he embarked a British infantry battalion at Mauritius and took it with him to Durban, where he arrived to learn that the C-in-C, Natal, Sir George White, was in great need of heavy artillery. Lambton then formed a naval brigade from *Powerful* and her intended relief, *Terrible*, equipped with naval 12-pdr and 4.7 inch guns on land carriages improvised by Captain Percy Scott of *Terrible*. This episode later became the theme for the Naval Field Gun Competition, a popular feature of the annual Royal Tournaments until these were discontinued in 1999. He reached Ladysmith just before the town was surrounded by the

Boers, and played an important part in its subsequent defence until it was relieved in February 1900.

At the end of 1900, in the "Khaki election", Lambton was persuaded by his family to stand for Parliament as the Liberal candidate for Newcastle-upon-Tyne, in the heartland of the Earl of Durham's political influence. It was hoped that as a war hero he would capture the patriotic vote, but this went to the governing Unionist (Conservative) party and Lambton was defeated. In April 1901 he was given command of the royal yacht *Victoria and Albert*, followed by appointment as Commodore, Royal Yachts, from July 1901 to April 1903, with promotion to rear-admiral on 3 October 1902. Between June 1903 and June 1904 he was second-in-command to his old friend Lord Charles Beresford in the battleship *Magnificent* in the Channel Fleet. Between November 1904 and December 1906 he commanded the Third Cruiser Squadron in the Mediterranean Fleet, with his flag in the armoured cruiser *Leviathan*. In 1906 he was elected a member of the Jockey Club, the governing body of British horse-racing. By this time Sir Hedworth Lambton had come to share Beresford's opposition to Fisher's naval reforms and also echoed Beresford's reservations about Prince Louis of Battenberg [74] on account of the latter's German origins. Lambton and Beresford had both been intimates of King Edward VII [44], but became estranged from him towards the end of his reign, not least over the King's support for Battenberg and Fisher. Lambton was promoted to vice-admiral on 1 January 1907 and served between January 1908 and April 1910 as C-in-C on the China station, with his flag in the armoured cruiser *King Alfred*.

In 1910 Lambton married the forty-year-old Viscountess Chelsea, whose first husband, second son of the fifth Earl Cadogan, had died two years earlier. The Chelseas had lived on the estate of Theobalds Park, Waltham Cross, Cheshunt, Hertfordshire, owned by Valerie, Lady Meux, the good-looking childless widow of the baronet Sir Henry Meux, the last of a rich brewing dynasty. This lady, of modest origins but determined character, had met her future husband in the bar of one of his own London taverns, the Horseshoe in Tottenham Court Road. She took control of his life and fortune (despite every effort by his family and business partners), kept her own racing stables and entertained lavishly. On the death of her weak-minded and alcoholic husband in 1900, she was left one of the wealthiest women in England. During the Anglo-Boer South African War, she commissioned and paid for a battery of naval 12-pdr guns on field carriages, made by the Elswick Ordnance factory, Tyneside. These guns, manned by men of the 1st Northumberland Volunteer Artillery, played a useful part in the South African campaign and Lambton had visited Lady Meux on his return from the war to express his appreciation of her patriotic gesture. The visit of this heroic scion of a noble house meant much to her, as, because of her background, she was not widely received in Society and had been given little official recognition of her contribution to the war effort. Their friendship, fostered by a common interest in racing, grew and, shortly

173

before her death in December 1910, she made a will leaving him the bulk of her estates and fortune, on condition that he took the name Meux. He did so in September 1911, after being promoted to admiral on 2 March 1911.

In December 1911 Sir Hedworth Meux, now a millionaire, was considered as a possible successor to Sir Arthur Wilson [59] as First Sea Lord, but his playboy image counted against him. A further difficulty was his opposition to Battenberg, the Second Sea Lord, on whom Winston Churchill, then First Lord of the Admiralty, placed great confidence. He was C-in-C, Portsmouth, from July 1912 to February 1916, with promotion to admiral of the fleet on 5 March 1915, and was responsible for the safe passage of the British Expeditionary Force to France on the outbreak of the First World War in August 1914 and the subsequent flow of shipping between Southampton and Le Havre. He also organized a flotilla of inshore vessels and yachts to form a lifeboat service. In August 1914, together with Sir George Callaghan [67], Meux headed an official enquiry into the failure of Rear-Admiral Troubridge to engage the German battlecruiser *Goeben* before she escaped into Turkish waters. They found Troubridge's decision "deplorable and contrary to the tradition of the British Navy", though a court-martial later found that Troubridge had acted in accordance with the orders that he had been given by Churchill and Battenberg. In October 1914, when Battenberg was forced to resign office as First Sea Lord on account of his German origins, George V [64] suggested that Meux (with whom the King was on cordial terms) should be appointed in his place, but Churchill refused to consider it. In January 1916, when Beresford was raised to the peerage, Meux was elected to his seat as Unionist (Conservative) Member for Portsmouth. He spoke in Parliament on naval questions, but was most noted for opposing the government's wartime ban on "treating" in public houses and restrictions on race-meetings.

Meux did not stand in the post-war General Election of 1918, and thereafter devoted himself to his racing stables and had numerous successes on the Turf. Like Valerie Meux before him, he proved a great benefactor to the people of Waltham Cross and Cheshunt and was locally much respected. He enlarged the ballroom of his house at Theobalds Park in order to give grand dances for the benefit of his five stepdaughters, all of whom made brilliant marriages. Sir Hedworth Meux died on 20 September 1929 at his country seat, Danebury, near Stockbridge, Hampshire, and was buried in the new churchyard of St Mary's, Cheshunt. With no children of his own, he left his estates in trust to his widow's young grandson, Ian Hedworth Gilmour, who many years later became a Conservative Cabinet minister and was awarded a life peerage in 1992.

MILFORD HAVEN
MARQUESS OF, see **BATTENBERG [74]**

MILNE
Sir ALEXANDER, 1st Baronet, GCB (1806–1896) [41]

Alexander Milne was born at Musselburgh, near Edinburgh, on 10 November 1806. His father was Captain (later Admiral Sir) David Milne, who served with much distinction during and after the Napoleonic wars. After attending the Royal Naval College, Portsmouth, from 1817 to 1819, Milne joined his father's flagship on the North America station, the 4th-rate *Leander*. He subsequently served in the 6th-rate *Conway*, the 3rd-rate *Ramillies*, the 2nd-rate *Ganges* and the 3rd-rate *Albion*, variously on the South America, Home and West Indies stations, until June 1827, when he became master's mate and acting lieutenant in the brig *Cadmus* on the coast of Brazil. He later recalled serving in this period under a captain who insisted on all his officers wearing white beaver hats, with even midshipmen going aloft being required to wear them. Milne was promoted to lieutenant on 8 September 1827 and, after returning home with *Cadmus*, became a commander on 25 November 1830.

In December 1836 Milne sailed for the West Indies in command of the sloop *Snake*. On anti-slave-trade patrol off the coast of Cuba he captured a Portuguese brigantine carrying 406 slaves in November 1837 and a Spanish schooner carrying another 259 in December 1837. He was promoted to captain on 30 January 1839 and appointed to the 6th-rate *Crocodile*, in which he served on fishery protection duties off Newfoundland and captured another Spanish slaver in the West Indies. In January 1841, while in the 6th-rate *Cleopatra*, he intercepted a Spanish schooner carrying 284 slaves. He then returned to fishery protection duties with *Crocodile* in the Gulf of St Lawrence, prior to returning home in November 1841. Between April 1842 and April 1845 Milne was flag captain to his father as C-in-C, Plymouth, and from October 1846 to December 1847 was flag captain to Sir Charles Ogle [21] as C-in-C, Portsmouth. He then became fourth naval lord in the Board of Admiralty headed by Lord Auckland, in Lord John Russell's first administration. Milne's appointment was a result of Auckland's policy of improving efficiency by bringing officers with recent sea experience onto the Board, irrespective of their political opinions. He proved a capable administrator and remained at the Admiralty until June 1859, serving under four different First Lords in three Liberal and two Conservative governments, at a time of numerous international crises, including the Crimean War of 1854–56. In 1850 he married Euphemia, daughter of Alexander Cochran of Ashkirk, Roxburghshire. They later had two daughters and a son who became a captain in the Navy. Milne became a rear-admiral on 2 January 1858 and a KCB in December 1858.

From 1860 to 1864 Sir Alexander Milne was C-in-C, North America and West Indies. During the American Civil War (April 1861-May 1865) relations between the United States and the United Kingdom came under severe strain, with the threat of hostilities on at least two occasions. He played an important part in avoiding clashes between his ships and those of the United States Navy, despite the provocation offered by British blockade runners carrying contraband to and from Confederate ports, and seeking the protection of the Royal Navy. He was given an extension of his command until the latter part of the war and was promoted to vice-admiral on 13 April 1865. Between June 1866 and December 1868 he was first naval lord in the Board of Admiralty headed by Sir J .Pakington, in the Earl of Derby's third administration. Milne served as C-in-C, Mediterranean, from April 1869 to September 1870, with promotion to admiral on 1 April 1870. At the end of this period he also commanded the Channel Squadron in joint exercises off the coast of Portugal and was asked to comment on the experimental *Captain*. He inspected her on 6 September 1870 and expressed his unease at her low freeboard when under sail in bad weather, a day before the ship was swamped with heavy loss of life. He was re-appointed first naval lord in 1872, where he remained in the Board under G J (later Viscount) Goschen, until the fall of Gladstone's first administration in February 1874, and then under G Ward Hunt in Disraeli's second administration until November 1876. He was then made a baronet and went on half-pay, remaining on the active list where he became an admiral of the fleet on 10 June 1881. Milne died of pneumonia, following a chill, at his family home, Inveresk House, Musselburgh, on 29 December 1896.

MORESBY
Sir FAIRFAX, GCB (1786–1877) [33]

Fairfax Moresby was born in 1786 in Calcutta, Bengal, the son of an East India merchant who retired with his fortune to Stow House, Lichfield, Staffordshire, where the young Moresby grew up. Through the patronage of a young neighbour, Captain William Parker [26], he joined the Navy on 21 December 1799, during the French Revolutionary War, entered on the books of the 2nd-rate *London* as an able seaman. He served in this ship as a midshipman in the unsuccessful British descent on the Spanish naval base of Ferrol (July–August 1800) and was subsequently transferred to the 1st-rate *Royal George*, where he remained until hostilities with France were ended by the Treaty of Amiens (27 March 1802). In March 1802 he joined Parker in the 6th-rate *Alarm* in the Channel Squadron and in November 1802 followed him to the 5th-rate *Amazon*. Moresby was disheartened by Parker's severe discipline and, after being twice disrated to able seaman, deserted while the ship was refitting at Portsmouth. He was found on the road to nearby Cosham by Captain Vansittart of the frigate *Fortunée*, who took pity on him, gave him a Bible to guide his future conduct and made his peace with Captain Parker.

When the war with France was renewed in May 1803 *Amazon* joined the Mediterranean Fleet, where Moresby was on a number of occasions made prize-master of small vessels taken by the ship. While so employed he was himself captured and taken to Malaga. There he was quartered with a rich Spanish merchant, who had a beautiful daughter. The two young people fell in love and, when the time came for Moresby's exchange, the merchant offered him the daughter's hand in marriage and the succession to his business if he remained. Nevertheless, Moresby felt obliged to return to duty and, in the summer of 1805, he was in *Amazon* in Nelson's fleet in the pursuit of the French to the West Indies and back. He was appointed master's mate in the 3rd-rate *Puissant* at Portsmouth in December 1805 and later moved to the 1st-rate *Hibernia*, flagship of the Earl of St Vincent [12], in which he was serving in the blockade of Brest when promoted to lieutenant in the 1st-rate *Ville de Paris* on 10 April 1806. In 1807 he joined the 3rd-rate *Kent*, in the blockade of Rochefort. This ship was subsequently deployed to the Mediterranean, where Moresby took part in a number of boat actions and was mentioned in despatches for his part in cutting out a convoy anchored at Nola, in French-occupied Naples (1 August 1808). He returned home with *Kent* in December 1809, before going back to the Mediterranean in the 3rd-rate *Repulse*.

Moresby was then appointed to the 3rd-rate *Sultan* from which he became acting commander of the sloop *Éclair* on 5 February 1811 and moved to the sloop *Acorn* a few days later. He served in the Adriatic, observing the French and Venetian ships that had survived their defeat at Lissa (13 March 1811) and taking more than sixty prizes. He was superseded in command of *Acorn* on 18 April 1811, when he was confirmed as a commander but placed on half-pay as there were others above him in that rank with a claim to a ship. He was soon given the sloop *Wizard*, in which he remained in the Mediterranean, operating against pirates in the islands of Turkish-ruled Greece, capturing three privateers and joining in the blockade of Toulon. Back in the Adriatic, he led another boat action (18 August 1813) at the entrance of the French-occupied Bocche di Cattaro (the Kotor inlet). In the same month Austria declared war on France. Moresby moved north to support the Austrians and served on shore in October 1813, in command of a heavy battery manned by British seamen at the siege of Trieste. In May 1814, in the distribution of honours after the fall of Napoleon, the Austrians created him a knight of the Order of Maria Theresa.

At Malta, in August 1814, Moresby married Eliza, youngest daughter of John Williams, Esquire, of Bakewell, Derbyshire. They later had three sons and two daughters, of whom the elder married an officer in the Navy. Two of the sons followed Moresby into the Navy. The elder, Commander Fairfax Moresby, was lost with all hands in the brig *Sappho* in the Bass Strait, off Tasmania, early in 1858. The younger became an admiral and, during 1871–74, surveyed the coast of New Guinea, where he named Port Moresby and Fairfax Harbour in honour of his family.

Moresby was promoted to captain on 7 June 1815, shortly before Napoleon's final defeat at Waterloo. He was appointed to the 6th-rate *Menai* in April 1819 and spent the following year as the senior naval officer at the Cape of Good Hope, with responsibility for guarding the approaches to St Helena, where Napoleon was in exile. From 1820 to 1823 he was the senior naval officer at Mauritius, formally transferred from France to the United Kingdom at the end of the Napoleonic Wars. Moresby's main task was the suppression of local slavers, who had carried on their business despite of the abolition of the slave trade in British dominions in 1807. In the course of these duties he cut out the fast schooner *Camilla* with a cargo of 140 slaves from the harbour of Zanzibar, despite her being protected by the local Arab governor. After negotiating anti-slaving treaties with Muscat and Madagascar, he returned home in September 1823.

Moresby had contracted fever while surveying off the Horn of Africa and spent the next five years recovering his health. He did not go back to sea until January 1837, when he was appointed to the 3rd-rate *Pembroke* in which he served in the Mediterranean, undertaking various minor diplomatic missions, until 1840. He was given command of the 3rd-rate *Canopus* in 1845 and was promoted to rear-admiral of the Blue on 20 December 1849. Between 1850 and 1853 he was C-in-C on the Pacific station and landed a naval brigade to protect British commercial interests at Valparaiso during a period of revolution in Chile. He became a rear-admiral of the White on 8 October 1852, a rear-admiral of the Red on 26 May 1854, and was awarded the KCB in 1855. Sir Fairfax Moresby was promoted to vice-admiral of the Blue on 12 November 1862, vice-admiral of the White on 10 September 1857 and vice-admiral of the Red on 12 June 1862, admiral of the Blue on 12 April 1862 and admiral of the White on 12 April 1863. The coloured squadrons used to denote different levels within each flag rank were abolished in 1864. Moresby was promoted to admiral of the fleet on 21 January 1870 and died on 21 January 1877.

MOUNTBATTEN
LOUIS ALEXANDER, HSH Prince Louis of Battenberg, 1st Marquis of Milford Haven, GCB, GCVO, KCMG (1854–1921)
[74]

Count (later Prince) Louis of Battenberg was born at Graz, Austria, on 24 May 1854, the eldest son of Prince Alexander of Hesse, a younger brother of Grand Duke Louis III of Hesse. Prince Alexander, a major general in the Russian Army, fell in love with Countess Julie von Hauke, a penniless maid of honour at the Russian Court, and, despite the Tsar's opposition to such a match, subsequently eloped with her. For his brother's sake, the Grand Duke of Hesse bestowed on Julie the title of Countess (later Her Serene Highness, Princess) of Battenberg, but her lack of royal birth meant that her marriage was morganatic, with the children taking her rank and title rather those of their father. For his behaviour Alexander was dismissed from the Russian Army, but his brother's influence brought him a commission in the Austrian Army, in which he commanded a division in the Austrian defeat at the battle of Solferino (24 June 1859). In 1862 he gave up his military career and retired to Hesse, in the same year that his cousin, Prince Frederick, later Louis IV of Hesse, married Queen Victoria's second daughter, Princess Alice. The Battenbergs thus became related, through marriage, to the British Royal Family.

In 1868 Prince Louis decided that he wished to make a career at sea and was encouraged by his aunt, Princess Alice, to join the Royal Navy, which offered better career prospects than the small coastal force operated by the North German Confederation of which Hesse had become part. Her brother, Captain Prince Alfred, later Duke of Edinburgh [49], supported the idea and, with Queen Victoria's consent, the young Battenberg entered the Navy as a cadet on 3 October 1868 and became a naturalized British subject. In January 1869, at the Austrian port of Trieste, Italy, he joined the Prince of Wales [44] in the frigate *Ariadne* as a midshipman, for a cruise in the Mediterranean and the Black Sea. After returning to the United Kingdom he joined the armoured ship *Royal Alfred*, flagship on the North America and West Indies station, in October 1869. Battenberg remained in this appointment for the next four and a half years, with intervals for home leave. In the first of these, visiting his parents in Hesse, he was overtaken by the outbreak of the Franco-Prussian War in July 1870 and was unable to rejoin his ship until October. In 1872 he went with his admiral when the flag was shifted to the sloop *Sirius* for a visit to British Guiana (Guyana).

Battenberg became an acting sub-lieutenant on 8 April 1874 at the beginning of his promotion courses. At this time Queen Victoria became alarmed by his friendship with her youngest daughter, Princess Beatrice, and gave orders for him to be sent abroad. The Prince of Wales then chose him as a member of his suite in an official tour of India and he accordingly embarked with it in the troopship *Serapis*. On 15 May 1876 he was promoted to lieutenant, followed by appointment to the armoured ship *Sultan*, commanded by the Duke of Edinburgh in the Mediterranean Fleet. In 1878, when there was a threat of war between the United Kingdom and Russia over the Turkish Question, *Sultan* was in the fleet sent to Constantinople (Istanbul), where it was met by a Russian army. Battenberg went ashore to visit his brother Prince Alexander, an officer in the Russian camp, and brought him back to be entertained in *Sultan*. These personal contacts were criticized in the English Press on the grounds that the Battenbergs were Russian spies, though Edinburgh himself was married to the daughter of the Russian Emperor. The British Ambassador complained that his negotiations were imperilled. Battenberg was transferred to another ship and, angered by this reflection on his family, considered resignation, a course in which he was encouraged by his father and by the Empress of Russia (his father's sister and Edinburgh's mother-in-law). Queen Victoria, who disapproved of any association with Russia, eventually chose to blame her son rather than the Battenbergs for the whole episode. After returning home with his ship in April 1878 Battenberg was sent back to serve in the armoured ship

Agincourt, flagship of the second-in-command of the Mediterranean Fleet, Rear-Admiral J E Commerell [48].

From April to October 1879 Battenberg was again with the Prince of Wales in the royal yacht *Osborne*, under command of Captain Lord Charles Beresford. He declined the offer of further employment in this ship and went on half-pay. In February 1880, accompanying members of his family to a banquet at St Petersburg, he narrowly escaped death when a bomb, intended for his uncle the Emperor of Russia, exploded shortly before the Imperial party arrived. After returning to London he began a brief *affaire* with Lily Langtry, a former mistress of the Prince of Wales. When Mrs Langtry became pregnant, Battenberg made appropriate financial provision for their child, a daughter, who was brought up as a member of a noble Scottish family. In August 1880 he was appointed to the frigate *Inconstant* in the Flying Squadron commanded by the Earl of Clanwilliam [50] and went round the world under sail. The same squadron included the corvette *Bacchante*, carrying the Prince of Wales's two eldest sons, Prince Albert Victor and Prince George [64]. When the squadron reached Gibraltar at the end of August 1882 *Inconstant* was detached to join the Mediterranean Fleet for operations against an Egyptian nationalist uprising led by Colonel Arabi ('Urbi) Pasha. Battenberg landed at Alexandria with a battery of Gatling guns in the force sent to protect the Khedive of Egypt, but was not engaged in combat. After returning to Portsmouth in October 1882 he went on half-pay and joined his family at Darmstadt, Hesse. In September 1883 he was appointed to the royal yacht *Victoria and Albert*.

In April 1884, at Darmstadt, he married his distant cousin Princess Victoria of Hesse, daughter of the Grand Duke Louis IV and Grand Duchess Alice (Queen Victoria's daughter). They later had a family of two sons and two daughters, one of whom married in 1903 Prince Andrew of Greece and later became the mother of Philip, Duke of Edinburgh [99]. Further marriage links between the Battenbergs and the British Royal Family were established in July 1885 when Princess Beatrice married Battenberg's younger brother, Prince Henry. Battenberg was promoted to commander on leaving *Victoria and Albert* on 30 August 1885 and went on half-pay, with intervals of training at Portsmouth in the gunnery school *Excellent* and the torpedo school *Vernon*.

In July 1887 Battenberg was appointed commander of the armoured ship *Dreadnought* in the Mediterranean, with his wife's distant cousin, Prince George of Wales, later George V [64], as one of his lieutenants. This led to an outcry in Parliament and the popular Press on the grounds that a German princeling was being selected over the heads of many better-qualified British officers. For the rest of his career his detractors asserted that his advancement was due to his royal connections, while his admirers claimed that he achieved it by his own merit. He returned to half-pay in January 1889. Meanwhile, in 1888, another of his wife's sisters married Prince Henry of Prussia [62], brother of the German Emperor William II [47]. Battenberg was given command in October 1889 of the cruiser *Scout*, in which he served in the Mediterranean and the Red Sea. He left this ship on promotion to captain on 31 December 1891 and spent most of the following year on half-pay before going to the War Office as naval adviser to the Inspector General of Fortifications. In October 1894 he was appointed to the light cruiser *Cambrian* in the Mediterranean. The extent to which senior officers sought his views led some of his contemporaries to attribute this to his position in Court circles and criticism began to be voiced about his German connections, which seemed all the closer because he never lost his German accent. The death of Prince Henry of Battenberg on active service with the British Army in West Africa in 1896 made no difference to these critics, who included Lord Charles Beresford and the Honourable Hedworth Lambton, later Sir Hedworth Meux [66].

From 1897 to June 1899 Battenberg commanded the battleship *Majestic*, flagship in the Channel Squadron, and then became Assistant Director of Naval Intelligence at the Admiralty. He was beside Edward VII at Windsor when the Royal Horse Artillery gun team pulling the cortege in Queen Victoria's funeral procession broke a trace and threatened to disrupt the solemnity of the occasion. Battenberg, with the King's approval, ordered a route-lining party of seamen to take the place of the team, so instituting the custom followed in all subsequent Royal funerals. In September 1901, after a few months on half-pay, he was appointed commodore, 2nd class, with command of the battleship *Implacable* in the Mediterranean Fleet under Sir John Fisher [58]. He returned to the Admiralty in November 1902 to become Director of Naval Intelligence. There he renewed his association with Fisher, who became second naval lord in the Board of Admiralty in February 1904 and First Sea Lord in October 1904. He spoke highly of Fisher's professional ability and took the same view of Beresford, despite the latter's continued personal hostility towards him, and blamed Fisher rather than Beresford for starting the feud that split the officers of the Navy into rival factions. Nevertheless, he opposed Fisher's decision to transfer eight battleships from the Channel Fleet to a new Home Fleet, on the grounds that, if hostilities with Germany began before the Home Fleet's reserve element was mobilized, they would be faced by sixteen efficient German battleships under his brother-in-law, Prince Henry of Prussia.

Battenberg returned to sea in February 1905, as acting rear-admiral in command of the Second Cruiser Squadron in the Atlantic Fleet, with his flag in the cruiser *Drake*. With his promotion confirmed on 1 July 1904, he was sent with his cruisers on a series of official visits, including Canada (where Fisher's decision to close the North America station had been taken badly) and the USA. On 24 February 1907 he became acting vice-admiral and second-in-command of the Mediterranean Fleet, with his flag in the battleship *Venerable*. In August 1907 he shifted his flag to the battleship *Prince of Wales* and remained in this ship when he was promoted to vice-admiral and became C-in-C of the Atlantic Fleet from 30 June 1908 to December 1910. In March 1911 he was given command of the Third and

Fourth Divisions of the Home Fleet. The German naval attaché reported on him as an officer who "unites a seaman's judgement, based on long experience in the best commands, with the inborn German thoroughness of a systematic worker".

In December 1911 the newly appointed First Lord of the Admiralty, Winston Churchill, made Battenberg Second Sea Lord. As this was only a few months after the Agadir crisis had threatened to lead to war between Germany and the United Kingdom, this decision led to renewed criticism of his German birth. One newspaper, under the headline "Bulldog breed or Dachshund", declared that it was a heavy strain to put on any German "to give him the key to our defences". Churchill's selection was based on recommendations from Fisher, who spoke highly of Battenberg's administrative ability and also of his enthusiasm for the creation of a naval staff organization, which Churchill had been appointed to introduce. Fisher also said that to appoint someone of German birth might show the pacifist wing of the ruling Liberal party that the Cabinet was not bent on war with Germany, though "in reality, he is more English than the English". Lord Selborne, who had been First Lord of the Admiralty from 1900 to 1905, told Churchill that "a better Englishman does not exist". Sir Francis Bridgeman, who became First Sea Lord November 1911, was not an admirer of Battenberg, but Churchill found Battenberg easier to work with than Bridgeman. In December 1912 Bridgeman was made to retire, ostensibly on medical grounds, and Battenberg was appointed in his place.

As First Sea Lord, Battenberg accepted Churchill's view that the First Lord should no longer be *primus inter pares* among the Lords of the Admiralty, but instead act as Minister for the Navy, with the Sea Lords acting as his professional advisers. When Churchill attempted to go beyond this by interfering in professional questions, Battenberg used his diplomatic skill to restrain him and so avoided any open breach between Churchill and the other members of the Board. In the summer of 1914, for reasons of economy, the annual fleet manoeuvres were replaced by a trial mobilization. The end of this exercise coincided with the assassination by Serb nationalists of Archduke Franz Ferdinand, heir to the Austro-Hungarian throne, at Sarajevo, Bosnia. With Churchill and the rest of the Cabinet out of London for the weekend, Battenberg ordered the fleet not to disperse as planned, but to remain at readiness. After the commencement of hostilities with Germany on 4 August 1914, Churchill threw himself into every aspect of naval operations, often drafting orders in person, confident that his policy was identical with that of the First Sea Lord, who mostly initialled them with the words "I concur". Nevertheless, a series of naval disasters in the opening months of the war shook public confidence in the Admiralty.

In the prevailing mood of anti-German hysteria, Battenberg's German birth again became an issue. He himself had long felt that his position would be difficult in the event of a war with Germany. The newspapers clamoured for his removal and rumours spread that he had been put in the

182

Tower of London for betraying naval secrets. The Cabinet had no doubts about his loyalty, but was less sure of his ability to cope with the hyper-active Churchill, whose own position as First Lord was being called into question. Battenberg decided that he could no longer continue in office and resigned at the end of October 1914. His decision was widely regretted within the Navy, where he was generally well liked. Anti-German feeling grew even stronger as the war continued. In July 1917 George V decided to disclaim his German names and titles and told his relatives to do like-wise. The Battenbergs accordingly anglicized their name to Mountbatten. From 14 to 17 July 1917 Prince Louis of Battenberg was briefly known as Sir Louis Mountbatten (he had been awarded the KCMG in 1905), after which he accepted a peerage as Marquess of Milford Haven, a title last previously held by George II before his accession in 1727. At the time of Battenberg's resignation there had been a suggestion that, after the end of the conflict with Germany, he would be offered another appointment. When that time came he was close to reaching his retirement age, and so retired voluntarily on 1 January 1919. A proposal for his promotion to Admiral of the Fleet on the retired list was widely welcomed as compen-sation for his having been driven to resign in 1914 and he was accordingly promoted on 4 August 1921. He died suddenly at his London home, Half Moon Street, Piccadilly, on 11 September 1921 and was buried at Whippingham, Isle of Wight. His elder son, Lieutenant-Commander the Earl of Medina, a veteran of Heligoland, the Dogger Bank and Jutland, succeeded to his peerage, and his younger son, Lord Louis Mountbatten [102], was later created Earl Mountbatten of Burma.

MOUNTBATTEN
Lord LOUIS FRANCIS ALBERT VICTOR NICHOLAS, 1st Earl Mountbatten of Burma, KG, GCB, OM, GCSI, GCIE, GCVO, DSO (1900–1979) [102]

Prince Louis of Battenberg was born at Frogmore House, Windsor, on 25 June 1900, the younger son in a family of four children of Admiral Prince Louis of Battenberg [74] and his wife, Princess Victoria of Hesse, a grand-daughter of Queen Victoria. He became a cadet at the Royal Naval College, Osborne, in May 1913, and was there when his father resigned office as First Sea Lord after the outbreak of the First World War, in response to popular disquiet at his German connections. He felt bitter at the wrong he considered that his father had suffered and the episode intensified his ambition to rise eventually to take his place. After going on to the Royal Naval College, Dartmouth, he was appointed in July 1916 as a midshipman in the battle-cruiser *Lion*, flagship of the Battle-cruiser Fleet. He was present at a minor action on 19 August 1916 and transferred to the battle-ship *Queen Elizabeth* in February 1917. In June 1917 his father renounced his German titles and took the surname Mountbatten, before being granted a peerage as Marquess of Milford Haven. Prince Louis ("Dickie" to his intimates, and, later, "Tricky Dickie" to his rivals) then became Lord Louis Mountbatten. He spent two months on detachment to the submarine *K6* and in October 1918 joined the patrol boat *P31* where he was promoted to sub-lieutenant on 15 January 1919. In October 1919 he was one of the young naval officers sent to complete their education at a university and went up to Christ's College, Cambridge, where he was elected to the committee of the Cambridge Union and gained a reputation for holding radical opinions.

In March 1920 Mountbatten joined the battle-cruiser *Renown* to accompany the Prince of Wales [84] during his visit to Australia. He established a friendship with the Prince, his distant cousin, and, after passing out first on his promotion course in March 1921, and commanding a platoon of stokers on strike-breaking duty, joined the battle-cruiser *Repulse* to accompany the Prince on his tour to India and Japan in the winter of 1921–22. He had already become close to the well-connected Edwina Ashley, who in 1921 became a millionairess on the death of her grandfather, Sir Ernest Cassel. She visited the Viceroy and Governor-General of India, Lord Reading, at the time of the Prince of Wales's tour and, while there, accepted Mountbatten's proposal. They were married soon after Mountbatten's return home in 1922, with the Prince of Wales acting as best man, and later had a family of two daughters. In subsequent years the question of his wife's infidelity, as well as Mountbatten's own, became the subject of widespread comment.

In January 1923 Mountbatten joined the battleship *Revenge* in the Mediterranean Fleet. He returned home in August 1924 and spent the next two years as a student at the signals school, Portsmouth, and the Royal Naval Staff College, Greenwich. In 1926 he was appointed to the battleship *Centurion* in the Reserve Fleet and in January 1927 became assistant to the Fleet Signals Officer in the Mediterranean. He was promoted lieutenant-commander on 15 April 1928, with appointment to the instructional staff of the signals school at Portsmouth in July 1929. While there, he learnt to fly at a private flying school. In August 1931 he became Fleet Signals Officer in the Mediterranean in the battleship *Queen Elizabeth* and on 31 December 1932 was promoted to commander and appointed to the battleship *Resolution*. He was given command in 1934 of the new destroyer *Daring* in the Mediterranean Fleet and soon afterwards transferred to the older destroyer *Wishart*. During his years with the Mediterranean Fleet Mountbatten established an image that lasted for the rest of his career. To his admirers he was a charismatic and inspiring leader, whose brilliant talents, charm and energy allowed him to excel in every field. To his detractors he was a fun-loving playboy who shamelessly exploited his royal connections and his wife's money in the ruthless pursuit of personal ambition.

In July 1936 Mountbatten was appointed to the Naval Air Division of the Admiralty and lobbied in support of the campaign to transfer the Fleet

Air Arm from the Royal Air Force to the Navy. With friends in the film industry, he set up the Royal Naval Film Corporation, allowing ships at sea to screen the latest popular releases. He was also given credit for advocating the adoption of the Oerlikon gun as the fleet's low-level air defence weapon. During the abdication crisis of 1936 he failed to dissuade his old companion, who had come to the throne as Edward VIII [84], from abdicating in order to marry Mrs Wallis Simpson, and soon afterwards became close to the new King, George VI [86].

In June 1939 Mountbatten assumed command of the new destroyer flotilla leader *Kelly*, in whose construction he had taken a keen interest. With the outbreak of the Second World War in September 1939 he became Captain (Destroyers) of the Fifth Destroyer Flotilla. One of his first tasks was to bring back the former Edward VIII, now Duke of Windsor, from his self-imposed exile in France. *Kelly* subsequently suffered storm-damage when proceeding at excessive speed after failing to intercept a captured British merchantman off Norway. After repairs she was damaged first by a mine in December 1939 and then by collision with the destroyer *Gurkha* on returning to sea in March 1940. Mountbatten's flotilla took part in the Norwegian campaign (9 April–9 June 1940), coming under German air attack and embarking French Chasseurs Alpins during the Allied evacuation of Namsos. On 9 May 1940, operating off the Dutch coast, *Kelly* was badly damaged by a torpedo and only reached safety after a tow of ninety-two hours. Mountbatten's personal courage and seamanship gained him the first of his several mentions in despatches, but he was denied a DSO, despite lobbying by the new Prime Minister, Winston Churchill and by the King's brother, the Duke of Kent. The C-in-C, Home Fleet, Sir Charles Forbes [90], held that other officers were more deserving and that Mountbatten's ship had been torpedoed in consequence of his own rashness. In July 1940, with the United Kingdom threatened by invasion, Mountbatten felt that his family would be singled out by the Nazis on account of his own German descent and his wife's Jewish grandparents. Lady Louis refused to leave her position in the St John Ambulance Brigade, but their two daughters were evacuated to the United States.

In October 1940 the Fifth Destroyer Flotilla, with Mountbatten commanding from the flotilla leader *Javelin*, moved from the North Sea to the Channel. On 28 November 1940 in an encounter with an inferior force of German destroyers, *Javelin* was disabled by a torpedo and the enemy escaped. Mountbatten was criticized by the Admiralty for faulty tactics, but was congratulated by Churchill for his dashing conduct. *Kelly*, with many of her old crew having volunteered to rejoin her, put to sea again in December 1940, only to suffer minor damage through ramming a merchantman. Mountbatten was exonerated and received his DSO in January 1941. His flotilla joined the Mediterranean Fleet at the end of April 1941 and took part in the defence of Malta and operations off the Libyan coast. On 23 May 1941, after giving naval gunfire support to the Army during the campaign in Crete, *Kelly* was sunk by German dive-bombers, with the loss of half her complement. Mountbatten and other survivors were machine-gunned in the water before being rescued by the destroyer *Kipling*. He briefly resumed command as Captain (Destroyers) before returning to London.

In August 1941 Mountbatten flew to the USA to take command of the aircraft carrier *Illustrious*, then under repair at Norfolk, Virginia. He made official visits to several naval establishments, including the fleet base at Pearl Harbor, which he thought was inadequately defended against surprise attack, and met a number of important personages, including President Roosevelt. He was recalled in October 1941, when he was selected by Churchill to succeed Sir Roger Keyes **[80]** as adviser to the Chiefs of Staff on Combined Operations, with promotion to commodore. This rapid advancement did not enhance his popularity with senior officers of any Service, especially when he established a large headquarters, staffed by his own nominees, including a number of scientists whose ideas were required for the development of special projects needed for large-scale amphibious warfare. Some condemned it as full of cranks and communists, and derided the results of early raids on the German-held coast. Nevertheless, Churchill was impressed by Mountbatten's achievements and in March 1942 appointed him Chief of Combined Operations, with full membership of the Chiefs of Staff Committee and acting promotion to vice-admiral, lieutenant general and air marshal. During 1942 Rank/Two Cities, with Admiralty co-operation, produced the successful and morale-boosting feature film *In Which We Serve*. The film was written and directed by Mountbatten's friend, the composer, playwright and entertainer Noel Coward. Mountbatten was involved in every aspect of filming the story, which was based on that of *Kelly*, and the set-piece dialogue of the leading character (played by Coward himself with his cap at the same jaunty angle affected by Mountbatten) included some of Mountbatten's own speeches to his crew.

The failure of the raid on Dieppe (19 August 1942) brought much criticism on Mountbatten and his Combined Operations organization, though many of the faulty decisions leading to the disaster were in fact the responsibility of others. For a time even Churchill seemed to lose confidence in his protégé and the newspaper magnate Lord Beaverbrook (at that time in the Cabinet) never forgave Mountbatten for the heavy casualties suffered by his fellow Canadians. Mountbatten, however, rose above these attacks, and secured the adoption of many techniques used in the successful landings in Normandy in June 1944. In August 1943 he accompanied the Prime Minister to the Quebec Conference, where, although not the first choice, he was appointed Supreme Allied Commander, South-East Asia, with acting promotion to admiral and the honorary ranks of lieutenant general and air marshal. He once more established a large headquarters, initially in the Indian capital, Delhi, but after April 1944 in Kandy, the ancient capital of Ceylon (Sri Lanka), with the intention (encouraged by Churchill) of personally directing the operations of all Allied forces in his Command area. He was defeated in this by the local C-in-Cs, who were supported by the Chiefs of Staff in London in their insistence that he should act as a chairman and co-ordinator.

Mountbatten's relations with the C-in-C, Eastern Fleet, Sir James Somerville [93], to whom he had originally written in fulsome terms, grew frosty when (with SEAC press releases referring to "Mountbatten's fleet") he claimed authority over what was in most respects an independent command directly under the Admiralty. Somerville's successor, Sir Bruce Fraser [95], appointed in September 1944, proved more tolerant of Mountbatten's pretensions. Most of the heavy units of the Eastern Fleet subsequently became the nucleus of the new British Pacific Fleet and the remainder, under Sir Arthur Power [97], was renamed the East Indies Fleet and mostly allotted to SEAC's amphibious operations. Mountbatten's Deputy Supreme Commander, the anglophobe United States General "Vinegar Joe" Stilwell, who was also chief of staff to the Chinese Nationalist Army, never succumbed to his famous charm, and blamed Mountbatten for his recall in October 1944.

Mountbatten defined the major problems facing his command as monsoon, malaria and morale. With the Indian Army's ablest field commander, Lieutenant General Sir William Slim, commanding the Fourteenth Army in Burma, he decided that the Allies would fight on through the monsoon of 1944–45 and gave the fullest support to improved medical services. While Slim rebuilt the morale of his own troops, Mountbatten toured more widely, addressing assembled sailors, soldiers and airmen in carefully staged "informal" talks, with the newsreel cameras in attendance, and assuring them of their ability to defeat the Japanese. In May 1945 General Sir Oliver Leese, Commander of Allied Land Forces, SEAC, decided that Slim, who had just reconquered Burma, should be removed from his Army command. Mountbatten, after consulting the Chief of the Imperial General Staff, Sir Alan Brooke, dismissed Leese (with whom he was already on bad terms) and secured the appointment of Slim in his place. Their intended invasion of Malaya was pre-empted by the Japanese capitulation in response to nuclear bombardment in August 1945. Outraged at the initial offer of a barony, Mountbatten settled with reluctance for a viscountcy in the 1946 New Year Honours, with a special remainder in favour of his daughter. He declined to use his new title (Viscount Mountbatten of Burma) and continued to be known as Lord Louis Mountbatten

With the end of the war, the SEAC area was increased to include the Dutch East Indies and French Indo-China. Mountbatten had insufficient Allied forces to maintain civil order and therefore made use of surrendered Japanese troops for this purpose. In these areas, as well as in Burma and Malaya, he actively sympathized with local nationalists and thought it unrealistic to attempt the re-establishment of European colonial rule. At the end of May 1946 he left his headquarters in Singapore to return home, with reversion to his substantive rank of rear-admiral. His progressive views were appreciated by the Labour Cabinet that had come to power in 1945 and he was offered the post of Viceroy and Governor-General of India.

Mountbatten assumed office in March 1947, enthusiastically committed to the Cabinet policy of ending British rule in India within the year. He soon became friends with the Hindu leader of the Congress party, Jawaharlal Nehru, as, to an even greater extent, did the Vicereine herself, but was unable to influence the Muslim leader, Muhammad Ali Jinnah. Faced with the collapse of imperial authority, he brought forward the date of independence to 15 August 1947. The partition of the Indian Empire into two successor states, a theocratic Muslim Pakistan and a secular, predominantly Hindu, India, was accompanied by a degree of "ethnic cleansing" that left some 250,000 dead and many more as refugees. Mountbatten's opponents argued that, under the influence of Nehru, and in a hurry to return to the Navy, he sacrificed the unity of the sub-continent, tore up British treaties with the Indian princes and failed to forestall inter-communal massacres. Against this, his sympathizers claimed that, had the nationalist leaders not been forced to accept their responsibilities without further delay, the bloodshed would have been worse, with no prospect of an orderly hand-over of power.

After the achievement of independence, Mountbatten remained as Governor-General of the new dominion of India and as chairman of a Joint Defence Council, set up to divide the assets of the British Indian Army. Pakistanis came to regard him as over-sympathetic to India, especially over the question of Kashmir, Nehru's homeland, where the population was largely Muslim, but the ruler was a Hindu. When the state was invaded by Pathan (Pashtun) tribesmen from Pakistan, Mountbatten insisted that Indian troops could only be sent to restore order after the ruler had acceded to India. The resulting issues of legitimacy led to a series of armed conflicts between India and Pakistan and to demands for Kashmiri self-determination that, more than fifty years later, still continue to be a cause of terrorism and international tension. By October 1947 Indian politicians had come to believe that Field Marshal Sir Claude Auchinleck, the Supreme Commander of the armies of both new dominions, was preju-diced in favour of Pakistan. Mountbatten arranged for his retirement and the disbandment of his headquarters, to the indignation of the Pakistanis. Auchinleck, who had come to despise Mountbatten, declined his offer to obtain him a peerage. Mountbatten himself received the customary award of governor-generals at the end of their period in office, by being advanced one step in the peerage. He was accordingly created Earl Mountbatten of Burma, again with a special remainder in favour of his daughter, on 14 August 1947.

During 1947 Mountbatten had the satisfaction of seeing his nephew, Prince Philip of Greece, **[99]** take the surname Mountbatten and, on 20 November 1947, marry Princess Elizabeth, heiress to George VI.

Mountbatten himself had spared no effort to encourage this match and would later insist that, after her accession as Elizabeth II, a Mountbatten sat on the throne of the United Kingdom and that the Royal Family's surname had become Mountbatten-Windsor. After leaving India at the end of June 1948 he was given command of the First Cruiser Squadron in the Mediterranean Fleet, with his flag in the cruiser *Newcastle*. He was promoted to vice-admiral on 22 June 1949 and from April to May 1950 was second-in-command of the Mediterranean Fleet. Between June 1950 and April 1952 he was Fourth Sea Lord at the Admiralty. On the Iranian nationalization of the British-owned Anglo-Iranian Oil Corporation, he argued that the British government should make the best of the situation, rather than use force to oppose what he saw as the spirit of the times. In June 1952 Mountbatten was given command of the Mediterranean Fleet, with his flag in the cruiser *Glasgow*, followed by the additional new NATO appointment of C-in-C, Allied Forces, Mediterranean, in January 1953. He was promoted to admiral on 27 February 1953 and in October 1954 was selected to be First Sea Lord in the Board headed by James Thomas (Lord Cilcennin) in Churchill's second administration.

Mountbatten fulfilled a lifetime's ambition to succeed his father in this office on 18 April 1955, with promotion to admiral of the fleet on 22 October 1956. He began with a vigorous justification of the Navy's needs at a time when British public opinion attributed the parlous state of the economy to excessive defence spending. The apparent uselessness of this expenditure was revealed when the Egyptian government nationalized the Suez Canal, and Anglo-French landings there in October 1956, though militarily successful, proved a political disaster. Mountbatten believed that the age of Empire was over and that the Cabinet should come to terms with nationalism in Egypt, just as he had in Burma and India. He twice offered to resign, but was persuaded that it was his duty to remain in post and was retained by Harold Macmillan when the latter succeeded Eden in January 1957. The new Minister of Defence, Duncan Sandys, was ordered to make drastic economies and to rationalize the whole defence system. Mountbatten resisted Sandys's view that the advent of nuclear missiles had made conventional forces obsolete and argued persuasively that there was still a requirement for strong naval forces in the Far East as well as in the Atlantic. He successfully campaigned for a new generation of aircraft carriers and the conversion of old ones into commando carriers, but failed in his bid to transfer land-based maritime aircraft from the RAF to the Navy. Always fascinated by uniforms, he changed the regulations for naval head-dress so that white-topped caps, previously worn in temperate climates only in summer, became the permanent pattern.

In July 1959 Mountbatten became Chief of the Defence Staff. He pushed on with the policy of unifying the defence establishment and his normal three-year tour of office was extended by Macmillan by a further two. In

1964 the Admiralty, the War Office and the Air Ministry were renamed the Navy, Army and Air Force Departments, and combined in a new Ministry of Defence. He failed in his plan to strengthen the position of the CDS at the expense of the Chiefs of Naval, General, and Air Staffs, and alienated these officers by his cavalier attitude to truthfulness and his habit of agreeing a policy with them but privately advising the Ministers against it. In 1964 Peter Thorneycroft, who had remained in office as Defence Minister when Macmillan was succeeded by Sir Alec Douglas-Home, arranged for Mountbatten to stay on as CDS for a sixth year, while the new MOD organization was carried into effect. On the fall of the Conservative government in October 1964, the new Prime Minister, Harold Wilson, with Denis Healey as Minister of Defence, honoured this decision, but when Mountbatten left office in July 1965 it was with the feeling that the work of unification was only half-completed. Nevertheless, the steps taken in that direction had made him unpopular with his Service colleagues, who suspected him of personal aggrandisement and bad faith.

After leaving the Defence Ministry he undertook a number of official tasks, including a report into prison security. He attended to his extensive archives, opened the country house and estate at Broadlands, (inherited from his wife) to the public, contributed to a television series, *The Life and Times of Lord Mountbatten*, and spoke extensively on defence subjects. He became a friend and counsellor to the young Prince of Wales and studied the genealogies of the many Royal Houses with which he was connected. On 27 August 1979, together with his grandson Nicholas Knatchbull and an Irish boy, Paul Maxwell, he was murdered when Irish extremists blew up his fishing boat off his country house near Mullaghmore in County Sligo. His daughter Patricia, her husband Lord Brabourne, and their other son were injured, and Lord Brabourne's mother died of her injuries. After a state funeral in Westminster Abbey, planned by himself, Earl Mountbatten was buried in Romsey Abbey, near Broadlands. His elder daughter, Patricia, Lady Brabourne, succeeded him as the second Countess Mountbatten. Of her father's many biographers, one of the most scholarly, Philip Zeigler, summed up his career thus. "He flared brilliantly across the face of the twentieth century; the meteor is extinguished but the glow lingers on in the mind's eye."

MUNDY
Sir GEORGE RODNEY, GCB (1805–1884) [38]

George Mundy was born on 19 April 1805. His father became a general, his uncle and namesake became an admiral, and his mother was the youngest daughter of Admiral Lord Rodney, victor of the battle of The Saints (Iles des Saintes). He was educated at the Royal Naval College, Portsmouth, from February 1818 to December 1819 and was then appointed a volunteer, with two years' seniority, in the 5th-rate *Phaeton* on the North America station. Between 1822 and 1824 he served in the Mediterranean as a midshipman in the 5th-rate *Euryalus* and the 2nd-rate *Rochfort*. He then moved to the South America station, where he was successively in the 5th-rate *Blanche*, the sloop *Jaseur*, the 3rd-rate *Wellesley* and the 2nd-rate *Cambridge*, serving at times as acting lieutenant before being confirmed in that rank on 4 February 1826. From July 1826 to September 1827 he was in the sloop *Eclair*. During 1828 Mundy was in the British fleet at Lisbon, successively in the 6th-rate *Challenger* and the 5th-rate *Pyramus*, before being promoted to commander on 25 August 1828. At the end of the Belgian War of Independence Mundy was in the 3rd-rate *Donegal* as a liaison officer in the Anglo-French operations to force the Dutch to surrender Antwerp. He was then a British representative in negotiations between the Belgian and Netherlands governments leading to the end of hostilities in May 1833.

In August 1833 Mundy was appointed to the sloop *Favorite* in which he served in the Mediterranean until returning home after his promotion to captain on 10 January 1837. In October 1842 he was appointed to command the 6th-rate *Iris*. After serving off the coast of West Africa in 1843 the ship was recalled to Portsmouth for a refit and to replace numerous losses from fever among her crew. She then sailed for the East Indies station, arriving at Singapore in July 1844. During 1846 *Iris* was in the river expedition led by Sir Thomas Cochrane **[28]** and James (later Rajah) Brooke against the Sultan of Brunei. Mundy commanded the boats of the larger warships and was mentioned in despatches for his part in assaulting shore positions and a subsequent pursuit of the Sultan through the swamps and rain forests of Borneo. Between August 1846 and February 1847 he commanded in further operations against the Borneo pirates and twice received the thanks of the Admiralty.

Mundy then returned home, where he remained on half-pay until July 1854, when, with the outbreak of the Crimean War, he was appointed to the 2nd-rate *Nile*. He served in the Baltic during 1854 and 1855 and, at the end of the war, was deployed to the West Indies in 1856. He was promoted to rear-admiral on 30 July 1857. Between 1859 and 1861, with his flag in the 2nd-rate *Hannibal*, he was second-in-command of the Mediterranean Fleet. This period coincided with the wars of Italian unification. In the south Garibaldi and his red-shirts crossed from Sicily under the guns of the Royal Navy and deposed the tyrannical King of Naples, Francis II, known to his subjects as "Bombino". Mundy was stationed at Palermo and Naples to protect British interests and played a part in the relief of local civilians caught up in the fighting. He was awarded the KCB in November 1862 and became a vice-admiral on 15 December 1863. Between 1867 and 1869 Sir George Mundy was C-in-C in the West Indies. He was promoted to admiral on 26 May 1869 and was C-in-C, Portsmouth, from 1872 to 1875. He then went onto the retired list, where he was promoted to admiral of the fleet on 27 December 1877. He died, unmarried, on 23 December 1884.

NICHOLAS II
HIM Emperor (Tsar) of Russia, KG (1868–1918) **[60]**

The future Emperor Nicholas II was born in St Petersburg on 18 May 1868, the eldest son of the then Tsarevich Alexander, who succeeded to the Russian throne as Alexander III on the assassination of his own father, Alexander II, in 1881. Alexander III rejected his father's liberal views and saw it as his duty to rule as an absolute monarch. Of impressive physical strength and size, he became an object of hero-worship to his small and slightly-built heir, who accepted without question his father's opposition to any kind of constitutional reform. In 1893 he visited London for the wedding of his cousin, the Duke of York, the future George V **[64]**, whom he physically much resembled. He became engaged to Princess Alix of Hesse-Darmstadt and returned to England with her to visit her sister, the wife of Prince Louis of Battenberg **[74]**. They were widely feted and a new horse-race, the Cesarewitch, was named (using the French system of transliteration) in Nicholas's honour.

Nicholas succeeded his father as Tsar on 1 November 1894. His reign began inauspiciously. Even before his coronation he alienated liberal opinion by declaring that the idea of representative government was a "senseless dream", ill-chosen words for which his wife, the new Tsarina Alexandra, as reactionary as she was wilful, was widely held to have been responsible. The disasters to Russian arms in the Russo-Japanese War of 1904–5 weakened imperial prestige, and the annihilation of the Baltic fleet at the battle of Tsushima (27/8 May 1905), after an epic voyage of 17,000 miles, was a particularly devastating blow. In international politics Germany's decision to build a strong navy drove the United Kingdom to settle its differences with France in 1904 and with Russia in 1907. To mark the new friendship between the two powers, Nicholas was appointed an honorary admiral of the fleet in the Royal Navy on 11 June 1908. The Tsarina, after producing four daughters, turned to religious mysticism in her anxiety for a male heir. In 1904 she bore the Tsarevich Alexei, but it soon became apparent that, as a grand-daughter of Queen Victoria, she carried the genes of haemophilia, a disease carried in the female line but apparent only in the male. Grigori Efimovich Rasputin, an uncouth Siberian holy man, appeared to be able to ameliorate the sufferings of the young Tsarevich and thereby gained great influence over the Imperial family.

In 1914, when Austria-Hungary gave an ultimatum to Serbia, Nicholas for once disregarded his wife and Rasputin and ordered mobilization to show support for a fellow Slav state. Then, in response to an appeal from his cousin, the German Emperor William II **[47]**, who foresaw that this would inevitably lead to a general European war, he reduced the order to partial mobilization. He subsequently restored the order to full mobilization, under pressure from his generals, who then disconnected his telephone in case he changed his mind again. When the war continued to go badly for Russia, with millions of casualties at the front, and food short-ages at home, public opinion turned against the Tsarist regime and Nicholas was forced to abdicate on 2 March 1917. He and his family were taken into custody and, after the October Revolution, subjected to increasing hardships and indignities. These were worsened by the hostility of Russian sailors who, in Baltic cruises before the war, had seemed especially devoted to the Imperial family. On 16 July 1918 Nicholas, Alexandra, their children and their personal attendants were murdered at Yekaterinburg. Eighty years later, after the fall of the Soviet system, their remains (except for those of the Tsarevich Alexis) were identified by analysis of genetic material, including that from a distant relative, HRH Philip, Duke of Edinburgh [99]. On 16 July 1998, in an act of atonement and reconciliation, the President of the Russian Federation, Boris Yeltsin, attended their re-interment in the cathedral of Saints Peter and Paul, St Petersburg.

NOEL
Sir GERARD HENRY UCTRED, KCB, KCMG (1845–1918)
[61]

Jerry (later nicknamed "Sharkey") Noel was born on 5 March 1845. His father was related through his father to the Earls of Gainsborough, and his mother was the only child of Admiral Lord Barham (Sir Charles Middleton). He joined the Navy in 1859 and became an acting sub-lieutenant in the frigate *Shannon* on the North America and West Indies station on 7 March 1864. He was appointed sub-lieutenant on 18 January 1865 in the paddle sloop *Basilisk* on the China station and was promoted to lieutenant on 30 June 1866 in the sloop *Rattler*, in which he remained on the same station until she was wrecked in September 1868. In October 1869 he joined the gunnery training school *Excellent* and, after qualifying there, became gunnery officer of the armoured ship *Minotaur*, flagship of Rear-Admiral Geoffrey Hornby [45] in the Channel Squadron, in February 1871. In August 1873 Noel married Rachel, the eldest daughter of F J Cresswell, Esquire, and later had with her a family of a son and two daughters. At the end of 1873 he was appointed to the corvette *Active* on the West Coast of Africa station, where he commanded a naval brigade during the Second Ashanti War and took part in the capture of Kumasi (4 February 1874). He was promoted to commander on 31 March 1874 and from July 1874 to 1876 served as commander of the frigate *Immortalité* based at Portsmouth.

Noel made a serious study of his profession and in 1874 gained a prize for an essay on the future of naval tactics, later published under the title *The Gun, Ram and Torpedo*. In 1875 he was awarded the gold medal of the Royal United Services Institute. Between 1878 and 1880 he served as commander of the royal yacht *Victoria and Albert*, based at Portsmouth,

193

from where he was promoted captain on 11 January 1881. He then went on half-pay and continued to be a prominent figure at the RUSI, where he lobbied for naval rearmament and, in a discussion on 26 November 1884, declared that "for the last fourteen years the Navy has been starved". From September 1885 to November 1888 he was in command of the corvette *Rover* in the Training Squadron. In October 1889 Noel was appointed to the battleship *Téméraire* in the Mediterranean and from June 1891 to November 1893 commanded the battleship *Nile* in the Mediterranean Fleet. In the disastrous fleet manoeuvres of 22 June 1893, when the flagship *Victoria* was rammed and sunk by her consort *Camperdown,* Noel's prompt avoiding action saved his ship from a similar fate. In November 1893 he became a junior naval lord at the Admiralty, with promotion to rear-admiral on 8 May 1896, and remained there until January 1898.

Noel was then appointed second-in-command of the Mediterranean Fleet, with his flag in the battleship *Revenge.* In 1897 a Greek invasion of the Turkish-ruled island of Crete was followed by the landing of a multi-national peace-keeping force and during 1898 the island was divided into British, Russian, French and Italian-occupied areas. In September 1898 Turkish Cretans protested by murdering a British vice-consul and attacking the Customs House in the capital, Candia (Heraklion), where a number of the British defenders were killed or wounded. Several hundred Greek Cretans were killed in the associated disturbances before the Turkish authorities restored order. Noel, in temporary command of the Mediterranean Fleet, was already at Candia. He sent an ultimatum demanding the surrender of the terrorist leaders, who were then handed over, tried by court-martial and hanged. He was much praised for his firmness and diplomacy during the international negotiations leading to establishment of Cretan autonomy in 1899 and was awarded the KCMG.

Sir Gerard Noel handed over his fleet to Sir John Fisher [58] in September 1899. At a time of international tension with France, he recommended to the Admiralty that the Channel and Mediterranean Fleets should be concentrated at Gibraltar, but with a strong detachment left at Malta in case the Russian Black Sea Fleet came out to support the French. The plan was supported by Fisher, under whom Noel resumed the post of second-in-command in the Mediterranean. Fisher's habit of criticizing the evolutions of his subordinate flag-officers by signals sent in clear for the whole fleet to read, did not impress Noel, who signalled back with equal spirit. This did him no harm with Fisher, who regarded him as a fellow-reformer, and spoke of him in 1901 as eminently gifted. By 1903, however, the two were no longer on cordial terms, probably over Noel's opposition to Fisher's reform of naval education, and by 1904 they were in open disagreement on naval policy generally. Prior to sailing for the East in January 1904 Noel warned Lord Selborne, First Lord of the Admiralty in Balfour's Cabinet, against appointing Fisher as First Sea Lord, and said that this view was shared by most reliable senior officers.

In May 1900 Noel was appointed Admiral Superintendent of Naval

Reserves, with promotion to vice-admiral on 2 November 1901. In December 1902 his appointment was given the added title of Vice-Admiral Commanding, Home Fleet, with his flag successively in the battleships *Alexandra* and *Revenge* in the coast guard at Portland. He was succeeded in May 1903 by Sir Arthur Wilson [59] and in January 1904 became C-in-C on the China station, with his flag in the battleship *Glory*. His time in this appointment included the period of the Russo-Japanese War, during which relations between the United Kingdom and Russia were severely strained, with the possibility of conflict in Far Eastern waters no less than nearer home. Late in 1905 he transferred his flag to the cruiser *Diadem*, when, as part of Fisher's reforms, the battleships were brought home and the China, East Indies, Pacific and Australian stations were grouped together as the Eastern Fleet. He returned home early in 1906 and was C-in-C, Nore, from 1 January 1907 to 2 December 1908, when he was promoted to admiral of the fleet. He continued from time to time to comment on naval affairs, but was not again employed. Noel had a reputation for being a hard man to serve, but personally kind beneath a gruff exterior. He retired to Fincham, near Downham Market, Norfolk, where he died on 23 May 1918.

NORRIS
Sir JOHN, Kt (1660–1749) [1]

John Norris, the third son of a landed proprietor, was born in Speke, Lancashire, in 1660, and joined the Navy in his late teens as one of the first volunteers by Order, or "King's Letter Boys". In the Glorious Revolution of 1688 he supported William of Orange and, in August 1689, during the War of the League of Augsburg, was appointed lieutenant of the 3rd-rate *Edgar*, commanded by the future Admiral Sir Clowdisley Shovell. Early in 1690 he was with Shovell in the 4th-rate *Moncke* off the coast of Ireland, in support of William III's campaign there. On 8 July 1690 Norris was given command of the fireship *Pelican*, in which he served at the battle between the Anglo-Dutch and French fleets off Beachy Head (10 July 1690). He was appointed to the fireship *Spy* in December 1691 and was in the British fleet under Admiral Russell (later Earl of Orford) at the battles of Barfleur and La Hogue (May 1692). Norris became captain of the 5th-rate *Sheerness* on 13 January 1693. He served at Lagos Bay, Portugal, in June 1693, when the rich Levant convoy under escort from Smyrna (Izmir) was taken by the French, and was commended for his part in collecting those merchantmen that managed to avoid capture. He subsequently commanded successively the 3rd-rates *Royal Oak* and *Sussex*, the 2nd-rate *Russell* (in the British fleet sent to the Mediterranean in 1694), the 4th-rate *Carlisle* and the 3rd-rate *Content*, which he had helped capture from the French in January 1695.

During 1697 Norris commanded a squadron sent to recapture British trading posts in Hudson's Bay, taken by the French, but, bound by the decision of a council of war, remained at St John's, Newfoundland, to protect the settlement there from the risk of a French descent. On his return, his conduct was investigated by Parliament, but he was exonerated through the influence of his old patron Russell, at that time First Lord of the Admiralty. After the end of the war in 1697 Norris was appointed to the 4th-rate *Winchester*. He remained there until the outbreak of the War of the Spanish Succession in 1702, when he was given command of the 3rd-rate *Orford* and served in a squadron under Sir George Rooke in an attack on Cadiz (August 1702). While so employed, he had a violent quarrel on the flag-ship's quarter-deck with Rooke's chief of staff, struck him, threw him over a gun and drew his sword on him. Norris was placed under arrest, but through the influence of the expedition commander, the Duke of Ormond, was allowed to return to duty after the sudden death of the aggrieved officer a few days later.

Norris remained in *Orford* in the Mediterranean and commanded the van squadron at Rooke's victory over the French at Malaga (24 August 1704). In 1705 he became flag captain of the 1st-rate *Britannia*, with Shovell and the Earl of Peterborough as joint C-in-Cs, and served at the capture of Barcelona in October 1705. He was sent home with the despatches as a mark of distinction and was further rewarded with a grant of 1,000 guineas and a knighthood on 5 November 1705. Sir John Norris was disliked by Lord Peterborough (who described him as a "governing coxcomb") and did not return to active duty until 10 March 1707. He then became rear-admiral of the Blue and, with his flag in the 2nd-rate *Torbay*, was appointed second-in-command to Shovell in the Mediterranean Fleet.

After various operations off the coast of southern France during 1707 Norris sailed for home with Shovell's fleet, much of which was lost off the Scillies, together with its commander. *Torbay* avoided this disaster and Norris survived to be appointed rear-admiral of the White on 8 January 1708 and vice-admiral of the White on 26 January 1708. He returned to the Mediterranean in 1708 as second-in-command, with his flag in the 2nd-rate *Ranelagh*. During 1709 he commanded a squadron operating in the Baltic Approaches to prevent Swedish grain ships reaching France. He was appointed admiral of the Blue on 21 December 1709. Early in 1710 he became C-in-C in the Mediterranean, where he remained, conducting various operations against the French, until the effective end of hostilities in October 1711.

In May 1715 Norris was sent to the Baltic with orders to protect merchant shipping from the activities of Swedish privateers in the Great Northern War (1700–21). This was partly to safeguard the supply of ship-building materials from the Baltic countries and partly to protect the interests of Hanover, whose Elector came to the British throne as George I in 1714. Norris and his fleet returned there in 1716 and formed part of a combined Russian, Danish and British naval force led by the Russian Emperor Peter the Great, with Norris as his deputy. Norris was appointed a lord commissioner of the Admiralty in March 1718 and retained this office until May 1730, though continuing to command fleets at sea at various times during that period. After the death of Charles XII of Sweden in December 1718 Norris was sent back to the Baltic to protect Sweden against Peter the Great, whose new navy was regarded as a threat to British control of the Baltic. He served there between 1719 and 1722, but the Russian commerce-raiders were able to evade Norris's heavy ships, so that his main contribution to affairs was as a commissioner in the negotiations leading to the Treaty of Nystad (1721). This ended the Great Northern War on terms favourable to Russia, but in 1727 renewed Anglo-Russian tension caused Norris again to be sent with a fleet to the Baltic.

Norris became admiral of the White on 20 January 1733. As Anglo-Spanish relations worsened, a fleet was put into commission and on 20 February 1734 Norris was appointed commander-in-chief and admiral of the fleet, a rank in abeyance since 1719. In 1735, with his flag in another 1st-rate, *Britannia*, Norris commanded a fleet sent to support Portugal against the threat of invasion by Spain. On the outbreak of hostilities between Spain and the United Kingdom in 1739 ("the War of Jenkins's Ear") Norris was given command of the fleet in the Channel. Very little activity took place in this theatre and critics argued that this was a result of a system which provided for an establishment of only nine flag officers, all appointed by seniority and, in consequence, too old for active service. Norris was at this time aged seventy-nine.

The War of Jenkins's Ear was soon overtaken by the outbreak of a wider European conflict, the War of the Austrian Succession. Norris became the Cabinet's adviser on maritime affairs, but in 1743, when he recommended that the fleet should be made ready for war with France, he was, in his own words, "treated as an old man that dreamed dreams". On 21 February 1744 a French fleet appeared off Dungeness. Norris, widely known as "Foulweather Jack", sailed to meet it, but a violent gale drove it down the Channel before the two sides could engage. The same gale destroyed a French invasion fleet assembled at Dunkirk, thus allowing the Admiralty to send ships from Norris's fleet to reinforce the Mediterranean theatre. Norris, whose notoriously fiery temper had not mellowed with age, resigned his command in protest and remained out of office until his death on 19 July 1749.

Norris was the first admiral of the fleet, apart from those killed in action or lost at sea, to retain his rank for life. He sat as Member of Parliament for Rye from 1708 to 1722, then for Portsmouth until 1734 and then again for Rye until his death. His wife was Elizabeth Aylmer, elder daughter of a former admiral of the fleet, Lord Aylmer, one of the principal agents of Admiral Russell and the Orange cause in James II's fleet at the beginning of Norris's career. Of their two sons, the younger became a vice-admiral and the elder, Captain Richard Norris, was among the officers cashiered for their conduct at the battle of Hyeres, Toulon (11 February 1744).

197

NUGENT
Sir CHARLES EDMUND, KCH (1759–1844) [16]

Charles Nugent was born in 1759, one of the illegitimate sons (another of whom rose to be a British field marshal) of the Honourable Edmund Nugent, a younger son of the first Earl Nugent. He joined the Navy in 1771 in the sloop *Scorpion*, commanded by the future Admiral Lord Keith. In 1772 he transferred to the 3rd-rate *Trident*, flagship in the Mediterranean, and in 1775, after the beginning of the American War of Independence, went to the North America station in the 4th-rate *Bristol* under the command of Sir Peter Parker [10]. He became an acting lieutenant in *Bristol* on 3 June 1776 and took part in Parker's unsuccessful attack on Charleston, South Carolina (28 June 1776). Nugent served under Parker in the capture of Long Island, New York, in August 1776 and (after transferring with him to his new flagship, the 4th-rate *Chatham* in September 1776) of Rhode Island in December 1776. When Parker became C-in-C in the West Indies at the end of 1777 Nugent again followed him and was promoted to commander on 26 May 1778. He became captain of the 6th-rate *Pomona* on 2 May 1779. While trying to find local pilots prior to the British descent on the Spanish port of Omoa, Honduras, in October 1779, Nugent attempted to land with a boat from the schooner *Racehorse*. He was captured and put in irons but, on the arrival of *Pomona* the next day, his guards fled, leaving him and his boat's crew to free themselves. He remained in the West Indies until returning home in 1782, as the war drew to its close. Between 1784 and 1790 he sat as Member of Parliament for Buckingham, a stronghold of his father's family. The seat was then taken over by his elder brother, the future field marshal.

After the outbreak of war with Revolutionary France on 1 February 1793 Nugent was given command of the 3rd-rate *Veteran*. During the first half of 1794 he served in the capture of the French West Indian colonies of Martinique, St Lucia and Guadeloupe, and was sent home with the despatches as a mark of distinction. In the spring of 1795 he was given command of the 3rd-rate *Caesar* in which he served in the Channel until 20 February 1797, when he became rear-admiral of the Blue. Nugent was promoted to rear-admiral of the Red on 14 February 1799, vice-admiral of the Blue on 1 January 1801 and vice-admiral of the White on 23 April 1804. During 1805 he took part in the blockade of Brest, as captain of the fleet to Sir William Cornwallis. Thereafter he remained ashore, rising to become vice-admiral of the Red on 9 November 1805, admiral of the Blue on 28 April 1808, admiral of the White on 31 July 1810, admiral of the Red on 12 August 1819 and admiral of the fleet on 24 April 1833. He became a Knight Grand Cross of the Guelphic Order of Hanover on 12 March 1834. Sir Charles Nugent was married with one daughter. He died on 7 January 1844.

OGLE
Sir Chaloner, KB (1681–1750) [2]

Chaloner Ogle came from a medical family, with one of his brothers a physician in Marlborough's army and another a physician in the fleet. He joined the Navy as a volunteer by Order, or "King's Letter Boy" in July 1697 and served during the War of the League of Augsburg successively in the 3rd-rates *Yarmouth* and *Restoration,* the 4th-rate *Worcester* and the 3rd-rate *Suffolk.* Following the outbreak of the War of the Spanish Succession he was appointed lieutenant of the 3rd-rate *Royal Oak* on 29 April 1702 and became commander of the sloop *San Antonio* (captured two years previously from the infamous pirate Captain William Kidd) on 24 November 1703. Ogle became captain of the 6th-rate *Deal Castle* in April 1705, but on 3 July 1706 was captured in an encounter with three French ships off Ostend. After being exchanged, he was acquitted by a court-martial and given command of the 6th-rate *Queenborough.* He was appointed captain with command of the 5th-rate *Tartar* on 14 March 1708 and served in the Mediterranean, where he took several valuable prizes before the end of hostilities in 1713. When British interest turned to the long-running Great Northern War, Ogle served in the Baltic, commanding successively the 4th-rates *Plymouth* and *Worcester.*

In March 1719 Ogle was given command of the 4th-rate *Swallow,* in which he served on trade protection duties in the North Atlantic and the Mediterranean prior to being sent to the coast of West Africa in 1721. Despite being short-handed through sickness (fifty of his original crew had died and a hundred were in hospital), he sailed in November 1721 in search of two pirate vessels under Bartholomew Roberts, a notorious buccaneer who had taken some four hundred ships in the previous four years. Ogle encountered him near Cape Lopez on 5 February 1722. When Roberts sent one of his ships to investigate, Ogle pretended to flee, before turning and capturing the pirate after a brisk fight. He then returned, flying the French flag and giving the impression that *Swallow* was a captured prize. Ogle closed with Roberts's ship, *Royal Fortune,* and hoisted his true colours before firing a broadside in which Roberts was killed. 254 prisoners were taken, of whom sixty were later hanged at Whydah (Ouidah), Benin. Ogle was awarded the KB in April 1723, the only naval officer to be so honoured specifically for anti-piracy activities. His subsequent wealth was said to have come not only from his extensive prize-money but also from a large quantity of gold dust found in Roberts's cabin. Sir Chaloner Ogle was subsequently given command of the 3rd-rates *Burford,* in the Channel, in 1729, and *Edinburgh,* in the Mediterranean, in 1732. Later in 1732 he became the senior naval officer at Jamaica, as a commodore, with his broad pendant in the 4th-rate *Kingston.*

In June 1739 Ogle was appointed to the 4th-rate *Augusta,* which became his flagship when he was promoted rear-admiral of the Blue on 11 July

1739. Increasing tension between Spain and the United Kingdom led to the outbreak in October 1739 of the War of Jenkins's Ear, soon overtaken by a wider conflict, the War of the Austrian Succession. Ogle served during 1739 with the Mediterranean and as third in command of the fleet in the Channel in 1740. At the end of 1741 he went with reinforcements to the West Indies, where the local C-in-C, Vice-Admiral Edward Vernon (known as "Old Grog" from his grogram boat-cloak, and the initiator of the practice of issuing diluted rum, thereafter called "grog"), had previously captured Porto Bello with six ships. Earlier the Duke of Newcastle, the secretary of state responsible for sending reinforcements to the fleet in the West Indies, had replied to a questioner in Parliament "You ask me why does not Sir Chaloner Ogle sail? I answer because he is not ready. If you ask another question, why is he not ready, to that I cannot answer." Ogle reached Jamaica in January 1742, but the campaign proved a disaster for the British. There were quarrels between the senior military and naval officers, with Ogle himself found guilty, by a civil jury, of assaulting the Governor of Jamaica. In October 1742, when Vernon was recalled, Ogle (rear-admiral of the Red since the previous March) again became C-in-C, Jamaica. With neither the British or the Spanish fleets able to spare ships for large-scale operations in the West Indies, naval activity was confined to trade-protection and commerce raiding.

Ogle was promoted to vice-admiral of the Blue on 11 August 1743 and admiral of the Blue on 23 June 1744. He returned home in the summer of 1745 and presided at the courts-martial of officers charged with misconduct at the battle of Hyeres, Toulon (11 February 1744). Ogle became admiral of the White on 15 July 1747 and admiral of the fleet on 19 July 1749. He sat as Member of Parliament for Rochester from 24 November 1746 until he died, in London, on 11 April 1750. He was married, but died without issue.

OGLE
Sir Charles, 2nd Baronet (1775–1858) [21]

Charles Ogle, born on 24 May 1775, was the eldest son of Sir Chaloner Ogle, later admiral of the Red, and a grandnephew of Admiral of the Fleet Sir Chaloner Ogle [2]. He entered the Navy in 1788 as captain's servant and served on the Coast of West Africa station successively in the 5th-rate *Adventure* and the 4th-rate *Medusa*, before becoming a midshipman in the 3rd-rate *Alcide* at Portsmouth in September 1791. He then served off Halifax, Nova Scotia, and in the Channel, successively in the 6th-rate *Winchelsea*, the 3rd-rate *Edgar* and the 2nd-rate *Boyne*. After the outbreak of the French Revolutionary War he was appointed on 14 November 1793 lieutenant in the 5th-rate *Woolwich* in the West Indies. In December 1793 Ogle moved to the 3rd-rate *Vengeance* and in January 1794 returned to *Boyne*, then flagship of Sir John Jervis [12], C-in-C in the West Indies. In the spring of 1794 he took part in the British capture of Martinique and Guadeloupe, where he led a storming-party. He was then briefly in command of the 5th-rate *Assurance*, prior to being appointed commander of the sloop *Avenger* on 21 May 1794. When Jervis became C-in-C of the Mediterranean Fleet in November 1795 Ogle followed him to become successively commander of the sloop *Peterel* and, on 11 January 1796, captain of the 5th-rate *Minerve*. During 1797 he moved to the 5th-rate *Meleager* and was commended by Jervis for his part in the blockade of Cadiz. He next commanded successively the 5th-rate *Greyhound*, with which he made several prizes, and the 5th-rate *Egyptienne*, where he was awarded a gold medal by the Ottoman government for supporting the British landing in Egypt in March 1801.

After peace with France was declared by the Treaty of Amiens (27 March 1802) Ogle married Charlotte, daughter of General the Honourable Thomas Gage, governor of Massachusetts at the beginning of the American War of Independence and sister of the future Sir William Gage [23]. Hostilities were renewed in May 1803, but Ogle did not return to sea until April 1805, when he was given command of the 5th-rate *Unité*, fitting out for the Mediterranean. In June 1806 he was appointed to the royal yacht *Princess Augusta*, where he remained for the rest of the war. Ogle commanded the 3rd-rate *Ramillies* in the Channel from August to November 1815, the 2nd-rate *Malta* at Plymouth from November 1815 to January 1816 and the 3rd-rate *Rivoli* at Portsmouth from January to September 1816. After succeeding to his father's baronetcy and estate Sir Charles Ogle became rear-admiral of the Blue on 12 August 1819, rear-admiral of the White on 19 July 1812 and rear-admiral of the Red on 27 May 1825. His wife died in 1814, leaving him with a young family of a son and two daughters, and in 1820, he married Letitia Burroughs, the daughter of a baronet.

Ogle was C-in-C on the North America station from April 1827 to July 1830 and became vice-admiral of the Blue on 22 July 1830. The second Lady Ogle died in 1832 and Ogle married in 1834 Mary, Lady Thorold, who herself had been twice widowed. He became vice-admiral of the Red on 10 January 1837, admiral of the Blue on 23 November 1841, admiral of the White in November 1846 and admiral of the Red on 26 June 1847. From 1845 to 1848 he was C-in-C, Portsmouth. He became admiral of the fleet on 8 December 1857 and died at Tunbridge Wells on 16 June 1858.

OLIVER
Sir HENRY FRANCIS, GCB, GCMG, CVO (1865–1965) [78]

Henry Oliver, the fifth child in the family of seven sons and three daughters of a prosperous Border farmer, was born at Kelso, Roxburghshire, on 22 January 1865. He joined the Navy as a cadet in the training ship *Britannia* in 1878 and was appointed to the battleship *Agincourt*, flagship of the second-in-command of the Channel Squadron, in September 1880, with promotion to midshipman on 21 January 1881. In March 1882 he joined the corvette *Amethyst* on the south-east coast of America and remained there until becoming an acting sub-lieutenant on 21 January 1885 at the beginning of his promotion courses. Oliver was appointed to the battleship *Triumph*, flagship of the Pacific station, in October 1886 with promotion to lieutenant on 30 June 1888. From April 1889 to February 1894 he served in the survey vessel *Stork* and subsequently qualified as a navigating officer. He was then appointed navigating lieutenant of the cruiser *Wallaroo*, assigned to the protection of seaborne trade in Australasian waters, from which he returned home to become navigating lieutenant of the cruiser *Blake*, in the Channel Squadron, in January 1898. At the end of 1898 he was turned over to the cruiser *Niobe*, in which he was detached to the Cape of Good Hope during the Anglo-Boer South African War, with promotion to commander on 31 December 1899. In September 1900 Oliver was appointed navigating commander in the battleship *Majestic*, flagship of Sir Arthur Wilson [59], C-in-C of the Channel Squadron, and contributed to Wilson's reputation as a skilful fleet handler. He was promoted to captain on 30 June 1903.

As part of the training reforms introduced by Sir John Fisher [58] as second naval lord, Oliver was appointed the first captain of a new school for navigators at Portsmouth, initially set up in the old cruiser *Mercury* and then ashore, in *Dryad*. From February 1907 to November 1908 he commanded the armoured cruiser *Achilles* in the Home Fleet. He then became Naval Assistant to the First Sea Lord, where he served under Fisher until 1910 and subsequently under Wilson until 1912. He was then given command of the new battleship *Thunderer* before returning to the Admiralty in 1913 as Director of Naval Intelligence, with promotion to rear-admiral on 3 December 1913. In June 1914 he married Beryl Carnegy White, of Lour, Angus.

Soon after the outbreak of the First World War in August 1914 Oliver went to Antwerp in advance of the naval brigade despatched by Winston Churchill, First Lord of the Admiralty. During September, with Belgian support, Oliver blew up the engine-rooms of thirty-eight German merchantmen stranded in Antwerp at the outbreak of hostilities. The Germans reached Antwerp in October 1914. Churchill landed in person and offered to lead its defence, a proposal received by his Cabinet colleagues with ill-concealed merriment. Most of the British naval brigade was forced into internment in the neutral Netherlands. Oliver served briefly as Churchill's Naval Secretary before becoming Chief of the War Staff at the Admiralty in November 1914.

Oliver remained there under Sir Henry Jackson [70], who succeeded Fisher as First Sea Lord in May 1915. He was one of the few officers over whom Jackson considered it unnecessary to exercise close personal control and was thus in charge of the Admiralty's part in the conduct of the battle of Jutland (31 May–1 June 1916). In June 1916 he was awarded the KCB. When Sir John Jellicoe [68] became First Sea Lord and Chief of the Naval

Staff in December 1916 Sir Henry Oliver was appointed to the new post of Deputy Chief of the Naval Staff, with a seat on the Board of Admiralty. Oliver's own reluctance to delegate, a characteristic he shared with Jackson, Jellicoe and most other senior officers of his day, placed him under steadily increasing strain. In January 1918 he left the Admiralty and commanded the First Battle-cruiser Squadron, with his flag in the battle-cruiser *Repulse*, from then until May 1919, when the Grand Fleet dispersed after the end of the war. On 1 December 1919 he was promoted to vice-admiral and appointed C-in-C, Home Fleet, subsequently combined with the Reserve fleet.

Oliver became Second Sea Lord in 1920. In 1922 the Committee on National Expenditure, headed by the eminent businessman, Sir Eric Geddes (a former First Lord of the Admiralty), recommended large-scale reductions in the number of public employees. As the member for personnel, Oliver was responsible for implementing the naval element of these cuts, as well as those resulting from the reduction of the fleet by the Washington Naval Treaty. He was promoted to admiral on 1 November 1923 and, after declining the appointment of C-in-C, Portsmouth, went back to sea as C-in-C, Atlantic Fleet, from 1924 to 1927. He was promoted to admiral of the fleet on 21 January 1928 and retired in 1933. He played no operational part in the Second World War, though he gave much encouragement to the Royal National Lifeboat Association and supported his wife, created Dame Beryl Oliver, in her London-based war work with the British Red Cross Society. He died at their home in London on 15 October 1965.

OSWALD
Sir JOHN JULIAN ROBERTSON, GCB (1933-) [114]

Julian Oswald, son of Captain George Hamilton Oswald, Royal Navy, of Newmore, Invergordon, Ross-shire, was born on 11 August 1933. After attending Beaudesert Park School, Minchinhampton, Gloucestershire, he joined the Navy as a cadet at the Royal Naval College, Dartmouth, on 1 May 1947. After sea training in the cruiser *Devonshire*, he became a midshipman on 1 January 1952 and served in the battleship *Vanguard* and the frigate *Verulam*. He was promoted to sub-lieutenant on 1 May 1953 and, after attending Junior Officers' courses, joined the aircraft carrier *Theseus*, flagship of the Training Squadron in the Home Fleet, in February 1955. He subsequently served between 1957 and 1959 in the cruiser *Newfoundland* and the minesweeper *Jewel*. In 1958 Oswald married Veronica ("Roni") Thompson, with whom he later had two sons and three daughters. During 1959 he joined the gunnery training school *Excellent*, where he qualified as a gunnery specialist. From 1960 until early 1962 he was in the aircraft carrier *Victorious*, prior to being given command of the minesweeper *Yarnton* in April 1962. He was promoted to lieutenant-commander on 1 June 1963 and qualified at the Royal Naval Staff College,

Greenwich, during 1964. In 1965 he returned to *Excellent* as the Air Weapons Officer.

Oswald returned to sea in September 1966 as first lieutenant of the frigate *Naiad*. He was appointed to the Ministry of Defence in August 1968 in the Directorate of Naval Plans, with promotion to commander on 31 December 1968. From January 1971 to 1972 he commanded the frigate *Bacchante*, after which he returned to the MOD to join the office of the Assistant Chief of the Defence Staff. He was promoted to captain on 31 December 1973 and remained at the MOD until the end of 1975. During 1976 he attended the Royal College of Defence Studies, London. Oswald commanded the guided weapons destroyer *Newcastle* from January 1977 to early 1979, when he joined the Royal Naval Presentation Team. He served as Captain of the Britannia Royal Naval College, Dartmouth, from 1980 until his promotion to rear-admiral on 2 September 1982 and then became Assistant Chief of the Defence Staff (Programmes) at the MOD, followed by appointment as ACDS (Policy and Nuclear) in 1985. From 1985 to 1987 he was Flag Officer, Third Flotilla and Commander, Anti-Submarine Warfare, Striking Fleet, with promotion to vice-admiral on 3 January 1986 and the award of the KCB in 1987. Sir Julian Oswald was promoted to admiral on 29 May 1987 and was between 1987 and 1989 C-in-C, Fleet, and NATO C-in-C, Channel (CINCHAN) and Eastern Atlantic Area (CINCEASTLANT).

Oswald was First Sea Lord from May 1989 to 2 March 1992, when he was promoted to admiral of the fleet and went on half-pay. During this period he had to deal with changes in defence policy arising from the collapse of the Soviet Union and also with the brief Gulf War following the Iraqi occupation of Kuwait. He was also responsible for the then controversial decision that members of the Women's Royal Naval Service (whose unofficial punning motto had previously been *"Never at Sea"*) could serve in sea-going ships. For many years he was President of the FRINTON (Former Russian Interpreters of the Navy) Society, originally composed of reservists who had learned the language during their National Service after the Second World War. After leaving the MOD Sir Julian Oswald undertook a variety of business and charitable activities, with especial emphasis on maritime benevolent and historical interests. He published *The Royal Navy-Today and Tomorrow* and numerous articles on strategy and defence policy. In 1994 he became President of the Sea Cadet Association. From his home in the Meon Valley, Hampshire, he remains active in all his sporting, family and other interests.

PARKER
Sir PETER, 1st Baronet (1721–1811) [10]

Peter Parker, born in 1721, joined the Navy under command of his father, Captain, later Rear-Admiral, Christopher Parker. He was appointed a commander on 17 March 1735 and is thought to have served in the fleet sent to the West Indies under Admiral Edward Vernon on the outbreak of war with Spain ("the War of Jenkins's Ear") in 1739. This was soon overtaken by a wider European conflict, the War of the Austrian Succession, in which he served in the Mediterranean, first in the 2nd-rate *Russell* and then in the bomb vessel *Firedrake*. In January 1744 he joined the 2nd-rate *Barfleur*, flagship of Rear-Admiral William Rowley [6], in which he took part in the battle of Hyeres, Toulon (11 February 1744). Parker joined the 2nd-rate *Neptune*, flagship of Vice-Admiral Richard Lestock, in March 1744, and subsequently returned home. He was promoted to become captain of the 6th-rate *Margate* on 6 May 1747 and spent the winter of 1747–48 on trade protection duty in the North Sea and the Channel. In the closing stages of the war *Margate* was re-deployed to the Mediterranean before returning home in April 1749. Parker remained ashore until 1755, when, with another French war approaching, he was given the 5th-rate *Woolwich* and deployed to the North Sea for trade protection duty.

In the Seven Years' War Parker served with *Woolwich* during 1757 in the West Indies. He was appointed to the 3rd-rate *Bristol* in January 1759 and took part in the unsuccessful British attack on Martinique, followed by the capture of Guadeloupe in May 1759. He then became captain of the 3rd-rate *Buckingham* with which he returned home in 1760. During 1761 he served in the capture of Belle-Ile, off the west coast of France and, from August 1762 to the end of the war in 1763, commanded the 3rd-rate *Terrible*. He was given a knighthood in 1772.

Sir Peter Parker was appointed in October 1773 to the 2nd-rate *Barfleur*, part of the squadron held in permanent readiness at Portsmouth. In October 1775, after the outbreak of the American War of Independence, he became a commodore, with his broad pendant in a new *Bristol*, a 4th-rate, ordered to the North America station. With transports carrying 2,500 men, he sailed to join General Sir Henry Clinton in support of a loyalist uprising in the Carolinas, but was delayed by storms and failed to arrive in time. He then persuaded Clinton to attack Charleston, South Carolina, on 28 June 1776. The troops were landed, but when they failed to reach the harbour defences Parker attacked with his ships alone. After several hours fighting, he was driven off with the loss of a frigate and nearly two hundred casualties, including forty-six dead on his own flagship. He himself was wounded in the thigh and was reported by the colonial newspapers as having lost his breeches. In the 4th-rate *Chatham*, he later took part in the capture of Long Island, New York, in August 1776 and of Rhode Island in December 1776.

Parker was promoted to rear-admiral of the Blue on 20 May 1777 and took up appointment as C-in-C, Jamaica, at the end of the year. He became a rear-admiral of the White on 23 January 1778, rear-admiral of the Red on 29 January 1778, vice-admiral of the Blue on 29 March 1779 and vice-admiral of the White on 26 September 1780. As hostilities in American waters drew to a close, he returned home in the 2nd-rate *Sandwich* in August 1782. His ship also carried the French Admiral De Grasse, taken prisoner at the Battle of The Saints (Iles des Saintes) (12 April 1782). Parker was awarded a baronetcy on 13 January 1783 and was promoted to admiral of the Blue on 24 September 1787. He sat as Member of Parliament for Seaford, Sussex, from 1784 to 1786, and for Maldon, Essex, from 1787 to 1790. At the beginning of the French Revolutionary War in 1794, Parker was appointed C-in-C, Portsmouth, where he remained, with promotion to admiral of the White on 12 April 1794 until 16 September 1796, when he became admiral of the fleet. He died at his house in Weymouth Street, London, on 21 December 1811.

He had a reputation for making full use of his powers of patronage, exemplified by his appointment in March 1779 of his son Christopher as a captain of a frigate at the age of 18, and of his nephew George as a lieutenant at the age of 13. He was also responsible for the early advancement of Horatio Nelson (nephew of the then Comptroller of the Navy) by taking him into his own flagship in July 1778 and giving him command of the brig *Badger* five months later. His wife Margaret, a member of the influential Nugent family, seems also to have taken a kindly interest in the young Nelson, and Sir Peter Parker was chief mourner at Nelson's funeral. They had one daughter and a son, Christopher, who, after his early promotion, rose to become a vice-admiral and predeceased his father in 1804. Christopher Parker's son, who inherited the baronetcy, became a captain in the Navy and was killed in a shore action during the American War of 1812.

PARKER
Sir WILLIAM, 1st Baronet, GCB (1781–1866) [26]

William Parker, the third son of a country gentleman, George Parker, of Almington, Staffordshire, and the grandson of Sir Thomas Parker, an influential Whig politician, was born on 1 December 1781. George Parker's sister, Martha, married Captain Sir John Jervis, the future Earl of St Vincent [12]. William Parker joined the Navy on 5 March 1793, shortly after the beginning of the French Revolutionary War, as captain's servant in the 3rd-rate *Orion*, commanded by Captain (later Admiral Sir) John Duckworth. After serving in this ship in the West Indies, he took part in the major fleet action of the Glorious First of June (1 June 1794) in the Channel. In March 1795 Parker followed Duckworth to the 3rd-rate *Leviathan* in which he returned to the West Indies and was present at the capture of numerous enemy vessels as well as the unsuccessful British attack on the French colonial port of Leogane, Haiti (21–23 March 1796).

Parker became an acting lieutenant in the 5th-rate *Magicienne*, followed by appointment in May 1798 as acting lieutenant in the 2nd-rate *Queen*, flagship of the C-in-C, West Indies, Sir Hyde Parker (no relation). He commanded successively the 6th-rate *Volage* and the sloops *Amaranthe* and *Pelican*, and was confirmed as lieutenant on 5 September 1799. He was promoted to commander on 10 October 1799 and was briefly in command of the 4th-rate *Abergavenny* before being appointed to the sloop *Stork* in November 1799. He served in this ship until 1801, serving in the West Indies, the Channel and the Mediterranean, taking the French packet *Légere* and supporting the capture of the Spanish privateer *El Cantara*. In October 1801 he became captain of the 5th-rate *Oiseau*, shortly before the armistice with France leading to the Treaty of Amiens (27 March 1802). An interesting legal problem arose in that Admiralty regulations required courts-martial to be composed of all captains present in the harbour where the proceedings took place. On the other hand, persons not having reached the age of legal majority (at that time twenty-one years) could not sit in judgement. As Parker was aged only nineteen on his first promotion to captain, the problem was solved by sending his ship to sea so that a court-martial could be convened in his absence.

Escaping the post-war reductions, Parker was given command of the 5th-rate *Alarm* in March 1802, where he remained until appointed in October 1802 to the 5th-rate *Amazon*, which he commanded for the next nine years. Following the renewal of hostilities with France in May 1803 he served under Nelson in the Mediterranean off Toulon, and was with him in the pursuit of the French fleet to the West Indies and back during the summer of 1805. His prizes included three privateers and a share in the French ship of the line *Marengo* and frigate *Belle Poule*, taken in March 1806. He was mentioned in despatches for this action and for landing with a party of seamen at Ferrol in the summer of 1809 to support the Spanish insurgency in Galicia. In June 1810, while *Amazon* underwent a lengthy refit at Plymouth, Parker married Frances Biddulph, the youngest daughter of a wealthy baronet. During 1811 he served in the blockade of Brest and captured the privateer *Cupidon*. After the worn-out *Amazon* was paid off in January 1812 Parker spent the rest of the Napoleonic war on half-pay. He used his prize money to buy an estate, Shenstone Lodge, near Lichfield, Staffordshire, a county where he had family connections, and settled there with his young wife to raise a family of two sons and six daughters.

Parker returned to sea in October 1827. He declined the offered appointment of C-in-C, Cape of Good Hope, on the grounds that no officer who had not previously commanded a ship of the line should serve as a commodore or flag officer, so instead was given the 3rd-rate *Warspite*. He then served in the Mediterranean under Vice-Admiral Edward Codrington and was on the coast of Greece during 1828, at a time of international tension with Turkey arising from the Greek War of Independence. Parker returned home late in 1828 and was appointed to the royal yacht *Prince Regent*. He became a rear-admiral of the Blue on 22 July 1830 and second-in-command in the Channel, again serving under Codrington, in April

1831, with his flag in the 1st-rate *Prince Regent*. Between September 1831 and June 1834, with his flag in the 2nd-rate *Asia*, he commanded a squadron in the mouth of the Tagus, during a civil war in Portugal ending with the accession of the British-supported Queen Maria II. He became a KCB in July 1834.

From July to November 1834 Sir William Parker was a Lord Commissioner of the Admiralty in the Board headed by Lord Auckland. When Sir Robert Peel became Prime Minister in December 1834 a new Board was formed, but in April 1835, after the fall of Peel's administration, Parker returned to the Admiralty with Auckland. He became rear-admiral of the White on 10 January 1837 and rear-admiral of the Red on 28 July 1838. Early in May 1841, during the First China War, he was appointed C-in-C, East Indies, with his flag in the 3rd-rate *Cornwallis*. He arrived at Canton (Guangzhou), on the south coast of China in July 1841, where, as the senior officer, he took over the supreme command of British forces there from Major General Hugh Gough. Parker was promoted to vice-admiral of the Blue on 23 November 1841. He got on well with the fire-eating Gough and both officers personally took part in combined operations along the coast of southern China and up the Yangtse River until the end of hostilities in August 1842.

Parker was granted a substantial pension in April 1844 and returned home with the award of a baronetcy in December 1844. He was appointed C-in-C, Mediterranean, with his flag in the 1st-rate *Hibernia*, in February 1845 and was given the additional command of the Channel Squadron in May 1846, at a period of renewed civil war in Portugal. Auckland, who returned to the Admiralty as a member of Lord John Russell's Cabinet in July 1846, then offered him the post of first naval lord, but he declined on the grounds that his health was not up to the work and that his eyesight could not cope with working by candlelight.

He became a vice-admiral of the White on 9 November 1846 and remained at sea (shifting his flag to the 1st-rate *Queen* in September 1849) until April 1852, becoming a vice-admiral of the Red on 8 January 1848 and an admiral of the Blue on 29 April 1851. Parker gained a reputation as an exacting C-in-C, demanding the highest standards of smartness in his fleet's sailing drill, forbidding officers in his flagship to use tobacco and encouraging officers to wear caps with slashed peaks (a style he pioneered, and which on that account became known as "promotion peaks"). He became an admiral of the White on 17 September 1853 and was C-in-C, Plymouth, from May 1854 to May 1857. During the Crimean War his advice was sought by the Admiralty on a proposal by the Earl of Dundonald (more famous as the dashing frigate captain, Lord Cochrane) for using poison gas against the Russian Baltic fleet. He became admiral of the Red on 25 June 1858 and admiral of the fleet on 27 April 1863. Parker died of bronchitis on 13 November 1866 and was buried in the parish church of St John the Baptist, Shenstone. He was succeeded as second baronet by his son, a captain (later admiral) in the Navy.

PHIPPS-HORNBY
GEOFFREY THOMAS, see **HORNBY**, Sir GEOFFREY
THOMAS PHIPPS **[45]**

PHILIP
HRH Duke of Edinburgh, KG, KT, OM, GBE, AC, QSO
(1921–) **[99]**

Prince Philip of Greece was born in Corfu on 10 June 1921, the only son
in a family of five children born to Prince Andrew of Greece and his wife
Princess Alice, a granddaughter of Queen Victoria. Prince Andrew was a
younger brother of King Constantine I of the Hellenes, and a nephew
of Alexandra, the queen of Edward VII **[44]** and daughter of Christian IV of
Denmark. Princess Alice, in her youth, was said to be the most beautiful
princess in Europe. A woman of determined character, who overcame the
challenge of being born profoundly deaf, she devoted much of her life to
charitable activities and worked with the Red Cross during the Balkan War
of 1912 nursing sick and wounded Greek soldiers. In later life she became
a nun and founded the Greek Orthodox Christian Sisterhood of Martha
and Mary. Her father, Prince Louis of Battenberg **[74]**, made his career in
the Royal Navy and became First Sea Lord but, after the outbreak of the
First World War in August 1914, was driven to resign from this office on
account of his German origins. When the British Royal Family disclaimed
its German titles in 1917 Battenberg anglicized his name as Mountbatten
and was granted a peerage as the Marquess of Milford Haven. The
marquess's younger son, Lord Louis Mountbatten, later created Earl
Mountbatten of Burma **[102]**, was thus a brother of Princess Alice of
Greece and the uncle of her only son, Prince Philip.

Prince Andrew, narrowly escaping execution at the hands of Greek
republicans for his part in a disastrous campaign against Turkey, went into
exile with his family in 1923. After escaping to Italy on the British cruiser
Calypso, they took refuge with relatives in Paris, from where Philip was sent,
in 1930, to Cheam Preparatory School. In 1934, he spent two terms in
Germany, before going to a new school at Gordonstoun in the Scottish
Highlands, founded by a prominent German educationalist. His four
sisters, one of whom was later killed with her husband and children in an
air crash in 1937, all married German princes.

Prince Philip decided on a naval career and became a cadet at the Royal
Naval College, Dartmouth, in May 1939. On the advice of Lord Louis
Mountbatten, he sought naturalization as a British subject when the
Second World War began in September 1939, but found that this process
had been placed in abeyance for the duration of hostilities. Like his contemporaries, he looked for employment in an active theatre of war, but as the
national of a neutral state, it was judged that it would be politically embar-
rassing if he fell into Axis hands. This was compounded by the

circumstance that, like other princes whose family ties stretched across international borders, his three surviving brothers-in-law were serving in the German Armed Forces, where one was later killed and two wounded. He was appointed to the battleship *Ramillies* on convoy escort duty in the Indian Ocean, and when *Ramillies* was temporarily sent to the Mediterranean, was transferred successively to the cruisers *Kent* and *Shropshire* on the East Indies station. In October 1940 the Italian invasion of Greece brought his native country into the war. This allowed his subsequent appointment to the battleship *Valiant* in the Mediterranean, in which he served at the battle of Matapan (28 March 1941) and was mentioned in despatches.

Prince Philip subsequently served in a troopship on passage home and to the West Indies, where, with others, he volunteered to take the place of a group of Chinese stokers who had deserted, and qualified as a coaltrimmer. After attending his promotion courses and enjoying occasional leave visits to the Royal Family at Windsor, he was promoted to lieutenant on 16 January 1942 and was appointed to the destroyer *Wallace*, based at Rosyth. During 1943 his ship was deployed to the Mediterranean and supported the invasion of Sicily (July 1943). In 1944 Philip was appointed first lieutenant of the destroyer *Whelp* and joined the Eastern Fleet. He served in this ship in the British Pacific Fleet in the closing stages of the war against Japan and was present at the signing of the instrument of Japanese surrender in the USS *Missouri* in Tokyo Bay (2 September 1945).

Prince Philip briefly commanded *Whelp* in reserve after returning home in 1946, followed by another brief appointment to the recruit training establishment *Glendower*, Pwllheli, Carnarvonshire, from which he transferred to the petty officers training school *Royal Arthur*, Corsham, Wiltshire. His name became increasingly linked with that of his distant cousin Princess Elizabeth, heiress to George VI [86]. After disclaiming his title as a prince of Greece and renouncing his place in the succession to the Greek throne, he was granted British citizenship in March 1947. Largely through the influence of his uncle, who had made the name famous by his exploits, he took the surname Mountbatten. Lieutenant Philip Mountbatten and Princess Elizabeth were married in Westminster Abbey on 20 November 1947. On the following day he was granted the style of Royal Highness and was created Duke of Edinburgh, a title dormant since the death of Queen Victoria's second son, Alfred [49]. Edinburgh returned to sea in October 1949 in the destroyer flotilla leader *Chequers* in the Mediterranean and was promoted to lieutenant-commander on 16 July 1950. From August 1950 to July 1951 he was the commanding officer of the frigate *Magpie*. Princess Elizabeth succeeded to the throne on 6 February 1952 and Edinburgh's naval career came to an end as he took up the duties of a Royal consort. He became an admiral of the fleet, a field marshal in the Army and a marshal of the Royal Air Force on 15 January 1953. His many interests included a special concern for young people, exemplified by his creation of the Duke of Edinburgh's Award scheme to encourage endeavour and self-reliance. In 1957, marking their tenth wedding anniversary, Queen Elizabeth II created her husband a prince of the United Kingdom.

POLE
Sir CHARLES MORICE, 1st Baronet, GCB (1757–1830) [15]

Charles Pole was born on 18 January 1757, the second son of Reginald Pole, Esquire, of Stoke Damerell, Devonshire. He attended the Royal Naval Academy, Portsmouth, from 1770 until 1772 and was then appointed to the 5th-rate *Thames*. In December 1773 he joined the 4th-rate *Salisbury* in which he served in the East Indies. After the outbreak of the American War of Independence he was promoted to lieutenant on 26 June 1777 in the 6th-rate *Seahorse*. In 1778 he was appointed to the 4th-rate *Ripon* under Commodore Sir Edward Vernon, C-in-C, East Indies, and served at sea against a French squadron off Pondicherry (9 August 1778), and ashore in the subsequent siege of Pondicherry (capitulated 17 October 1778). He was then given command of the sloop *Cormorant* and sent home with the despatches as a mark of distinction. On 22 March 1779 Pole became captain of the 1st-rate *Britannia*, flagship of the second-in-command in the Channel. In 1780 he was appointed to the 6th-rate *Hussar*, in which he was wrecked off Hell Gates, New York. He was acquitted at the subsequent court-martial and given the 5th-rate *Success*. In May 1782, while escorting the storeship *Vernon* to the blockaded fortress of Gibraltar, he encountered the large Spanish frigate *Santa Catalina* in the Bay of Biscay on 16 March 1782. Determined to save *Vernon*, he approached under Dutch colours, and then revealed his true ones and opened fire simultaneously. After an engagement lasting some hours, the Spanish ship was dismasted and surrendered. She later sank after being set on fire on the approach of an unidentified squadron, which, too late, was found to be British. Pole thus not only lost his prize-money but was left with so many prisoners as to threaten the security of his own ship.

After the conclusion of hostilities in 1783 he commanded the 3rd-rate *Crown* for three years and then in 1788 was appointed groom of the bedchamber to Prince William, Duke of Clarence [11]. During 1790, when there was a threat of war with Spain over the possession of Nootka Sound (Vancouver, British Columbia), Pole was appointed to the 5th-rate *Melampus* and deployed to observe the French fleet at Brest. In 1791 he commanded the 3rd-rate *Illustrious* and in 1792 he married Henrietta, the daughter of John Goddard, a wealthy merchant of Woodford Hall, Essex.

Following the outbreak of the French Revolutionary War in February 1793 Pole was given command of the 3rd-rate *Colossus* and sent to the Mediterranean, where he captured the small French privateer *Vanneau* on 6 June 1793 and served from August to December 1793 in the blockade of Toulon. During 1794 he was with *Colossus* in the Channel fleet, off Ushant.

He became rear-admiral of the Blue on 1 June 1795 and from November 1795 to October 1796 was second-in-command on the West Indies station, with *Colossus* as his flagship. In March 1797 he was appointed first captain (captain of the fleet) in the 1st-rate *Royal George*, flagship of Lord Bridport (Sir Alexander Hood) as C-in-C in the Channel. A month later he was despatched in haste from Portsmouth to inform Earl Spencer, First Lord of the Admiralty, that the Channel fleet was in a state of mutiny. Pole returned with a party of flag officers sent to negotiate with the seamen's delegates, but when his senior officer, Vice-Admiral Sir Alan Gardner, threatened to hang every fifth man in the fleet, the talks ended in a scuffle and the negotiators were put ashore. He became a rear-admiral of the White on 14 February 1799 and joined the blockade of Rochefort, with his flag in *Royal George*.

During 1800 Pole served as Governor of Newfoundland, until his promotion to vice-admiral of the Blue on 1 January 1801. In June 1801 he succeeded Nelson in command of the Baltic fleet, with his flag in the 2nd-rate *St George*. On the re-establishment of friendly relations with Russia he brought the fleet home in July 1801 and was praised for his seamanship in exiting the Baltic through the Great Belt against a contrary wind. He was created a baronet in September 1801. After the Treaty of Amiens (27 March 1802) ended the war with revolutionary France Sir Charles Pole entered Parliament and sat as Member for Newark from 1802 to 1806 and Plymouth from 1806 to 1818. The war was renewed in May 1803 and Pole became an admiral of the Blue on 9 November 1805. Between February and October 1806 he was a lord commissioner of the Admiralty in the Board headed by Viscount Howick (later Earl Grey) during the "Ministry of all the Talents". He became admiral of the White on 31 July 1810 and admiral of the Red on 4 June 1814, but the war ended in 1815 without him again going to sea. He was made an admiral of the fleet on 22 July 1830, one of the three officers promoted to that rank to mark the accession of William IV [11]. He died at Denham Abbey on 6 September 1830. He had two daughters, but no male heir, and his baronetcy became extinct.

POLLOCK
Sir MICHAEL PATRICK, GCB, LVO, DSC (1916-) [108]

Michael Pollock, born on 19 October 1916, joined the Navy in May 1930 as a cadet in the Royal Naval College, Dartmouth. In January 1934 he joined the training cruiser *Frobisher* and became a midshipman on 1 September 1934, when he was appointed to the battleship *Nelson*, flagship of the Home Fleet. Between September 1935 and January 1936 he served in the destroyer *Express* in the Mediterranean, during a period when there was a threat of war between the United Kingdom and Italy following the Italian invasion of Abyssinia (Ethiopia). Pollock then returned to *Nelson* until the beginning of his promotion courses as an acting sub-lieutenant in

January 1936. He was promoted to sub-lieutenant on 1 May 1937 and joined the cruiser *York*, flagship of the America and West Indies station, at Bermuda in October 1937. After promotion to lieutenant on 1 August 1938 he returned home and was appointed to the battleship *Warspite*, flagship of the Mediterranean Fleet, at Malta in June 1939. Soon after the outbreak of the Second World War in September 1939 he was appointed first lieutenant of the destroyer *Vanessa* in which he served from October 1939 in Atlantic and Channel convoys and patrols off the east coast of Britain, with the threat of invasion after the German occupation of France and the Low Countries in May and June 1940. *Vanessa* was disabled by German air attack in July 1940. In 1940 Pollock married Margaret Steacy, of Bermuda, with whom he later had two sons and a daughter. He joined the gunnery school *Excellent* in January 1941 where he qualified as a gunnery officer before joining the junior instructional staff there. He was appointed in March 1942 to the cruiser *Arethusa* and served first in the North Atlantic and then in the Mediterranean, based at Alexandria, from where he took part in the bombardment of Rhodes and escorted convoys to the besieged island of Malta. On 18 November 1942, on convoy escort duty, *Arethusa* was torpedoed by enemy aircraft and set on fire. Badly damaged, with the loss of 155 out of her complement of 500, she then survived a stern tow in a rising gale to reach Alexandria three days later. The ship was sent to refit in Charleston, South Carolina, from where Pollock returned to *Excellent* in July 1943. He was appointed gunnery officer of the cruiser *Norfolk* in the Home Fleet in October 1943 and took part in North Atlantic and Arctic convoys and the sinking of the German battlecruiser *Scharnhorst* (27 December 1943). In this operation *Norfolk* was hit by *Scharnhorst*'s 11-in guns, and had one turret and most of her radars put out of action. She returned to Newcastle-upon-Tyne for extensive repairs and modernization, with Pollock, who was awarded the DSC, left in the ship in charge of the Seaman aspect of the refit, and in command for part of the time. *Arethusa* rejoined the fleet late in 1944 and subsequently took part in convoy actions and raids on enemy shipping off the Norwegian coast. Pollock was promoted to acting lieutenant-commander on 1 May 1945 and sailed with his ship to join the British Pacific Fleet. After the end of hostilities with Japan in August 1945 and minor operations against nationalist insurgents in Malaya and Java, he returned home by troopship in December 1945, having been mentioned in despatches three times in the course of the war.

Pollock returned to *Excellent* in January 1946 as an assistant instructor on the Long Gunnery Course, with his promotion to lieutenant-commander confirmed on 1 June 1946. In August 1947 he became an application officer at the Admiralty Signals Research Establishment, Hazlemere, Buckinghamshire, before returning to *Excellent* where he was between May and October 1949 in charge of the Fire Control section. In October 1949 he joined the cruiser *Glasgow*, flagship of the America and West Indies station, as fleet gunnery officer to the C-in-C. He was promoted to commander on 30 June 1950 and was appointed in November

1950 to be Commander (G) at the Chatham gunnery school. In September 1952 he became commander of the Junior Officers' War Course at the Royal Naval College, Greenwich. Pollock's first wife had died in 1951 and in 1954 he married Mrs Majory Helen Reece, acquiring with her a step-daughter. He was appointed commander of the cruiser *Newcastle*, flagship of the Far East station in June 1954. This ship served off the coast of Korea at the end of the Korean War and in 1955 took part in the Malayan insurgency campaign, giving gunfire support to the ground forces.

Pollock was promoted to captain on 30 June 1955 and from January 1956 to January 1957 was Assistant Director of Plans (Warfare) at the Admiralty. In February 1958 he became Captain (D) at Portsmouth, commanding the destroyer *Vigo*. He was next appointed Director, Surface Weapons, in the Admiralty's outstation at Bath, Somerset, in January 1960. In October 1962 he was given command of the cruiser *Blake* and was sent on a tactical course in that capacity, but in December 1962 his appointment was changed to command of the aircraft carrier *Ark Royal*, which from time to time was flagship of the Flag Officer, Aircraft Carriers. Pollock commanded this ship during 1963 on the Far East station and off the coasts of East Africa and the Middle East until returning home in January 1964. Between April 1964 and April 1966 he served in the Navy Department of the Ministry of Defence (as the Admiralty became in 1964) as Assistant Chief of the Naval Staff, with promotion to rear-admiral on 7 July 1964. Pollock then became Flag Officer second-in-command of the Home Fleet (renamed the Western Fleet on the demise of the Mediterranean Fleet in 1967), with his flag in the cruiser *Tiger*. He was promoted to vice-admiral on 26 December 1967, when he was appointed Flag Officer, Submarines, and NATO Allied Commander (Submarines), Eastern Atlantic Area (COMSUBEASTLANT), at the submarine base *Dolphin*, Gosport. He was awarded the KCB in 1968.

In January 1970 Sir Michael Pollock became Controller of the Navy, with promotion to admiral on 21 April 1970. From there in March 1971 he was appointed First Sea Lord, where he remained until leaving office and becoming an admiral of the fleet on 1 March 1974. Undertaking many charitable and civic activities, he settled at his home in Churchstoke, Montgomery, Powys.

POUND
Sir ALFRED DUDLEY PICKMAN ROGERS, GCB, OM, GCVO (1877–1943) [89]

Dudley Pound was born at Wraxall, near Ventnor, Isle of Wight, on 29 August 1877. His father, a country gentleman, played little part in public affairs, though he spent a year in the Colonial Service in British Guiana (Guyana), and on returning home via the United States met his future wife, Elizabeth Pickman Rogers, who came from a family of wealthy merchants in Salem, Massachusetts. A woman of strong will, eccentric behaviour and extravagant habits, she eventually separated from her husband, who settled at Buckfastleigh, Devon, where Pound grew up. On 15 January 1891 he joined the training ship *Britannia* at Dartmouth, where he passed in first in the order of merit and retained that position on passing out in December 1892. On 5 January 1893 he was appointed midshipman in the battleship *Royal Sovereign*, flagship of the Channel Squadron, from which he was transferred in May 1894 to the cruiser *Undaunted* and sailed for the China station. After returning home in the full-rigged cruiser *Leander*, he joined her sister ship, the cruiser *Calypso*, in the Training Squadron.

Pound was promoted to acting sub-lieutenant on 29 August 1896, at the beginning of his promotion courses, and joined the destroyer *Opossum* in October 1897. He joined the battleship *Magnificent*, flagship of the second-in-command of the Channel Squadron, in January 1898, in which he was promoted to lieutenant on 29 August 1898. He was appointed flag lieutenant and, despite frequently being placed under arrest by his irascible admiral (on one occasion twelve times while *Magnificent* sailed the three miles between the Hamoaze and Plymouth Sound), received a favourable report. In September 1899 he joined the torpedo school *Vernon* from which, after qualifying in December 1901, he was appointed as torpedo lieutenant to the cruiser *Grafton*, flagship on the Pacific station.

Pound returned home to serve as torpedo lieutenant in the battleship *King Edward VII*, flagship of the Atlantic Fleet, in January 1905 to March 1907. Between then and October 1908 he was torpedo lieutenant in the battleship *Queen* in the Mediterranean Fleet. There he married Betty, the daughter of an old Ventnor neighbour, Dr John Whitehead. They later had a family of two sons and a daughter. Pound joined the staff of the Ordnance Department at the Admiralty in January 1909. In May 1911 he became commander of the battleship *Superb* in the Home Fleet. There he gained the medal of the Royal Humane Society for leading the attempted rescue of four men, three of whom subsequently died, overcome by foul air in the ship's potato hold, in June 1911. Early in 1913 he joined the staff of the Naval War College, Portsmouth, from which he was appointed commander of the battleship *St Vincent* in the Home Fleet in April 1914.

Following the outbreak of the First World War in August 1914 Pound served in *St Vincent* in the Grand Fleet until promoted to captain on 31 December 1914. He was then appointed additional Naval Assistant to Lord Fisher [58], who had returned to office as First Sea Lord in the Board of Admiralty headed by Winston Churchill. Pound went back to the Grand Fleet in May 1915 on appointment to the battleship *Colossus* as flag captain to the second-in-command of the First Battle Squadron, Rear-Admiral Ernest Gaunt, his former captain in *Superb*. Pound served at the battle of Jutland (31 May–1 June 1916), where *Colossus* contributed to the sinking of the German cruiser *Wiesbaden* and destroyer *V48* and sustained several casualties. After the battle he was appointed to a committee to examine the use of wireless to control gunfire. In July 1917 he returned to the Admiralty as the head of a newly-formed Planning Section in the Operations Division. Shortly afterwards he became Assistant Director of its successor, the Plans Division, under Rear-Admiral Roger Keyes [80]. In January 1918, when Keyes was given command of the Dover Patrol, Pound became Director of the Operations Division (Home) and worked closely with Keyes in planning his raid on Zeebrugge (23 April 1918). After the end of the war he remained at the Admiralty until July 1919.

Between October 1920 and June 1923 Pound was captain of the battle-cruiser *Repulse* in the Atlantic Fleet. He then became Director of Plans at the Admiralty and attended the final session of the Lausanne conference, convened to settle outstanding international differences with Turkey. During 1924 he attended the League of Nations meeting at Geneva, where a proposed Protocol to promote peaceful settlement of international disputes by negotiation, mutual support and disarmament was causing anxiety at the Admiralty. With the termination of the Anglo-Japanese alliance of 1902, he urged the building of a naval base at Singapore. From April 1925 to February 1926 Pound served as chief of staff to Keyes as C-in-C, Mediterranean Fleet, in the battleship *Warspite*, with promotion to commodore on 2 July 1925 and rear-admiral on 1 March 1926. In April 1926 he became Assistant Chief of the Naval Staff at the Admiralty. During the abortive Geneva Naval Conference Pound took the place of the Deputy Chief of the Naval Staff, Vice-Admiral Sir Frederick Field [81], when the latter became ill in July 1927.

In May 1929, Pound was given command of the Battle-cruiser Squadron, with his flag in the battle-cruiser *Renown*, and became second-in-command of the Atlantic Fleet. He implemented a policy of realistic training, with special emphasis on night exercises, despite the risk of collision between darkened ships. He was promoted to vice-admiral on 15 May 1931 and handed over command of his squadron to his old friend Rear-Admiral Wilfred Tomkinson in May 1931. After a period on half-pay he was appointed Second Sea Lord in August 1932, as part of a general reconstruction of the Board of Admiralty in the aftermath of the mutiny of the Atlantic Fleet at Invergordon. When Tomkinson (who had been in temporary command of the fleet at the time of the mutiny) was made the scapegoat, he appealed to Pound, as the Sea Lord responsible for personnel matters, but Pound refused to support him. After being awarded the KCB in 1934 Sir Dudley Pound was promoted to admiral on 16 October 1935 and went to succeed Admiral Sir William Fisher as C-in-C, Mediterranean Fleet. A sudden increase in international tension following Italy's invasion of Abyssinian (Ethiopia) led to the decision that Fisher should remain in post until the crisis was resolved. Pound thereupon volunteered to act as his chief of staff until eventually succeeding him in March 1936.

Pound trained his fleet hard for likely operations against the Italian Navy and continued his emphasis on night exercises. During the Spanish Civil War of 1936–39 he was involved in the protection of British shipping off the Spanish coast and in the joint British, French and Italian patrols against "pirate" (actually Italian) submarines that attacked merchantmen carrying supplies for the Spanish republican government. He gained a reputation as an exacting, even harsh, disciplinarian, ready to criticize officers and ratings alike if they failed to reach the standards he required, while at the same time keeping in his own hands decisions that could have been delegated to a lower level. With his flag at various times in the battleships *Queen Elizabeth*, *Barham* and *Warspite*, and the cruiser *Galatea*, he remained in command as the international situation grew worse. After the Munich crisis of 1938, he was told that his tenure would be extended until April 1940, but in June 1939 he was recalled to succeed the ailing Sir Roger Backhouse [88] as First Sea Lord in the Board headed by Lord Stanhope in Chamberlain's Cabinet. He was promoted to admiral of the fleet on 31 July 1939.

On the outbreak of the Second World War in September 1939, Stanhope was succeeded by Winston Churchill, under whom Pound had served at the Admiralty in 1915. The signal "Winston's back", has been attributed to Pound, with the suggestion that he intended it as much as a caution as a cause for celebration. His approach towards the naval strategies advanced by Churchill, either as First Lord or, after May 1940, Prime Minister, was to give them fair consideration and offer a reasoned response, so that he became "Churchill's anchor". Nevertheless, he was seen by some as allowing Churchill to interfere in the details of operational matters and as attempting himself to exercise too close a control over ships at sea. He was hampered by Churchill's habit of giving senior posts to his personal favourites, such as the Earl of Cork and Orrery [87] as Flag Officer, Narvik, in April 1940; Keyes as Chief of Combined Operations in July 1940 and Lord Louis Mountbatten [102] as Keyes's successor in 1941.

Pound was criticized by Cork for the Admiralty's part in the conduct of the Norwegian campaign, in which the Navy suffered heavy losses. Ever mindful of the need for convoy escorts in the battle of the Atlantic, he was reluctant to lose more destroyers in the evacuation of the British Expeditionary Force from Dunkirk (26 May–4 June 1940), but was persuaded by Vice-Admiral Sir Bertram Ramsay, Flag Officer, Dover, to accept the risks. He gave full support to the attack on the French fleet at Mers-el-Kebir on 3 July 1940, to ensure that its ships did not fall into German hands, and later dismissed Admiral Sir Dudley North, Flag Officer, Gibraltar, for failing to take action to prevent the passage of a French squadron into the Atlantic on 11 September 1940. At the end of 1940 he despatched Lord Cork to Gibraltar to enquire into the conduct of Vice-Admiral Sir James Somerville [93], whom Churchill had wished to court-martial for failing to pursue a defeated Italian fleet. By the convention of each Service holding this post in turn, Pound became chairman of the Chiefs of Staff Committee in the summer of 1941. As Chief of the Naval Staff, he was responsible for the strategic deployment of units involved in the sinking of the German battleship *Bismarck* on 27 May 1941. Later he was criticized for having agreed, under pressure from Churchill, to send the battleship *Prince of Wales* and the battle-cruiser *Repulse,* without air cover, to the Far East, where they were sunk off Malaya on 10 December 1941. He was also blamed for failing to prevent the passage of the German battle-cruisers *Scharnhorst* and *Gneisenau* through the Channel in February 1942 and for personally ordering the Arctic convoy PQ17 to scatter in the face of a threat from German surface raiders in July 1942. In the Chiefs of Staff committee he waged a long campaign against the Royal Air Force giving priority to the strategic bomber offensive at the expense of Coastal Command, and argued that to lose the battle of the Atlantic would be to lose the war.

At the time of his appointment as First Sea Lord Pound was already suffering from problems with his left hip and had begun to walk with the aid of a stick. His practice of sleeping on a camp bed at the Admiralty, so as to be immediately available, meant that he did not rest well, and his habit of closing his eyes to concentrate his mind during important meetings led some to suppose that he was asleep. The strain of working with Churchill, whose eccentric hours of work and insistent demands for information and action told heavily on all the Chiefs of Staff, left him increasingly tired. This, together with the successful "Channel dash" of *Scharnhorst* and *Gneisenau,* was one of the factors that led Churchill in December 1942 to replace him as Chairman of the Chiefs of Staff Committee by General Sir Alan Brooke, the new Chief of the Imperial General Staff. His last important official meeting was the Quebec Conference between President Franklin D Roosevelt and Churchill in August 1943. There he began to lose sensation on his right side and, on returning to London, was diagnosed as suffering from a malignant brain tumour. He resigned office on 20 September 1943 and was immediately admitted to the Royal Masonic Hospital, London. He declined the offer of a peerage, but accepted the Order of Merit. Pound died on 2 October 1943. After a funeral in Westminster Abbey, his ashes were taken aboard the cruiser *Glasgow* at Portsmouth and scattered in the Solent.

POWER
Sir ARTHUR JOHN, GCB, GBE, CVO (1889–1960) [97]

Arthur Power, the son of a corn merchant, was born in London on 12 April 1889 and joined the Navy as a cadet in the training ship *Britannia* in 1904. He became a cadet captain in his second term and chief cadet captain in his third, and gained the King's Medal, awarded to the best cadet of each intake. He was promoted to midshipman on 15 September 1905 and was appointed to the battleship *King Edward VII,* flagship of Lord Charles Beresford in the Channel Fleet. On 15 January 1909 he became an acting sub-lieutenant at the beginning of his promotion courses, and on 15 April 1910 was promoted to lieutenant and appointed to the battle-cruiser *Indomitable* in the Home Fleet. From there in October 1912 Power became the first lieutenant of the destroyer *Nautilus*. In 1913 he joined the gunnery training school *Excellent* and qualified as a gunnery officer. During the First World War he served in the battleship *Magnificent*, the cruiser *Royal Arthur*, the monitor *Raglan*, in which he took part in the Dardanelles campaign, and the battle-cruiser *Princess Royal* in the Battle-cruiser Fleet in the North Sea. He was promoted to lieutenant-commander on 15 April 1918 and married Amy Bingham, the daughter of a Territorial lieutenant-colonel, and later had with her a family of three sons. He remained in *Princess Royal* after the end of hostilities in November 1918 and, in August 1920, joined the instructional staff at *Excellent*. Power was promoted to commander on 31 December 1922 and then served from January 1923 to August 1924 as Assistant Director in the Naval Ordnance Department at the Admiralty. After attending the Royal Naval Staff College, Greenwich, he served from 1925 to July 1927 as commander of the battle-cruiser *Hood*, flagship of the Battle-cruiser Squadron in the Atlantic Fleet. From 1927 to his promotion to captain on 30 July 1929 he was employed at the Royal Naval Staff College, Greenwich. Power then joined the Ordnance Committee at the Royal Arsenal, Woolwich, before returning to sea in April 1931 as flag captain of the Second Cruiser Squadron in the Home Fleet, in the cruiser *Dorsetshire*. In July 1933 he was appointed to the Imperial Defence College and in October 1935 became the captain of *Excellent*.

Power left *Excellent* in September 1937, prior to appointment as captain of the new aircraft carrier *Ark Royal,* then under construction at Birkenhead. He assumed command in July 1938 and later became flag captain to the Rear-Admiral commanding aircraft carriers in the Home Fleet. After the outbreak of the Second World War in September 1939 he remained in *Ark Royal* until returning to the Admiralty in May 1940 as Assistant Chief of the Naval Staff (Home) with promotion to rear-admiral on 25 June 1940. In August 1942 he was given command of the Fifteenth Cruiser Squadron in the Mediterranean, with his flag in the cruiser *Cleopatra*. Early in 1943 he became flag officer commanding the Malta-based Force K, with acting promotion to vice-admiral, confirmed on 4 August 1943. As flag officer, Malta, he played an important part in planning the seaborne invasions of Sicily (10 July 1943) and Southern Italy (3–9 September 1943). Following the Italian surrender on 8 September 1943, Power commanded the naval forces in the landing of V British Corps at Taranto. He subsequently became head of the Allied military mission to the Italian government and was for a short while second-in-command of the Mediterranean Fleet. In January 1944, with his flag in the battle-cruiser *Renown*, he was given command of the First Battle Squadron and appointed second-in-command of the newly re-established Eastern Fleet, with the award of the KCB. Sir Arthur Power became C-in-C, East Indies, in November 1944 and continued the policy of naval strikes against the Japanese in Borneo and Malaya. After the Japanese surrender Power entered Singapore harbour on 3 September 1945, with his flag in *Cleopatra*, the first major ship of the Navy to return there since the defeats of February

219

1942. His happiness was marred by the death of Lady Power in 1945.

After returning home Power was promoted to admiral on 6 May 1946 and served as Second Sea Lord from 1946 to 1948. As the member of the Admiralty responsible for personnel matters, he completed the demobilization of men and women engaged for the duration of hostilities only and the reduction of the Navy's manpower to its peacetime establishment. In 1947 he married Second Officer Margaret Watson, WRNS. From May 1948 to May 1950 he was C-in-C, Mediterranean Fleet, followed by appointment in September 1950 as C-in-C, Portsmouth. He was promoted to admiral of the fleet on 22 April 1952 and became NATO Allied Commander, Channel and Southern North Sea (CINCHAN). Sir Arthur Power went on half-pay after hauling down his flag at Portsmouth in September 1952. He died at the Royal Naval Hospital, Haslar, Gosport, on 28 January 1960.

RICHARDS
Sir FREDERICK WILLIAM, GCB (1833–1912) [52]

Frederick Richards was born at Ballyhally, County Wexford, on 30 November 1833. His father, a captain in the Royal Navy, and his mother, daughter of the Dean of Killala, County Mayo, both came from the Anglo-Irish Protestant Ascendancy. He was educated at the Naval School, New Cross, Greater London (now Goldsmiths' College, University of London) and joined the Navy as a cadet in 1848. He subsequently served on the Australian station, where on 8 January 1854 he was appointed acting mate in the sloop *Fantome*. He was promoted to lieutenant on 31 October 1855 and returned home in 1856. Richards was appointed to the 2nd-rate *Ganges*, flagship of the C-in-C on the China station, in 1857 and became the flag lieutenant in April 1859 and commander of the paddle-sloop *Vixen*, during the Second China War, on 9 February 1860. After returning home with *Vixen* in 1861 he commanded the gunboat *Dart* on the West Coast of Africa station from March 1862 to January 1866. He was promoted to captain on 6 February 1866 and married Lucy Fayle, the young widow of a clergyman and heiress to her father's estate of Horton Court, Chipping Sodbury, Gloucestershire. He then went on half-pay until 1870 when he was appointed to the Indian troopship *Jumna*, an unattractive post, as this class of vessel was not a combatant but a transport, and there were constant disputes between the naval and military officers over the command of the troops on board.

At the end of three years in the troopship service Richards was rewarded in June 1873 with command of the turret ship *Devastation*, the first British battleship to be powered by steam alone. He served in this ship in the Mediterranean from 1874 to June 1877 and became commodore and senior officer on the West Coast of Africa, with his broad pendant in the corvette *Boadicea*, in October 1878. He arrived at the Cape of Good Hope at the end of January 1879 to learn that, in the Zulu War, a British force had been wiped out at Isandhlwana, and another was besieged at Eshowe. Richards moved up to Natal, where he landed at the head of a small naval brigade and served at the battle of Gingindlovu (2 April 1879) and the relief of Eshowe (3 April 1879). He returned to Natal with a naval brigade in January 1881 on the outbreak of the Boer (First Anglo-Boer) War and, after taking part in the battle of Laing's Nek (28 January 1881), was awarded the KCB later in the year.

Sir Frederick Richards returned home with promotion to rear-admiral on 9 June 1882 and subsequently served as junior naval lord at the Admiralty until May 1885, when he was appointed C-in-C, East Indies, with his flag in the corvette *Bacchante*. During the Third Burma War he provided a naval brigade to support the British advance up the Irrawaddy River to Mandalay, ending with the annexation of Burma (Myanmar) to the British Indian Empire.

After completing this command in April 1888 Richards was appointed to a committee investigating the state of the fleet. Queen Victoria's Golden Jubilee Review at Spithead in 1887 had mustered an impressive number of ships, but only thirty-five were major combatants, including nine without armour. The committee's findings questioned the ability of the Navy to meet the combined fleets of any other two Powers (the "two-Power standard"), regarded as essential for the safety of British interests) and led to a general demand for naval rearmament. This was met by the Naval Defence Act of 1889, providing for the construction of eight battleships of the new *Royal Sovereign* class. The Chancellor of the Exchequer, George Goschen, funded this with a new tax, estate duty, payable at a rate of 1 per cent by the inheritors of estates with a value above £10,000. Richards was promoted to vice-admiral on 27 October 1888. From 1890 to June 1893 he was C-in-C on the China station and then returned to the Admiralty as second naval lord.

Richards was promoted to admiral on 1 September 1893 and became first naval lord in November 1893, in the Board headed by Earl Spencer in Gladstone's fourth Cabinet. He remained at the Admiralty during a new building programme, caused by advances in naval artillery. The collision of two battleships in June 1893, with *Victoria* sunk and *Camperdown* damaged, had revealed how quickly the Navy's numerical superiority might be reduced, so that an entire squadron, eventually built as the *Magnificent* class, was needed. To fund this, Gladstone's Chancellor of the Exchequer, Sir William Harcourt, brought in a new tax, death duties, levied on all forms of property before the residue was passed on to inheritors. During the course of the next century this measure became a means for the redistribution of wealth and led to the break-up of the landed estates that, with their great country houses, had been an important feature in British history. At the time it was opposed by Gladstone on the grounds that it would allow uncontrolled increases in public expenditure. Defeated in Cabinet on the naval issue, he resigned in March 1894 and was succeeded by Lord

Rosebery. When Rosebery's administration fell in June 1894 Richards, with the other naval lords, remained at the Admiralty under Goschen, who became First Lord in Salisbury's third administration and continued the previous ministry's naval programme. On 20 October 1898, shortly before Richards reached the compulsory retirement age for his rank, Goschen arranged for him to be promoted admiral of the fleet, passing over the two admirals senior to him, so that he could remain on the active list and thus continue as first naval lord. Richards finally left the Admiralty in August 1899, when Goschen decided to replace him by Lord Walter Kerr [56]. He retired to his home at Horton Court, where he died, without offspring, on 28 September 1912. A trust fund was set up in his memory, to make charitable grants to officers of the Royal Navy and Royal Marines and their dependants.

ROWLEY
Sir William, KB (c.1690–1768) [6]

Will Rowley, a native of Essex, joined the Navy as a volunteer by Order, or "King's Letter Boy", in 1704, in the 3rd-rate *Orford*, commanded by Captain John Norris [1]. He served in the Mediterranean during the War of the Spanish Succession and was appointed lieutenant in the 3rd-rate *Somersett* in December 1708. After the end of the war he was promoted on 26 June 1716 to be captain of the 6th-rate *Biddeford*, based at Gibraltar. From then until February 1719 he was engaged in trade protection duties against pirates operating from S'la (Sallee) on the west coast of Morocco. In September 1719 Rowley was given command of the 6th-rate *Lively*, in which he was employed, mostly in anti-smuggling duties, in the Irish Sea until June 1728. On the outbreak of the War of Jenkins's Ear he was appointed to a ship in September 1739, but declined it on the grounds that he was involved in expensive litigation in Dublin. He did not again go to sea until 1741, when he was given command of the 2nd-rate *Barfleur* in the Mediterranean, during the War of the Austrian Succession (1740–48).

Rowley remained in *Barfleur* when promoted to rear-admiral of the White on 7 December 1743. His promotion directly to the White squadron was a consequence of the increase in the establishment of flag officers from nine to twenty-five earlier that year. He took part in the battle of Hyeres, Toulon (11 February 1744) and was, together with Captain Edward Hawke [7], one of the few officers to emerge from that engagement with credit. He was promoted to vice-admiral of the Blue on 23 June 1744 and became C-in-C, Mediterranean, in August 1744. He maintained the blockade along the French Riviera and watched the Republic of Genoa, in case it abandoned its policy of neutrality. In February 1745, at Gibraltar, he was given the task of investigating the questionable conduct of Captain Richard Norris at the battle of Hyeres. Rowley released him from arrest pending the outcome of the investigation, but Norris then took the chance to escape to Spain. He was the elder son of Sir John Norris (Rowley's old captain) who was also, at the time, the commander-in-chief and admiral of the fleet, and there was a strong suspicion that Rowley had been in some way influenced by this. Rowley became a vice-admiral of the White on 23 April 1745, but the Admiralty decided that, in view of the Norris affair, he could not be relied on to maintain impartial discipline in a fleet. He was accordingly removed from his command on 29 May 1745.

Although he never again commanded at sea, Rowley nevertheless rose to become admiral of the Blue on 15 July 1747, admiral of the White on 12 May 1748 and a lord commissioner of the Admiralty, in the Board headed by Admiral George Anson [5], on 22 June 1751. Apart from a brief period out of office between November 1756 and April 1757, he remained in the Admiralty until July 1757. He was awarded the KB on 12 December 1753 and sat as Member of Parliament for Portsmouth from 1750 to 1754 and for Taunton from 1754 to 1761. On the death of Lord Anson Sir William Rowley succeeded him as C-in-C and admiral of the fleet on 17 December 1762. He died on 1 January 1768. With his wife, Arabella, the daughter of a landholder in County Londonderry, he had four sons and a daughter. Their second son, Joshua, became a baronet and rear-admiral of the White, and their daughter Arabella married a captain in the Navy.

RYDER
Sir Alfred Phillipps, KCB (1820–1888) **[43]**

Alfred Ryder, the seventh son of the Honourable Henry Ryder, Bishop of Lichfield and Coventry, was born on 27 November 1820. The bishop's elder brother, through whom he was connected by marriage to several other noble families, was the first Earl of Harrowby. Alfred Ryder's sister became the wife of the Whig politician and Cabinet minister, Sir George Grey. Ryder himself never married. He joined the Navy on 6 May 1833 and was promoted to lieutenant on 2 July 1841, appointed to the 5th-rate *Belvidera*, commanded by the Honourable George Grey, and served in the Mediterranean from 1841 to 1845. He was promoted to commander on 26 May 1847 and was given command of the steam sloop *Vixen* on the North America and West Indies station. At the beginning of 1848 he was in a small British force sent to Nicaragua (a region in which at that time both the British and the United States were interested as a possible route across Central America) following the arrest of two British subjects in the port of San Juan del Norte (Greytown). The local Nicaraguan commander, Colonel Salas, retreated thirty miles up the rapids and waterfalls of San Juan River to a fort at Serapaqui, where Ryder followed him in his ship's boats. After a short action (12 February 1848), the Nicaraguans were driven into the surrounding rain-forest and the fort was destroyed. Ryder was promoted to captain on 2 May 1848 in recognition of his services.

In 1853 Ryder was appointed to the frigate *Dauntless* in the Channel. After the outbreak of the Crimean War in 1854 *Dauntless* formed part of the fleet sent to the Baltic under Sir Charles Napier. Along with Captain Henry Codrington [35], Ryder was criticized by Napier for failing to bring his ship up to the required standard, but like Codrington, was sufficiently well connected to retain the confidence of the Admiralty. In the closing stage of the war he served with *Dauntless* in the Black Sea and took part in the capture of Kinburn (Pokrovskiy), guarding the strategically important Russian port of Ochakov in the Dnepr estuary (Dneprovskiy Liman). From 1863 to 2 April 1866, when he was promoted to rear-admiral, he was Controller of the Coastguard. During 1868–69 Ryder was second-in-command in the Channel . He subsequently became naval attaché at Paris, at the time of the Franco-Prussian War (July 1870- February 1871). He was promoted to vice-admiral on 7 May 1872 and served as C-in-C on the China station from 1872 and 1874. Ryder became an admiral on 5 August 1875 and was C-in-C, Portsmouth, from 1879 to 1884, with the awarded of the KCB in May 1884, followed by promotion to admiral of the fleet on 29 April 1885. During April 1888 Sir Alfred Ryder sought medical treatment in London for depression. He drowned in the Thames near Vauxhall, after falling from a river steamer, and was buried on 5 May 1888 in the churchyard of St Mary the Virgin, Hambleden, Buckinghamshire.

SALMON
Sir Nowell, VC, GCB (1835–1912) **[53]**

Nowell Salmon, son of the Reverend Henry Salmon, Rector of Swarrington, Hampshire, and his wife Emily, the daughter of Admiral Nowell, was born on 20 February 1835. After attending Marlborough College, Wiltshire, he joined the Navy in May 1847 and was appointed midshipman and mate in the 2nd-rate *James Watt* in March 1854. After serving in the Baltic in 1854 and 1855 during the Crimean War Salmon was promoted to lieutenant in January 1856 and joined the frigate *Shannon* for service in the East Indies. During the Indian Mutiny campaign of 1857 Salmon served in command of a rifle company in a naval brigade in Oude (Awadh). At the first relief of Lucknow in November 1857 he was awarded the Victoria Cross for climbing a tree under heavy fire in order to observe the fall of shot despite being wounded in the thigh by a musket ball. He took part in the British recapture of Lucknow in March 1858 and, in recognition of his services, was promoted to commander on 22 March 1858. In November 1859 Salmon was given command of the sloop *Icarus* on the West Indies and North America station. There, during 1860, he was sent from Belize to deal with W W Walker, the colourful American adventurer and former president of Nicaragua, who had turned to piracy and raided the Honduran city of Truxillo. Salmon intercepted his ship, overpowered his crew and handed him over to the Honduran authorities, who had him court-martialled and shot.

Salmon was promoted to captain on 12 December 1863. In January 1866 he married Emily Augusta Saunders, the daughter of a country gentleman, and later had with her a family of a son and a daughter. Between March 1869 and May 1873 Salmon commanded the armoured ship *Defence* in the Mediterranean, after which he served from April 1874 to May 1877 as captain of the armoured ship *Valiant*, stationed at Foynes on the River Shannon, Ireland. On 28 November 1877 he was given command of the battleship *Swiftsure* in the Mediterranean, where he served until returning home in 1878. He was promoted to rear-admiral on 2 August 1879. Between April 1882 and April 1885 Salmon was C-in-C, Cape of Good Hope and the West Coast of Africa, with his flag in the corvette *Boadicea*. He was promoted to vice-admiral on 1 July 1885 and awarded the KCB in June 1887. Sir Nowell Salmon was C-in-C on the China station from December 1887 to the end of 1890, with his flag in the armoured cruiser *Impérieuse*. He was promoted to admiral on 10 September 1891 and C-in-C, Portsmouth, from June 1894 until August 1897, with his tenure extended by two months beyond the usual three years, so that he could command the Diamond Jubilee Review at Spithead, with a line of warships twenty-five miles long. He became an admiral of the fleet on 18 January 1899 and retired in February 1905. Sir Nowell Salmon died of bronchitis at his home in Clarence Parade, Southsea, Hampshire, on 14 February 1912 and was buried in St Peter's churchyard, Curdridge, near Southampton.

ST VINCENT
EARL OF, see **JERVIS**, Sir JOHN

SARTORIUS
Sir GEORGE ROSE, GCB (1790–1885) [32]

George Sartorius, the son of an engineer officer in the East India Company's service and his wife Arabella, was born in 1790 and entered the Royal Navy in June 1801, during the French Revolutionary War, as a volunteer in the yacht *Mary*. In May 1802, surviving the post-war reductions following the Treaty of Amiens (27 March 1802), he joined the 5th-rate *Fisguard*. After the renewal of war with France in May 1803 he became a midshipman in the 5th-rate *Naiad*, from which he moved to the 3rd-rate *Tonnant* in October 1804. Sartorius was in this ship at the battle of Trafalgar (21 October 1805) and afterwards formed part of the prize crew of the captured Spanish ship *Bahama*. In June 1806 he was appointed to the 6th-rate *Daphne*, in which he served in the River Plate during 1807 in operations against the Spanish colonial cities of Montevideo, Uruguay, and Buenos

Aires, Argentina. In 1808, when the Spanish rose against French occupation, British operations against Spain and her colonies came to an end.

Sartorius was promoted to lieutenant in the 5th-rate *Success* on 5 March 1808, and spent the next year on fishery protection duties off Greenland, before joining the fleet in the Mediterranean. He took part in the landing of a British army on the islands of Ischia and Procida, Naples, in June 1809, and was subsequently deployed in the defence of Sicily against the threat of invasion from the French-occupied mainland. During 1810 he took part in a number of boat actions and cutting-out expeditions along the Italian coast and was mentioned in despatches. After serving with the flotilla in the defence of Cadiz, where a combined Spanish, British and Portuguese garrison was under siege by the French, Sartorius was promoted to commander on 1 February 1812. His next appointments were successively to the sloops *Snap* in August 1812 and *Avon* in July 1813. He was promoted to captain on 6 June 1814, two months after Napoleon's abdication. Between December 1814 and August 1815 he commanded the 6th-rate *Slaney* and was off Rochefort, in company with the 3rd-rate *Bellerophon*, when Napoleon surrendered himself to these ships after his final defeat at Waterloo. During 1828, Sartorius commanded the 5th-rate *Pyramus* in the British fleet at Lisbon.

In 1831 Sartorius became of one of the many unemployed veterans who, with the approval of the British government, served in the civil wars in Spain and Portugal. He was given command of the fleet of the exiled Regent of Portugal, the constitutionalist Dom Pedro, with the rank of admiral, and landed his army at Oporto in July 1832. Pedro's brother and rival, the absolutist Dom Miguel, besieged the city until July 1833, while Sartorius protected it from the sea. When funds to pay his men were not forthcoming, he was forced to use his own money to keep them from mutiny and desertion, and threatened to sail away, taking the fleet with him, unless he was reimbursed. Pedro sent two other British officers to relieve him of his command, but Sartorius, with the full approval of his crews, arrested them. In June 1833 he was succeeded by Sir Charles Napier, who insisted on full payment before destroying the Miguelist fleet off Cape St Vincent (5 July 1833).

Sartorius was restored to the Navy List in 1836. He married Sophia, a daughter of John Lamb, Esquire, in 1839 and later had with her a family of three sons, who all joined the Army and two of whom won the Victoria Cross. In 1841 he was awarded a knighthood and was appointed to the 3rd-rate *Malabar*, which he commanded in the Mediterranean until 1844. Sir George Sartorius received the thanks of the United States government for his efforts to save the frigate *Missouri*, lost by fire off Gibraltar, but saw no more active service. He became a rear-admiral on 9 May 1849, vice-admiral on 31 January 1856, admiral on 11 February 1861 and was awarded the KCB in March 1865. Sartorius was promoted to admiral of the fleet on 3 July 1869. He died at his house, East Grove, Lymington, Hampshire, on 13 April 1885.

SEYMOUR
Sir EDWARD HOBART, GCB, OM, GCVO (1840–1929) [57]

Edward Seymour, second son of the rector of Kinwarton, was born at Kinwarton, Warwickshire, on 30 April 1840. His grandfather was Rear-Admiral Sir Michael Seymour, a veteran of the Napoleonic wars, and his uncle became Admiral Sir Michael Seymour. After attending Radley School, Oxfordshire, and Eastman's Naval Academy, Southsea, he joined the Navy late in 1852 on appointment to the screw corvette *Encounter*. In January 1854 he became a midshipman in the paddle frigate *Terrible*, in which he served in the Black Sea from April 1854 to 1856 during the Crimean War, and during 1857 sailed in the sloop *Cruizer* to join his uncle's flagship *Caledonia* on the China station. He served in several engagements during the Second China War, including an attack on a fleet of war-junks at Fat-shan Creek in the estuary below Canton (Guangzhou) (1 June 1857), where his boat was sunk by gunfire; the capture of Canton (29 December 1857), where he served in the artillery of the naval brigade alongside Midshipman Arthur Wilson [59]; and the capture of the Taku Forts, at the mouth of the Peiho River, northern China (20 May 1858). He was subsequently sent home in the frigate *Pique*, suffering from the effects of heat stress.

After returning to Portsmouth Seymour was appointed to the steam frigate *Mersey*, from which he went to study at the cadet training ship *Illustrious* and the gunnery school *Excellent*. Having qualified for promotion to lieutenant in all respects except age, he became a mate in June 1859 and rejoined *Mersey* in the Channel. With the renewal of the Second China War in the same month, he was appointed to the frigate *Impérieuse*. On passage to the China station he earned the medal of the Royal Humane Society for diving into the shark-infested waters of Rhio (Riau) Bay, near Singapore, in an unsuccessful bid to rescue a marine who had fallen overboard. After reaching Hong Kong Seymour was appointed lieutenant by the local C-in-C, Sir James Hope [39], in his flagship, the frigate *Chesapeake*, and took part in the capture of the Taku Forts (21 August 1860). He subsequently served in the river paddle steamer *Waterman* at Canton, first as second-in-command and then as commanding officer, with his promotion to lieutenant confirmed on 11 February 1861. He was then appointed to the paddle sloop *Sphinx* as first lieutenant, in which he visited the Philippines and Guam, where, at an impressionable age, he fell in love with several Spanish ladies in the local colonial society. After four and a half months in *Sphinx* Seymour returned to *Impérieuse*, which had become Hope's flagship, and from which he landed with various shore parties during 1862 to assist the Imperial Chinese authorities during the Taiping rebellion.

From 1863 to 1866 Seymour was flag lieutenant to his uncle as C-in-C, Portsmouth, with a brief attachment in 1865 to the royal yacht *Victoria and Albert*. He became commander on 5 March 1866 in one of the promotions customarily allotted to a C-in-C on hauling down his flag. On half-pay, he spent some time in the Peterhead whaling ship *Mazinthien*, to gain experience of navigating in icy waters, in the hope of joining an Arctic expedition. In 1868 he was appointed to the Coast Guard in Ireland followed in June 1869 by command of the gunboat *Growler* on the West Coast of Africa. In 1870, in operations against African pirates on the Congo coast, he was shot in the leg, but received no treatment as his ship's surgeon had taken to drink and was unfit for duty. After being invalided home, Seymour returned to half-pay and during 1871, visited France and Switzerland and became fluent in French. From January 1872 until his promotion to captain on 13 March 1873 he commanded successively the paddle despatch vessels *Vigilant* and *Lively* in the Channel. He then spent a year at the Royal Naval College, Greenwich, and resumed his travels in France and Italy. Between 1876 and 1879 he commanded the troopship *Orontes*. After again travelling abroad, he returned to sea in April 1880 in command of the cruiser *Iris* in the Mediterranean Fleet.

From November 1882 to February 1885 Seymour commanded the battleship *Inflexible*, remaining in the Mediterranean. Late in 1885, when there was a threat of war between the United Kingdom and Russia over the disputed control of Penjdeh on the borders of Afghanistan and Turkmenistan, he was given a brief command of the armed merchant cruiser *Oregon*, a converted liner intended to counter Russian commerce raiders. He served as flag captain to the C-in-C, Portsmouth, from May 1886 to December 1887 and then became assistant to the Admiral Superintendent of Naval Reserves and Coast Guards. Seymour was promoted to rear-admiral on 14 July 1889. On half-pay, he again travelled abroad and visited France, Russia, the West Indies and the United States. He remained a keen linguist and felt strongly that all naval officers should be able to converse in at least one foreign language. In July 1892 he commanded a squadron in the annual fleet exercises, with his flag in the battleship *Swiftsure* and from then until April 1894 was second-in-command of the Channel Squadron, with his flag successively in the battleships *Anson* and *Empress of India*. He was then appointed Admiral Superintendent of Naval Reserves, with promotion to vice-admiral on 9 November 1895. Seymour commanded the Reserve Fleet in its annual exercises, with his flag in the battleship *Alexandra*, and achieved a notable success over the Channel Fleet in the manoeuvres of 1896. He was awarded the KCB in 1897.

Sir Edward Seymour was appointed C-in-C on the China station in December 1897, with his flag in the battleship *Centurion*. In May 1898 he took possession of Wei-hai-wei on the coast of northern China, acquired by the British in response to the occupation of Kiao-Chow (Jiaozhou) by the Germans and of Port Arthur (Lushun) by the Russians. Chinese resentment at the growth of Western ideas and influence led to the growth of an anti-foreign movement, the Fists of Righteous Harmony, or Boxers. At the end of May 1900, when Boxer rebels murdered the German minister and laid siege to the diplomatic quarter of Peking (Beijing), Seymour sailed for the Taku Forts at the mouth of the Peiho River, where he was joined by warships from several other nations. At the head of a naval brigade composed of some two thousand seamen and marines from the ships of eight different nations, he proceeded overland to the relief of the legations, but was met by strong opposition at Lang Fang (11 June 1900) and had to fall back to Tientsin (Tienjin). He captured the arsenal of Hsiku and withstood a three-day siege by Boxers and Imperial Chinese troops until, having suffered nearly three hundred casualties, he was relieved by a Russian column. Seymour was promoted to admiral on 24 May 1901 and returned home after a six-month extension in command. He was C-in-C, Plymouth, from March 1903 to February 1905 and, in recognition of his services in China, was extended in appointment for a month after his promotion to admiral of the fleet on 20 February 1905, to allow him to fly his flag in that rank. He returned briefly to sea in 1909, with his flag in the new battlecruiser *Inflexible*, in command of a squadron sent to attend celebrations at Boston, Massachusetts. He retired in 1910 and died, unmarried, at his home in Maidenhead, Berkshire, on 2 March 1929.

SEYMOUR
Sir GEORGE FRANCIS, GCB, GCH (1787–1870) [29]

George Seymour was born on 17 September 1787, the eldest son of Vice-Admiral Lord Hugh Seymour (fifth son of the first Marquess of Hertford). Lord Hugh was an intimate of the Prince of Wales, but had been rescued from his irregular lifestyle by his marriage to Anne, third daughter of the second Earl Waldegrave. Seymour's other family connections included the Duke of Grafton, five marquesses, three earls, two viscounts and a baron. He joined the Navy in October 1797 as a first class volunteer in the yacht *Princess Augusta* in the Thames. In March 1798 he joined his father's flagship, the 3rd-rate *Sanspareil* in the Channel and subsequently went with him to the 2nd-rate *Prince of Wales*, on his appointment as C-in-C, Leeward Islands and Jamaica. He was at the Dutch surrender of Surinam in August 1799 and was appointed midshipman in the 5th-rate *Acasta* at the beginning of 1800. After Lord Hugh Seymour's death from yellow fever in September 1801 George Seymour remained in *Acasta* until the end of the French Revolutionary War in March 1802. During the next two years he served on the Home, Newfoundland and Mediterranean stations, in the 4th-rates *Endymion* and *Isis*.

After the renewal of war with France in May 1803 Seymour was in *Endymion* at the capture of the corvettes *Colombe* and *Bacchante*, the storeship *Adour* and the privateer *Général Moreau*. He then moved to the 1st-rate *Victory*, flagship of Viscount Nelson, from which he became acting lieutenant in the 4th-rate *Madras* in February 1804 and the 3rd-rate *Donegal* in March 1804. He was confirmed as lieutenant in *Donegal* on 12 October

1804 and was at the capture of two Spanish frigates, *Matilda* and *Amfitrate*, before going with the rest of Nelson's fleet in the pursuit of the French Admiral Villeneuve to the West Indies and back during the summer of 1805. Immediately after the battle of Trafalgar (21 October 1805) he was at the capture of the Spanish 100-gun ship *El Rayo*. In January 1806 Seymour joined the 3rd-rate *Northumberland*, flagship in the West Indies. He served at the battle of Santo Domingo (6 February 1806), off Spanish-held eastern Hispaniola, in the last major fleet action of the Napoleonic wars, where he was wounded in the jaw with the loss of several teeth and was mentioned in despatches. He was promoted to commander on 22 January 1806 and appointed to command the sloop *Kingfisher*, in which he sailed to join Rear-Admiral Edward Thornbrough's squadron blockading Rochefort. Thornbrough came to consider Seymour imprudent and ordered him not to go closer inshore than the Ile d'Aix. On 14 May 1806, when the dashing Lord Cochrane's frigate, the 5th-rate *Pallas*, was disabled by coast artillery while attempting to capture the French frigate *Minerve*, Seymour disregarded these orders and towed *Pallas* to safety.

Seymour was promoted captain on 29 July 1806 on appointment to the 6th-rate *Aurora* in the Mediterranean. In February 1808 he was given command of *Pallas* in which he served in the Channel under Lord Gambier [14] and took part in Lord Cochrane's attack on a French squadron in the Basque Roads on 11–12 April 1809. Cochrane later accused Gambier of failing to support him and Seymour gave evidence on Cochrane's side at the court-martial convened to clear Gambier's name. Seymour's opinion does not seem to have been held against him, and he was appointed to the 5th-rate *Manilla* at Lisbon in September 1809. In March 1811 he married his cousin Georgina, eldest daughter of Vice-Admiral Sir George Berkeley. They later had a family of three daughters and three sons, of whom the eldest eventually succeeded to the peerage as fifth Marquess of Hertford and the second became a captain in the Navy. *Manilla* was lost off the Texel in January 1812, during Seymour's absence, and he was given another ship, the 5th-rate *Fortunée*, in June 1812. During the American War of 1812 he was appointed captain of the 5th-rate *Leonidas* in January 1813 and served in the West Indies, where he captured the United States privateer *Paul Jones* (23 May 1813).

Seymour became sergeant-at-arms to the House of Lords (where his uncle, the Marquess of Hertford, was Lord Chamberlain) in 1818 and remained in that office, with an absence of a few months during 1827, in command of the 5th-rate *Briton*, until 1841. He became a knight commander of the Guelphic Order of Hanover, with a British knighthood, in 1831. Sir George Seymour was from September 1841 to September 1844 a lord commissioner of the Admiralty in the Board headed by the Earl of Haddington in Sir Robert Peel's second Cabinet. He became a rear-admiral of the Blue on 23 November 1841, rear-admiral of the White on 9 November 1846 and rear-admiral of the Red on 26 July 1847. Between 1844 and 1848 he was C-in-C, Pacific station, with his flag in the 3rd-rate

Collingwood. During this period there were strained relations with the French over Tahiti in 1844 and with the United States over Oregon in 1845–6, and Seymour's ships played a valuable part in projecting British power. He was promoted to vice-admiral of the Blue on 27 March 1850. Between January 1851 and November 1853 he was C-in-C, North America and West Indies station, and from January 1856 to March 1859 C-in-C, Portsmouth, with promotion to admiral on 14 May 1857. Seymour was promoted to admiral of the fleet on 30 November 1866. He died of bronchitis on 20 January 1870 and was buried at Holy Trinity church, Arrow, near his family's estate at Alcester, Warwickshire.

SOMERVILLE
Sir JAMES FOWNES, GCB, GBE, DSO (1882–1949) [93]

James Somerville was born on 17 July 1882, at Weybridge, Surrey, the second son of Arthur Somerville of Dinder House, Wells, Somerset. His grandmother was a descendant of the Hood family, two of whose members had been admirals in the Napoleonic wars. Somerville entered the Navy in 1897 as a cadet in the training ship *Britannia.* After serving as a midshipman successively in the cruisers *Royal Arthur* in the Channel and *Warspite* in the Pacific, he was promoted to sub-lieutenant on 15 December 1901 at the beginning of his promotion courses. He became a lieutenant on 15 March 1904 and joined the armoured cruiser *Sutlej* on the China station, in which he served until returning home in 1907 to attend the torpedo school *Vernon* at Portsmouth. After qualifying as a torpedo officer, he remained at *Vernon* (at that time responsible for most aspects of electrical training) to work on the development of wireless telegraphy. He met Mary (Molly) Main, the good-looking and spirited daughter of a retired colonel of Royal Engineers living in Botley, Hampshire, and, after a prolonged friendship, and some prompting by her family, married her in 1913. They later had a daughter and a son who followed him into the Navy.

After the outbreak of the First World War in August 1914 Somerville served first as wireless officer in the battleship *Marlborough* in the Grand Fleet, then as fleet wireless officer in the successive flagships of Vice-Admiral De Robeck [77] in the Dardanelles campaign, the battleship *Queen Elizabeth,* the battle-cruiser *Inflexible* and the cruiser *Chatham.* He was promoted to commander on 31 December 1915 and was awarded the DSO in 1916. Somerville joined the Grand Fleet with De Robeck in January 1917, in the battleship *King George V,* flagship of the Second Battle Squadron, where he contributed to the development of wireless fire control systems. At the end of 1917 he joined the Signals School, Portsmouth, where responsibility for wireless telegraphy had been transferred from *Vernon,* and remained there after the war ended in November 1918.

In March 1920 Somerville became commander of the battleship *Ajax* in the Mediterranean, from which he moved to the battleship *Emperor of India,* flagship of the Mediterranean Fleet. He was promoted to captain on 31 December 1921 and, during 1922, served at the Admiralty as Deputy Director of the Signals Division. He then returned to the Mediterranean as flag captain of the battleship *Benbow*, flagship of his old friend (later Sir) John Kelly **[85]**, commanding the Fourth Battle Squadron. From early 1925 to 1927 Somerville was Director of Signals at the Admiralty. He then became flag captain and chief of staff to Kelly as second-in-command of the Mediterranean Fleet, first in the battleship *Warspite* and then, after *Warspite* was damaged by striking an uncharted rock, the battleship *Barham*. He was a member of the directing staff at the Imperial Defence College, London, from 1929 to 1931. In the aftermath of the mutiny of the Atlantic Fleet at Invergordon, Somerville, together with Captain John Tovey **[92]**, was selected by Kelly, the new C-in-C, to enquire into the seamen's problems. He next commanded the cruiser *Norfolk* in the Home Fleet, prior to appointment as commodore of the naval barracks at Portsmouth in October 1932.

Somerville was promoted to rear-admiral on 12 October 1933. In May 1934 he returned to the Admiralty as Director of Personal Services, where he introduced a seamen's welfare scheme that stemmed from his findings after the Invergordon mutiny. From 1936 to 1938 he was flag officer (Destroyers) in the Mediterranean Fleet, with his flag in the light cruiser *Galatea*, at a time of international tension arising from the Italian campaign in Abyssinia (Ethiopia) and the Spanish Civil War. He was promoted to vice-admiral on 11 September 1937 and became C-in-C, East Indies, with his flag in the cruiser *Norfolk* in July 1938. There he was diagnosed as suffering from pulmonary tuberculosis and invalided to the retired list. Despite the opinion of eminent civilian specialists that he had fully recovered, he was not re-instated, though he was awarded the KCB in 1939. On the outbreak of the Second World War in September 1939 Sir James Somerville reported to the Admiralty for active duty, and, as a wireless specialist, worked on the development of radar. During the evacuation of the British Expeditionary Force from Dunkirk in May 1940 he joined Vice-Admiral Sir Bertram Ramsay, Flag Officer, Dover, and helped him carry the burden of continuous command at this critical period.

With the fall of France in June 1940, Somerville was given command of Force H, a detached squadron based at Gibraltar, composed initially of an aircraft carrier and three capital ships. The British government, concerned to prevent the French fleet at Mers-el-Kebir from falling into Axis hands, offered it the choice of continuing the fight, sailing to the West Indies, or handing over its ships to British control. When no satisfactory answer was received, Somerville, with his flag in the battle-cruiser *Hood*, was ordered to sink the French ships at their moorings. After several hours of negotiation with the French and exchanging signals with the Admiralty in the hope that his orders would be changed, he eventually bombarded the harbour on 3 July 1940, followed by an air attack on 6 July 1940. In August 1940 he transferred his flag to the battle-cruiser *Renown*. Under Somerville, Force H was primarily deployed in the western Mediterranean and eastern Atlantic, providing escorts for important convoys to Malta and attacking Italian shore installations. At the battle of Cape Spartivento (27 November 1940) he put to flight a faster Italian fleet that had threatened a British convoy, but was unable to bring it to battle before it reached the protection of its air-bases and light craft. The Prime Minister, Winston Churchill, was critical of Somerville for not continuing the pursuit and sought his court-martial. The First Sea Lord, Sir Dudley Pound [89], sent the Earl of Cork and Orrery [87] to Gibraltar in December 1941 to conduct an enquiry. Cork considered that Somerville's decision was entirely sound and reported accordingly. In May 1941 Somerville hoisted his flag briefly in the aircraft carrier *Ark Royal*, prior to taking fighter reinforcements to Malta. From 24 to 27 May 1941, with Force H, he took part in the destruction of the German battleship *Bismarck*. In August 1941 he transferred his flag to the battleship *Nelson* and, after *Nelson* was damaged while escorting a Malta convoy on 27 September 1941, successively to the battleships *Rodney* and *Malaya*.

Somerville was ordered to the Indian Ocean as C-in-C, Eastern Fleet, in March 1942, with promotion to admiral (retired) on 6 April 1942. Early in April 1942, when a superior Japanese fleet threatened Ceylon (Sri Lanka), Somerville, with his flag in the battleship *Warspite*, sailed to meet it, but failed to make contact. Shortly afterwards he was given discretion to withdraw to Kilindini, (Mombasa, Kenya) where for the next two years he had to adopt the strategy of avoiding action, so as to keep his ships as a "fleet in being". Early in 1944 the improved Allied position in Europe allowed the Eastern Fleet to be reinforced with powerful modern ships and Somerville, with his flag in the battleship *Queen Elizabeth*, went onto the offensive by launching air strikes on Sabang (17 April 1944 and 25 July 1944) and Surabaya (17 May 1944). Somerville's relations with the Allied Supreme Commander, South-East Asia, Lord Louis Mountbatten [102], appointed in August 1943, were initially cordial, but became frosty when Mountbatten (considerably junior to Somerville as a flag officer) attempted to claim the Eastern Fleet as part of his own Command. Somerville was succeeded by Sir Bruce Fraser [95] in August 1944, after being restored to the active list.

Somerville became head of the British naval delegation at the Combined Chiefs of Staff committee in Washington in October 1944. He remained there for the rest of the war, with promotion to admiral of the fleet on 8 May 1945, until returning home in December 1945. He undertook no further naval duties, but played a full part in civic life from his home at Dinder House, Somerset, where he died of coronary thrombosis on 19 May 1949. Slight of build and stature, but always physically active and extrovert, Somerville was a trusted and popular leader, despite his abrasive tongue and blue language. His salty, even earthy, sense of humour endeared him to the lower deck, and he greatly relished the signal he received from Sir

Andrew Cunningham [91] on being awarded the KBE in 1941 "What, twice a knight at your age?".

STAVELEY
Sir WILLIAM DOVETON MINET, GCB (1928–1997) [113]

William Staveley was born on 10 November 1928, the son of an admiral and grandson of Sir Doveton Sturdee [73]. After attending West Downs School at Winchester, Hampshire, he joined the Navy as a cadet at the Royal Naval College, Dartmouth, in 1942. After the end of the Second World War he was promoted to midshipman on 1 September 1946 and appointed to the cruiser *Ajax* in the Mediterranean Fleet. He became an acting sub-lieutenant on 1 January 1948, under training in the destroyer *Zephyr*, and with his promotion confirmed on 1 January 1948, served from 1949 to 1951 successively in the cruisers *Nigeria* and *Bermuda* in the South Atlantic. He was promoted to lieutenant on 1 September 1950. From 1952 to 1954 Staveley was flag lieutenant to the C-in-C, Home Fleet, Sir George Creasy [101], successively in the aircraft carrier *Indomitable* and the battleship *Vanguard*. In 1954 he married Bettina Shuter and later had with her a son and a daughter. Between 1954 and 1956 he was an instructor at the Royal Naval College, Dartmouth, and during 1957 was in the royal yacht *Britannia*. He served on the Far East station as first lieutenant of the destroyer *Cavalier* from November 1957 until his promotion to lieutenant-commander on 1 September 1958, and was present at the British hydrogen bomb tests at Christmas Island on the Pacific. During 1959 he qualified at the Royal Naval Staff College, Greenwich, and between 1959 to 1961 was on the staff of the C-in-C, Nore.

Staveley was promoted to commander on 31 December 1961 and in January 1965 became commanding officer of the minesweeper *Houghton* and Senior Officer, 104th (later Sixth) Minesweeping Flotilla in the Far East Fleet. After operational service during the Brunei counter-insurgency campaign in 1962 and the confrontation with Indonesia in Malaysia in 1963 he was Commander, Sea Training, at the working-up base, Portland, from 1964 to 1966. He commanded the destroyer *Zulu* on the Home and Middle East stations between January and October 1967, when he was appointed Assistant Director of Naval Plans at the Ministry of Defence, with promotion to captain on 31 December 1967. From November 1970 to April 1972 he was flag captain to the second-in-command, Far East Fleet, in the assault ship *Intrepid*, and was then captain of the commando carrier *Albion* from May 1972 until she was decommissioned in 1973.

Staveley then attended the Royal College of Defence Studies before returning to the MOD as Director of Naval Plans (later Director of Naval Future Policies) from February 1974 until 1976, when he became Flag Officer, Second Flotilla. He was promoted to rear-admiral on 7 January 1977 and was appointed Flag Officer, Carriers and Amphibious Ships, and

NATO Allied Commander, Carrier Striking Group Two, based at Portsmouth, in March 1977. In October 1978 he became chief of staff to the C-in-C, Fleet, Sir Henry Leach [111], who had been Director of Naval Plans during Staveley's period as Assistant Director. Between 1980 and 1982 Staveley was a member of the Admiralty Board at the MOD as Vice-Chief of the Naval Staff. He was promoted to vice-admiral on 11 April 1980 and awarded the KCB in 1981. An announcement of reductions in the Navy by John Nott, Defence Secretary in Margaret Thatcher's first Cabinet, was followed by the Argentine occupation of the Falkland Islands (1–2 April 1982). Sir William Staveley regretted that, as VCNS, he was unable to play an operational role in the subsequent campaign and so emulate his grandfather with another British victory in the Falklands. He was promoted to admiral on 29 October 1982 on appointment as C-in-C, Fleet, and NATO Allied C-in-C, Channel (CINCHAN) and Eastern Atlantic Area (CINCEASTLANT). He drew attention to the inadequacy of his resources to meet the Warsaw Pact's threat to NATO sea communications and thereby caused irritation to British ministers anxious to reduce defence expenditure. From 1985 to 1989 he was First Sea Lord under successive Conservative ministers and continued to press for a fleet capable of meeting its NATO and other international commitments. Staveley left the Ministry of Defence with promotion to admiral of the fleet on 25 May 1989. He subsequently held a number of public appointments, including senior posts in the administration of the National Health Service. He died of a heart attack on 13 October 1997.

STEUART
JAMES, (c.1690–1757) [3]

James Steuart or Stewart, born in about 1690, became captain of the 5th-rate *Greyhound* on 14 January 1709, during the War of the Spanish Succession. He was later given command of the 4th-rate *Dartmouth*, in which he spent the rest of the war in the Mediterranean. During 1716 he commanded the 6th-rate *Aldborough* off the Scottish coast, in anti-Jacobite patrols. He was captain of the galley *Royal Anne* in the squadron that escorted George I on his return from Hanover in 1717, but held no recorded naval appointments during "the long peace" that followed. Following the outbreak of the War of the Austrian Succession in 1740 he was given command of the 3rd-rate *Cumberland*, in which he served in the Channel in 1741 and the West Indies in 1742. Between 1741 and 1747 Steuart was Member of Parliament for Weymouth and Melcombe Regis, Dorset. He became rear-admiral of the Blue on 6 April 1742, rear-admiral of the White on August 1743, vice-admiral of the Blue on 7 December 1743 and vice-admiral of the Red on 19 June 1744. In 1744 he was second-in-command of a fleet sent to Lisbon to support the Portuguese government against a threatened invasion from Spain. Steuart did not again go to sea.

He was promoted to admiral of the White on 15 July 1747 and became admiral of the fleet on 22 November 1750. He died in March 1757.

STEWART
Sir HOUSTON, GCB (1791–1875) [34]

Houston Stewart, a younger son of a Scottish baronet, was born on 3 August 1791. He joined the Navy during the Napoleonic wars, as a first class volunteer in the 5th-rate *Medusa*, on 5 February 1805. His first long cruise was to Calcutta, then the capital of British India, escorting the newly appointed Governor-General of Bengal, Lord Cornwallis. *Medusa* then returned home in what was, for the period, the short time of eighty-three days for the round trip. Stewart transferred to the 3rd-rate *Revenge* in which he served in the blockade of Brest and Lorient and was present at the capture of four French frigates by Sir Samuel Hood (later Viscount Hood) on 25 September 1806. In October 1806 he joined the 5th-rate *Impérieuse*, commanded by Lord Cochrane (later Earl of Dundonald), one of the most dashing frigate captains of his day, under whom he took part in a series of raids and boat actions along the west coast of France. Stewart was mentioned in despatches for his part in the destruction of Fort Roquette, Arcachon, on 7 January 1807. In the Mediterranean, during November 1808, he served with Cochrane in a landing party alongside the Spanish defenders of Rosas. He was then given command of a small vessel, *Julie,* used as an armed tender until damaged by coastal artillery fire. He rejoined *Impérieuse*, commanded by Cochrane's successor, Thomas Garth, and took part in the British expedition to Walcheren (July-September 1809). At a critical point in the attack on Flushing (Vlissingen) he was commended for suggesting the use of explosive shells (remaining from the incendiary Cochrane's period in command) with which *Impérieuse* destroyed an opposing shore battery.

From November 1809 to January 1810 Stewart was in the 4th-rate *Adamant,* flagship of Rear-Admiral Edward Nagle at Leith. In May 1810 he joined the 6th-rate *Hussar*, in which he served in the North Sea and the Baltic. He was subsequently appointed to the 1st-rate *Royal William* at Portsmouth and the 5th-rate *Alexandria* at Leith, in which he became a lieutenant on 1 August 1811. A fortnight later he was transferred to the 3rd-rate *Tigre*, in which he took part in the continuing blockade of Rochefort. In May 1812 he joined the 1st-rate *San Josef,* flagship of Lord Keith, in the Channel, and in January 1813 became Keith's signal-lieutenant in the 1st-rate *Queen Charlotte*. Stewart was briefly detached in March 1814 as acting captain of the 3rd-rate *Clarence*, blockading Brest, and in June 1814 as acting captain of the sloop *Podargus* off Finisterre. Stewart was promoted to commander on 13 August 1814 and, at the time of Napoleon's final defeat in June 1815, was serving in the West Indies.

There, between January 1815 and April 1818, he commanded in succession the sloops *Shark*, *Royalist* and *Rifleman*, followed by acting command successively of the 5th-rate *Pique* and the 4th-rate *Salisbury*. He was promoted to captain on 10 June 1817. After returning home, he married in 1819 Martha Miller, the daughter of a Scottish baronet, and later had with her a family of three sons, of whom the eldest became an admiral.

From October 1823 to December 1826 Stewart commanded the 6th-rate *Menai* on the North America station, based at Halifax, Nova Scotia. He returned to sea in April 1839, in command of the 3rd-rate *Benbow* in the Mediterranean. At this time Mehemet Ali, the Albanian ruler of Egypt, had conquered Palestine and Syria and threatened to unseat his nominal overlord, the Sultan of Turkey. The French supported Mehemet Ali, but the other Great Powers were determined to protect the Sultan. While France prepared for war, a combined British, Austrian and Turkish fleet appeared off Beirut, Lebanon. This encouraged a general rising throughout Syria against Mehemet Ali's oppressive rule. Stewart, at the head of a small squadron, delivered arms to the Arabs, rescued the consuls of Aleppo (Haleb, Syria) and Alexandretta (Iskenderun, Turkey), and bombarded the Egyptian garrison in Tripoli (Tarabulus, Lebanon). With the main fleet, he took part in the bombardment and capture of Acre, Palestine (Akko, Israel) in November 1840. The rapid collapse of Mehemet's forces pre-empted a war in Europe and, in the early part of 1841, Stewart commanded the British and Austrian squadrons observing the Egyptian withdrawal. Later that year he played a part in rescuing Greek nationalists from Candia (Heraklion, Crete), following an unsuccessful rebellion against Turkish rule.

From May to July 1846 Stewart was acting Superintendent of Woolwich Dockyard and captain of the yacht *William and Mary*. He was Comptroller General of the Coast Guard from November 1846 to 1850, when he was appointed a lord commissioner of the Admiralty. Between 1850 and 1852 he sat as a Tory Member of Parliament for Greenwich. He served at the Admiralty, with promotion to rear-admiral on 16 June 1851, until the Earl of Derby's first administration fell in December 1852. From 1853 to 1855 he was Superintendent of Malta Dockyard. Following the outbreak of the Crimean War in March 1854, a British fleet was sent to the Black Sea, where he became second-in-command in January 1855. During October 1855 Stewart commanded a squadron in the successful allied landings at Kinburn (Pokrovskiy), guarding the strategically important Russian port of Ochakov in the Dnepr estuary (Dneprovskiy Liman). He was awarded the KCB in July 1855 and during 1856 served as Superintendent of Devonport Dockyard. From November 1856 to January 1860 Sir Houston Stewart was C-in-C on the North America station with promotion to vice-admiral on 30 July 1857. He was C-in-C, Plymouth, from October 1860 to October 1863, with promotion to admiral on 10 November 1862. He became an admiral of the fleet on 20 October 1872 and died on 10 December 1875.

STEWART
JAMES, see **STEUART**, JAMES **[3]**

STURDEE
Sir FREDERICK CHARLES DOVETON, 1st Baronet, GCB, KCMG, CVO (1859–1925) **[73]**

Frederick Sturdee, the eldest son of a captain in the Navy, was born at Charlton, near Woolwich, on 9 June 1859. He attended the Royal Naval School at New Cross, Greater London (now the campus of Goldsmiths' College, University of London) and joined the Navy in July 1871 as a cadet in the training ship *Britannia*. He passed out first in his class and became a midshipman on 19 July 1873. He served in the frigate *Undaunted*, flagship on the China station, from 1876 until returning home to become an acting sub-lieutenant on 9 June 1878 at the beginning of his promotion courses. Sturdee was promoted to lieutenant on 7 Feb 1880, with appointment in May 1880 to the brig *Martin*, tender to the training ship for boys at Portsmouth. Between February 1881 and September 1882 he was in the torpedo depot ship *Hecla* under Captain Arthur Wilson **[59]** in the Mediterranean. There he took part in the British operations at Alexandria in July 1882, undertaken in response to the Egyptian nationalist revolution led by Colonel Arabi (' Urbi) Pasha. Sturdee then joined the torpedo school *Vernon* at Portsmouth, where he remained until December 1885 and qualified as a torpedo officer. In 1882 he married Marion Andrews, of Fortis Green, Middlesex, and later had with her a son and a daughter.

Sturdee was from 1886 to 1889 the torpedo lieutenant in the battleship *Bellerophon*, flagship on the North America and West Indies station. He rejoined *Vernon* in 1889 and remained on the staff there until promoted to commander on 30 June 1893. He was then appointed to the Admiralty as a torpedo specialist in the Directorate of Naval Ordnance and served there until November 1897, when he became commanding officer of the cruiser *Porpoise* on the Australia station. At the beginning of 1899 he was involved in a war of succession in Samoa, for long an area of disputed influence between Germany, the United States and the United Kingdom. Landing parties from United States and British warships supported one party, while the other was encouraged by the Germans. Sturdee's contribution to Anglo-American diplomacy, which included the bombardment of Apia by the USS *Philadelphia* and his own participation in a violent argument with the local German representatives, was rewarded by his promotion to captain on 30 June 1899. The Samoan islands were subsequently partitioned between the United States and Germany, with the German element, to Sturdee's great satisfaction, falling to New Zealand soon after the outbreak of the First World War.

Sturdee returned to the Admiralty during 1902 as Assistant Director of Naval Intelligence. In November 1903 he was given command of the armoured cruiser *Bedford* in the Home Fleet, and in May 1905 became chief of staff to Lord Charles Beresford, C-in-C, Mediterranean Fleet, in the battleship *Bulwark*. He followed Beresford in 1907, when the latter became C-in-C, Channel Fleet, and commanded successively the battleships *King Edward VII* and *New Zealand* until his promotion to rear-admiral on 12 September 1908. In 1910, with his flag in the battleship *St Vincent*, Sturdee was appointed to command the First Battle Squadron in the Home Fleet. He expressed doubts about the advantages claimed for the new Dreadnought class battleships, armed predominantly with long-range guns, on the grounds that the weather conditions in the North Sea usually restricted visibility to a range when this advantage would count for little. He also supported the strategy of a close blockade of German ports, as planned by his C-in-C, Sir Henry May [65] and the First Sea Lord, Sir Arthur Wilson [59] (his old captain in *Hecla*). During 1911 Sturdee was president of an Admiralty committee on submarines and then returned to the Home Fleet in December 1911 to command the Third Cruiser Squadron, with his flag in the cruiser *Shannon*. Sturdee impressed the fleet second-in-command, Sir John Jellicoe [68], with his careful study of naval tactics and gained a reputation as a skilful squadron leader. In 1913 he transferred with *Shannon* to command the Second Cruiser Squadron where he remained, with the award of the KCB, until promoted to vice-admiral on 13 December 1913.

Sir Doveton Sturdee succeeded Sir Henry Jackson [70] as Chief of War Staff at the Admiralty in July 1914. On the outbreak of the First World War in the following month he was handicapped both by the lack of a fully-developed staff organization and his own insistence on conducting most of the staff work in person. His immediate superior, the First Sea Lord, Prince Louis of Battenberg [74], was driven to resign on account of his German origins at the end of October 1914 and was succeeded by Lord Fisher [58]. A few days later, at the battle of Coronel (1 November 1914), the German East Asiatic Squadron inflicted the first defeat the Navy had suffered since the American War of 1812. Fisher had already decided to replace Sturdee, whom he regarded as an ally of Sir Charles Beresford, his opponent in a feud that had divided the Navy into two factions. Winston Churchill, the First Lord of the Admiralty, had worked closely with Sturdee since the beginning of the war and refused to let him be made the scapegoat for the Coronel disaster. He accordingly offered him command of the China station, enlarged by responsibility for naval operations in the Pacific. Sturdee declined, as this would have meant being based ashore, and declared his willingness to remain in post under Fisher.

When Fisher decided to send the battle cruisers *Invincible* and *Inflexible* from the Grand Fleet to the South Atlantic, Sturdee commented that this was the course he had previously advised. Fisher was provoked into declaring that he would no longer retain Sturdee on his staff. Churchill thereupon gave Sturdee command of the two ships, with which he proceeded (with his flag in *Invincible*) to the South Atlantic. While Sturdee's ships were coaling at Port Stanley, Falkland Islands, the German squadron appeared on the horizon. Sturdee remained calm and, as the Germans turned away on discovering the presence of the battle-cruisers, put to sea to avenge Coronel at the ensuing battle of the Falkland Islands (8 December 1914). At the end of the action he remarked to his flag captain "Well, Beamish, we were sacked from the Admiralty, but we've done pretty well today". He returned home a hero and, despite further petty criticism and complaints from Fisher, became the first admiral since the Napoleonic Wars to receive the baronetcy conventionally awarded for victory in a naval engagement. At the end of January 1915 Sir Doveton Sturdee was given command of the Fourth Battle Squadron in the Grand Fleet, with his flag in the battleship *Benbow*.

Sturdee remained in the Grand Fleet, in which he served at the battle of Jutland (31 May–1 June 1916) until promoted to admiral on 17 May 1917. He was C-in-C, Nore, from 1 March 1918 and retained this post after the end of the war in November 1918 until his promotion to admiral of the fleet on 5 July 1921. He retired to his home at Wargrave House, Camberley, Surrey, and died on 7 May 1925. He was buried in the nearby parish churchyard of St Peter's, Frimley. His son, a future rear-admiral, succeeded to his baronetcy, and had a daughter who became an officer in the Women's Royal Naval Service and married the future Sir Edward Ashmore [109]. Sturdee's own daughter married a future admiral and became the mother of Sir William Staveley [113].

SYMONDS
Sir THOMAS MATTHEW CHARLES, GCB (1813–1894) [40]

Thomas Symonds was born on 15 July 1813. His grandfather had been a captain in the Navy, and his father, (later Rear-Admiral Sir) William Symonds, as Surveyor of the Navy from 1832 to 1847, became the designer of a series of warships whose sailing abilities were the cause of much controversy. Symonds joined the Navy in April 1825 and rose to become a lieutenant on 5 November 1832. He was appointed in April 1833 to the 6th-rate *Vestal* at Portsmouth, and then moved to the Mediterranean, where he joined the 4th-rate *Endymion* in September 1833 and the 1st-rate *Britannia* in July 1834. From December 1834 until his promotion to commander on 21 October 1837 he was in the 6th-rate *Rattlesnake* on the East Indies station. In August 1838 Symonds was given command of the sloop *Rover* on the North America and West Indies station, where he remained prior to being promoted to captain on 22 February 1841. In September 1845 he married Anna Heywood, the daughter of a captain in the Navy.

Symonds returned to sea in the 6th-rate *Spartan*, an appointment arranged by his father to ensure that this ship (one of his designs) was given a fair chance in trials against the 6th-rate *Eurydice* (designed by a rival

240

officer, the Honourable Sir George Elliot). He commanded *Spartan* in the Mediterranean from May 1846 to 1849 and, after returning home, was appointed in January 1850 to the 4th-rate *Arethusa*. He went back to the Mediterranean in *Arethusa* during 1852 and, after the outbreak of the Crimean War in 1854, took part in operations in the Black Sea. Symonds became a rear-admiral on 1 November 1860 and a vice-admiral on 2 April 1866. He was awarded the KCB in March 1867 and commanded in the Channel from December 1867 to July 1870. Sir Thomas Symonds was promoted to admiral on 14 July 1871 and was C-in-C, Devonport, from November 1871 to November 1875. He became an admiral of the fleet on 15 July 1879 and died at Torquay on 14 November 1894.

TOVEY
Sir JOHN CRONYN, Baron Tovey, GCB, KBE, DSO
(1885–1971) **[92]**

John Tovey was born at Borley Hill, Rochester, Kent, on 7 March 1885, the youngest in a family of four daughters and seven sons of a colonel of the Royal Engineers and his Canadian wife. He was educated at Durnford House School, Langton Matravers, Dorset, and joined the Navy as a cadet in the training ship *Britannia* in January 1900. He served as a midshipman successively in the battleship *Majestic*, flagship of the Channel Squadron, and the cruiser *Ariadne*, flagship on the North America and West Indies station, and was promoted to acting sub-lieutenant on 15 July 1904 at the beginning of his promotion courses. Tovey was promoted to lieutenant on 15 July 1906 and served from 1908 to 1910 in the armoured cruiser *King Alfred*, flagship of the C-in-C on the China station. Between April 1910 and June 1911 he was on the staff of the Royal Naval College, Osborne, and from then until July 1912 he served in the cruiser *Bellona*, leader of the Second Destroyer Flotilla in the Home Fleet. In November 1911 he was appointed first lieutenant of the scout *Patrol* in the Home Fleet. Tovey subsequently qualified as a gunnery officer and in April 1913 became gunnery lieutenant of the light cruiser *Amphion* in the Home Fleet.

With the outbreak of the First World War in August 1914 Tovey became lieutenant-commander of the destroyer flotilla leader *Faulknor*. In January 1915 he was given command of the destroyer *Jackal* in the Grand Fleet, in which he served until appointed on 7 May 1916 to command the destroyer *Onslow*. He took part in the battle of Jutland (31 May–1 June 1915) where, as part of the Thirteenth Destroyer Flotilla, he torpedoed the German light cruiser *Wiesbaden* and went on to attack the main battle line before being stopped by hits on his ship's boiler room. As the battle fleets moved on, *Onslow* was given a tow by the damaged destroyer *Defender* and reached Aberdeen forty-eight hours later. Tovey was subsequently awarded the DSO and the first of his four mentions in despatches. In March 1916 he married Aida Rowe, the daughter of a private gentleman settled in

Plymouth. In October 1917 he was appointed to the new destroyer *Ursa* and subsequently moved to the destroyer *Wolfhound*, where he remained after the end of hostilities in November 1918, until joining the Royal Naval Staff College, Greenwich, in May 1919.

Between June 1920 and June 1922 Tovey was at the Admiralty in the Operations Division. He was promoted to captain on 31 December 1923 and from 1925 to 1926 was based at Port Edgar, Edinburgh, as Captain (Destroyers) of the Eighth Destroyer Flotilla in the Atlantic Fleet, in the flotilla leader *Bruce*. During 1927 he attended the Imperial Defence College, London, and subsequently returned to the Admiralty as Naval Assistant to the Second Sea Lord. He then commanded the battleship *Rodney* from April 1932 until January 1935, when he was appointed commodore of the naval barracks, Chatham.

Tovey was promoted to rear-admiral on 27 August 1935. In March 1938, he became Rear-Admiral (Destroyers) in the Mediterranean Fleet with his flag first in the depot ship *Woolwich* and then in the cruiser *Galatea*, and was promoted to vice-admiral on 3 May 1939. Following the entry of Italy into the Second World War and the fall of France in June 1940 Tovey was appointed second-in-command of the Mediterranean Fleet. He was given command of the fleet's light forces and took part in the battle of Calabria (9 July 1940), with his flag in the cruiser *Orion*.

At the end of 1940 Tovey was appointed C-in-C, Home Fleet, with the acting rank of admiral. In May 1941 he commanded the operations against the German battleship *Bismarck* and, with his flag in the battleship *King George V*, was present at her destruction on 27 May 1941, for which he was awarded the KBE. In the aftermath of this action, the First Sea Lord, Sir Dudley Pound [89], considered court-martialling Captain J C Leach of the battleship *Prince of Wales* for breaking off action after *Bismarck* had sunk his consort, the battle-cruiser *Hood*. Tovey declared that in such a case he would haul down his flag and appear in court as prisoner's friend, with the result that the idea was dropped. Following the entry of the Soviet Union into the war in June 1941 the Home Fleet assumed the added task of escorting Arctic convoys to Northern Russia. Sir John Tovey was promoted to admiral on 30 October 1942. He later lost favour with the Prime Minister, Winston Churchill, who described him as "foolish and obstinate" for his continued argument that the battle of the Atlantic rather than the strategic bomber offensive should have priority in the allocation of aircraft. He advocated greater use of the fleet to attack the German battleship *Tirpitz*, based in the Norwegian fjords, but was ordered to concentrate on convoy protection.

In July 1943 Tovey hauled down his flag in the battleship *Duke of York* and left the Home Fleet to become C-in-C, Nore, with promotion to admiral of the fleet on 22 October 1944. There he was responsible for coastal operations in support of the Allied advance into the Low Countries in late 1944, and the protection of the lines of communication across the North Sea. He remained at the Nore following the end of hostilities in 1945 until going on half-pay in April 1946, with the grant of a peerage as Baron Tovey of Langton Matravers. He died, without offspring, at Funchal, Madeira, on 12 January 1971 and his peerage became extinct.

TYRWHITT
Sir REGINALD YORKE, 1st Baronet, GCB, DSO (1870–1951)
[82]

Reginald Tyrwhitt, the fifth son of the vicar of St Mary Magdalene, Oxford, was born at Oxford on 10 May 1870. He joined the Navy as a cadet in the training ship *Britannia* in July 1883 and was appointed to the battleship *Alexandra*, flagship of the C-in-C, Mediterranean Fleet, in August 1885. In November 1888 he joined the cruiser *Calypso* in the Training Squadron and was promoted to acting sub-lieutenant at the beginning of his promotion courses on 14 December 1889. He took part in manoeuvres in the armoured cruiser *Australia* in 1889 and in the battleship *Ajax* in 1890, and in March 1892 was appointed to the brig *Pilot*, tender to the training ship for boys at Plymouth. Tyrwhitt was promoted to lieutenant on 25 August 1892 and served in the light cruiser *Cleopatra* on the North America and West Indies station until the end of 1895. In January 1896 he was given command of the destroyer *Hart*, from where he moved at the end of the year to be first lieutenant of the despatch vessel *Surprise* in the Mediterranean. In December 1899 he became first lieutenant of the cruiser *Indefatigable* on the North America and West Indies station and remained there until promoted to commander on 1 January 1903. He was then appointed commander of the cruiser *Aurora*, tender to the training ship *Britannia*, and in the same year married Angela Corbally of Rathbeale Hall, Swords, County Dublin, with whom he later had a family of two daughters and a son.

From 1904 to 1905 Tyrwhitt commanded the torpedo-boat destroyer *Waveney*, followed by command successively of the scouts *Attentive* in 1906 and *Skirmisher* in 1907. He was promoted to captain on 30 June 1908, followed by appointment as Captain of the Fourth Destroyer Flotilla, based at Portsmouth, in the cruiser *Topaze*. From 1910 to 1912 he served in the Mediterranean as flag captain successively of the cruisers *Bacchante* and *Good Hope* and then joined the Home Fleet as Captain of the Second Destroyer Flotilla, in the flotilla leader *Bellona*. In 1914 he became commodore of all destroyers in the Home Fleet. On the outbreak of the First World War in August 1914 he was appointed commodore of the Harwich Force, with the First and Third Destroyer Flotillas under his command and his broad pendant in the light cruiser *Amethyst*.

Tyrwhitt proved an able leader of light forces. Together with Commodore Roger Keyes **[80]**, whose submarine flotilla was based at Harwich, he proposed an action that became the first major naval engagement of the war, the battle of Heligoland Bight (28 August 1914).With his broad pendant in the new light cruiser *Arethusa*, he led a force of thirty-one destroyers in an attack on German torpedo-boats, provoking a response by German light cruisers who, in turn, were outmatched by the Battle-cruiser Squadron under Rear-Admiral David Beatty [69]. *Arethusa* was hit in the engine-room, but Tyrwhitt returned with only two other ships damaged. At the battle of the Dogger Bank (24 January 1915) Tyrwhitt's force was again in close co-operation with Beatty's battle-cruisers. In March 1916 he escorted the seaplane carrier *Vindix* to the Skagerrak to attack the German airship base at Cuxhaven. Two collisions delayed his return, but bad weather intervened before the German surface fleet could reach him.

The German High Seas Fleet again put to sea on 24 April 1916, planning to bombard the coast of East Anglia and so draw British ships out to be defeated in detail. Intercepted radio transmissions revealed the German intentions to the Admiralty and the whole Grand Fleet sailed to meet the Germans. The Harwich Force was ordered to join it, but Tyrwhitt instead headed for Lowestoft, where the German battle-cruisers began their bombardment. He tried, without success, to lure them to the south, but then followed them to Yarmouth, where his attack on the accompanying German light cruisers forced the battle-cruisers to break off their bombardment and go to their rescue. They then fell back on the High Seas Fleet, followed by Tyrwhitt until the Admiralty ordered him to break contact. At the battle of Jutland (31 May–1 June 1916) Tyrwhitt, with his five light cruisers and nineteen destroyers, sailed from Harwich on his own initiative, only to be recalled by the Admiralty in case a part of the German fleet moved south. The Germans made another sortie on 19 August 1916, during which one of their airships mistakenly reported the Harwich Force as a detached battle squadron. On discovering that the Grand Fleet was approaching from a different direction, the Germans suspected a trap and headed for home. Tyrwhitt planned to attack with torpedoes, but broke off contact when the light failed, judging that to continue would amount to suicide. His critics later argued that he should have pressed on with the attack, but his decision was approved by the C-in-C, Grand Fleet, Sir John Jellicoe [68], who had signalled to Tyrwhitt that the fleet was too far away to come to his support. Tyrwhitt was awarded the DSO in 1916 and the KCB in 1917.

Sir Reginald Tyrwhitt remained in command of the Harwich Force for the rest of the war, taking part in several destroyer actions in the southern North Sea and receiving acting promotion to rear-admiral in 1918. At the end of hostilities in November 1918 the German submarine force was required to sail to Harwich and surrender. Tyrwhitt was awarded a baronetcy in the post-war honours, with promotion to rear-admiral on 2 December 1919. He subsequently became Senior Naval Officer, Gibraltar, followed by appointment in 1921 as Flag Officer commanding the Third Light Cruiser Squadron in the Mediterranean Fleet, with his flag in the light cruiser *Cardiff*. He next served as Admiral Superintendent, Rosyth Dockyard, from early in 1923 until promoted vice-admiral on

18 February 1925. Between 1927 and 27 February 1929, when he was promoted to admiral, Tyrwhitt was C-in-C on the China station, with his flag in the cruiser *Hawkins*, at a time of increasing tension arising from civil war in China. From 1930 to 1933 he was C-in-C, Nore, followed by promotion to admiral of the fleet on 31 July 1936. On the outbreak of the Second World War in September 1939 he was too old for service with the Navy, but in 1940, when invasion seemed likely, he volunteered to join the Home Guard, and for a short while commanded the 3rd Kent Battalion. Sir Reginald Tyrwhitt died at his home in Sandhurst, Kent, on 30 May 1951. He was succeeded in his baronetcy by his son, who had followed him into the Navy and later became Second Sea Lord. His elder daughter, Dame Mary Tyrwhitt, joined the Army and became Director of the Women's Royal Army Corps.

VIAN
Sir PHILIP LOUIS, GCB, KBE, DSO (1894–1968) [98]

Philip Vian, the son of a company secretary, was born in London on 15 June 1894. After attending Hillside School and the Royal Naval Colleges at Osborne and Dartmouth from 1907 to 1911, he went to sea in the training cruiser *Cornwall*, only to find his cruise cut short when she ran aground off the Canadian coast. He was appointed a midshipman in the battleship *Lord Nelson* in the Home Fleet on 15 January 1912. On mobilization in the outbreak of the First World War in August 1914 *Lord Nelson*, too old to join the Grand Fleet, remained at Portland. Vian, promoted to acting sub-lieutenant (confirmed on 15 June 1915), was initially appointed to the cruiser *Argonaut*, intended for service in hunting for German commerce- raiders. Making use of a chance acquaintance with the First Sea Lord, Lord Fisher [58], he soon succeeded in obtaining a transfer to the Grand Fleet, in which he was appointed to the destroyer *Morning Star*. He was present at the battle of Jutland (31 May–1 June 1916) and was promoted to lieutenant on 15 September 1916. He subsequently served as first lieutenant successively of the destroyers *Ossory* and *Sorceress*.

After the conclusion of hostilities Vian was appointed to the naval barracks at Chatham in April 1919 and subsequently qualified as a gunnery specialist. In 1921 he was lent to the Royal Australian Navy for service as gunnery lieutenant successively of the battle-cruiser *Australia* and the light cruiser *Adelaide*. He was promoted to lieutenant-commander on 15 February 1924 and was appointed to the battleship *Thunderer* in the Reserve fleet, where he remained until December 1924. Vian next served as gunnery officer successively of the battleship *Emperor of India* in the Mediterranean Fleet, from May 1925 to February 1927, and of the cruiser *Kent*, flagship on the China station, from November 1927 to May 1928. After returning home with promotion to commander on 30 December 1929 he married Marjorie Haig, the daughter of a war-time colonel in the

Cameronians (Scottish Rifles), and later had with her a family of two daughters.

Between March 1930 and March 1933 Vian was employed at the Admiralty in the Training and Staff Duties Division, preparing tables for gunnery engagements. He was then given command of the destroyer *Active* in the Mediterranean Fleet, followed by promotion to captain on 31 December 1934. In October 1935 reinforcements were despatched to the Mediterranean at a time of international tension arising from the Italian invasion of Abyssinia (Ethiopia). Vian was appointed Captain (Destroyers) of the Nineteenth Destroyer Flotilla, mobilized from the Reserve fleet, and commanded it in the Mediterranean from the flotilla leader *Douglas*. After returning home in the destroyer *Keppel* late in 1936, in command of the First Destroyer Flotilla, he attended the Senior Officers' War Course. In March 1937 he became flag captain and chief of staff of the Third Cruiser Squadron of the Mediterranean Fleet, in the cruiser *Arethusa*, and was involved in the protection of British and neutral shipping during the Spanish Civil War.

Shortly before the outbreak of the Second World War on 3 September 1939 Vian was appointed to the destroyer *Mackay* and given command of a flotilla of destroyers from the Reserve Fleet, based at Liverpool and deployed as escorts with North Atlantic convoys. Early in 1940 he was transferred to the destroyer *Cossack*, based at Rosyth and deployed to escort convoys to the neutral Scandinavian countries. In February 1940 he was ordered to intercept the German freighter *Altmark*, known to be carrying captured seamen from British merchant ships sunk by the armoured ship *Admiral Graf Spee*. On 16 February 1940 he pursued *Altmark* into Josing (Josen) Fjord, near Stavanger and, notwithstanding Norwegian protests at this infringement of their neutrality, came alongside and boarded her. Vian, by his own account, was not the best of ship handlers, but on this occasion judged his distance to perfection. After a short fight the 290 prisoners of war were transferred to *Cossack*, and taken home. The phrase "The Navy's here", shouted to the prisoners by the boarding party, passed into legend. Vian himself became famous as "Vian of the *Cossack*". He was awarded the DSO to which he subsequently gained two bars.

Vian subsequently moved to the destroyer *Afridi* in which he served in Norwegian waters following the German invasion of Norway (partly in response to the *Altmark* incident) on 9 April 1940. After taking part in numerous coastal actions and in the evacuation of Allied troops from Namsos, Vian survived the sinking of *Afridi* by German aircraft on 3 May 1940. He returned to *Cossack*, based first at Scapa Flow and then at Rosyth, preparing for deployment further south in the event of a German invasion after the fall of France in June 1940. In late May 1941 he led his flotilla to replace the destroyer screen of the battleships of the Home Fleet hunting for the German battleship *Bismarck*, but, receiving an aircraft sighting report, changed course on his own initiative to intercept her. He launched several torpedo attacks and remained in contact until the main fleet arrived.

Vian was promoted to rear-admiral on 8 July 1941 and sent to the Soviet Union (invaded by Germany on 22 June 1941) for discussions on maritime co-operation. After a brief visit, in which he found himself treated with suspicion, he returned home and was given command of a force based at Scapa Flow, with his flag in the cruiser *Nigeria*. In August 1941 he destroyed the coal mines on the demilitarized island of Spitsbergen, from where he evacuated the Norwegians and escorted the Russians to the Soviet Union. While returning home, he made an attack on enemy naval units in the Norwegian Leads, in which the German training cruiser *Bremse* was rammed and sunk. In October 1941, Vian was given command of the Fifteenth Cruiser Squadron in the Mediterranean Fleet, with his flag in the cruiser *Naiad*. In December 1941, on his own initiative, he bombarded Derna, Libya, and later escorted an eastbound convoy to Malta despite Italian air attack. In the course of this operation, at the first battle of Sirte (17 December 1941), he exchanged fire with a more powerful Italian fleet, but contact was lost as the Italians were escorting their own convoy to North Africa. Vian survived the sinking of *Naiad* on 11 March 1942 and transferred his flag to the cruiser *Dido* in which he returned to Alexandria. At the second battle of Sirte (21 March 1942), with his flag in the cruiser *Cleopatra*, escorting a convoy of three merchantmen, he drove off a more powerful Italian fleet, for which he received a special message of congratulations from the Prime Minister, Winston Churchill, and was later awarded the KBE.

Sir Philip Vian was ordered home in September 1942, but contracted malaria while staging through West Africa. In April 1943, unfit for sea duty, he was nominated to the planning staff for the Allied invasion of Europe. The death in an air crash of the commander of an amphibious force in the Mediterranean led to Vian being appointed in his place, with his flag in the headquarters landing ship *Hilary*. After the Allied invasion of Sicily in July 1943 Vian was given command in August 1943 of a light aircraft carrier squadron tasked to provide fighter and ground attack support during the Allied landings at Salerno (9–16 September 1943).

Vian declined Churchill's offer of the post of Chief of Combined Operations in succession to Lord Louis Mountbatten [102] on the grounds that it would be a shore appointment. Instead, he spent the latter part of 1943 training an amphibious force for the Allied invasion of Normandy. In January 1944 he was given command of the Eastern (British) Task Force for this operation, with his flag in the cruiser *Scylla*, in which he gave close support to the landings in June 1944. In November 1944 he was given command of the First Aircraft Carrier Squadron and sailed to join the British Pacific Fleet. With his flag in the aircraft carrier *Indomitable*, he launched raids against Japanese-held oil refineries in Sumatra in December 1944 and January 1945 and operated on the flank of the United States invasion of Okinawa (1 April–2 July 1945). With the flag transferred to the aircraft carrier *Formidable*, his ships spent the final weeks of the war in the United States fleet, attacking the Japanese home islands, and came under attack from Japanese bombers and kamikaze aircraft. Vian, promoted to vice-admiral on 8 May 1945, returned home in time to take part in the Victory Parade in London.

Between 1946 and 1948 Vian was a member of the Board of Admiralty as Fifth Sea Lord, responsible as such for naval aviation. He found this a frustrating time and, with his habit of speaking his mind freely, was not temperamentally suited to departmental desk duties. He was promoted to admiral on 26 September 1948 and returned to sea in 1950 as C-in-C, Home Fleet, with his flag successively in the aircraft carriers *Implacable* and *Indomitable* until promoted to admiral of the fleet on 1 June 1952 on completing his tenure of command. He retired to his home at Ashford Hill, near Newbury, Berkshire, where he died on 27 May 1968. Vian was remembered by many officers as an exacting senior, capable of expressing himself in unpleasant terms to those who failed to reach the high standards he required. Despite his boldness in combat, he was nevertheless noted as being careful of his ships and their companies, both in peace and war.

WALLIS
Sir PROVO WILLIAM PARRY, GCB (1791–1892) [37]

Provo Wallis was born on 12 April 1791 at Halifax, Nova Scotia, the only son of the chief clerk of the Naval Commissioner at Halifax. One of his grandfathers had been a master shipwright at Halifax and the other a major in the Halifax Provincial Regiment. During the French Revolutionary War, he was at school in the United Kingdom, while his name was carried on the books of several Halifax-based ships. He was listed as an able seaman in the 5th-rate *Oiseau* in May 1795 and as a first class volunteer successively in the 5th-rate *Prévoyante* from May 1798 to September 1799 and the 3rd-rate *Asia* until September 1800. In October 1804, after the renewal of war with Napoleonic France, he was appointed midshipman in the 5th-rate *Cleopatra* at Halifax. While on passage to the West Indies his ship attacked the more heavily armed French frigate *Ville de Milan*, but was captured after an action lasting nearly three hours (16 February 1805). A week later the severely damaged *Ville de Milan* and *Cleopatra* were both taken without a fight by the 4th-rate *Leander* and Wallis, along with his shipmates, was liberated. *Milan* was subsequently taken into the Navy as a 5th-rate and remained on the North America station with Wallis as one of her midshipmen.

In November 1806 Wallis was appointed acting lieutenant of the 3rd-rate *Triumph* under Captain Thomas Masterman Hardy (formerly Nelson's flag captain), but was superseded by an established lieutenant in February 1808 and re-assigned as master's mate in the 3rd-rate *Bellona*. He became a lieutenant in the brig *Curieux* on 30 November 1808, in which he was wrecked while blockading Guadeloupe on 3 November 1809. Wallis was appointed to the 5th-rate *Gloire* on 29 December 1809 and during the following years served in the sloops *Observateur, Driver* and *Emulous*. In January 1812 he joined the 5th-rate *Shannon*, under Captain Philip Broke, one of the Navy's efficient gunnery enthusiasts. In the American War of 1812, after three British frigates in succession had been defeated in single-ship actions against frigates of the United States Navy, Broke challenged the frigate USS *Chesapeake* to a duel off Boston. His capture of this ship after a combat lasting fifteen minutes (1 June 1813) was a famous victory and did much to restore the Navy's prestige. Broke himself was badly wounded and his first lieutenant killed, so that it was under Wallis's command that, after the battle, *Shannon* returned to base at Halifax. Wallis was rewarded by promotion to commander on 9 July 1813 and returned home in January 1814 to command the sloop *Snipe*, in which he served at Sheerness until the end of the Napoleonic Wars in 1815. During 1817 he married Juliana Massey, second daughter of the Archdeacon of Barnstaple, and later had with her a family of two daughters.

Wallis was promoted to captain on 12 August 1819 and later commanded successively the 6th-rate *Nieman* at Halifax from June 1824 to September 1826 and the 5th-rate *Madagascar* on the North America and West Indies station from April 1838 to September 1839. At Vera Cruz, he gained the thanks of the British merchants of the city for protecting their interests when a French fleet bombarded the city to enforce long-standing claims for damages suffered during the Mexican insurrection of 1828. Between October 1843 and April 1846 he was Senior Naval Officer, Gibraltar, in the 3rd-rate *Warspite*. During 1844 he was the British observer at the French bombardment of Tangiers and Mogador, Morocco (mounted from Gibraltar) and in 1845 was the senior British officer off the coast of Syria, at a time of civil war between the local Druse and Maronite Christians. After the death of his first wife, Wallis married in 1849 Jemima, daughter of Sir Robert Wilson, the then governor of Gibraltar. He was promoted to rear-admiral on 27 August 1851. At the beginning of 1857 he became C-in-C on the South-east Coast of America, but was recalled on promotion to vice-admiral on 10 September 1857 and was awarded the KCB in May 1860. Sir Provo Wallis thereafter remained on half-pay, with promotion to admiral on 2 March 1863.

On the introduction of a compulsory age-related retirement system in 1851, officers who had commanded a rated ship before the end of the Napoleonic War in 1815 were allowed to retain their existing right to remain on the active list and be promoted, by seniority, to vacancies as these occurred. Because Wallis had been in command of *Shannon* during the few days after her victory over *Chesapeake* he was able to benefit from this concession and so rose to become admiral of the fleet on 11 December 1877. He remained on the active list, holding one of the three established posts in this rank, until his death at his home in Funtington, near Chichester, Sussex, on 13 February 1892, at the age of 101. He was buried at St Mary's Church, Funtington.

WEMYSS
Sir ROSSLYN ERSKINE, 1st Baron Wester Wemyss, GCB, CMG, MVO (1864–1933) [71]

"Rosy" Wemyss, the posthumous youngest son of the laird of Wemyss Castle, Fife, and his wife, a granddaughter of the Duke of Clarence (later William IV) [11] and Mrs Jordan, was born in London on 12 April 1864. His paternal grandfather, a distant relation of the Earls of Wemyss, was a rear-admiral. Wemyss joined the Navy as a cadet in the training ship *Britannia* on 15 July 1877. In July 1879 he was appointed to the corvette *Bacchante*, with his distant cousins Prince Albert Victor, heir apparent to the Prince of Wales [44] and Prince George of Wales, later George V [64], with promotion to midshipman on 23 September 1879. During the next three years they undertook a series of cruises that took them round the world under sail in the Flying Squadron. In 1883 Wemyss was appointed to the battleship *Northumberland* in the Channel, before joining the corvette *Canada* on the North America and West Indies station. He became an acting sub-lieutenant on 24 September 1883 at the beginning of his promotion courses and in 1885 was appointed to the torpedo depot ship *Hecla* in the Mediterranean Fleet. He was promoted to lieutenant on 31 March 1887 and served in the royal yacht *Osborne* from October 1887 until September 1889.

Wemyss then became flag lieutenant in the battleship *Anson*, flagship of the second-in-command of the Channel Squadron. Between 1890 and 1892 he served in the armoured cruiser *Undaunted*, commanded by Captain Lord Charles Beresford in the Mediterranean, and from 1892 to 1895 in the battleship *Empress of India*, flagship of the second-in-command of the Channel Squadron. Between 1895 and 1896 he was in the cruiser *Astraea* in the Mediterranean and then served as the senior lieutenant in the royal yacht *Victoria and Albert* until his promotion to commander on 31 August 1898. Wemyss then became commander of the cruiser *Niobe*, first in the Channel and subsequently at the Cape of Good Hope during the Anglo-Boer South African War, in which he was employed in the transport of Boer prisoners of war to St Helena. He returned home at the end of 1900 and was invited by his old ship-mate, Prince George, who had become Duke of York, to be second-in-command of the passenger ship *Ophir* in his cruise to open the new Australian Parliament. At the end of this cruise, he was promoted to captain on 6 November 1901.

Wemyss was selected to be the first Captain of the newly-created Royal Naval College for junior cadets at Osborne, Isle of Wight, and held this appointment for two years from August 1903. In 1903 he married Victoria Morier, the only daughter of a leading diplomat, and later had with her a daughter, their only child. He commanded successively the cruiser *Suffolk* in the Mediterranean Fleet and the battleship *Implacable*, flagship of the Atlantic Fleet, in which he was flag-captain from March 1909 to May 1910. The Prince of Wales (the former Duke of York) then invited Wemyss to go with him as captain of the liner *Balmoral Castle* on his cruise to open the new South African Parliament. The death of Edward VII brought the Prince to the throne as George V and Wemyss sailed instead with the new King's younger brother, the Duke of Connaught. He was promoted to rear-admiral on 19 April 1911 and commanded the Second Battle Squadron in the Home Fleet from October 1912 to September 1913, with his flag in the battleship *Orion*.

On the outbreak of the First World War in August 1914 Wemyss was given command of the Twelfth Cruiser Squadron in the Channel, with his flag in the cruiser *Charybdis*. After escorting troopships from Canada to the United Kingdom he returned to the Channel, with his flag in the cruiser *Euryalus*. In February 1915 he was sent to the Mediterranean with the task of establishing a base at Mudros for an attack on the Dardanelles. This base was on the Turkish island of Lemnos (Limnos), occupied since 1913 by the Greeks, who were persuaded to leave so that the Allies could use it without infringing Greek neutrality. Wemyss, with his flag in the gunboat *Hussar*, was installed as the Allied governor, and the departure on medical grounds of the Allied Naval C-in-C for this campaign, Vice-Admiral Carden, left him the senior naval officer on the station. Wemyss volunteered to remain as governor at Mudros and the seagoing command was given to Carden's second-in-command, Rear-Admiral John De Robeck [77]. With his flag again in *Euryalus*, Wemyss commanded a squadron at the British landings on Cape Helles on 25 April 1915, and was mentioned in despatches for his support to the landings at Suvla Bay, Gallipoli (Gelibolu), on 9 August 1915. He became acting vice-admiral during De Robeck's absence on leave in November 1915, and urged that one more attempt should be made to force a passage through the Dardanelles by the fleet alone, but the proposal was not accepted. The Cabinet decided to abandon the whole expedition and Wemyss became responsible for the successful re-embarkation of the troops from Suvla Bay and Anzac Cove (Ari Burnu) on the night of 20 December 1915. He was awarded the KCB in January 1916.

Sir Rosslyn Wemyss was then appointed C-in-C, East Indies and Egypt station, with his flag still in *Euryalus*. He supported the Army in operations against Senussi tribesmen raiding Egypt from Libya (ceded to Italy by Turkey in 1912) and against the Turks in the Sinai peninsula. He also supported the campaign in Mesopotamia (Iraq) and went up the Tigris in a river gunboat as part of an unsuccessful attempt to relieve the British garrison of Kut-el-Amara, before its surrender at the end of April 1916. Wemyss spent the summer on a tour of the East Indies station and returned to Egypt in August 1916, where he co-operated with the British advances in Palestine and the Arab revolt led by the Emir Faisal and Colonel T E Lawrence. His promotion to vice-admiral was confirmed on 6 December 1916. He was appointed C-in-C, Mediterranean in June 1917, shortly before the Prime Minister of the day, David Lloyd George, installed an eminent railwayman, Sir Eric Geddes, as First Lord of the Admiralty.

Wemyss's spirited contribution to the Middle East campaign, the only land or sea theatre where British forces seemed to be achieving a victory, drew him to the notice of the Prime Minister. Geddes considered that the First Sea Lord, Sir John Jellicoe [68], lacked flexibility and imagination. Unable immediately to remove him from office, he decided to create a new post, Deputy First Sea Lord, to which Wemyss was appointed in the hope that this would bring a new spirit to the Naval Staff. Jellicoe declined to hand any of his own responsibilities to Wemyss and eventually Geddes dismissed Jellicoe on Christmas Eve 1917 and appointed Wemyss in his place.

Wemyss disliked the circumstances of his appointment, but accepted Geddes's constitutional position and established cordial relations with him. He made a number of changes at the Admiralty with the intention of delegating and decentralizing command to trusted subordinates. He also appointed Commodore Roger Keyes [80] to command the Dover Patrol (Jellicoe's support for the previous flag officer there had caused the final break with Geddes) and ordered him to implement the plans for more vigorous operations in the Channel that had been drawn up at the Admiralty by Keyes himself. At the end of the war, when the Germans asked for an Armistice early in November 1918, Wemyss ensured that British naval interests were fully represented. As neither the United States nor France was enthusiastic at the prospect of the German battle fleet falling into British hands, the wily Lloyd George arranged for its ships to be interned rather than formally surrendered, but nevertheless to be anchored under the guns of the Royal Navy. Wemyss, representing the Allied Navies, was one of the signatories at the Armistice agreement. When the German naval representative asked if it was right for the ships of the High Seas Fleet to be interned when they had not been defeated, Wemyss dryly remarked "they had only to come out".

A capable diplomat, he played a full part in framing the naval articles of the Versailles Treaty and was promoted to admiral on 21 February 1919. In the same period he became increasingly at odds with Sir David Beatty [69], C-in-C, Grand Fleet, to whom Geddes had promised the post of First Sea Lord prior to his own departure to the Ministry of Transport in November 1919. A campaign against Wemyss's retention of office began in the Press and in London society, and the two admirals' ladies, neither of whom had ever liked the other, ceased to be on speaking terms. Wemyss himself indicated his readiness to combine the governorship of Malta with naval command in the Mediterranean, but Winston Churchill, at this time Secretary of State for War, insisted that the governorship continue to be filled by a general. He therefore remained at the Admiralty, where he had to deal with the problems of demobilization and financial reductions at a time of continued operational commitments in the Mediterranean and Black Sea, coupled with the determination of the United States to establish parity with the British Navy. In April 1919 he used the threat of resignation to overcome the Treasury's delay in funding a recommended increase in naval pay.

Wemyss again offered to resign in July 1919, when his name did not appear in the Victory Honours list, though the other two Service Chiefs were given baronetcies and monetary awards. He was persuaded to remain in office until 1 November 1919, when he was promoted to admiral of the fleet, and accepted a barony as Lord Wester Wemyss, in lieu of the viscountcy he thought his due. He lost favour with Lloyd George and had never had any with Bonar Law, who became Prime Minister in October 1922, so thereafter remained on half-pay. He took up directorships with the Cable and Wireless Company and in the oil industry, and joined the retired list in 1929. After leaving office he lived mostly at Cannes, France, where he died in his garden on 24 May 1933. He was buried at his family home, Wemyss Castle, and, with no male heir, his peerage became extinct.

WEST
Sir JOHN, GCB (1774–1862) [22]

John West, the son of a lieutenant colonel in the First Foot Guards, nephew of the future Admiral Temple West and grandson of Vice-Admiral Temple West, was born on 28 July 1774. More remotely, he could claim family connections with the Pitts (Earls of Chatham), and Admiral Sir Alexander Hood (later Viscount Bridport). He joined the Navy in 1788 as a first class volunteer and served on the coast of West Africa in the 6th-rate *Pomona*, commanded by one of Hood's followers. During the next two years he served first in the 4th-rate *Salisbury*, flagship on the North America station, and then, as a midshipman, in the 2nd-rate *London*, Hood's flagship in the Channel. From July 1790 to the outbreak of the French Revolutionary War in February 1793 he was in Captain Alexander Hood's 5th-rate *Hebe* in the Channel. After serving in the 4th-rate *Romney* in the Mediterranean and the 1st-rate *Royal George* in the Channel he was promoted to lieutenant on 27 July 1793 and appointed to the 3rd-rate *Saturn*, at Portsmouth, in November 1793. In February 1794 he rejoined Viscount Bridport in *Royal George*, his flagship in the Channel, and later was present at Bridport's action off the Ile de Groix, Lorient, when three French ships of the line were captured (23 June 1795). West was made a commander on 7 September 1795 and assumed command of the sloop *Diligence*, in the West Indies, on 11 December 1795. He was promoted to captain of the 6th-rate *Tourterelle* on 15 November 1796 and returned home in 1798.

During the brief peace with France following the Treaty of Amiens (27 March 1801) West commanded the 3rd-rate *Utrecht* at Chatham. The war was renewed in May 1803, but he was not again employed until January 1807, when he became captain of the 3rd-rate *Excellent*. In November 1808, with the Spanish national uprising against French occupation, he operated off the coast of Catalonia and landed with 250 marines and seamen to support the defenders of Rosas, where he had his horse shot under him leading a sortie for which he was mentioned in despatches. He then joined the blockade of Toulon and subsequently served in the Adriatic until he was appointed to the 3rd-rate *Sultan* in December 1809. West commanded this ship in the Mediterranean, the Channel and the West Indies until March 1814, when Napoleon's defeat and abdication brought the war at sea to an end.

In 1817 West married Harriet Adams, the daughter of a Northamptonshire landowner, and later had with her a family of three sons and two daughters. He became a rear-admiral of the Blue on 12 August 1819, rear-admiral of the White on 19 July 1825, rear-admiral of the Red on 27 May 1825, vice-admiral of the Blue on 22 July 1830, vice-admiral of the White on 10 January 1837 and vice-admiral of the Red on 28 June 1839. He was awarded the KCB in July 1840 and was promoted to be admiral of the Blue on 23 November 1841. Sir John West was C-in-C, Portsmouth, from April 1845 to April 1848. He became an admiral of the White on 20 November 1846, admiral of the Red on 15 September 1849, admiral of the fleet on 25 June 1858 and died at his home in Eaton Square, London, on 14 April 1862.

WHITSHED
Sir JAMES HAWKINS, 1st Baronet, GCB (1762–1849) [17]

James Hawkins, born in 1762, was the third son of the bishop of Raphoe, County Donegal, and came from a prominent family in the Anglo-Irish Protestant Ascendancy. He joined the Navy in 1773 and was carried successively on the books of the sloop *Ranger*, on the Irish station, and then on those of the 3rd-rate *Kent* at Plymouth, where he escaped injury when an accidental explosion killed or wounded forty-two members of her crew. After the beginning of the American War of Independence in 1775 he served off the North American coast, first as midshipman and later as acting lieutenant, successively in the schooner *Canada* (wrecked in a violent gale), the 4th-rate *Romney*, the 6th-rate *Aldborough* and the 5th-rates *Diamond* and *Rainbow*. He became a lieutenant on 4 September 1778 in the 5th-rate *Amazon* in the Channel, before transferring to the 2nd-rate *Sandwich*, flagship of Sir George Rodney, and taking part in operations leading to the relief of Gibraltar early in 1780. At Gibraltar he was appointed commander of the captured sloop *San Vincente*, in which he sailed with Rodney's fleet to the West Indies and was present at an indecisive fleet action off Dominica (17 April 1780). He was promoted to be captain of the 6th-rate *Deal Castle* on 18 April 1780.

Left behind with several other major combatants when Rodney moved his main force to North America, *Deal Castle* was at St Lucia when a hurricane struck the West Indies in October 1780. The British naval base at Barbados was destroyed, along with six rated ships. Hawkins's consort, the sloop *Camelion*, was lost without trace. His own ship was dismasted and, after several days at sea, was wrecked on the Spanish-held island of Puerto

254

Rico. Hawkins and his crew reached the shore on rafts, with the loss of only three men, and spent two months as prisoners of war, before being exchanged and sent to the nearby British Virgin Islands. He was acquitted by court-martial for any blame in the loss of his ship and, after recovering from fever, was sent home with despatches as a mark of distinction. In July 1781 he was given command of the 5th-rate *Ceres* and sailed for New York, where he remained until 1783, when the war came to an end. Between 1784 and 1786 he commanded the 6th-rate *Rose*, based at Leith.

Hawkins spent the next few years on half-pay. He attended lectures on astronomy at Oxford University, and visited the Baltic, Denmark and Russia. In 1791, as a condition of an inheritance from his cousin, he took the surname Whitshed, belonging to his maternal grandmother, and married Sophia Bentinck, a distant relative of the Earls of Portland. She was the daughter of a naval captain (the inventor of the chain-pump) who had died in 1775, the sister of a future vice-admiral and the sister-in-law of Sir George Martin [18]. They later had a family of four daughters and two sons, of whom the elder was killed in action as a midshipman in December 1813. After the outbreak of the French Revolutionary War in February 1793, Whitshed was appointed to the 3rd-rate *Arrogant*, in which he served in the Channel until early 1795, when he transferred to the 2nd-rate *Namur*. He was in a squadron sent to reinforce Sir John Jervis [12] at Lisbon in 1796, and served under him at the battle of St Vincent (14 February 1797), for which, along with the other captains, he was awarded a gold medal. He remained in the Channel in command successively of the 3rd-rate *Ajax* and the 2nd-rate *Formidable*, before becoming rear-admiral of the White on 14 February 1799. In April 1800, with his flag in the 1st-rate *Queen Charlotte*, he led a squadron of four ships of the line and two frigates to join Jervis (Earl of St Vincent), under whom he served first in the Mediterranean and then in the blockade of Brest.

Whitshed became rear-admiral of the Red on 1 January 1801 and continued in the Channel in the 2nd-rate *Téméraire*. With the fleet reduced following the conclusion of peace with France by the Treaty of Amiens (27 March 1802), he declined the appointment of C-in-C at Halifax, Nova Scotia, and went on half-pay. When war with France was renewed in 1803 he was appointed naval adviser to the government of Ireland, responsible for coastal defences, the Sea Fencibles, and the construction of signal stations and Martello towers at vulnerable points around Dublin. He was promoted to vice-admiral of the Blue on 23 April 1804 and vice-admiral of the White on 9 November 1805. Between 1807 and 1810 Whitshed was C-in-C, Cork. He became vice-admiral of the Red on 28 April 1808, admiral of the Blue on 31 July 1810 and admiral of the White on 12 August 1812 and, after the defeat of Napoleon, was awarded the KCB in April 1815. Sir James Whitshed was C-in-C, Portsmouth from 31 January 1821 to 12 April 1824 and was promoted to admiral of the Red on 19 July 1821. He became a baronet in May 1834, a baron of the kingdom of Hanover in 1843 and an admiral of the fleet on 8 January 1844. He died at his home in Cavendish Square, London, on 28 October 1849 and his baronetcy was inherited by his younger son.

WILLIAM IV
WILLIAM HENRY, HM King of Great Britain and Ireland (1765–1837) [11]

Prince William Henry, born at Buckingham Palace, London, on 21 August 1765, was the third son of George III and Queen Charlotte. The King decided that, with his eldest son destined for the throne and his second for the Army, his third should make a career in the Navy. After receiving a general education from his tutors, Prince William joined the Navy on 14 June 1779, carried on the books of the 2nd-rate *Prince George* at Portsmouth as an able seaman. During the American War of Independence he served in the Channel in August 1779 and as a midshipman at the relief of Gibraltar in January 1780. There he was arrested in a tavern brawl with a group of common soldiers who had spoken slightingly of the Navy's performance in the relief operations and was only released after the intervention of his admiral. Prince William returned with the fleet to England, where a London theatre crowd hailed him as a hero, but was soon again arrested for disorderly conduct in a public pleasure garden. The King ordered him back to his ship, so that he spent the summer of 1780 at sea in the Channel.

In January 1781 Prince William met and fell in love with an attractive teenage debutante, Julia Fortescue. He spoke of marrying her, at which her parents removed her to Scotland, while the King sent William to the North America station, where he arrived at New York at the end of August 1781. There, in March 1782, he became the target of a kidnap plan, authorized by George Washington, but the scheme was discovered by British Intelligence officers. The prince was immediately ordered to sea in the 4th-rate *Warwick*, in which he served in an action off the Delaware. On 4 November 1782 he moved to the 2nd-rate *Barfleur*, flagship in the West Indies. Hostilities with Spain ended in January 1783 and William, escorted by his new friend Captain Horatio Nelson, made an official visit to the Spanish colony of Cuba. There he was greatly attracted by Maria Solano, daughter of a Spanish admiral, and succeeded in luring her away from her duennas. This caused much offence to the Spaniards and Nelson was obliged to hurry him back to naval duty.

After William's return home in June 1783 the King decided that he should go to Hanover. He spent the next two years on the Continent, where his itinerary included a visit to Frederick the Great (who reproved him for not having read *Candide*) and the Grand Tour through Italy. He was nearly involved in a duel with Baron Hardenberg, a card-sharp who allowed him to win the first few hands, only to find that William left the table with his winnings rather than playing on to be fleeced. He found the German aristocracy haughty and over-punctilious, and they in turn were offended by his coarse language, a failing that he had picked up at sea and one that remained with him throughout his life. Nevertheless, he embarked on numerous flirtations and *affaires*, and had at least one natural son, for whom he later provided. His wild conduct distressed his mother and angered his father. Eventually their second son, the Duke of York, persuaded the King that a return to duty with the fleet would give William a sense of self-discipline and his repeated requests to leave Hanover were granted in 1785. He was kept away from London society while he studied for his promotion examination and on 17 June 1785 was appointed third lieutenant of the 5th-rate *Hebe*. After a circumnavigation of Great Britain he returned to Portsmouth, where he became attached to Sarah Martin, the daughter of the resident Commissioner to the Navy, and spoke of marrying her. The horrified commissioner sent his daughter to stay in London and the equally horrified King sent his son to Plymouth.

William was appointed captain of the 6th-rate *Pegasus* on 10 April 1786 and sailed for the North American station three months later. From Nova Scotia he was sent to the Leeward Islands, where he found himself under command of his old friend Nelson. Despite Nelson's guidance, William proved a severe disciplinarian. He introduced numerous petty regulations, including a prohibition on using the term "bugger" (at that time a common term of abuse in the fleet) and ordered floggings for the least transgression. He soon became as unpopular with his officers as with his men. The ship's schoolmaster tried to murder him, but was prevented by an alert Marine sentry. The first lieutenant, an experienced officer, tried to reduce the extent of the punishments ordered by his captain, only to be publicly over-ruled. William complained that this officer, Lieutenant Isaac Schomberg, constantly challenged his authority. Schomberg, an officer of whom Nelson had a high opinion, asked for a court-martial and was promptly placed under arrest. After being persuaded to apologize, he was transferred to *Barfleur* and, to the prince's chagrin, became flag lieutenant to the distinguished admiral, Lord Hood. In another incident, William's third officer, Lieutenant William Hope, who was generally thought to have been subjected to harsh treatment, also later left the ship. Off-duty, William enjoyed attending official and private balls, banquets and similar events in polite colonial Society. In March 1787 he gave away the widowed Mrs Frances Nesbit at her marriage to Nelson. In less polite circles he frequented houses of ill-repute and was sued by the proprietress of one in Bridgetown, Barbados, for extensive damage caused by him and his companions. He also underwent treatment for a social disease at this time. *Pegasus* was then sent to Canada, where he had an *affaire* with Mrs Wentworth, the wife of a senior colonial official. This caused his ship's sudden recall to England at the end of 1787.

William then applied to go to the East Indies station, but was refused. He had the sympathy of his elder brothers, but this only made his position worse in the eyes of the King, who regarded them as a bad influence. On

1 March 1788 he became captain of the 5th-rate *Andromeda*, taking the crew of *Pegasus* with him. During July 1788 he put to sea with the rest of his squadron for exercises in the Channel. At the same time the King learnt of an *affaire* between William and Sally Winne, daughter of a naval victualling contractor. *Andromeda* was ordered to sail immediately to Halifax, Nova Scotia, despite William's protest that his officers and men, who had expected to return home after a short deployment, would be unable to make provision for their families. At Halifax he found that Mrs Wentworth had transferred her affections to another officer. He resumed his round of balls and parties, maintaining his reputation as a hard drinker, and celebrating the King's birthday with a cannonade that drowned the signal guns of a vessel sinking in full view of his own. He then sailed for Jamaica, where he was already a local favourite from his earlier service there. Dining with the planters, he spoke in defence of slavery (already under attack from abolitionists in British society) and was acclaimed by them as an ideal future Governor.

William was recalled home early in 1789, after George III had become seriously ill with what is now believed to be porphyria. The King had recovered his mind by the time that *Andromeda* arrived in April 1789, but was then faced with a demand by William for the peerage customarily given to princes on their coming of age, and therefore, in his case, overdue. With some reluctance, the King created him Duke of Clarence (the first since Edward IV's brother drowned in a butt of Malmsey in the Tower of London in 1478) on 20 May 1789. In 1789 Clarence set up house in Richmond, Surrey, with a noted courtesan, Polly Finch, but she became bored with the rural surroundings, by the lack of company and by his custom of reading Campbell's *The Lives of the Admirals* to her. On discovering that there was a second volume, she fled back to London. Between May and November 1790 he commanded the 3rd-rate *Valiant* in the fleet assembled at the time of a threatened war with Spain over the possession of Nootka Sound (Vancouver, British Columbia).

Clarence was promoted rear-admiral of the Blue on 3 December 1790. In 1793, after the outbreak of the French Revolutionary War, he was appointed to command the 2nd-rate *London*, then fitting out. The refit was cancelled when Clarence made a speech in the House of Lords calling for peace and criticizing the war policy of the Prime Minister, William Pitt the Younger. He was never again given a seagoing command, though he rose steadily in rank to became rear-admiral of the Red on 1 February 1793, vice-admiral of the Blue on 12 April 1794, vice-admiral of the White on 4 July 1794, vice-admiral of the Red on 1 June 1795, admiral of the Blue on 14 February 1799, admiral of the White on 1 January 1801 and admiral of the Red on 9 November 1805. On the death of Sir Peter Parker **[10]** he became admiral of the fleet on 24 December 1811, at the age of 46. During this period, from 1791 onwards, he kept house with an actress, Mrs Dorothy Jordan. They had a family of ten children, who took the surname FitzClarence. In 1811 he suddenly ended their relationship, though making financial provision for her and their children. She made an unsuccessful return to the stage and died in misery at St Cloud, France, five years later. Clarence flew his flag as admiral of the fleet in the 2nd-rate *Impregnable* in 1814, when, after the fall of Napoleon, he conveyed Louis XVIII to France and the Emperor Alexander I of Russia and King Frederick William III of Prussia to England. The Prince Regent, who had designed the baton awarded to field marshals, presented a naval version to Clarence, who continued to figure in Society as "the Royal Tar" or "Old Tarrybreeks".

In 1817 Princess Charlotte of Wales, the Prince Regent's only legitimate offspring, died in childbirth. As the Duke of York had long been estranged from his childless wife, the succession to the throne lay with Clarence and his younger brothers. Clarence himself (like all his brothers, hopelessly in debt) sought the hand of an English heiress, Sophia Wykeham of Thame Park, Oxfordshire. After the Prince Regent forbade this match, Clarence married the twenty-six-year-old Princess Adelaide of Saxe-Meiningen on 13 July 1818. Between 1819 and 1822 she suffered two miscarriages and bore two daughters, of whom one died at birth and the other lived for only three months. On 17 April 1827, after the death of the Duke of York made Clarence heir presumptive, the ancient office of Lord High Admiral was revived for his benefit. Nevertheless, it was intended that he should carry out his duties only on the advice of a Council, led by the forceful Admiral Sir George Cockburn [20]. A junior member was Vice-Admiral Sir William Hope, who had been Clarence's third lieutenant in *Pegasus* but seemed not to bear his old captain a grudge.

Clarence insisted on taking the duties seriously, touring dockyards and introducing reforms into the promotion system. First Lieutenants of ships of the line became commanders, both in title and in rank. Four admirals and six captains were made naval aides-de-camp to the Lord High Admiral (later to the King), a new appointment devised by Clarence with appropriate embellishments of uniform, a subject that always fascinated him. In a practical measure, he introduced a uniform peaked cap to replace the variety of head-gear previously worn by officers on informal occasions instead of the full dress cocked hat. After the battle of Navarino (20 October 1827), where his old friend Admiral Sir Edward Codrington embarrassed the British Cabinet by destroying a combined Turkish and Egyptian fleet, Clarence sent him personal congratulations and distributed honours on an unprecedented scale. Despite his reputation as a stern captain, he now drastically reduced the number of offences for which men could be flogged. Cockburn repeatedly reminded Clarence that he had no powers to act without the agreement of his Council, but Clarence disregarded him. Finding a small squadron waiting at Portsmouth for the arrival of its appointed admiral, he put to sea with it so that for ten days the Admiralty had no idea where he and the ships had gone.

In 1828 Clarence, who stressed the importance of good gunnery, set up a committee to improve this aspect of the fleet's training. This involved financial costs about which his Council had not been consulted. The Duke of Wellington, as Prime Minister, was already alarmed at the cost of Clarence's dockyard visitations. Always a strict constitutionalist, he informed King George IV that, if his brother did not resign, his ministers would. Clarence accordingly left office on 17 September 1828, though his concern for gunnery was shared by others and played a part in the establishment in 1830 of a gunnery training school at Portsmouth in the hulk *Excellent*.

Clarence succeeded to the throne on his brother's death on 26 June 1830. Never one for court etiquette, he entirely agreed with the government's economies in the costs of his coronation, which he regarded as a waste of money. Many traditional ceremonies were abolished and Queen Adelaide provided the jewels for her own crown. On his accession he gave up his position as admiral of the fleet, and bestowed this rank on the three senior admirals of the Red, Williams Freeman [13], Lord Gambier [14] and Sir Charles Pole [15]. Still interested in uniforms, he changed the Royal Navy's facings from white to scarlet, as more appropriate to a Royal Service (a decision reversed under his successor). William IV was soon faced by a constitutional crisis over the question of parliamentary reform. Despite a majority in the Commons in favour of the Reform Bill, supported by public opinion in the country as a whole, the measure was repeatedly rejected by the Lords. Reluctantly, he was persuaded by Wellington, who feared a breakdown of public order, to declare that, if necessary, he would create enough new pro-Reform peers to ensure the Bill's passage. Rather than see the emergence of a permanent Liberal majority in the Lords, the Opposition finally gave way and allowed the measure to be carried. During the rest of William IV's reign he acted as a constitutional monarch, accepting the advice of his ministers and enjoying a modest degree of popularity among his subjects. He died on 20 June 1837 from pneumonia brought on by heart disease and other factors, and was buried at Windsor. He was succeeded by Victoria, only child of his deceased younger brother, the Duke of Kent.

WILLIAM (WILHELM) II
HM German Emperor and King of Prussia FREDERICK WILLIAM VICTOR ALBERT, KG, GCVO (1859–1941) [47]

Prince William of Prussia, the future German Emperor William II (Kaiser Wilhelm II), was born in Berlin on 27 January 1859. He was the first child of Frederick, Crown Prince of Prussia, and Princess Victoria, eldest daughter of Queen Victoria. His birth, to a teenage mother, was a difficult one and caused him to be born with a left arm that never developed to its full size, and possibly with brain damage contributing to his violent mood swings in later life. Hopes that Frederick, who succeeded as German Emperor in 1888, would, under the influence of his forceful wife, turn the new Germany into a liberal and pro-British nation ended with his death at the age of 55 from cancer of the throat, after a reign of ninety-nine days.

William succeeded his father on 15 June 1888 and began his reign by impressing all whom he met with his personal charm, energy and breadth of new ideas for a new empire. With nobody willing to contradict him, he came to believe himself an expert on every subject. At the opening of the Kiel Canal, he insisted on piloting his yacht, *Hohenzollern*, as the first vessel through. It was widely believed that the ship's officers disconnected the controls on the bridge and navigated her from a different position. Hastening to Queen Victoria's deathbed (he was always proud that she died with his arm supporting her), he first drove the train and then took the helm as his ship crossed the Channel. In foreign policy his capricious character led him to alternate between chauvinism and conciliation, and served only to create tension between Germany and the other Great Powers. William's attitude towards the British was one of extremes. On the one hand he admired British power and gloried in his descent from Queen Victoria. On the other hand he resented the British reluctance to accept that the new Germany was a World, rather than merely a European, Power. His open sympathy for the Boer republics in their struggle with the British in South Africa, though it reflected the views of many of his subjects, placed a considerable strain on Anglo-German relations.

William's enthusiasm for the Imperial German Navy, a new service created for the new empire and officered largely by the sons of its rising industrial and commercial middle class, alienated the British still further. As a small boy his first uniform had been a sailor suit and, with his younger brother, Prince Henry [62], he had played in a small-scale replica of a Royal Navy frigate. On 2 August 1889, at the Royal Regatta at Cowes, Isle of Wight, (the first in his series of regular attendances at this event) Queen Victoria appointed him an honorary admiral of the fleet. This honour, one that had never previously been bestowed on any foreign sovereign, delighted William and he immediately began work on a plan to improve the British Navy. Influenced by the United States Admiral Alfred Mahan's book *The Importance of Sea Power*, William became convinced that, as a Great Power, Germany must herself have a Navy to match her imperial status. He saw the need for cruisers to protect her large merchant fleet and her new colonial possessions in Africa and the Pacific, and battleships to show the British that Germany's friendship was worth having. This only triggered a costly naval race between the two nations, as the British insisted on retaining their existing margin of superiority. Intending to usher in an era of international peace, to be kept by British supremacy at sea and German supremacy on land, he only drove the British into the arms of France and Russia, the ancient foes of the British and Germans alike.

When the British ambassador to Berlin pointed out that, if the German fleet maintained its rate of expansion, by 1912 it would have more modern battleships than the British, he replied that, as an admiral of the English fleet, he knew that this was nonsense. He remained well disposed towards the Royal Navy and when he encountered a British fleet while cruising in *Hohenzollern*, had to be talked out of inviting its admiral to dine with him.

Although William was superficially on good terms with his uncle, Edward VII [44], the two monarchs came to dislike each other. William disapproved of his uncle's womanizing and playboy life-style (though in his own private life he himself had a taste for unconventional sexual practices), while Edward took his sister Victoria's part in her quarrel with her son. Moreover, Edward's queen, Alexandra, was a Danish princess who never forgave Prussia for defeating Denmark in the war of 1864. The prospect of warmer relations between William and George V [64], who succeeded Edward VII in 1910, was blighted by the continued naval race. Winston Churchill, as First Lord of the Admiralty, expressed the British point of view in 1912. For Britain, he said, a powerful fleet was a necessity. For Germany, it was a luxury.

The approach of the First World War in 1914 found William cruising in the Baltic. Shocked and surprised by the rapid escalation of the crisis, he first tried to persuade his cousin, the Emperor Nicholas II of Russia [60], not to mobilize, but failed both in this and in his subsequent attempt to persuade his own generals to march against Russia rather than France. When the British declared war on Germany William repudiated his position as a British admiral of the fleet and field marshal. Although he was constitutionally Supreme War Lord, his generals excluded him from any part in framing military strategy. He exercised greater influence over his admirals and was instrumental in May 1916 in calling off the submarine campaign against unarmed merchant shipping. In January 1917 he approved the renewal of the campaign, having been persuaded that, even if it provoked the United States into entering the war, his U-boats would sink the American troopships before they reached France.

Throughout the war William insisted that the High Seas Fleet must be kept as a fleet in being, to inhibit the Royal Navy's use of its own supremacy, and to remain as a bargaining counter in any post-war negotiations. At the beginning of November 1918 news that his government was seeking an armistice had a shattering effect throughout Germany. Sailors of the very fleet on which he had lavished so much enthusiasm began the slide into revolution. On 9 November 1918, following the declaration of a German republic, William abdicated and fled to the neutral Netherlands. He was given refuge by the Dutch government and lived in exile as a private gentleman. His empress, Augusta Victoria of Schleswig-Holstein-Sonderburg-Augustenburg, with whom he had six sons and a daughter, died in 1921. In 1922 he married Princess Hermine of Reuss, a capable thirty-four-year-old widow with five children. William died at Doorn on 4 June 1941 and was buried in the grounds of his estate there, in an impressive tomb of his own design.

WILLIAMS
WILLIAM PEERE, see **FREEMAN**, WILLIAM PEERE WILLIAMS [13]

WILLIS
Sir ALGERNON USBORNE, GCB, KBE, DSO (1889–1976)
[96]

Algernon Willis, the younger son in a family of three children of a London businessman, was born in Hampstead on 17 May 1889. After attending Eastbourne College he entered the Navy in 1903 as a cadet in the training ship *Britannia* and became a midshipman on 15 September 1905, appointed to the battleship *Hindostan* in the Channel. In September 1907 he joined the battleship *Glory* in the Mediterranean Fleet, from where he returned home with promotion to acting sub-lieutenant on 18 November 1908 at the beginning of his promotion courses. Willis was promoted to lieutenant on 15 November 1909 and was appointed to the armoured cruiser *Donegal* in the Home Fleet in May 1910. During 1911 he served in the armoured cruiser *Good Hope*, flagship of the Fifth Cruiser Squadron in the Atlantic Fleet, and in August 1912 joined the torpedo school *Vernon* at Portsmouth, where he qualified as a torpedo specialist and remained until 1914.

On 28 July 1914, a week before the outbreak of the First World War, Willis was appointed torpedo lieutenant in the battleship *Magnificent*, which on mobilization became part of the Grand Fleet. He returned to *Vernon* in the spring of 1915 and subsequently served in the cruiser *Donegal* in the Atlantic and in the torpedo school *Defiance* at Plymouth before joining the destroyer flotilla leader *Fearless*, in which he was present at the battle of Jutland (31 May–1 June 1916). In 1916 he married the daughter of a Hampstead businessman and later had with her a family of two daughters. Her twin sister married Major Clement Attlee, a future Labour Prime Minister. Willis returned to *Vernon* after Jutland, with the award of the DSO and promotion to lieutenant-commander on 15 November 1915. He remained on the staff there until September 1918, when he was appointed to the destroyer flotilla leader *Saumarez*, where he remained after the end of the war in November 1918. Willis joined the flotilla leader *Wallace* in November 1919 and was with the British naval force sent to the Baltic at a time of disorder following the collapse of the Russian and German empires.

During 1920 Willis was in the battle-cruiser *Renown* in the visit to Australia and New Zealand of the Prince of Wales. He subsequently rejoined the staff of *Vernon* and was promoted to commander on 30 June 1922, before attending the Royal Naval Staff College, Greenwich. He was then appointed torpedo officer in the light cruiser *Coventry*, flagship of the destroyer flotillas in the Atlantic Fleet, where he served from December 1923 to November 1925. Between October 1927 and the summer of August 1929 he commanded his old ship *Wallace* in the Atlantic Fleet. Willis was promoted to captain on 30 June 1929 and served from February 1930 to August 1932 on the staff of the Royal Naval War College, Greenwich. In January 1933 he was appointed flag captain in the cruiser *Kent*, flagship of the Fifth Cruiser Squadron and the C-in-C on the China station, from which he returned home to become flag captain of the battle-ship *Nelson*, flagship of the C-in-C, Home Fleet, in May 1934. Between September 1935 and April 1938 he was captain of *Vernon* and then returned to the Mediterranean as captain of the battleship *Barham*. In July 1938 he became flag captain to the second-in-command of the Mediterranean Fleet. On 2 February 1939 he was appointed commodore and chief of staff to the C-in-C, Mediterranean, where he served first under Sir Dudley Pound [89] and later (after June 1939) Sir Andrew Cunningham [91], in the battleship *Warspite*.

On the outbreak of the Second World War in September 1939 Willis remained in the Mediterranean on Cunningham's staff. He was promoted to rear-admiral on 5 January 1940 and, after Italy entered the war in June 1940, was involved in planning operations against the Italian fleet. During 1941 he was given acting promotion to vice-admiral as C-in-C, South Atlantic, and early in 1942, with his flag in the battleship *Resolution*, became second-in-command of the Eastern Fleet, a force hastily assembled to counter the advancing Japanese. He became a substantive vice-admiral on 3 April 1943, with command of Force H, a powerful formation based at Gibraltar, from where he took part in the Allied landings in North Africa, Sicily and Italy. He was awarded the KBE in 1943. In 1944 Sir Algernon Willis joined the Admiralty as Second Sea Lord where he remained until early in 1946. As chief of naval personnel, he was responsible for finding manpower for the final campaigns against Japan and then, after the end of hostilities in August 1945, for dealing with the post-war demobilization and reductions in naval manpower. He was promoted to admiral on 16 October 1945.

Willis served as C-in-C, Mediterranean, from April 1946 to 1948, where his problems included the requirement to prevent unlawful Jewish immigration into Palestine while it remained a British mandate, tension in the Balkans and nationalist opposition to the British presence in Egypt. He was C-in-C, Portsmouth, from 1948 to 1950, with promotion to admiral of the fleet on 20 March 1949. After going onto half-pay he played a leading role in the Royal Naval Benevolent Trust and was chairman of the trustees of the Imperial War Museum, Lambeth. He died on 12 April 1976 in the Royal Naval Hospital, Haslar, Gosport.

WILSON
Sir ARTHUR KNYVET, 3rd Baronet, VC, GCB, OM, GCVO (1842–1921) [59]

Arthur Knyvet Wilson was born at Swaffham, Norfolk, on 4 March 1842, the third son of Rear-Admiral George Knyvet Wilson (nephew of a Norfolk peer, Lord Berners) and his wife (younger daughter of the Reverend William Yonge, Chancellor of Norwich, who held the living of Swaffham for sixty-five years). The Chancellor's sister was married to the Reverend

William Nelson, who became Earl Nelson after his brother Horatio's death at Trafalgar, and there were several other naval connections in the family. Arthur Wilson attended Eton College as a day-boy prior to joining the Navy in 1855. He served in the Crimean War as a midshipman in the 2nd-rate *Algiers* and was present at the bombardment and capture of Kinburn (Pokrovskiy), guarding the Dnepr estuary (Dneprovskiy Liman) in October 1855. In March 1856 he returned home and served for a week under his father in the 2nd-rate *Rodney* before transferring with the Honourable Henry Keppel [36], a family relation, when the latter was given command of the 3rd-rate *Colossus*. This ship was intended to lead an inshore flotilla in the Baltic campaign, but, with the end of hostilities, was sent to assist in the British evacuation of the Crimea. Wilson went ashore at Balaklava to look for an army officer's dog. He found the dog, but lost his ship, which sailed in his absence.

In September 1856 Keppel took Wilson into his new command, the frigate *Raleigh*, along with a number of other well-connected young officers. Hastening to join the Second China War, the ship struck an uncharted rock near Hong Kong and became a total loss, though all her crew was saved. Wilson was assigned to the flagship, the 2nd-rate *Calcutta*. The flag captain had served under Wilson's father twenty-seven years earlier and repaid the kindness shown to him then by keeping a close eye on his son and employing him as a signal midshipman. Wilson served ashore in command of a gun in a naval brigade in the capture of Canton (29 December 1857), and the Taku Forts at the mouth of the Peiho River (20 May 1858). He returned home in August 1859 and, after six weeks ashore, was appointed to the steam frigate *Topaze*, in which he served on the Pacific station, based at Esquimalt, British Columbia. He was promoted to acting sub-lieutenant on 4 March 1861 and to acting lieutenant during his ship's passage home at the end of 1863. He then passed his promotion examinations with high marks and became a lieutenant with seniority backdated to 11 December 1861.

Wilson was then appointed to the paddle frigate *Gladiator* in which he served until April 1865, when he joined the gunnery school *Excellent* at Portsmouth. There he became friends with a junior member of the instructional staff, Lieutenant John Fisher [58], with whom he would serve later in his career. In May 1867 he was selected as one of the officers lent to Japan as instructors at the new naval college at Yedo. He learnt Japanese and began his classes in January 1868, but political disturbances in Japan caused the mission to be withdrawn. Wilson was appointed as first lieutenant of the cadet training ship *Britannia* in January 1869. During 1870 he was the junior member of a committee to examine the new Whitehead torpedo and was involved in its trials in the Medway. At the end of these trials he was appointed gunnery lieutenant in the armoured ship *Caledonia* in which he served in the Mediterranean until returning home in September 1872. Wilson was appointed in October 1872 as first lieutenant of the frigate *Narcissus*, flagship of a flying squadron deployed under sail on a long cruise to the West Indies and Halifax, Nova Scotia. In a violent storm in the Bay of Biscay he was lowered over the bows to re-secure the bowsprit, which was in danger of being carried away and taking the foremast with it. From Halifax the squadron was sent to Gibraltar to protect British interests at a time of civil unrest in Spain leading to the abdication of King Amadeus in February 1873.

Wilson was promoted to commander on 18 September 1873 and shortly afterwards was appointed to the new steam frigate *Raleigh*. This ship cruised under sail to the Falkland Islands as part of a flying squadron, before escorting the Prince of Wales on his official visit to India in the cold weather of 1875–76. In March 1876 Wilson joined the torpedo school *Vernon* at Portsmouth, previously a tender of *Excellent* but about to become a separate establishment under Captain W Arthur (after whom Port Arthur, Northern China, was named). He was appointed commander and chief instructor, and pioneered a number of advances in underwater warfare, including mine-laying and mine counter-measures. He remained there until 20 April 1880, when he was promoted to captain and given command of the torpedo depot ship *Hecla* in the Mediterranean Fleet. In the summer of 1882 an Egyptian nationalist rising led by Colonel Arabi ('Urbi) Pasha was followed by anti-European riots at Alexandria. *Hecla* was ordered to take ammunition to the fleet there and arrived thirty minutes before the British bombardment (11 July 1882). Wilson afterwards spoke highly of the Egyptian coast artillerymen, who had few armour-piercing guns, but continued to fight until these were dismounted by naval gunfire. In the subsequent landings, together with Captain John Fisher, Wilson installed a heavy gun on a railway carriage and improvised an armoured train. During the early part of August 1882 he took part in a number of combats alongside the army and joined in a raid to destroy Egyptian naval explosives. After refitting at Malta, *Hecla* moved to Port Said at the end of October 1882, where Wilson spent a fortnight in control of the city under the nominal authority of the Egyptian governor.

In 1884 Wilson was sent with *Hecla* to Trinkitat on the Red Sea coast of the Sudan, to support the Anglo-Egyptian forces defending Suakin against Mahdist attack. He attached himself to the naval brigade in the second battle of El Teb (29 March 1884) where he was wounded in hand-to-hand combat and awarded the Victoria Cross. As a special concession, the Admiralty allowed the officers of *Vernon* to present him with a new sword to replace the one broken in the battle. A similar presentation by the wives of his brother officers on *Hecla*'s return to Malta was considered not to need Admiralty permission. With his ship back in the Channel, he continued to carry out torpedo exercises and occasionally went underwater as a diver. Wilson left *Hecla* at the end of July 1885, but returned to sea in March 1886 as flag captain to the C-in-C, Cape of Good Hope, in his old ship *Raleigh*. In April 1887 he accepted the appointment of Director of Torpedoes at the Admiralty, but discovered on arrival that Fisher, the new Director of Naval Ordnance, had added Torpedoes to his own title, so that Wilson's post became Assistant Director of Torpedoes. It was explained to him that this was a device to secure Treasury funding for two new posts rather than one. He remained there until 1889, when he was appointed captain of *Vernon*.

On leaving *Vernon* in 1892 Wilson was given command of the battleship *Sans Pareil* in the Mediterranean Fleet. He commanded a detached squadron on various official visits in the eastern Mediterranean and, with Lord Charles Beresford of the cruiser *Undaunted* in charge of the attacking force, conducted an important exercise to test the use of torpedo-boats against an anchored fleet. In June 1893 he witnessed the loss of the battleship *Victoria*, flagship of the C-in-C, Mediterranean Fleet, Sir George Tryon, who had a few weeks earlier, to Wilson's annoyance, poached his commander, John Jellicoe [68], from *Sans Pareil*. Jellicoe, weak and ill with dysentery, was given accommodation in Wilson's own cabin. Tryon himself was lost with his flagship, and his successor, Sir Michael Seymour, hoisted his flag in *Sans Pareil*, with Wilson as flag captain, until the arrival of the battleship *Ramillies* later in the year. Wilson drew the lesson that, as a torpedo would inflict at least as much damage as a ram, additional watertight compartments should be fitted, to prevent the rapid sinking that had caused such loss of life below decks. He continued to serve as senior captain in the Mediterranean Fleet until returning home in March 1895.

Wilson was promoted to rear-admiral on 20 June 1895. He was given command of an experimental torpedo squadron, with his flag in the cruiser *Hermione*, and carried out trials that led to the gradual replacement of torpedo-boats by destroyers. During the fleet manoeuvres of 1896, with his flag in *Sans Pareil*, he was second-in-command of the Reserve Fleet. In 1897 Wilson was appointed to the Admiralty in succession to Fisher as Controller of the Navy and third naval lord. There he soon incurred criticism for failing to consult his fellow lords of the Admiralty and for centralizing the work of his subordinates in his own hands. As Controller he was responsible for ship-building and design, so that he was held to blame for delays in the programme of naval rearmament, about which public opinion was becoming increasingly agitated, and also for the top-heaviness discovered when the new royal yacht neared completion. In March 1901 the Earl of Selborne, who became First Lord in October 1900, gave him command of the Channel Squadron and appointed Rear-Admiral Henry May [65] in his place.

Wilson was promoted to vice-admiral on 24 May 1901. With his flag in the battleship *Majestic* and his base at Bere Haven, County Cork, he soon established a reputation as a brilliant fleet commander. He practised various tactical evolutions in all sailing conditions, including the fogs and limited sea-room of the Channel itself, and on manoeuvres against the Mediterranean Fleet. He was awarded the KCB in 1902. In May 1903 Sir Arthur Wilson was appointed C-in-C, Home Fleet, with his flag successively in the battleships *Revenge* and *Exmouth*. This command was enlarged and renamed the Channel Fleet in December 1904, as part of the reorganization introduced by Fisher soon after becoming First Sea Lord.

Wilson was promoted to admiral on 24 February 1905 and to admiral of the fleet on 1 March 1907 at the end of his command. He was offered the appointment of President of the Naval War College, Greenwich, but, after being persuaded that he would be standing in the way of a younger officer, declined and went to live with his sister at Swaffham.

On 25 January 1910 Wilson was persuaded to return to the Admiralty as First Sea Lord in succession to Fisher. His appointment was seen as a short-term one, as he would reach retiring age in just over three years. It was hoped that, as one of the few admirals not to have been caught up in the rivalry between Fisher and Lord Charles Beresford, he would be able to reconcile the two factions into which they had split the Navy. Fisher himself saw Wilson as one who would maintain the momentum of his reforms and persuaded the First Lord of the day, Reginald McKenna, to hasten Wilson's appointment so that he would be in post before an imminent General Election. Fisher's main concern was the likelihood that, if the Unionists (Conservatives) came into office, they would appoint a Beresford supporter to succeed him. Wilson was reluctant to accept, but was finally persuaded by an appeal to his sense of duty, and undertook to follow existing policy. Once installed, however, he revived the Navy's traditional strategy by planning for a close blockade of the German coast, with the main fleet deployed in support of the blockading ships. His previous experience in the early days of underwater warfare led him to minimize the threat posed by German submarines and he had no doubt that the Navy would defeat the Germans in any surface battle.

Wilson proved no easier a colleague at the Admiralty than he had previously been. His toughness of character, no less than his insistence on realistic training when commanding his fleet, gained him the punning nickname " 'ard Art" (other nicknames were "Tug" or "Old Tugs"). There were complaints that he would neither consult nor compromise, and that he disregarded any opinion not in accord with his own. Indeed, he was even more difficult than before, as he treated the other Sea Lords as if they were subordinate flag officers in a fleet under his command. Once more he attempted to take all the decisions himself and once more the business of the Admiralty was held up while he did so. In the fleet manoeuvres off Portugal in March 1910 he controlled every movement of ships forming the Second Battle Squadron by wireless from the Admiralty. At the time of the Agadir crisis in 1911, when there was a risk of war with Germany, Wilson refused to place the fleet on alert, or even to allow it to rig its anti-torpedo nets. This weakened his esteem in the eyes of other senior admirals, who saw this as deference to ministerial views that such precautions would be regarded by Germany as evidence of warlike intent.

Wilson's reluctance to discuss his decisions extended into the political sphere. It was claimed that he kept the Navy's war plans either in his own head or in a safe to which he alone had the key. Indeed, in the emergency meeting of the Committee of Imperial Defence held on 23 August 1911 to consider the lessons of the Agadir crisis, he gave the impression that naval plans were none of the Committee's business. His taciturn approach compared unfavourably with that of his namesake, the voluble, quick-witted and politically adroit Brigadier General Henry Wilson, Director of Military Operations. An enthusiastic francophile, Henry Wilson produced detailed plans for the continental strategy that, with no case presented for the alternative of a maritime strategy, was eventually followed by the Cabinet. At the time, however, Sir Arthur Wilson made it clear that he could not guarantee the safe passage of a British Expeditionary Force to France without preparations that would be interpreted abroad as steps towards war.

The Prime Minister, Herbert Asquith, responded to this apparent unreadiness by deciding that the Navy should have a War Staff, corresponding to the General Staff (copied from the German model) recently created for the Army. In October 1911 he appointed Winston Churchill as First Lord of the Admiralty with a remit to establish such an organization. Wilson refused to hear of it, mostly on the grounds that it would divide control of naval strategy between the First Sea Lord and the proposed Naval War Staff (eventually created by Churchill out of the existing Naval Intelligence Department). He also believed strongly that the German concept of an elite corps of staff officers had no place in naval warfare and declared, "The Service would have the most supreme contempt for any body of officers who professed to be specially trained to think. There is no Service where there is more thinking done, but officers are judged by what they can do when afloat." Wilson's views were in contrast to those of Prince Louis of Battenberg [74], who had become Churchill's favourite and been appointed Second Sea Lord. Wilson was therefore removed from office at the beginning of December 1911 and went onto the retired list. His successor, Sir Francis Bridgeman, was forced into retirement by Churchill in December 1912, ostensibly on medical grounds, to allow Battenberg to become First Sea Lord in his place.

On the outbreak of the First World War in August 1914 Churchill recalled Wilson to the Admiralty as an adviser on strategy to the First Sea Lord. Wilson accepted on condition that he was not paid or appointed to an established post. Younger admirals greeted his return to a position of influence with dismay. Some even doubted his sanity when, in September 1914, he revived his old plan of seizing Heligoland (ceded by the United Kingdom to Germany in 1890 in return for concessions in Africa) to use as a base for an inshore blockading squadron. In May 1915 one of the six demands that Fisher (re-appointed First Sea Lord when Battenberg resigned in October 1914) made as a condition of remaining in office was that Wilson must leave the Admiralty and cease distracting him with schemes for the bombardment of Heligoland. When Fisher resigned, Churchill proposed re-appointing Wilson as First Sea Lord. Sir John Jellicoe, C-in-C, Grand Fleet, declared that the flag officers afloat trusted Wilson (his old captain in *Sans Pareil*) even less than they did Churchill and would regard his return to office as a national disaster. Wilson therefore remained as an adviser until the end of the war in November 1918.

In 1858, his uncle, Archdale Wilson, had been created a baronet for services in the Indian Mutiny campaign, with a special remainder in favour of his brother's sons in default of male issue of his own. Arthur Wilson's eldest brother died at a young age in a mountaineering accident, and the baronetcy was in due course inherited by his next brother, Roland. Sir Arthur Wilson succeeded him as third baronet in October 1919 and died at Swaffham on 25 May 1921. He was unmarried and his baronetcy became extinct. Churchill said of him, "he was the most selfless man I have ever met or even read of . . . everything was duty . . . [to him] there was nothing else". Jellicoe's view was that, if the politicians appealed to his sense of duty, he would agree to anything they wanted.

TABLE 1

A SENIORITY LIST OF THE ADMIRALS OF THE FLEET

1.	Norris, Sir John (c.1660–1749)	*20 Feb 1734*
2.	Ogle, Sir Chaloner (1681–1750)	*19 Jul 1749*
3.	Stueart, James (c.1690–1757)	*22 Nov 1751*
4.	Clinton, the Honourable George (1686–1761)	*Mar 1757*
5.	Anson, George, Lord Anson, Baron of Soberton (1697–1762)	*30 Jul 1761*
6.	Rowley, Sir William, KB (1690–1768)	*17 Dec 1762*
7.	Hawke, Sir Edmund, 1st Baron Hawke (1705–1781)	*15 Jan 1768*
8.	Forbes, the Honourable John (1714–1796)	*24 Oct 1781*
9.	Howe, Sir Richard, Earl Howe, KG (1726–1799)	*12 Mar 1796*
10.	Parker, Sir Peter, 1st Baronet (1721–1811)	*16 Sep 1799*
11.	William IV, HM King of Great Britain and Ireland, King of Hanover (1765–1837)	*24 Dec 1811*
12.	Jervis, Sir John, Earl of St Vincent, GCB (1735–1823)	*19 Jul 1821*
13.	Freeman, William Peere Williams (1742–1832)	*28 Jun 1830*
14.	Gambier, James, Baron Gambier, GCB (1765–1833)	*22 Jul 1830*
15.	Pole, Sir Charles Morice, 1st Baronet, GCB (1757–1830)	*22 Jul 1830*
16.	Nugent, Sir Charles Edmund, KCH (1759–1844)	*24 Apr 1833*
17.	Whitshed, Sir James Hawkins, 1st Baronet, GCB (1761–1849)	*8 Jan 1844*
18.	Martin, Sir George, GCB, GCMG (1764–1847)	*9 Nov 1846*
19.	Martin, Sir Thomas Byam, GCB (1773–1854)	*13 Oct 1849*
20.	Cockburn, the Right Honourable Sir George, 2nd Baronet, GCB (1772–1853)	*1 Jul 1851*
21.	Ogle, Sir Charles, 2nd Baronet (1775–1858)	*18 Dec 1857*

22.	West, Sir John, KCB (1774–1862)	*25 Jun 1858*
23.	Gage, Sir William Hall, GCB, GCH (1777–1864)	*20 May 1862*
24.	Hamond, Sir Graham Eden, 1st Baronet, GCB (1779–1862)	*10 Nov 1862*
25.	Austen, Sir Francis William, GCB (1774–1863)	*27 Apr 1863*
26.	Parker, Sir William, 1st Baronet, GCB (1781–1866)	*27 Apr 1863*
27.	Curtis, Sir Lucius, 2nd Baronet, KCB (1786–1869)	*11 Jan 1864*
28.	Cochrane, Sir Thomas John, GCB (1789–1872)	*12 Sep 1865*
29.	Seymour, Sir George Francis, GCB, GCH (1787–1870)	*30 Nov 1866*
30.	Gordon, Sir James Alexander, GCB (1782–1869)	*30 Jan 1868*
31.	Bowles, Sir William, KCB (1780–1869)	*15 Jan 1869*
32.	Sartorius, Sir George Rose, KCB (1790–1885)	*3 Jul 1869*
33.	Moresby, Sir Fairfax, GCB (1786–1877)	*21 Jan 1870*
34.	Stewart, Sir Houston, GCB (1791–1875)	*20 Oct 1872*
35.	Codrington, Sir Henry John, KCB (1808–1877)	*22 Jan 1877*
36.	Keppel, Sir Henry, GCB (1809–1904)	*5 Aug 1877*
37.	Wallis, Sir Provo William Parry, GCB (1791–1892)	*11 Dec 1877*
38.	Mundy, Sir George Rodney, GCB (1805–1884)	*27 Dec 1877*
39.	Hope, Sir James, GCB (1808–1881)	*15 Jun 1879*
40.	Symonds, Sir Thomas Matthew Charles, GCB (1813–1894)	*15 Jun 1879*
41.	Milne, Sir Alexander, 1st Baronet, GCB (1806–1896)	*10 Jun 1881*
42.	Elliot, the Honourable Sir Charles Gilbert John Brydone, KCB (1818–1895)	*1 Dec 1881*
43.	Ryder, Sir Alfred Phillipps, KCB (1820–1888)	*29 Apr 1885*
44.	Edward VII, HM King of Great Britain and Ireland (1841–1910)	*18 Jul 1887*
45.	Hornby, Sir Geoffrey Thomas Phipps, GCB (1825–1895)	*1 May 1888*
46.	Hay, the Right Honourable Lord John, GCB (1827–1916)	*8 Dec 1888*
47.	William (Wilhelm) II, HM German Emperor and King of Prussia, KG, GCVO (1859–1941)	*2 Aug 1889*
48.	Commerell, Sir John Edmund, VC, GCB (1829–1901)	*14 Feb 1892*
49.	Alfred Ernest Albert, HRH Duke of Edinburgh, HSH Duke of Saxe-Coburg and Gotha, KG, KT, KP, GCB, GCSI, GCMG, GCIE, GCVO (1844–1900)	*3 Jun 1893*
50.	Meade, the Right Honourable Richard James,	

	4th Earl of Clanwilliam, GCB, KCMG	
	(1832–1907)	*20 Feb 1895*
51.	Lyons, Sir Algernon McLennan, GCB	
	(1833–1908)	*23 Aug 1897*
52.	Richards, Sir Frederick William, GCB (1833–1912)	*29 Nov 1898*
53.	Salmon, Sir Nowell, VC, GCB (1835–1912)	*13 Jan 1899*
54.	Erskine, Sir James Elphinstone, KCB (1838–1911)	*3 Oct 1902*
55.	Hotham, Sir Charles Frederick, GCB, GCVO	
	(1843–1925)	*30 Aug 1903*
56.	Kerr, the Right Honourable Lord Walter Talbot	
	(1839–1927)	*16 Jun 1904*
57.	Seymour, Sir Edward Hobart, GCB, OM, GCVO	
	(1840–1929)	*20 Feb 1905*
58.	Fisher, Sir John Arbuthnot, 1st Baron Fisher	
	of Kilverstone, GCB, OM, GCVO (1841–1920)	*4 Dec 1905*
59.	Wilson, Sir Arthur Knyvet, 3rd Baronet,	
	VC, GCB, OM, GCVO (1842–1921)	*1 Mar 1907*
60.	Nicholas II, HIM Emperor of Russia (1868–1918)	*11 Jun 1908*
61.	Noel, Sir Gerard Henry Uctred, KCB, KCMG	
	(1845–1918)	*2 Dec 1908*
62.	Henry (Heinrich) of Prussia, HRH Prince,	
	KG, GCB (1862–1929)	*27 Jan 1910*
63.	Fanshawe, Sir Arthur Dalrymple, GCB, GCVO	
	(1847–1936)	*30 Apr 1910*
64.	George V, HM King of Great Britain and Ireland	
	(1865–1936)	*6 May 1910*
65.	May, Sir William Henry, GCB, GCVO	
	(1849–1930)	*20 Mar 1913*
66.	Meux, the Honourable Sir Hedworth Lambton,	
	GCB, KCVO (1856–1929)	*5 Mar 1915*
67.	Callaghan, Sir George Astley, GCB, GCVO	
	(1852–1920)	*2 Apr 1917*
68.	Jellicoe, Sir John Rushworth, 1st Earl Jellicoe,	
	GCB, OM, GCVO (1859–1935)	*3 Apr 1919*
69.	Beatty, Sir David, 1st Earl Beatty,	
	GCB, OM, GCVO, DSO (1871–1936)	*3 Apr 1919*
70.	Jackson, Sir Henry Bradwardine, GCB, KCVO,	
	(1855–1929)	*31 Jul 1919*
71.	Wemyss, Rosslyn Erskine, 1st Baron Wester	
	Wemyss, GCB, CMG, MVO (1864–1933)	*1 Nov 1919*
72.	Burney, Sir Cecil, KCB (1858–1929)	*24 Nov 1920*
73.	Sturdee, Sir Frederick Charles Doveton,	
	1st Baronet, GCB, KCMG, CVO (1859–1925)	*5 Jul 1921*
74.	Mountbatten, Louis Alexander, HSH Prince Louis	
	of Battenberg, 1st Marquess of Milford Haven,	
	GCB, GCVO, KCMG (1854–1921)	*4 Aug 1921*

75.	Madden, Sir Charles Edward, 1st Baronet, GCB, OM, GCVO, KCMG (1862–1935)	*31 Jul 1924*
76.	Gough-Calthorpe, the Honourable Sir Somerset Arthur, GCB, GCMG, CVO (1864–1937)	*8 May 1925*
77.	De Robeck, Sir John Michael, 1st Baronet, GCB, GCMG, GCVO (1862–1928)	*24 Nov 1925*
78.	Oliver, Sir Henry Francis, GCB, GCMG (1865–1965)	*21 Jan 1928*
79.	Brock, Sir Osmond de Beauvoir, GCB, KCVO (1869–1947)	*31 Jul 1929*
80.	Keyes, Sir Roger, 1st Baron Keyes, 1st Baronet, GCB, KCVO, DSO (1872–1945)	*8 May 1930*
81.	Field, Sir Frederick Lawrence, GCB, KCMG (1871–1945)	*21 Jan 1933*
82.	Tyrwhitt, Sir Reginald Yorke, 1st Baronet, GCB, DSO (1870–1951)	*31 Jul 1934*
83.	Chatfield, Sir Alfred Ernle Montacute, 1st Baron Chatfield, GCB, KCMG, CVO (1873–1967)	*3 May 1935*
84.	Edward VIII, HM King of Great Britain and Ireland, HRH Duke of Windsor (1894–1972)	*21 Jan 1936*
85.	Kelly, Sir John Donald, GCB, GCVO (1871–1936)	*12 Jul 1936*
86.	George VI, HM King of Great Britain and Ireland (1895–1952)	*11 Dec 1936*
87.	Boyle, William Henry Dudley, 12th Earl of Cork and Orrery, GCB, GCVO (1873–1967)	*21 Jan 1938*
88.	Backhouse, Sir Roger Roland Charles, GCB, GCVO, CMG (1879–1939)	*7 Jul 1939*
89.	Pound, Sir Alfred Dudley Pickman Rogers, GCB, OM, GCVO (1877–1943)	*31 Jul 1939*
90.	Forbes, Sir Charles Morton, GCB, DSO (1880–1960)	*8 May 1940*
91.	Cunningham, Sir Andrew Browne, Viscount Cunningham of Hyndhope, 1st Baronet, KT, GCB, OM, DSO (1883–1963)	*21 Jan 1943*
92.	Tovey, Sir John Cronyn, Baron Tovey, GCB, KBE, DSO (1885–1971)	*22 Oct 1943*
93.	Somerville, Sir James, GCB, GBE, DSO (1882–1949)	*8 May 1945*
94.	Cunningham, Sir John Henry Dacres, GCB, MVO (1885–1962)	*21 Jan 1948*
95.	Fraser, Sir Bruce Austin, Baron Fraser of North Cape, GCB, KBE (1888–1981)	*22 Oct 1948*
96.	Willis, Sir Algernon Usborne, GCB, KBE, DSO (1889–1976)	*20 Mar 1949*

97.	Power, Sir Arthur John, GCB, GBE, CVO (1889–1960)	*22 Apr 1952*
98.	Vian, Sir Philip Louis, GCB, KBE, DSO (1894–1968)	*1 Jun 1952*
99.	Philip, HRH Duke of Edinburgh, KG, KT, OM, GBE, AC, QSO (1921–)	*15 Jan 1953*
100.	McGrigor, Sir Rhoderick Robert, GCB, DSO (1893–1959)	*1 May 1953*
101.	Creasey, Sir George Elvey, GCB, CBE, MVO, DSO (1895–1972)	*22 Apr 1955*
102.	Mountbatten, Lord Louis, 1st Earl Mountbatten of Burma, KG, GCB, OM, GCSI, GCIE, GCVO, DSO (1900–1979)	*22 Oct 1956*
103.	Lambe, Sir Charles Edward, GCB, CVO (1900–1960)	*10 May 1960*
104.	John, Sir Caspar, GCB (1903–1984)	*23 May 1962*
105.	Begg, Sir Varyl Cargill, GCB, DSO, DSC (1908–1995)	*12 Aug 1968*
106.	Le Fanu, Sir Michael, GCB, DSC (1913–1970)	*3 Jul 1970*
107.	Hill-Norton, Sir Peter John, Baron Hill-Norton, GCB (1915–)	*12 Mar 1971*
108.	Pollock, Sir Michael Patrick, GCB, LVO, DSC (1916–)	*1 Mar 1974*
109.	Ashmore, Sir Edward Beckwith, GCB, DSC (1919–)	*9 Feb 1977*
110.	Lewin, Sir Terence Thornton, Baron Lewin, KG, GCB, LVO, DSC (1920–1999)	*6 Jul 1979*
111.	Leach, Sir Henry Conyers, GCB (1923–)	*1 Dec 1982*
112.	Fieldhouse, Sir John, Baron Fieldhouse, GCB, GBE (1928–1992)	*2 Aug 1985*
113.	Staveley, Sir William Doveton Minet, GCB (1928–1997)	*25 May 1989*
114.	Oswald, Sir John Julian Robertson, GCB (1933–)	*2 Mar 1992*
115.	Bathurst, Sir David Benjamin, GCB (1936–)	*10 Jul 1995*

TABLE 2

THE CATALOGUE OF THE SHIPS

SEAGOING SHIPS OF THE ROYAL NAVY IN WHICH THE ADMIRALS OF THE FLEET SERVED

The descriptions of the ships listed below are intended only as a general guide to the importance of the ships in which the admirals of the fleet served at various stages in their career. Designations such as destroyer, corvette, cruiser, frigate and sloop each had different meanings at different times. In many cases the classification, tonnage, armament and even names were changed in the course of a ship's life. Prior to 1873 tonnages were given in builders' measurement. From then until 1926 they were given in displacement tonnage, and thereafter, under international rules, in standard displacement. Where two methods were used during the years that a ship was in service, both are given. The first date given is in most cases that of launch. The second is that of the ship ceasing to be an effective unit of the fleet. The names of the admirals of the fleet shown in this table are those by which they were known at the end of their careers.

ABERGAVENNY 4th-rate; 1,182; 1795–1807 *William Parker*

ABOUKIR [1] 3rd-rate; 1,703; 1807–24 *Cockburn; Thomas Martin*
        [2] 2nd-rate; 3,091; 1848–77 *Erskine*
        [3] armoured cruiser; 12,000; 1900–1914 *Beatty; Chatfield*

ACASTA 5th-rate; 1,127; 1797–1821 *Bowles; George Seymour*

ACHERON submarine; 11,120; 1945–67 *Fieldhouse*

ACHILLES armoured cruiser, 13,550; 1905–21 *Oliver*

ACORN sloop; 430; 1807–19 *Moresby*

ACTIVE [1] 6th-rate; 594; 1758–78 *Freeman*
      [2] 5th-rate; 1,058; 1799–1826 *Gordon*

[3] corvette (3rd-class cruiser); 3,080; 1869–1906 *Brock;*
Cork and Orrery; Jackson; Noel
[4] destroyer; 1,350; 1929–47 *Vian*

ADAMANT 4th-rate; 1, 060; 1780–1809 *Stewart*

ADELAIDE (HMAS) light cruiser; 5,440; 1918–49 *Vian*

ADVENTURE [1] 4th-rate; 438; 1646–1709 *Norris*
[2] 5th-rate; 896; 1784–1801 *Charles Ogle*
[3] minelayer; 6,740; 1924–44 *John Cunningham*

AENEAS submarine; 1,120; 1945–74 *Fieldhouse*

AEOLUS 5th-rate; 1,078; 1801–17 *Pole*

AFRICA battleship; 16,350; 1905–20 *McGrigor; Milford Haven*

AFRIDI destroyer; 1,870; 1937–40 *Vian*

AGAMEMNON [1] 2nd-rate; 3,102; 1852–70 *Fisher*
[2] battleship; 16,500; 1906–20 *McGrigor*

AGINCOURT [1] 3rd-rate; 1,747; 1817–48 *Cochrane*
[2] battleship; 6,621 (10,690); 1865–1904 *Commerell;*
De Robeck; Jellicoe; Kelly; Meux; Milford
Haven;Oliver

AIGLE 5th-rate; 1,003; 1780–1809 *Hamond*

AJAX [1] 3rd-rate; 1,953; 1798–1807 *Cochrane; Whitshed*
[2] battleship; 8,600; 1880–1904 *Tyrwhitt*
[3] battleship; 23,000; 1912–26 *Somerville*
[4] cruiser; 6,985; 1934–49 *Staveley*

AKBAR 4th-rate; 1,388; 1801–24 *Thomas Martin*

ALACRITY despatch vessel; 1,700; 1885–1913 *Brock, Callaghan*

ALARM 5th-rate; 683; 1758–1812 *Moresby; William Parker; St Vincent*

ALBEMARLE battleship; 14,000; 1901–19 *Chatfield; Jellicoe*

ALBION [1] 3rd-rate; 1,743; 1802–31 *Cockburn; Milne*
[2] 2nd-rate; 3,111;1842–84 *Lyons*
[3] battleship; 12,950; 1898–1919 *Field*

[4] commando carrier; 22,000; 1947–1973 *Ashmore; Leach; Staveley*

ALCIDE 3rd-rate; 1,625; 1779–1817 *Charles Ogle*

ALDBOROUGH [1] 6th-rate; 288; 1706–43 *Steuart*
           [2] 6th-rate; 440; 1756–77 *Whitshed*

ALERT [1] brig-sloop; 205; 1779–92 *George Martin*
    [2] sloop; 751; 1856–84 *May*
    [3] frigate; 1,500; 1945–71 *Ashmore*

ALEXANDRA battleship; 9,490; 1875–1908 *Alfred, Duke of Edinburgh; Chatfield; Fanshawe; George V; Hay; Hornby; Hotham; Jellicoe; Madden; Meux; Noel; Edward Seymour; Tyrwhitt*

ALEXANDRIA 5th-rate; 662; 1806–18 *Stewart*

ALGIERS 2nd-rate; 3,340; 1854–70 *Codrington; Wilson*

AMARANTHE brig-sloop; 290; 1796–99 *William Parker*

AMAZON [1] 5th-rate; 687; 1773–94 *Whitshed*
        [2] 5th-rate; 1,038; 1799–1817 *Moresby; William Parker*

AMERICA 3rd-rate; 1,370; 1777–1800 *Gage*

AMETHYST [1] corvette (3rd-class cruiser); 1,970; 1873–87 *Oliver*
          [2] 3rd-class cruiser; 3,000; 1903–20 *Tyrwhitt*

AMPHION [1] 5th-rate; 909; 1798–1820 *Bowles*
        [2] scout cruiser; 3,440; 1911–14 *Tovey*

AMPHITRITE 1st-class cruiser; 11,000; 1898–1920 *De Robeck*

ANDROMEDA 5th-rate; 721; 1784–1808 *Austen; Thomas Martin; William IV*

ANGLER torpedo-boat destroyer; 310; 1897–1920 *De Robeck*

ANSON [1] battleship; 10,600; 1886–1909 *Kelly; Edward Seymour; Wemyss*
      [2] battleship; 35,000; 1940–57 *Fraser*

ANTELOPE 4th-rate; 858; 1741–81 *Hawke*

278

ANTRIM [1] armoured cruiser; 10,850; 1903–22 *Madden*
      [2] guided missile destroyer; 5,600; 1967–84 *Ashmore*

APOLLO 5th-rate; 1,086; 1805–46 *Codrington*

AQUILON 5th-rate; 724; 1786–1815 *Bowles; Hamond*

ARETHUSA [1] 4th-rate; 2,132; 1849–74 *Symonds*
      [2] light cruiser; 3,500; 1913–16 *Tyrwhitt*
      [3] cruiser; 5,220; 1934–50 *Pollock; Vian*

ARGONAUT 1st-class cruiser, 11,000; 1898–1920 *Vian*

ARIADNE [1] frigate; 3,214; 1859–84 *Milford Haven*
      [2] 1st-class cruiser; 11,000; 1898–1917 *Tovey*
      [3] frigate; 2,500; 1971–92 *Bathurst*

ARIEL sloop; 314; 1781–1802 *Cockburn*

ARK ROYAL [1] aircraft carrier; 22,000; 1937–41 *Power; Somerville*
      [2] aircraft carrier; 36,800; 1950–80 *Ashmore;*
        Hill-Norton; Leach; Pollock

ARROGANT [1] 3rd-rate; 1,644; 1761–1801 *Gordon; Whitshed*
      [2] 2nd-class cruiser; 5,750; 1896–1923 *Beatty*

ARTOIS 5th-rate; 984; 1794–97 *Thomas Martin*

ASHANTI destroyer; 1,870; 1937–49 *Lewin*

ASIA [1] 3rd-rate; 1,364; 1764–1804 *Wallis*
      [2] 2nd-rate; 2,289; 1824–58 *Codrington; Hornby; William Parker*

ASSISTANCE troopship; 2,515; 1874–97 *Madden*

ASSURANCE 5th-rate; 898; 1790–98 *Charles Ogle*

ASTRAEA 2nd-class cruiser; 4,360; 1893–1920 *Cork and Orrery; Wemyss*

ASTUTE submarine; 1,120; 1945–70 *Fieldhouse*

ATTENTIVE scout cruiser; 2,670; 1904–20 *Tyrwhitt*

AUDACIOUS battleship; 3,774 (6,010); 1869–1902 *De Robeck; Ryder*

AUGUSTA 4th-rate; 1,068; 1739–65 *Chaloner Ogle*

AURORA [1] 6th-rate; 596; 1777–1814 *George Seymour*
    [2] armoured cruiser; 5,600; 1887–1907 *Fanshawe; Tyrwhitt*
    [3] cruiser; 5,270; 1936–48 *Cork and Orrery; Le Fanu*

AUSTRALIA [1] armoured cruiser; 5,600, 1886–1905 *Tyrwhitt*
    [2] (HMAS) battle-cruiser; 18,000; 1911–24 *Vian*

AVENGER sloop; 330; 1794–1802 *Charles Ogle*

AVON brig-sloop; 1805–14 *Sartorius*

BACCHANTE [1] corvette (3rd-class cruiser); 2,679 (4,130); 1876–97
      George V; Richards; Wemyss
    [2] 1st-class cruiser; 12,000; 1901–20 *Jackson; Tyrwhitt*
    [3] frigate; 2,500; 1968–82 *Oswald*

BAHAMA 3rd-rate; 1,772; 1805-09 *Sartorius*

BALTIMORE sloop; 251; 1742–62 *Howe*

BANTERER gunboat; 232; 1855–72 *Fisher*

BARFLEUR [1] 2nd-rate; 1,551; 1716–64 *Anson; Peter Parker; Rowley*
    [2] 2nd-rate; 1,947; 1768–1819 *George Martin; Thomas
      Martin; Peter Parker; William IV*
    [3] battleship; 10,500; 1892–1910 *Beatty; Field*

BARHAM battleship; 27,500; 1914–41 *Pound; Somerville; Willis*

BASILISK paddle sloop; 1,031; 1848–82 *Noel*

BAT torpedo-boat destroyer; 360; 1896–1919 *Keyes*

BEDFORD [1] 3rd-rate; 1,606; 1775–1801 *Gage; Hamond*
    [2] armoured cruiser; 8,900; 1901–10 *Sturdee*

BELFAST cruiser; 10,000; 1938–71 *Lewin*

BELLEISLE 3rd-rate; 1,889; 1795–1814 *Cockburn*

BELLEROPHON battleship; 4,270 (7,550); 1865–1904 *Burney;
      Callaghan; Clanwilliam; Fisher; Lyons; Ryder; Sturdee*

BELLONA [1] 3rd-rate; 1,615; 1760–1814 *Gage; Wallis*
    [2] scout cruiser; 3,350; 1909–21 *Tovey; Tyrwhitt*
    [3] light cruiser; 5,950; 1942–59 *Lewin*

BELVIDERA 5th-rate; 946; 1809–46 *Ryder*

BENBOW [1] 3rd-rate; 1,773; 1813–48 *Stewart*
        [2] battleship; 25,000; 1913–31 *Lambe; Somerville;*
             Sturdee

BERMUDA cruiser; 8,000; 1941–65 *Staveley*

BERWICK [1] 3rd-rate; 1,147; 1723–43 *Clinton*
         [2] 3rd-rate; 1,280; 1743–60 *Hawke*
         [3] 1st-class cruiser; 9,800; 1902–1920 *John Cunningham*

BIDDEFORD (BIDEFORD) 6th-rate; 282; 1711–36 *Rowley*

BIRMINGHAM cruiser; 9,000; 1937–60 *Ashmore*

BLACK PRINCE armoured ship; 6,109 (9,137); 1861–99 *Alfred, Duke*
             of Edinburgh; Hay

BLACKPOOL frigate; 1,180; 1955–76 *Ashmore*

BLAKE [1] 1st-class cruiser; 9,000; 1889–1908 *Oliver*
       [2] cruiser; 9,550 1961–82; *Leach; Lewin; Pollock*

BLANCHE [1] 5th-rate; 951; 1800-05 *Hamond*
         [2] 5th-rate; 1,074; 1819–52 *Mundy*

BOADICEA [1] corvette (3rd-class cruiser); 2,679 (4,140);
              1875–1905 *Erskine; Richards; Salmon*
          [2] scout; 3,300; 1908–26 *Fraser*

BOMBAY screw ship; 2,782; 1861–64 *Elliot*

BOURDELOIS 6th-rate; 625; 1799–1804 *Gordon*

BOYNE 2nd-rate; 2,010; 1790–95 *Charles Ogle; St Vincent*

BRISTOL [1] 4th-rate; 1,021; 1746–68 *Peter Parker*
         [2] 4th-rate; 1,049; 1775–94 *Nugent; Peter Parker*
         [3] frigate; 3,027 (4,020); 1861–83 *Hornby*
         [4] destroyer; 6,100; 1969–90 (still in commission at date of
             publication as an immobile tender for Sea Cadet training,
             Portsmouth harbour) *Ashmore*

BRITANNIA [1] 1st-rate; 1,708; 1682–1715 *Norris*
           [2] 1st-rate; 1,894; 1719–45 *John Forbes; Norris*

[3] 1st-rate; 2,116; 1773–1825 (renamed PRINCESS
ROYAL 1812) *Cockburn; Hamond; Pole*
[4] 1st-rate ; 2,626; 1820–59 *Symonds*
[5] royal yacht; 3,990; 1953–97 *Lewin; Staveley*

BRITON 5th-rate; 1,080; 1821–41 *Codrington; George Seymour*

BRUCE destroyer flotilla leader; 1,800; 1918–39 *Tovey*

BUCKINGHAM 3rd-rate; 1,436; 1751–77 *Peter Parker*

BULLDOG destroyer; 1,340; 1930–46 *Le Fanu*

BULWARK [1] battleship; 15,000; 1899–1914 *Brock; Milford
Haven; Sturdee*
[2] commando carrier; 22,000; 1960–84 *Ashmore*

BURFORD 3rd-rate; 1,147; 1722–52 *John Forbes; Howe; Chaloner Ogle*

CADMUS [1] brig-sloop; 237; 1808–35 *Milne*
[2] corvette (3rd-class cruiser); 1,466; 1856–79 *Jackson*

CAESAR [1] 3rd-rate; 1,792; 1793–1814 *Nugent*
[2] battleship; 14,900; 1896–1921 *Callaghan; Chatfield;
Madden*

CAIRO light cruiser; 4,190; 1918–42 *Cork and Orrery*

CALCUTTA [1] 2nd-rate; 2,299; 1831–65 *Clanwilliam; Fisher;
Ryder; Edward Seymour; Wilson*
[2] light cruiser; 4,190; 1918–41 *Cunningham of
Hyndhope*

CALEDONIA [1] 1st-rate; 2,602; 1808–58 *Austen; Bowles;
Codrington; Gambier; Milne*
[2] armoured ship; 4,125 (6,832); 1862–86 *Wilson*

CALLIOPE corvette (3rd-class cruiser); 2,770; 1884–1951 *Kelly*

CALYPSO corvette (3rd-class cruiser); 2,770; 1883–1902 *Pound;
Tyrwhitt*

CAMBRIAN [1] 4th-rate; 1,148; 1797–1828 *Bowles; Hope*
[2] 5th-rate; 1,622; 1841–72 *Lyons*
[3] 2nd-class cruiser; 4,360; 1893–1916 *Brock; Milford
Haven*

CAMBRIDGE 3rd-rate; 2,139; 1815–56 *Mundy*

CAMELION sloop; 307; 1777–80 *George Martin*

CAMPBELL destroyer flotilla leader; 1,800; 1918–47 *McGrigor*

CAMPERDOWN battleship; 10,600; 1885–1908 *Beatty*

CANADA [1]3rd-rate; 1,605; 1765–1810 *Thomas Martin*
    [2] corvette (3rd-class cruiser); 2,380; 1881–97 *George V;*
    Wemyss

CANOPUS 3rd-rate; 2,270; 1798–1862 *Austin; George Martin; Moresby*

CAPTAIN 3rd-rate; 1,632; 1787–1809 *Bowles; Gage; Cockburn*

CARDIFF light cruiser; 4,190; 1917–46 *Chatfield; Tyrwhitt*

CARLISLE 4th-rate; 912; 1693–96 *Norris*

CARNARVON armoured cruiser; 10,850; 1903–21 *De Robeck; Charles*
    Forbes

CARNATIC 3rd-rate; 1,720; 1783–1825 *St Vincent*

CARYSFORT corvette (3rd-class cruiser); 2,380; 1878–99 *Brock;*
    Burney

CAVALIER destroyer; 1,710; 1944–77 *Staveley*

CENTURION [1] 3rd-rate; c.1,000; 1733–69 *Anson*
    [2] battleship; 10,500; 1892–1910 *Jellicoe; Edward*
    Seymour
    [3] battleship; 23,000; 1911–40 *John; Keyes;*
    Mountbatten

CERES 5th-rate; 692; 1781–1804 *Whitshed*

CHALLENGER 6th-rate; 603; 1826–35 *Mundy*

CHAMPION 6th-rate; 519; 1779–1810 *Hamond*

CHARYBDIS [1] corvette (3rd-class cruiser); 1,506 (2,187);
    1859–80 *Hotham; Lyons*
    [2] 2nd-class cruiser; 4,360; 1893–1918 *Wemyss*
    [3] frigate; 2,350; 1968–92 *Lewin*

CHATHAM [1] 4th-rate; 1750–93 *Nugent; Peter Parker*
[2] 2nd class cruiser; 5,400; 1911–20 *De Robeck; Somerville*

CHEQUERS destroyer flotilla leader; 1,710; 1944–66 *Leach; Lewin; Philip, Duke of Edinburgh*

CHESAPEAKE frigate; 2,377; 1855–67 *Fisher; Hope; Edward Seymour*

CHILDERS brig-sloop; 385; 1827–65 *Keppel*

CLARENCE 3rd-rate; 1,749; 1812–28 *Stewart*

CLEOPATRA [1] 5th-rate; 689; 1779–1814 *Wallis*
[2] 6th-rate; 918; 1835–62 *Hornby; Milne*
[3] corvette (3rd-class cruiser); 2,380; 1878–1905 *Chatfield; Tyrwhitt*
[4] cruiser; 5,450; 1940–58 *Power; Vian*

CODRINGTON [1] 3rd-rate; 2,589; 1841–67 *George Seymour*
[2] destroyer flotilla leader; 1,540; 1929–40 *Creasy*

COLCHESTER 4th-rate; 756; 1721–42 *Clinton*

COLLINGWOOD [1] 3rd-rate; 2,589; 1841–67 *Hornby; George Seymour*
[2] battleship; 19,350; 1908–23 *George VI*

COLOSSUS [1] 3rd-rate; 1,703; 1787–98 *Gage; George Martin; Thomas Martin; Pole*
[2] 3rd-rate; 2,590; 1848–67 *Keppel; Wilson*
[3] battleship; 9,510; 1882–1908 *Cork and Orrery; Gough-Calthorpe; Jellicoe*
[4] battleship; 20,000; 1910–28 *Keyes; Pound*

COMET fireship/bomb vessel; 275; 1742–9 *Howe*

COMUS [1] ex-COMET sloop; 462; 1828–62 *Commerell*
[2] corvette (3rd-class cruiser); 2,380; 1878–1904 *Backhouse; Burney*

CONQUEROR battleship; 22,500; 1911–22 *Creasy*

CONQUEST light cruiser; 3,750; 1915–30 *Backhouse*

CONSTANCE [1] frigate; 2,132; 1846–72 *Fanshawe*
[2] 3rd-class cruiser; 2,380; 1880–89 *Field*
[3] light cruiser; 3,750; 1915–36 *Cork and Orrery*

CONTENT 3rd-rate; 1,130; 1695–1703 *Norris*

CONWAY 6th-rate; 451; 1814–25 *Milne*

CORDELIA corvette (3rd-class cruiser); 2,380; 1881–1904 *De Robeck*

CORMORANT [1] sloop; 304; 1776–81 *Pole*
[2] gun-vessel; 675; 1856–59 *Hope*

CORNWALL 2nd-rate; 1,350; 1692–1761 *Howe*

CORNWALLIS [1] 3rd-rate; 1,809; 1813–65 *Commerell; Kerr; William Parker*
[2] battleship; 14,000; 1901–17 *Kelly*

COROMANDEL despatch vessel; 303; 1855–66 *Fisher*

CORUNNA destroyer; 2,400; 1945–74 *Lewin*

COSSACK destroyer; 1,870; 1937–41 *Vian*

COURAGEOUS aircraft carrier; 22,500; 1928–39 *John*

COVENTRY light cruiser; 4,190; 1917–42 *Cunningham of Hyndhope; Charles Forbes; Lambe; Willis*

CREOLE 5th-rate; 949; 1813–33 *Bowles; Thomas Martin*

CRESCENT 1st-class cruiser; 7,700; 1892–1921 *Erskine; George V*

CRESSY 3rd-rate; 2,359; 1853–67 *Elliot*

CROCODILE 6th-rate; 500; 1825–50 *Milne*

CROWN 3rd-rate; 1,387; 1782–98 *Austen; Pole*

CULLODEN 3rd-rate; 1,487; 1747–70 *St Vincent*

CUMBERLAND [1] 3rd-rate; 1,308; 1710–60 *Norris; Steuart*
[2] 3rd-rate; 1,718; 1807–30 *George Martin*
[3] armoured cruiser; 9,800; 1902–21 *George VI*
[4] cruiser; 9,750; 1926–59 *Hill-Norton*

CURACOA frigate; 1,570; 1854–69 *Hotham*

CURIEUX brig-sloop; 315; 1804-09 *Wallis*

DAPHNE [1] 6th-rate; 574; 1796–98 *Bowles*
  [2] 6th-rate; 540; 1806–16 *Sartorius*
  [3] sloop; 1,140; 1888–1918 *Cork and Orrery*

DARING destroyer; 1,375; 1932–40 *Mountbatten*

DART brigantine (gunvessel WV 26); 319; 1847–75 *Richards*

DARTMOUTH 4th-rate; 681; 1698–1747 *Steuart*

DAUNTLESS frigate; 1,432; 1847–85 *Commerell; Ryder*

DEAL CASTLE [1] 6th-rate; 240; 1697–1706 *Chaloner Ogle*
  [2] 6th-rate; 400; 1756–80 *Whitshed*

DEFENCE [1] 3rd-rate; 1,603; 1763–1811 *Gambier; Gordon*
  [2] armoured ship; 3,270; 1861–98 *Salmon*

DEFENDER destroyer; 2,610; 1950–70 *Ashmore*

DESPATCH [1] brig; 187; 1779–98 *Austen*
  [2] light cruiser; 4,765; 1919–46 *Cunningham of Hyndhope*

DESPERATE torpedo-boat destroyer; 310; 1896–1920 *De Robeck*

DEVASTATION turret ship; 9,330; 1871–1908 *Brock; Richards*

DEVONSHIRE [1] 3rd-rate; 1,471; 1745–72 *Hawke; St Vincent*
  [2] cruiser; 10,850; 1904–21 *Kelly*
  [2] cruiser; 9,850; 1927–54 *John Cunningham; Oswald*
  [3] guided missile destroyer; 5,600; 1960–84
    Ashmore, Bathurst

DIADEM 1st-class cruiser; 11,000; 1896–1921 *Cunningham of
  Hyndhope; Noel*

DIAMOND [1] 5th-rate; 595; 1723–44 *Anson*
  [2] 5th-rate; 710; 1774–84 *Whitshed*

DICTATOR 3rd-rate; 1,388; 1783–1817 *Thomas Martin*

DIDO [1] 5th-rate; 734; 1836–60 *Keppel*
[2] cruiser; 5,450; 1939–58 *Vian*

DILIGENCE brig-sloop; 320; 1795–1800 *West*

DIOMEDE frigate; 2,350; 1969–88 *Fieldhouse*

DOLPHIN [1] 6th-rate; 511; 1751–77 *Howe*
[2] sloop; 925; 1882–1907 *Meux*

DOMINION battleship; 16,350; 1903–21 *De Robeck; Charles Forbes*

DONEGAL [1] 3rd-rate; 1,901; 1798–1845 *Mundy; George Seymour*
[2] 1st-rate; 3,245 (5,481); 1858–1925 (renamed
VERNON torpedo school 1886) *Fisher*
[3] armoured cruiser; 9,800; 1902–20 *Willis*

DORIS 2nd-class cruiser; 5,600; 1896–1919 *Cunningham of Hyndhope*

DORSETSHIRE cruiser; 9,975; 1929–42 *Le Fanu; Power*

DOUGLAS destroyer flotilla leader; 1,800; 1918–45 *Vian*

DRAGON paddle frigate; 1,270; 1845–64 *Commerell*

DRAKE armoured cruiser; 14,100; 1901–17 *Jellicoe; Milford Haven*

DREADNOUGHT [1] battleship; 5,030 (10,820); 1875–1903 *Field;*
George V; Gough-Calthorpe; Milford Haven
[2] battleship; 17,900; 1906–21 *Backhouse;*
Madden; May
[3] fleet submarine; 3,000; 1960–85
Fieldhouse

DRIVER sloop; 402; 1797–1824 *Bowles; Wallis*

DUBLIN [1] 3rd-rate (reduced to 5th-rate in 1826); 1,772;
1812–45 *Hamond*
[2] 2nd-class cruiser; 5,400; 1912–26 *Burney; Kelly*

DUKE 2nd-rate; 1,931; 1777–99 *Hamond*

DUKE OF YORK battleship; 35,000; 1938–58 *Ashmore; Creasy; Fraser;*
Leach; Le Fanu; McGrigor; Tovey

DUNCAN battleship; 13,550; 1903–20 *Callaghan; Field*

DUNEDIN light cruiser; 4,650; 1918–41 *Lambe*

DUNKIRK [1] 4th-rate; 1,246; 1754–78 *Howe*
        [2] destroyer; 2,380; 1945–65 *Leach*

DURBAN cruiser; 5,800; 1919–44 *Begg*

EAGLE aircraft carrier; 36,800; 1946–78 *Ashmore; Bathurst; Hill-Norton;*
        Le Fanu

ECHO sloop; 341; 1797–1809 *Hamond*

ECLAIR brig-sloop; 387; 1807–31 *Moresby; Mundy*

ECLIPSE corvette (3rd-class cruiser); 1,273 (1,755); 1867–88 *Erskine*

EDGAR [1] 3rd-rate; 1,046; 1688–1711 *Norris*
       [2] 3rd-rate; 1,644; 1779–1813 *Charles Ogle*
       [3] 2nd-rate; 3,094; 1858–70 *Erskine; Hornby*
       [4] 1st-class cruiser; 7,350; 1890–1921 *Callaghan*

EDINBURGH 3rd-rate; 952; 1702–71 *Hawke; Chaloner Ogle*

EFFINGHAM cruiser; 9,750; 1921–40 *Cork and Orrery; Fraser*

EGMONT 3rd-rate; 1,648; 1768–99 *Gage*

EGYPTIENNE 5th-rate; 1,430; 1801–17 *Charles Ogle*

ELEPHANT 3rd-rate; 1,604; 1786–1830 *Austen*

ELTHAM 5th-rate; 678; 1736–63 *Howe*

EMERALD [1] 5th-rate; 934; 1795–1836 *George Martin*
         [2] frigate; 2,913; 1856–69 *Kerr*

EMPEROR OF INDIA battleship; 25,000; 1913–31 *Lambe; Somerville;*
        Vian

EMPRESS OF INDIA battleship; 14,500; 1893–1913 *Burney; Edward*
        Seymour; Wemyss

EMULOUS brig-sloop; 384; 1806–12 *Wallis*

ENCHANTRESS Admiralty yacht; 3,470; 1903–35 *Brock*

ENCOUNTER corvette (3rd-class cruiser); 953; 1846–66 *Edward Seymour*

ENDYMION [1] 4th-rate; 1,277; 1797–1860 *George Seymour; Symonds*
    [2] frigate; 2,486; 1865–85 *Meux*
    [3] 1st-class cruiser; 7,350; 1891–1920 *Callaghan*

ESPOIR gunboat; 465; 1880–95 *De Robeck*

ESSEX 3rd-rate; 1,226; 1679–1759 *Howe*

ETHALION 5th-rate; 996; 1802–35 *Cochrane*

EURYALUS [1] 5th-rate; 946; 1803–26 *Mundy*
    [2] frigate; 2,371; 1853–67 *Alfred, Duke of Edinburgh*
    [3] armoured cruiser; 12,000; 1901–20 *Wemyss*

EURYDICE 6th-rate; 521; 1781–1834 *Gordon*

EXCELLENT 3rd-rate; 1,645; 1787–1830 *Curtis; West*

EXETER cruiser; 8,390; 1929–42 *John*

EXMOUTH battleship; 14,000; 1901–20 *Wilson*

EXPERIMENT 6th-rate; 445; 1740–63 *St Vincent*

EXPRESS destroyer; 1,400; 1934–56 *Pollock*

FAME torpedo-boat destroyer; 340; 1896–1921 *Keyes*

FANTOME brig-sloop; 483; 1839–64 *Richards*

FAULKNOR destroyer flotilla leader; 1,694; 1914–20 *Tovey*

FAVORITE sloop; 434; 1829–59 *Mundy*

FEARLESS [1] scout cruiser; 3,440; 1912–21 *Keyes; Willis*
    [2] assault ship; 10,000; 1963–2002 *Ashmore; Lewin*

FIFE guided missile destroyer; 5,600; 1964–87 *Ashmore; Lewin*

FIREBRAND paddle frigate; 1,190; 1842–64 *Commerell; Hope; Lyons*

FISGARD 5th-rate; 1,182; 1797–1814 *Sartorius; Thomas Martin*

FLAMBOROUGH 6th-rate; 377; 1707–48 *Hawke*

FLORA 5th-rate; 698; 1761–78 *Williams*

FORMIDABLE [1] 2nd-rate; 1,945; 1777—1813 *Whitshed*
           [2] 2nd-rate; 2,289; 1814–69 *Hornby*
           [3] battleship; 15,000; 1898–1915 *McGrigor*
           [4] aircraft carrier; 23,000; 1939–53 *Vian*

FORTE [1] 5th-rate; 1,155; 1814–44 *Cochrane; Hope*
     [2] frigate; 2,364 (3,456); 1858–80 *Keppel*
     [3] 2nd-class cruiser; 4,360; 1893–1922 *Kelly*

FORTH frigate (converted to steam mortar-frigate 1856); 1,215;
     1833–69 *Hay*

FORTUNEE 5th-rate; 921; 1800–21 *George Seymour*

FOUDROYANT 2nd-rate; 1,978; 1758–87 *St Vincent*

FOX 2nd-class cruiser; 4,360; 1893–1920 *Cork and Orrery; Cunningham
of Hyndhope*

FOXHOUND destroyer; 953; 1909–21 *McGrigor*

FROBISHER cruiser; 9,860; 1920–49 *Ashmore; Cork and Orrery; Creasy;
Lewin; Pollock*

FURIOUS [1] paddle frigate; 1,287; 1850–67 *Fisher*
      [2] 2nd-class cruiser; 5,750; 1896–1915 *Cork and Orrery*

FURY paddle sloop; 1,124; 1845–64 *Commerell*

GALATEA [1] 5th-rate; 947; 1810–36 *Keppel*
       [2] frigate; 3,227; 1859–83 *Alfred, Duke of Edinburgh*
       [3] light cruiser; 3,500; 1914–21 *Charles Forbes*
       [4] cruiser; 5,220; 1934–41 *Cunningham of Hyndhope;
Pound; Somerville; Tovey*
       [5] frigate; 2,350; 1964–88 *Leach*

GANGES [1] 3rd-rate; 1,679; 1782–1811 *Thomas Martin*
      [2] 2nd-rate; 2,248; 1821–65 *Milne; Richards*

GARLAND 6th-rate; 375; 1724–44 *Anson*

GARNET corvette (3rd-class cruiser); 2,120; 1877–1904 *Erskine*

GIBRALTAR 1st-class cruiser; 7,700; 1892–1914 *John Cunningham*

GIPSY destroyer; 380; 1897–1921 *Fraser*

GLADIATOR paddle frigate; 1,190; 1844–79 *Wilson*

GLASGOW cruiser; 9,100; 1936–58 *Begg; Mountbatten; Pollock*

GLOIRE 5th-rate; 1,153; 1806–12 *Wallis*

GLORIOUS aircraft carrier; 18,600; 1930–40 *Fraser; John*

GLORY [1] 5th-rate; 748; 1747–63 *Howe*
       [2] 2nd-rate; 1,932; 1788–1809 *Austen; George Martin*
       [3] battleship; 12,950; 1899–1920 *Noel; Willis*

GLOUCESTER 4th-rate; 968; 1747–63 *Hawke; St Vincent*

GOLIATH [1] 3rd-rate; 1,604; 1781–1815 *Gordon*
         [2] battleship; 12,950; 1898–1915 *Fraser*

GOOD HOPE armoured cruiser; 14,100; 1901–14 *Burney; Cork and Orrery; Chatfield; Madden; Tyrwhitt; Willis*

GOSPORT 5th-rate; 691; 1741–68 *St Vincent*

GRAFTON 1st-class cruiser; 7,350; 1892–1920 *Pound*

GRAMPUS 4th-rate; 1,114; 1802–20 *Cockburn*

GRENVILLE destroyer flotilla leader; 1,485; 1935–40 *Creasy*

GREYHOUND [1] 5th-rate; 494; 1703–11 *Steuart*
           [2] 5th-rate; 682; 1783–1808 *Charles Ogle*
           [3] sloop; 880 (1,260); 1859–69 *Hornby*

GROWLER gunvessel; 584; 1868–87 *Edward Seymour*

GUERNSEY 4th-rate; 863; 1698–1769 *John Forbes*

HALCYON torpedo gunboat; 1,070; 1894–1920 *Gough-Calthorpe*

HAMPSHIRE 4th-rate; 690; 1698–1739 *Anson*

HANNIBAL [1] 2nd-rate; 3,136 (4,735); 1854–74 *Mundy*
        [2] battleship; 14,000; 1896–1920 *Cunningham of
        Hyndhope; Fraser*

HART torpedo-boat destroyer; 295; 1895–1912 *Keyes; Tyrwhitt*

HAUGHTY [1] gunboat; 232; 1856–67 *Elliot*
        [2] destroyer; 290; 1895–1912 *Cork and Orrery*

HAWKE 1st class cruiser; 7,350; 1891–1914 *Burney; Cunningham of
        Hyndhope; Kelly*

HAWKINS cruiser; 9,750; 1917–47 *Lambe; Tyrwhitt*

HAZARD [1] sloop; 431, 1837–66 *Elliot*
        [2] torpedo gunboat; 1,070; 1894–1918 *Cork and Orrery*

HEBE [1] 5th-rate; 1,063; 1782–1811 *Cockburn; West; William IV*
      [2] torpedo gunboat; 810; 1892–1919; *John Cunningham*

HECLA torpedo depot ship; 6,400; 1878–1926 *Sturdee; Wemyss; Wilson*

HERCULES [1] battleship; 5,234 (8,680); 1868–81 *Alfred, Duke of
        Edinburgh; Clanwilliam; Fisher; Kerr; May*
        [2] battleship; 20,000; 1910–21 *Callaghan; Jellicoe*

HERMES [1] aircraft carrier; 10,950; 1919–42 *John*
       [2] aircraft carrier; 22,500; 1953–86 *Ashmore; Fieldhouse;
       Le Fanu; Lewin*

HERMIONE 2nd-class cruiser; 4,360; 1893–1921 *Callaghan; Kelly;
        Wilson*

HIBERNIA [1] 1st-rate; 2,530; 1804–55 *Moresby; William Parker; St
        Vincent*
        [2] battleship; 16,350; 1905–21 *Cork and Orrery*

HIGHFLYER [1] frigate; 1,1153; 1851–71 *Fisher*
        [2] 2nd-class cruiser; 5,600; 1898–1921 *McGrigor*

HIGHLANDER destroyer; 1,340; 1939–46 *Lewin*

HILARY amphibious landing HQ ship; 8,036, 1938–49 *Vian*

HINDOSTAN battleship; 16,350; 1903–21 *Edward VIII; Gough-
        Calthorpe; Willis*

HONG KONG river paddle steamer; 1856–58 *Keppel*

HOOD battle-cruiser; 41,200; 1918–41 *Cunningham of Hyndhope; John Cunningham; Pound; Power; Somerville*

HORNET sloop; 753; 1854–68 *Clanwilliam*

HOTSPUR armoured ram (turret ship); 2,637 (4,010); 1870–1904 *Hay*

HOUGHTON minesweeper; 360; 1957–71 *Staveley*

HOWE [1] store-ship; 1,048; 1805–19 *Cockburn*
　　　 [2] battleship; 35,000; 1940–58 *Hill-Norton; Le Fanu*

HUSSAR [1] 6th-rate; 627; 1763–80 *Pole*
　　　　 [2] 5th-rate; 1,077; 1807–33 *Charles Ogle; Stewart*
　　　　 [3] torpedo gunboat; 170; 1894–1920 *Cork and Orrery; Wemyss*

HYDRA 5th-rate; 1,017; 1797–1820 *Bowles*

ICARUS sloop; 580; 1858–1904 *Salmon*

ILLUSTRIOUS [1] 3rd-rate; 1,746; 1789–95 *Pole*
　　　　　　　 [2] battleship; 14,900; 1896–1920 *Callaghan; John Cunningham*
　　　　　　　 [3] aircraft carrier; 23,000; 1939–56 *Mountbatten*

IMMORTALITE [1] frigate; 3,984; 1859–83 *Lyons; Noel*
　　　　　　　 [2] armoured cruiser; 5,600; 1887–1907 *Burney*

IMPERIEUSE [1] 5th-rate; 1,046; 1804–38 *Stewart*
　　　　　　　[2] frigate; 2,147; 1852–67 *Clanwilliam; Edward Seymour*
　　　　　　　[3] armoured cruiser; 8,400; 1883–1905 *De Robeck; Field; Gough-Calthorpe; Charles Forbes; May; Salmon*

IMPETUEUX 3rd-rate; 1,884; 1794–1813 *George Martin; Thomas Martin*

IMPLACABLE [1] 3rd-rate; 1,882; 1805–55 *Cockburn; Thomas Martin*
　　　　　　　[2] battleship; 15,000; 1899–1921 *Cunningham of Hyndhope; Milford Haven; Wemyss*
　　　　　　　[3] aircraft carrier; 26,000; 1944–55 *Ashmore; Vian*

IMPREGNABLE 2nd-rate; 2,406; 1810–62 *Thomas Martin; William IV*

293

INCONSTANT [1] 5th-rate; 890; 1783–1817 *Cockburn; Thomas Martin*
[2] frigate; 4,066 (5,700); 1868–98 *Clanwilliam; George V; May; Milford Haven*

INDEFATIGABLE 2nd-class cruiser; 3,600; 1891–1913 *John Cunningham; Tyrwhitt*

INDOMITABLE [1] battle-cruiser; 17,250; 1907–21 *Power*
[2] aircraft carrier; 23,000; 1940–55 *Staveley; Vian*

INDUS 3rd-rate; 1,756; 1812–40 *Gage*

INFLEXIBLE [1] battleship; 11,880; 1876–1903 *Fisher; Edward Seymour*
[2] battle-cruiser; 17,250; 1907–21 *De Robeck; Edward Seymour; Somerville*

INTREPID assault ship; 10,000; 1964- *Ashmore; Staveley*

INVINCIBLE [1] 3rd-rate; 1,631; 1765–1801 *Gordon*
[2] battle-cruiser; 17,250; 1907–16 *Sturdee*

IPHIGENIA [1] 5th-rate; 870; 1808–33 *Curtis*
[2] 2nd-class cruiser; 3,600; 1910–18 *John Cunningham*

IRIS [1] 6th-rate; 906; 1840–69 *Mundy*
[2] 2nd-class cruiser; 3,730; 1877–1905 *Edward Seymour*

IRON DUKE [1] battleship; 6,010; 1870–1906 *Chatfield*
[2] battleship; 25,000; 1912–32 *Backhouse; Beatty; Brock; Callaghan; De Robeck; Charles Forbes; Gough-Calthorpe; Jellicoe; John; Madden*

IRRESISTIBLE 3rd-rate; 1,643; 1782–1806 *Hamond; George Martin*

ISIS 4th-rate; 1,051; 1774–1810 *George Seymour*

JACKAL destroyer; 745; 1911–20 *Tovey*

JALOUSE brig-sloop; 384; 1797–1807 *Curtis*

JAMES WATT 2nd-rate; 3,083; 1853–75 *Salmon*

JASEUR [1] brig-sloop; 387; 1813–45 *Mundy*
[2] gun-vessel; 427; 1862–74 *Hotham*

JASON 5th-rate; 661; 1804–15 *Cochrane*

JAVELIN destroyer flotilla leader; 1,690; 1938–41 *Mountbatten*

JERSEY 4th-rate; 1,065; 1736–71 *Chaloner Ogle*

JEWEL minesweeper; 860; 1944–67 *Oswald*

JUMNA Indian troopship; 4,173 (6,211); 1866–97 *Fanshawe*

JUNO [1] 5th-rate; 689; 1780–1811 *Mundy; Thomas Martin*
      [2] 2nd-class cruiser; 5,600, 1895–1920 *Beatty*

JUPITER destroyer; 1,760; 1939–41 *Ashmore, Mountbatten*

KATOOMBA 3rd-class cruiser; 2,575; 1889–1906 *Kelly*

KELLY destroyer flotilla leader; 1,695; 1938–41 *Mountbatten*

KEMPENFELDT destroyer flotilla leader; 1,390; 1931–45 *McGrigor*

KENT [1] 3rd-rate; 1,617; 1762–84 *St Vincent; Whitshed*
      [2] 3rd-rate; 1,694; 1798–1856 *Moresby*
      [3] cruiser; 9, 850; 1926–48 *McGrigor; Philip, Duke of Edinburgh; Vian; Willis*
      [4] guided missile destroyer; 5,600; 1961–80 *Ashmore; Hill-Norton*

KEPPEL destroyer flotilla leader; 1,861; 1915–45 *Vian*

KING ALFRED armoured cruiser; 14,100; 1901–20 *Meux; Tovey*

KING EDWARD VII battleship; 16,350; 1903–16 *Brock; Burney; Callaghan; May; Milford Haven; Pound; Power; Sturdee*

KING GEORGE V; battleship; 23,000; 1911–26 *De Robeck; Field; Lambe; Oliver; Somerville*

KINGFISHER sloop; 370; 1804–16 *George Seymour*

KINGSALE (KINSALE) 5th-rate; 762; 1703–39 *Hawke*

KINGSTON 4th-rate; 1,068; 1697–1762 *Hawke, Chaloner Ogle*

LANCASTER [1] 3rd-rate; 1,430; 1797–1815 *Curtis*
        [2] armoured cruiser; 9,800; 1902–20 *Fraser*

LARK sloop; 423; 1794–1809 *Austen*

LEANDER [1] 4th-rate; 1,045; 1780–1806 *Bowles*
       [2] 4th-rate; 1,572; 1813–30 *Milne*
       [3] cruiser; 7,270; 1931–49 *Fraser*
       [4] frigate; 2,350; 1961–89 *Ashmore*

LEONIDAS 5th-rate; 1,067; 1807–72 *George Seymour*

LEOPARD [1] 4th-rate; 762; 1703–39 *Hawke*
       [2] 4th-rate; 1,045; 1790–1814 *Austen*

LEVIATHAN [1] 3rd-rate; 1,707; 1790–1816 *William Parker*
         [2] armoured cruiser; 14,100; 1902–20 *Callaghan; Meux*

LIFFEY frigate; 2,126; 1856–77 *May*

LIGAERA (LIGERA) 6th-rate; 440; 1804–14 *Gordon*

LION [1] 3rd-rate; 906; 1709–38 *John Forbes*
    [2] 3rd-rate; 1,378; 1777–1816 *Hamond*
    [3] battle-cruiser; 26,350; 1912–24 *Backhouse; Beatty; Chatfield; Cork and Orrery; John Cunningham; Mountbatten*

LIVELY [1] 6th-rate; 279; 1713–38 *Rowley*
     [2] 6th-rate; 438; 1756–84 *Freeman*
     [3] 5th-rate; 806; 1794–98 *St Vincent*
     [4] 5th-rate; 1,076; 1804–10 *Hamond*
     [5] paddle despatch vessel; 985; 1870–83 *Edward Seymour*
     [6] torpedo-boat destroyer; 400; 1900–22 *Creasy*

LIVERPOOL frigate; 2,656; 1860–75 *Hornby*

LIZARD gunboat; 715; 1886–1905 *Cork and Orrery*

LOCUST torpedo-boat destroyer; 385; 1896–1919 *Cunningham of Hyndhope*

LONDON [1] 2nd-rate; 1,871; 1766–1811 *Austen; Moresby; West; William IV*
        [2] battleship; 15,000; 1899–1920 *Chatfield*
        [3] cruiser; 9,850; 1927–50 *Hill-Norton*
        [4] guided missile destroyer; 5,600; 1961–82 *Lewin*

LONDONDERRY frigate; 2,150; 1958–89 *Ashmore*

LORD NELSON battleship; 16,500; 1906–20 *Burney; Vian; Wemyss*

LORD WARDEN battleship; 4,080; 1865–89 *Kerr*

LURCHER destroyer; 765; 1912–22 *Keyes*

MACKAY destroyer flotilla leader; 1,861; 1915–45 *Vian*

MADAGASCAR [1] 5th-rate; 1,114; 1811–19 *Curtis; Gordon*
                 [2] 5th-rate; 1,167; 1822–53 *Codrington; Elliot;*
                      Wallis

MADRAS 4th-rate; 1,426; 1795–1803 *George Seymour*

MAEANDER [1] 6th-rate; 1,067; 1813–17 *Gordon*
            [2] 5th-rate; 1,221; 1840–59 *Keppel*

MAGICIENNE [1] 5th-rate; 968; 1781–1810 *Curtis; William Parker;*
               George Martin
              [2] 5th-rate; 949; 1831–45 *Keppel*
              [3] paddle frigate; 1,258; 1849–66 *Commerell*

MAGNANIME 3rd-rate; 1,823; 1748–75 *Freeman; Howe*

MAGNIFICENT battleship; 14,900; 1894–1918 *Fanshawe; Charles*
                Forbes; Meux; Pound; Power; Willis

MAGPIE sloop (later frigate); 1,350; 1943–59 *Philip, Duke of Edinburgh*

MAIDSTONE 5th-rate; 947; 1811–32 *Hope*

MAJESTIC [1] 2nd-rate; 2,589; 1853–68 *Hope*
         [2] battleship; 14,900; 1895–1915 *Kerr; Milford Haven;*
              Oliver; Tovey; Wilson

MALABAR [1] 3rd-rate; 1,715; 1818–48 *Sartorius*
          [2] Indian troopship; 4,173 (6,211); 1866–1901 *Fanshawe*

MALAYA battleship; 27,500; 1915–48 *Backhouse; George VI; John;*
          McGrigor; Somerville

MALCOLM destroyer flotilla leader; 1,804; 1919–45 *Creasy*

MALTA 2nd-rate; 1,670; 1785–1831 *Charles Ogle*

MANILLA 5th-rate; 947; 1809–12 *George Seymour*

MARGATE 6th-rate; 438; 1746–49 *Peter Parker*

MARLBOROUGH [1] 2nd-rate; 1,567; 1732–63 *Clinton*
[2] 3rd-rate; 1,754; 1807–35 *Cockburn*
[3] battleship; 25,000; 1912–32 *Begg; Burney;
Field; Madden; Somerville*

MAURITIUS cruiser; 8,530; 1939–65 *Leach*

MEDINA royal yacht (chartered passenger liner); 12,500; 1911 *Chatfield*

MEDUSA [1] 4th-rate; 910; 1785–98 *Charles Ogle*
[2] 5th-rate; 910; 1801–13 *Bowles; Stewart*

MELAMPUS 5th-rate; 947; 1785–1815 *Pole*

MELEAGER 5th-rate; 682; 1785–1801 *Cockburn; Charles Ogle*

MELVILLE brig-sloop; 353; 1805-08 *Cochrane*

MENAI 6th-rate; 449; 1814–31 *Moresby; Stewart*

MERCURY 6th-rate; 594; 1779–1814 *Gordon*

MERMAID destroyer; 335; 1898–1919 *De Robeck*

MERSEY frigate; 3,733; 1858–75 *Edward Seymour*

MIDDLETON destroyer; 1,050; 1941–55 *Ashmore*

MILAN 5th-rate; 1,086; 1805–1815 *Bowles; Wallis*

MILNE destroyer; 1,110; 1914–21 *Creasy*

MINERVA [1] 5th-rate, 929; 1780–1803 *Austen*
[2] 2nd-class cruiser; 5,600; 1895–1920 *Fraser*
[3] frigate; 2,350; 1964–84 *Bathurst*

MINERVE 5th-rate; 1,102; 1795–1814 *Cockburn; Gage; Charles Ogle*

MINOTAUR armoured ship; 6,621 (10,690); 1863–1904 *Alfred, Duke of
Edinburgh; Field; Fisher; Hay; Hornby; Jellicoe; Madden; Noel*

MONARCH [1] 3rd-rate; 1,612; 1765–1813 *George Martin*
[2] armoured turret ship; 5,102 (8,320); 1868–97
Commerell; Cork and Orrery; Jellicoe; Lyons

MONCKE 4th-rate; 684; 1659–1720 *Clinton; Norris*

MODESTE 5th-rate; 940; 1793–1814 *Thomas Martin*

MONMOUTH 3rd-rate; 944; 1700–16 *Anson*

MONTAGUE [1] 4th-rate; 914; 1716–49 *Anson*
　　　　　　[2] 3rd-rate; 1,631; 1779–1818 *George Martin*

MONTROSE destroyer flotilla leader; 1,800; 1918–46 *McGrigor*

MORNING STAR destroyer; 1,025; 1915–21 *Vian*

NAIAD [1] 5th-rate; 1,020; 1797–1847 *Codrington; Sartorius*
　　　　[2] cruiser; 4,450; 1939–42 *Vian*
　　　　[3] frigate; 2,350; 1963–90 *Oswald*

NAMUR 2nd-rate; 1,814; 1756–1807 *Gordon; Whitshed*

NARCISSUS frigate; 2,665; 1859–83 *Elliot; Wilson*

NELSON [1] armoured ship; 7,320; 1876–1902 *Erskine*
　　　　　[2] battleship; 33,500; 1925–49 *Backhouse; Begg;*
　　　　　　Chatfield; Cork and Orrery; Charles Forbes; Kelly; McGrigor;
　　　　　　Pollock; Somerville; Willis

NEPTUNE [1] 2nd-rate; 1,573; 1730–84 *Hawke; Peter Parker;*
　　　　　　　St Vincent
　　　　　[2] 2nd-rate; 2,111; 1797–1813 *Austen; Gambier*
　　　　　[3] 1st-rate; 2,830; 1832–75 *Hornby; Kerr*
　　　　　[4] battleship; 19,900; 1909–22 *Backhouse; Callaghan*
　　　　　[5] cruiser; 7,175; 1933–41 *John Cunningham*

NEW ZEALAND battleship (renamed ZEALANDIA in 1911); 16,350;
　　　　　1904–21 *Sturdee*

NEWCASTLE [1] frigate; 3,053; 1860–89 *Jellicoe; May*
　　　　　　　[2] cruiser; 9,100; 1936–59 *Leach; Mountbatten;*
　　　　　　　Pollock
　　　　　　　[3] guided missile destroyer; 3,850; 1975- *Oswald*

NEWFOUNDLAND cruiser; 8,800; 1941–59 *Ashmore; Oswald*

NIEMAN 6th-rate; 502; 1820–28 *Wallis*

NIGER 5th-rate; 679; 1759–1810 *Hamond*

NIGERIA cruiser; 8,000; 1939–57 *Hill-Norton; Staveley; Vian*

NILE [1] 2nd-rate; 2,598; 1839–76 *Mundy*
    [2] battleship; 11,940; 1888–1912 *Beatty; Noel*

NIMROD sloop; 395; 1799–1811 *Cochrane*

NIOBE 1st-class cruiser; 11,000; 1897–1922 *Oliver; Wemyss*

NONSUCH destroyer; 1,025; 1915–21 *Creasy*

NORFOLK [1] 3rd-rate; 1,393; 1693–1777 *John Forbes*
    [2] cruiser; 9,925; 1928–50 *Fieldhouse; Leach; McGrigor;*
    Pollock; Somerville
    [3] guided missile destroyer; 5,600; 1967–82 *Bathurst*

NORTHAMPTON armoured ship; 7,630; 1876–1905 *Cunningham of*
    Hyndhope; Fisher; Gough-Calthorpe

NORTHUMBERLAND [1] 3rd-rate; 1,907; 1798–1827 *Cochrane;*
    Cockburn; George Martin; George Seymour
    [2] armoured ship; 6,621 (10,780);
    1866–98 *George V; Hay; Wemyss*

NOTTINGHAM 4th-rate; 928; 1719–73 *Clinton; St Vincent*

OBSERVATEUR brig-sloop; 303; 1806–14 *Wallis*

OCEAN [1] armoured ship; 4,047 (6,832); 1863–82 *Fanshawe;*
    Fisher; Hornby
    [2] aircraft carrier; 13,190; 1944–62 *John*

ODIN paddle frigate; 1,326; 1846–65 *Hay*

OISEAU 5th-rate; 913; 1793–1810 *William Parker; Wallis*

OLMEDA fleet auxiliary (tanker); 10,980 (36,000 fully laden); 1964–95
    Lewin

ONSLOW destroyer; 1,025; 1916–21 *Tovey*

OPHELIA destroyer; 1,025; 1915–21 *Cunningham of Hyndhope*

OPPOSSUM destroyer; 320; 1895–1920 *Keyes; Pound*

ORESTES [1] brig-sloop; 367; 1781–99 *Cockburn*
    [2] sloop; 460; 1824–52 *Codrington*

ORFORD 3rd-rate; 1,326; 1698–1709 *Norris; Rowley*

ORION [1] 3rd-rate; 1,646; 1787–1814 *William Parker*
     [2] battleship; 22,500; 1910–22 *Wemyss*
     [3] cruiser; 7,215; 1932–49 *Tovey*

ORONTES Indian troopship; 5,600; 1862–93 *Edward Seymour*

ORWELL torpedo-boat destroyer; 360; 1898–1920 *Cunningham of Hyndhope*

OSBORNE royal yacht; 1,860; 1870–1908 *Meux; Milford Haven; Wemyss*

P31 patrol boat; 613; 1916–26 *Mountbatten*

PALLAS [1] 5th-rate; 667; 1804–19 *George Seymour*
     [2] corvette (3rd-class cruiser); 2,372; (3,661); 1865–86 *Fisher*

PANTHER destroyer; 360; 1897–1920 *Backhouse*

PATROL scout cruiser; 2,940; 1904–20 *Tovey*

PEARL [1] 4th-rate; 595; 1708–44 *Howe*
     [2] 5th-rate; 683; 1762–1832 *Cockburn*
     [3] corvette (3rd-class cruiser); 1,469; 1855–84 *Fisher*

PEGASUS 6th-rate; 594; 1779–1816 *Thomas Martin; William IV*

PELICAN [1] fireship; 200; 1690-92 *Norris*
     [2] brig-sloop; 365; 1795–1806 *William Parker*

PEMBROKE 3rd-rate; 1,758; 1812–58 *Moresby*

PENELOPE corvette (3rd-class cruiser); 3,096 (4,394); 1867–97 *Alfred, Duke of Edinburgh*

PERSEVERANCE 5th-rate; 572; 1781–1806 *Austen*

PETEREL (PETREL) sloop; 361; 1794–1811 *Austen; Charles Ogle*

PHAETON [1] 5th-rate; 944; 1782–1827 *Cockburn; Hamond; Mundy*
     [2] light cruiser; 3,500; 1914–23 *Cork and Orrery*

PHOEBE cruiser; 5,450; 1939–56 *Begg*

PIQUE [1] 5th-rate; 1,028; 1800–19 *Stewart*
       [2] 5th-rate; 1,633; 1834–72 *Edward Seymour*

PLANTAGENET 3rd-rate; 1,770; 1801–17 *Hamond*

PLOVER [1] sloop; 422; 1796–1819 *Cockburn*
        [2] gunboat; 232; 1855–59 *Hope*

PLYMOUTH 4th-rate; 922; 1708–64 *Chaloner Ogle*

PODARGUS brig-sloop; 254; 1808–33 *Stewart*

POLYPHEMUS torpedo-ram; 2,640; 1881–1903 *May*

POMONA 6th-rate; 594; 1778–1811 *Nugent; West*

POMPEE 3rd-rate; 1,901; 1793–1817 *Cockburn*

POOLE 5th-rate; fireship; 381; 1696–1737 *John Forbes*

PORCUPINE [1] sloop; 314; 1746–63 *St Vincent*
           [2] 6th-rate; 520; 1777–1805 *George Martin*

PORPOISE torpedo cruiser; 1,770; 1886–1905 *Sturdee*

PORT MAHON 6th-rate; 277; 1711–40 *John Forbes*

PORTLAND 4th-rate; 772; 1693–1743 *Hawke*

POWERFUL [1] 2nd-rate; 2,296; 1826–60 *Hay*
          [2] 1st-class cruiser; 14,200; 1895–1919 *Meux*

PRESIDENT 4th-rate; 1,537; 1829–62 *Cockburn*

PRESTON; 4th-rate; 1,044; 1757–85 *George Martin*

PRETORIA CASTLE trials aircraft carrier; 19,650; 1943–46 *John*

PREVOYANTE 5th-rate; 803; 1795–1809 *Wallis*

PRINCE [1] 2nd-rate; 1,677; 1750–75 *St Vincent*
        [2] 2nd-rate; 2,080; 1788–1837 *Curtis; St Vincent*

PRINCE FREDERICK [1] 3rd-rate; 1,111; 1699–1740 *Clinton*
                  [2] 3rd-rate; 1,270; 1796–1817 *Thomas Martin*

PRINCE GEORGE [1] 2nd-rate; 1,567; 1723–50 *Anson*
[2] 2nd-rate; 1,935; 1772–1817 *Austen;*
Gambier; William IV
[3] battleship; 14,900; 1895–1921 *Fraser*

PRINCE OF WALES [1] 2nd-rate; 2,010; 1794–1822 *Thomas*
Martin; George Seymour
[2] battleship; 15,000; 1902–20 *Burney;*
Callaghan; Jellicoe; Milford Haven

PRINCE REGENT [1] royal yacht; 282; 1820–36 *William Parker*
[2] 1st-rate; 2,613; 1823–73 *Codrington; Kerr;*
William Parker

PRINCESS AMELIA 3rd-rate; 1,579; 1757–88 *Freeman; Howe; Williams*

PRINCESS AUGUSTA royal yacht; 184; 1773–1818 *Charles Ogle;*
George Seymour

PRINCESS CHARLOTTE 1st-rate; 2,443; 1825–58 *Hornby*

PRINCESS ROYAL [1] 2nd-rate; 1,973; 1773–1807 *Gage; George*
Martin
[2] 2nd-rate; 3,129; 1853–72 *Kerr*
[3] battle-cruiser; 26,350; 1911- 22 *Beatty;*
Brock; Kelly; Power

PROSERPINE 6th-rate; 596; 1777–99 *Gage*

PUISSANT 3rd-rate; 1,794; 1793–1816 *Moresby*

PYRAMUS [1] 5th-rate; 920; 1810–32 *Mundy; Sartorius*
[2] 3rd-class cruiser; 2,135; 1897–1920 *De Robeck*

QUEEN [1] 2nd-rate; 1,867; 1769–1821 *George Martin; William Parker*
[2] 1st-rate; 3,104; 1839–71 *Codrington; William Parker;*
West
[3] battleship; 15,000; 1902–20 *Backhouse; Beatty; Burney;*
Pound

QUEEN CHARLOTTE 1st-rate; 2,289; 1790–1800 *Curtis; Hamond;*
Howe; Stewart; Whitshed

QUEEN ELIZABETH battleship; 27,500; 1913–48 *Beatty; Brock;*
Chatfield; Creasy; Cunningham of Hyndhope; John

Cunningham; De Robeck; Charles Forbes; Madden;
Mountbatten; Pound; Somerville

QUEENBOROUGH 6th-rate; 262; 1694–1719 *Chaloner Ogle*

RACER [1] brig-sloop; 431; 1833–52 *Hope*
       [2] sloop; 579; 1857–76 *Lyons*

RACOON [1] brig-sloop; 317; 1795–1806 *Gordon*
        [2] corvette (3rd-class cruiser); 1,467; 1857–77 *Alfred,*
           Duke of Edinburgh

RAGLAN monitor; 6,150; 1915–18 *Power*

RAINBOW 5th-rate; 831; 1747–84 *Freeman; Whitshed*

RALEIGH [1] 5th-rate; 697; 1778–83 *Gambier*
        [2] frigate; 1,939; 1845–57 *Clanwilliam; Keppel; Wilson*
        [3] frigate; 3,215 (5,200); 1873–1905 *Brock; Keyes;*
           Madden; Wilson
        [4] light cruiser; 9,750; 1919–22 *Lambe*

RAMILLIES [1] 2nd-rate; 1,689; 1664–1760 *Hawke*
          [2] 3rd-rate; 1,670; 1785–1831 *Gordon; Milne; Charles*
            Ogle
          [3] battleship; 14,150; 1892–1913 *Brock; Jellicoe; May*
          [4] battleship; 25,750 (29,150); 1916–48
            Hill-Norton, Philip, Duke of Edinburgh

RANELAGH 2nd-rate; 1,199; 1697–1764 (later renamed PRINCESS
    CAROLINE) *Norris*

RANGER sloop; 142; 1752–83 *Whitshed*

RATTLER sloop; 950; 1862–68 *Noel*

RATTLESNAKE [1] 6th-rate; 503; 1822–45 *Symonds*
             [2] corvette (3rd-class cruiser); 1,705 (2,431);
               1861–82 *Commerell*
             [3] destroyer; 946; 1910–21 *Cunningham of*
               Hyndhope

RELENTLESS destroyer (after 1950, frigate); 2,300; 1942–71 *Le Fanu*

RENOWN [1] battleship; 12,350; 1895–1914 *Brock; Fisher*
        [2] battle-cruiser; 26,500; 1916–48 *John Cunningham;*

Fraser; *John*; *McGrigor*; *Mountbatten*; *Pound*; *Power*;
Somerville; *Willis*

REPULSE [1] 3rd-rate; 1,727; 1803–20 *Moresby*
        [2] 2nd-rate; 6,190 (3,749);1853–73 *Burney*
        [3] battleship; 14,150; 1892–1911 *Backhouse*; *Brock*
        [4] battle-cruiser; 26,500; 1916–41 *Cork and Orrery*;
          Oliver; *Mountbatten*; *Pound*

RESOLUTION battleship; 25,750 (29,150); 1915–45 *Cork and Orrery*;
          John Cunningham; *Fraser*; *Mountbatten*; *Willis*

RESTORATION 3rd-rate; 1,018; 1678–1703 *Chaloner Ogle*

REVENGE [1] 3rd-rate; 1,954; 1805- 49 *Stewart*
        [2] battleship; 14,150; 1892–1919 *Noel*; *Wilson*
        [3] battleship; 25,750 (29,150); 1915–48
          Backhouse; *Burney*; *Field*; *Charles Forbes*; *Madden*;
          Mountbatten

REVOLUTIONNAIRE 5th-rate; 1,148; 1794–1822 *Gordon*

RIFLEMAN brig-sloop; 387; 1809–36 *Stewart*

RIPPON (RIPON) [1] 4th-rate; 1,021; 1712–51 *Howe*
               [2] 4th-rate; 1,229; 1758–1801 *Pole*

RIVOLI 3rd-rate; 1,804; 1812–19 *Hamond*; *Charles Ogle*

ROCHFORT 2nd-rate; 2,082; 1814–26 *Mundy*

RODNEY [1] 3rd-rate; 1,754; 1809–36 *George Martin*
        [2] 2nd-rate; (rebuilt as screw ship); 2,770;
          1833–84 *Elliot*; *Keppel*; *Wilson*
        [3] battleship; 34,000; 1925–48 *Ashmore*; *Backhouse*;
          Chatfield; *Creasy*; *Cunningham of Hyndhope*; *Charles*
          Forbes; *Fraser*; *Hill-Norton*; *Leach*; *Somerville*; *Tovey*

ROEBUCK destroyer; 400; 1901–21 *Cunningham of Hyndhope*

ROMNEY 4th-rate; 1,046; 1762–1804 *Cockburn*; *Freeman*; *West*;
          Whitshed

ROSE [1] 6th-rate; 594; 1783–94 *Whitshed*
     [2] sloop; 367; 1805–17 *Curtis*

ROTHESAY frigate; 2,150; 1957–88 *Ashmore*

ROVER [1] sloop; 316; 1777–80 *George Martin*
     [2] sloop; 590; 1832–45 *Symonds*
     [3] corvette (3rd-class cruiser); 3,460; 1874–93
        Gough-Calthorpe; Jackson; Noel

ROXBURGH armoured cruiser; 10,850; 1904–21 *Gough-Calthorpe*

ROYAL ALBERT 1st-rate; 3,726 (5,517); 1854–84 *Lyons*

ROYAL ALFRED armoured ship; 4,068 (6,707), 1864–84 *Fanshawe;*
        Milford Haven

ROYAL ARTHUR 1st-class cruiser; 7,700; 1891–1920 *Fanshawe; Kelly;*
        Power; Somerville

ROYAL GEORGE [1] 1st-rate; 1,801; 1673–1767 (renamed
           ROYAL ANNE 1756) *Howe; St Vincent*
        [2] 1st-rate; 2,066; 1756–82 *Anson; Hawke*
        [3] 1st-rate; 2,286; 1788–1822 *Thomas Martin;*
           Moresby; Pole; St Vincent; West
        [4] 1st-rate; 2,616; 1827–75 *Codrington*

ROYAL KATHERINE 2nd-rate; 1664–1702 *Aylmer*

ROYAL OAK [1] 3rd-rate; 1,017; 1674–1764 *Norris; Chaloner Ogle*
       [2] battleship, 14,150; 1892–1914 *Charles Forbes*

ROYAL SOVEREIGN [1] royal yacht; 278; 1804–49 *Thomas Martin*
         [2] battleship; 14,150; 1891–1913 *Chatfield;*
           Madden; Pound

ROYAL WILLIAM 1st-rate; 1,918; 1719–1813 *Stewart*

ROYALIST brig-sloop; 385; 1807–19 *Stewart*

RUBY [1] 4th-rate; 704; 1708–48 *Anson*
    [2] corvette (3rd-class cruiser); 2120; 1876–1904 *Beatty,*
    Callaghan; Hotham; Madden

RUSSELL [1] 2nd-rate; 1,188; 1692–1762 *Norris; Chaloner Ogle;*
       Peter Parker
       [2] 3rd-rate; 1,462; 1764–1811 *George Martin*
       [3] battleship; 14,000; 1901–16 *Backhouse; John*
       Cunningham

SABRINA 6th-rate; 427; 1806–16 *George Martin*

ST ALBANS 3rd-rate; 1,366; 1764–1814 *Austen*

ST GEORGE [1] 1st-rate; 1,655; 1687–1774 *Hawke; St Vincent*
         [2] 2nd-rate; 1,950; 1765–1811 *Pole*
         [3] 1st-rate(after 1859, screw ship); 2,864; 1840–83
             Alfred, Duke of Edinburgh; Hay
         [4] 1st-class cruiser; 7,700; 1892–1920
             Gough-Calthorpe

ST JEAN D'ACRE 1st-rate; 3,199; 1853–75 *Keppel*

ST VINCENT [1] 1st-rate; 2,601; 1815–62 *Codrington; Milne*
           [2] battleship; 19,250; 1908–21 *Gough-Calthorpe;*
               Madden; Pound; Sturdee

SALISBURY [1] 4th-rate; 1,051; 1769–96 *Pole; West*
          [2] 4th-rate; 1,199; 1814–37 *Stewart*

SAN ANTONIO sloop; 67; 1700–07 *Chaloner Ogle*

SAN JOSEF 1st-rate; 2,457; 1797–1837 *Stewart*

SAN VINCENTE sloop; 276; 1780–83 *Whitshed*

SANDWICH 2nd-rate; 1759–90 *George Martin; Peter Parker; Whitshed*

SANSPAREIL (SANS PAREIL) [1] 3rd-rate; 2,245; 1794–1810
                             George Seymour
                         [2] battleship; 10,470; 1887–1902
                             Jellicoe; Wilson

SANTA MARGARETA 5th-rate; 993; 1779–1817 *Thomas Martin*

SAPPHO 2nd-class cruiser; 3,400; 1891–1921 *Burney*

SATURN 3rd-rate; 1,646; 1782–1825 *West*

SAUMAREZ destroyer flotilla leader; 1,673; 1916–31 *Willis*

SCARBOROUGH 6th-rate; 378; 1711–39 *Anson; Hawke*

SCEPTRE 3rd-rate; 1,727; 1802–21 *Cockburn*

SCORPION [1] sloop; 276; 1746–62 *St Vincent*
          [2] sloop; 294; 1771–80 *Nugent*
          [3] turret ship; 1,857; 1845–64 *Commerell*
          [4] destroyer; 916; 1910–21 *Cunningham of Hyndhope*

SCOUT torpedo cruiser; 1,580; 1885–1904 *Milford Haven*

SCYLLA [1] 2nd-class cruiser; 3,400; 1891–1914 *Cunningham of Hyndhope*
       [2] cruiser; 5,450; 1940–50 *Vian*

SEAFIRE destroyer; 1,075; 1918–36 *Cunningham of Hyndhope*

SEAHORSE [1] 6th-rate; 282; 1712–48 *Hawke*
          [2] 6th-rate; 519; 1748–84 *Pole*
          [3] 5th-rate; 984; 1794–1819 *Austen; Gordon*

SERAPIS troopship; 4,173 (6,211); 1866–94 *Burney; Milford Haven*

SEVERN [1] 4th-rate; 853; 1695–1747 *John Forbes; Howe*
       [2] 4th-rate; 1,061; 1747–59 *St Vincent*

SHAKESPEARE destroyer flotilla leader; 1,750; 1917–36 *Cunningham of Hyndhope*

SHANNON [1] 5th-rate; 800; 1796–1802 *Austen*
          [2] 5th-rate; 1,066; 1806–32 *Wallis*
          [3] frigate; 2,667; 1855–71 *Kerr; Noel; Salmon*
          [4] frigate; 5,439; 1875–99 *De Robeck*
          [5] armoured cruiser; 14,100; 1906–22 *Callaghan; Gough-Calthorpe; Madden; Sturdee*

SHARK sloop; 304; 1779–1818 *Stewart*

SHEERNESS 5th-rate; 359; 1691–1744 *Norris*

SHROPSHIRE cruiser; 9,830; 1928–55 *Begg; Philip, Duke of Edinburgh*

SIRIUS sloop; 1,268; 1868–85 *Milford Haven*

SKIRMISHER scout; 2,895; 1905–20 *Cork and Orrery; Tyrwhitt*

SLANEY 6th-rate; 460; 1813–32 *Sartorius*

SNAKE [1] brig-sloop; 434; 1832–47 *Milne*
       [2] gun-vessel; 480; 1854–64 *Commerell*

SNAP brig; 181; 1812–27 *Sartorius*

SNIPE gun-brig; 185; 1801–16 *Wallis*

SOMERSETT (SOMERSET) 3rd-rate; 1,263; 1698–1715 *Rowley*

SOUTHAMPTON [1] 5th-rate; 671; 1757–1812 *Thomas Martin*
[2] 2nd-class cruiser; 5,400; 1912–26 *Chatfield*
[3] cruiser; 9,100; 1936–41 *Cork and Orrery*

SPARTAN 6th-rate; 911; 1841–62 Elliot; Symonds

SPARTIATE 3rd-rate; 1,949; 1798–1832 *Hamond*

SPEAR destroyer; 1,075; 1918–26 *John*

SPEEDWELL [1] 5th-rate; 274; 1702–20 *Clinton*
[2] gun-vessel; 322 (570); 1861–77 *Erskine*

SPEEDY brig-sloop; 208; 1782–1801 *Cockburn*

SPHINX 6th-rate; 520; 1748–70 *St Vincent*

SPITEFUL paddle sloop; 1,054; 1842–83 *Cochrane; Hay*

SPRIGHTLY destroyer; 400; 1900–20 *Keyes*

SPY fireship; 253; 1690–93 *Norris*

SQUIRELL (SQUIRREL) 6th-rate; 377; 1727–49 *Anson*

STORK [1] sloop; 427; 1796–1816 *William Parker*
[2] gunboat; 465; 1882–1913 *Oliver*

STUART destroyer flotilla leader; 1,800; 1918–33 *Lambe*

SUBTLE submarine, 640; 1944–59 *Fieldhouse*

SUCCESS 5th-rate; 683; 1781–1814 *Pole; Sartorius*

SUFFOLK [1] 3rd-rate; 1,401; 1680–1765 *Chaloner Ogle; Howe*
[2] 3rd-rate; 1,606; 1765–1803 *George Martin*
[3] armoured cruiser; 9,800; 1903–20 *Beatty; Cunningham of Hyndhope; Wemyss*

SULTAN [1] 3rd-rate; 1,751; 1807–60 *Moresby; West*
      [2] battleship; 5,234 (9,286); 1870–1906 *Alfred, Duke of Edinburgh; Milford Haven*

SUPERB [1] battleship; 18,600; 1907–22 *Charles Forbes; Gough-Calthorpe; Pound*
      [2] cruiser; 8,885; 1943–60 *Le Fanu*

SURPRISE [1] 5th-rate; 1,072; 1812–22 *Cochrane*
      [2] despatch vessel; 1,650; 1885–1919 *Tyrwhitt*

SUSSEX [1] 3rd-rate; 1,203; 1693–94 *Norris*
      [2] cruiser; 9,830; 1928–50 *Creasy; Hill-Norton*

SUTHERLAND 4th-rate; 675; 1704–44 *Clinton*

SUTLEJ armoured cruiser; 12,000; 1899–1924 *Kelly; Somerville*

SUVA armed merchant cruiser; 1915–19 *Cork and Orrery*

SWALLOW 4th-rate; 612; 1703–28 *Chaloner Ogle*

SWIFTSURE [1] armoured ship; 3,893 (6,660); 1870–1904 *Lyons; Salmon; Edward Seymour*
      [2] cruiser; 8,800; 1943–62 *Ashmore*

SYBILLE [1] 5th-rate; 1,091; 1794–1833 *Codrington*
      [2] 5th-rate; 1,633; 1847–66 *Elliot*

TALBOT 6th-rate; 500; 1824–55 *Codrington; Elliot*

TAMAR 5th-rate; 999; 1796–1810 *Thomas Martin*

TARBAT NESS fleet auxiliary; 15,000; 1967–81 *Lewin*

TARTAR [1] 5th-rate; 420; 1702–32 *Chaloner Ogle*
      [2] frigate; 2,300; 1960–84 *Ashmore*

TEMERAIRE [1] 2nd-rate; 2,121; 1798–1813 *Whitshed*
      [2] barbette ship; 8,540; 1876–1904 *Brock; Noel*

TENBY frigate; 2,150; 1955–75 *Lewin*

TERMAGANT [1] sloop; 378; 1780–95 *Cockburn*
      [2] destroyer; 1,098; 1915–21 *Cunningham of Hyndhope*

TERPSICHORE 5th-rate; 683; 1785–1818 *Gage*

TERRIBLE [1] 3rd-rate; 1,644; 1762–81 *Peter Parker*
　　　　　[2] paddle frigate; 1,858; 1845–79 *Commerell; Edward Seymour*
　　　　　[3] 1st-class cruiser; 14,200; 1895–1920 *Madden*

THAMES 5th-rate; 656; 1758–1803 *Pole*

THESEUS [1] 3rd-rate; 1,653; 1786–1814 *Bowles*
　　　　　[2] aircraft carrier; 13,350; 1944–62 *Oswald*

THETIS [1] 5th-rate; 946; 1782–1814 *Cochrane; Gage*
　　　　　[2] 5th-rate; 1,086; 1817–30 *Mundy*
　　　　　[3] 5th-rate; 1,524; 1846–55 *Codrington*

THRUSH gunboat; 805; 1889–1917 *George V*

THULE submarine; 1,090; 1942–62 *Fieldhouse*

THUNDER bomb vessel; 305; 1779–81 *Gambier*

THUNDERER [1] turret ship; 4,407; 1872–1909 *George V*
　　　　　　[2] battleship; 22,500; 1911–26 *Oliver; Vian*

TIGER [1] 5th-rate; 613; 1647–1743 *John Forbes*
　　　　[2] (captured TIGRE) 3rd-rate; 1,887; 1795–1817 *Stewart*
　　　　[3] battle-cruiser; 28,500; 1913–32 *Cork and Orrery*
　　　　[4] cruiser; 8,800; 1945–80 *Pollock*

TIPTOE submarine; 1,090; 1944–71 *Fieldhouse*

TISIPHONE 6th-rate; 425; 1781–1816 *Thomas Martin*

TOBAGO brig-sloop; 1777–83 *George Martin*

TONNANT 3rd-rate; 2,281; 1798–1821 *Sartorius*

TOPAZE [1] frigate; 2,659; 1858–84 *Wilson*
　　　　[2] 3rd-class cruiser; 3,000; 1903–21 *Tyrwhitt*

TORBAY [1] 2nd-rate; 1,202; 1693–1749 *Norris*
        [2] 2nd-rate; 1,573; 1730–84 *Hawke*

TOTEM submarine; 1,090; 1943–73 *Fieldhouse*

TOURTERELLE 6th-rate; 581; 1795–1816 *West*

TRAFALGAR battleship; 11,940; 1887–1911 *Beatty; Brock; Kerr*

TRIBUNE corvette (3rd-class cruiser); 1,570; 1853–66 *Clanwilliam;*
        Hay; Hornby

TRIDENT 3rd-rate; 1,366; 1768–1816 *Nugent*

TRITON (TRYTON) [1] 6th-rate; 620; 1745–58 *Howe*
                 [2] 5th-rate; 849, 1796–1803 *Austen*

TRIUMPH [1] 3rd-rate; 1,825; 1764–1813 *Wallis*
         [2] battleship; 6,040; 1870–1904 *Erskine; Oliver*
         [3] battleship; 11,800, 1903–15 *Burney; Fraser*
         [4] aircraft carrier (after 1964, repair ship); 13,350;
             1944–81 *Ashmore; Begg*

TURQUOISE corvette (3rd-class cruiser); 2,120; 1876–92 *Keyes*

TWEED 6th-rate; 500; 1823–52 *Keppel*

TYNE 6th-rate; 633; 1826–47 *Bowles*

ULYSSES 5th-rate; 887; 1779–1816 *George Martin*

UNDAUNTED [1] 5th-rate; 1,086; 1807–56 *Hope*
           [2] frigate; 3,039 (4,020); 1861–82 *Fanshawe; Meux;*
               Sturdee
           [3] armoured cruiser; 5,600; 1886–1907 *Wemyss;*
               Pound

UNITE 5th-rate; 1,040; 1793–1832 *Charles Ogle*

URANIE 5th-rate; 1,110; 1797–1807 *Gage*

URCHIN destroyer (later frigate); 1,710; 1943–67 *Lewin*

URSA [1] destroyer; 1,085; 1917–29 *Tovey*
      [2] frigate; 1,710; 1943–67 *Ashmore*

UTRECHT 3rd-rate; 1,331; 1799–1810 *West*

VALIANT [1] 3rd-rate; 1,799; 1759–99 *William IV*
[2] armoured ship; 3,893 (6,713); 1863–88 *Salmon*
[3] battleship; 27,500; 1914–48 *Lewin; Philip, Duke of Edinburgh*

VALOROUS paddle frigate; 1,257 (2,300); 1851–91 *Erskine; Fisher*

VANESSA destroyer; 1,300; 1918–47 *Pollock*

VANGUARD [1] 3rd-rate; 1,644; 1787–1812 *Hamond*
[2] battleship; 42,500; 1944–60 *Creasy; Oswald; Staveley*

VENERABLE battleship; 15,000; 1899–1920 *Chatfield; Milford Haven*

VENGEANCE [1] 3rd-rate; 1,627; 1774–1808 *Charles Ogle*
[2] battleship; 12,950; 1899–1923 *De Robeck*
[3] aircraft carrier; 13,190; 1944–56 *Ashmore; John; Lambe*

VENUS [1] 5th-rate; 722; 1758–1817 *Freeman*
[2] 2nd-class cruiser; 5,600; 1895–1921 *Keyes*

VERNON 4th-rate; 2,080 (2,388); 1832–76 *Cockburn*

VERSATILE destroyer; 1,300; 1917–47 *McGrigor*

VERULAM frigate; 1,710; 1943–72 *Oswald*

VESTAL 6th-rate; 913; 1833–62 *Symonds*

VETERAN 3rd-rate; 1,397; 1787–99 *Nugent*

VICTORIA [1] 1st-rate; 4,127 (6,959); 1859–87 *May*
[2] battleship; 10,470; 1887–93 *Jellicoe*

VICTORIA AND ALBERT royal yacht; 2,470 (2,345); 1855–1904
Beatty; Burney; Kerr; May; Meux; Milford Haven; Noel; Wemyss

VICTORIOUS [1] 3rd-rate; 1,724; 1808–26 *Hamond*
[2] battleship; 14,900; 1895–1916 *Backhouse*
[3] aircraft carrier; 30,530; 1939–69 *Ashmore; Fraser; Oswald*

313

VICTORY 1st-rate; 2,124; 1765–1824 (still in commission at date of publication); *Cockburn; Gage; Howe; St Vincent; George Seymour*

VIGILANT paddle despatch vessel; 835 (1,000); 1871–86 *Edward Seymour*

VIGO destroyer; 2,315; 1945–64 *Pollock*

VILLE DE PARIS 1st-rate; 2,351; 1795–1825 *Moresby*

VINDICTIVE 4th-rate; 1,741; 1813–62 *Austen*

VIXEN paddle sloop; 1,054; 1841–62 *Richards; Ryder*

VOLAGE [1] 6th-rate; 523; 1798–1804 *William Parker*
[2] 2nd-class cruiser; 3,080; 1869–1922 *Field; Kelly*

VULTURE [1] frigate; 1,191; 1843–66 *Commerell*
[2] torpedo-boat destroyer; 300; 1898–1919 *Cunningham of Hyndhope*

WALLACE destroyer flotilla leader; 1,750; 1918–45 *Cunningham of Hyndhope; Philip, Duke of Edinburgh; Willis*

WALLAROO 2nd-class cruiser; 2,575; 1890–1906 *Oliver*

WALRUS submarine; 1,605; 1959–87 *Fieldhouse*

WARRIOR armoured ship; 6,109 (9,210); 1860–1902 *Fisher*

WARSPITE [1] 3rd-rate; 1,881; 1807–62 *Bowles; Codrington; Elliot; Gage; William Parker; Wallis*
[2] armoured cruiser; 8,400; 1884–1905 *Chatfield; Hotham, Meux; Somerville*
[3] battleship; 27,500 (31,100); 1913–46 *Begg; Creasy; Cunningham of Hyndhope; Fraser; Kelly; Le Fanu; Pollock; Pound; Somerville; Willis*

WARWICK [1] 4th-rate; 1,073; 1767–1802 *William IV*
[2] destroyer; 1,300; 1917–44 *Willis*

WASP sloop; 973; 1850–69; *Hay*

WAVENEY torpedo-boat destroyer; 550; 1903–20 *Tyrwhitt*

314

WEAZEL (WEASEL) sloop; 102; 1721–32 *Anson*

WELLESLEY 3rd-rate; 1,746; 1815–54 *Hamond; Mundy*

WESER paddle gun vessel; 590; 1855–66 *Commerell*

WEYMOUTH 2nd-class cruiser; 5,250; 1910–28 *Kelly*

WHELP destroyer; 1,710; 1943–53 *Philip, Duke of Edinburgh*

WHIRLWIND frigate; 1,760; 1943–74 *Ashmore*

WHITSHED destroyer; 1,325; 1919–47 *Le Fanu*

WILLIAM AND MARY royal yacht; 199; 1807–49 *Bowles; Stewart*

WINCHELSEA 6th-rate; 679; 1764–1805 *Charles Ogle*

WINCHESTER [1] 4th-rate; 673; 1698–1774 *Norris*
           [2] 4th-rate; 1,487; 1822–61 *Hornby*

WISHART destroyer; 1,350; 1919–45 *Mountbatten*

WIZARD brig-sloop; 283; 1805–16 *Moresby*

WOLF sloop; 244; 1731–41 *Hawke*

WOLFHOUND destroyer; 1,300; 1918–48 *Tovey*

WOLVERENE (WOLVERINE) [1] brig-sloop; 428; 1836–55
                    Hornby
                  [2] corvette (3rd-class cruiser); 1,703
                  (2,431); 1863–81 *Callaghan*

WOOLASTON coastal minesweeper; 360; 1958–80 *Bathurst*

WOOLWICH [1] 5th-rate; 825; 1749–62 *Peter Parker*
          [2] 5th-rate; 907; 1785–94 *Charles Ogle*
          [3] depot ship; 8,750; 1934–62 *Tovey*

WORCESTER 4th-rate; 694; 1698–1733 *Chaloner Ogle*

YARMOUTH [1] 3rd-rate; 1,058; 1695–1740 *Chaloner Ogle*
          [2] 3rd-rate; 1,359 tons; 1745–83 *Anson; Gambier*

YARNTON minesweeper; 360; 1956–86 *Oswald*

YORK cruiser; 8,250; 1928–41 *John; Le Fanu; Pollock*

ZEALOUS 3rd-rate; 1,607; 1785–1816 *Hamond*

ZEBRA bomb vessel; 315; 1779–1812 *Bowles*

ZEPHYR destroyer; 1,710; 1943–58 *Staveley*

ZULU frigate; 2,300; 1962–84 *Staveley*

BIBLIOGRAPHY

REFERENCE PUBLICATIONS

Bruce's Peerage and Baronetage, London, 1886.

Debrett's Peerage and Baronetage, London, 1990.

Dictionary of National Biography, 77 vols., London, 1885–1990.

Navy Lists, published by authority, annually, half-yearly or quarterly, London, 1800–2001.

Who's Who, published annually, London, 1974–2001.

Chesneau, Roger, and Kolesnik, Eugene M., (ed.), *Conway's All the World's Fighting Ships 1922–1946*, London, 1980.

Chesneau, Roger, *Conway's All the World's Fighting Ships 1860–1905*. London, 1979.

Chumbley, Stephen, (ed.), *Conway's All the World's Fighting Ships 1947–95*, London, 1995.

Colledge, J.J., *Ships of the Royal Navy. The Complete Record of all Fighting Ships of the Royal Navy from the Fifteenth Century to the Present*, 2 vols., London, 1987.

Fryde, E.B.(ed.), *Handbook of British Chronology*, London, 1986.

Greenwood, Douglas, *Who's buried where in England*, 2nd edition, London, 1990.

Lyon, David, *The Sailing Navy List. All the Ships of the Royal Navy – Built, Purchased and Captured, 1688–1860*, London, 1993.

Montgomery-Massingberd, Hugh, *Burke's Royal Families of the World*, London, 1978.

Natkiel, Richard, and Preston, Antony, *The Weidenfeld Atlas of Maritime History*, London, 1986.

Pope, Stephen, and Wheal, Elizabeth-Anne, *The Macmillan Dictionary of the First World War*, London, 1995.

Raimo, John W., *Biographical Directory of American Colonial and Revolutionary Governors 1607–1789*, Westport, Conn., 1980.

Sanderson, Michael, *Sea Battles: a Reference Guide*, London, 1975.

Saunders, David, *Britain's maritime memorials and mementoes*, Sparkford, Yeovil, 1996.

Wheal, Elizabeth-Anne, and Pope, Stephen, *The Macmillan Dictionary of the Second World War*, London, 1989.

Williamson, David, *Brewer's British Royalty*, London, 1996.

Young, Peter, *A Dictionary of Battles*, London, 1977.

BIOGRAPHIES

Allen, W.Gore, *King William IV*, London, 1960.

Altham, Edward, *Jellicoe*, London, 1938.

Anson, Walter Vernon, *The Life of Admiral Lord Anson. The father of the British Navy, 1697–1762*, London, 1912.

—— *The Life of John Jervis, Admiral Lord St. Vincent*, London, 1913.

Applin, Arthur, *Admiral Jellicoe*, London, 1915.

Aspinall, Arthur, *Mrs Jordan and her family; being the unpublished correspondence of Mrs Jordan and the Duke of Clarence, later William IV*, London, 1951.

Aspinall-Oglander, Cecil Faber, *Roger Keyes; being the biography of Admiral of the Fleet Lord Keyes*, London, 1951.

Bacon, Reginald, *The Life of Lord Fisher of Kelverstone, Admiral of the Fleet*, 2 vols., London, 1929.

—— *The Life of John Rushworth, Earl Jellicoe*, London, 1936.

Baker, Richard, *Dry Ginger. The biography of Admiral of the Fleet Sir Michael Le Fanu*, London 1977.

Barker, Dudley, *Prominent Edwardians* [inc AF Lord Fisher], London, 1963.

Barrow, John, *The Life of Richard, Earl Howe*, London, 1838.

—— *The Life of George, Lord Anson*, London, 1839.

Berckman, Evelyn Domenica, *Nelson's Dear Lord. A portrait of St. Vincent*, London, 1962.

Bonner-Smith, David, (ed.), *Letters of Admiral of the Fleet the Earl of St. Vincent while First Lord of the Admiralty, 1801–1804*, 2 vols., Navy Records Society, London, 1922–27.

Bourchier, Jane, *Selections from the letters (private and professional) of Sir Henry Codrington*, London, 1880.

Boyle, William, *My Naval Life* [autobiography of AF the Earl of Cork and Orrery], London, 1943.

Bradford, Edward, *Admiral of the Fleet Sir Arthur Knyvett-Wilson*, London, 1923

Brenton, Edward Pelham, *Life and Correspondence of John, Earl of St. Vincent, GCB, Admiral of the Fleet*, 2 vols., London, 1838.

Brighton, J. G., *Admiral of the Fleet Sir Provo Wallis; A Memoir*, 1892.

Brodhurst, Robin, *Churchill's Anchor. The biography of Admiral of the Fleet Sir Dudley Pound OM, GCB, GCVO*, Barnsley, 2000.

Burrows, Montagu, *The Life of Edward, Lord Hawke. Admiral of the Fleet*, London, 1904.

Cecil, Lamar, *Wilhelm II Prince and Emperor 1859–1908*, Chapel Hill N.C. and London, 1989.

Chalmers, W.S. *The Life and letters of David, Earl Beatty*, London, 1951.

Charnock, John, *Biographia Navalis*, 6 vols., London, 1794–98.

Chatfield, Alfred, *The Navy and Defence. The autobiography of Admiral of the Fleet Lord Chatfield, Vol. I*, London, 1943.

—— *It might happen again. The autobiography of Admiral of the Fleet Lord Chatfield, Vol. II*, London, 1947.

Chatterton, Henrietta, *Memorials, personal and historical, of Admiral Lord Gambier*, 2 vols., London, 1861.

Cochrane, Thomas, 10th Earl of Dundonald, *The Autobiography of a Seaman*, 2 vols., London, 1860.

Connell, Brian, *Manifest Destiny: A Study in five Profiles of the Rise and influence of the Mountbatten Family*, London, 1953.

Cunningham, A.B., *A Sailor's Odyssey* [autobiography of AF Viscount Cunningham of Hyndhope], London, 1951.

Egerton. F., *Admiral of the Fleet Sir Geoffrey Phipps Hornby, GCB. A Biography*, London, 1894.

Fisher, John A., *Memories* [memoirs of AF Lord Fisher], London, 1919.

—— *Records*, London, 1919.

Grove, Eric, *The Battle and the Breeze. The naval reminiscences of Admiral of the Fleet Sir Edward Ashmore*, Stroud, (Royal Naval Museum), 1997.

Halpern, Paul G., (ed.), *The Keyes Papers*, 3 vols., London, 1979–81.

Hamilton, Richard Vesey, *Letters and Papers of Admiral of the Fleet Sir Thomas Byam Martin*, 3 vols., London, 1898–1903.

Hatch, Alder, *The Mounbattens*, London, 1965.

Heald, Tim, *The Duke. A portrait of Prince Philip*, London, 1991.

Heaps, Leo, *Log of the "Centurion", based on the original papers of Captain Philip Saumarez on board HMS Centurion, Lord Anson's flagship, etc.* London, 1973.

Hill, Richard, *Lewin of Greenwich. The authorized biography of Admiral of the Fleet Lord Lewin*, London, 2000.

Hollis, Leslie, *The Captain General. A Life of HRH Prince Philip, Duke of Edinburgh*, London, 1961.

Hough, Richard, *First Sea Lord, an authorized biography of Admiral Lord Fisher*, London, 1969.

—— *Louis and Victoria. The First Mountbattens*, London, 1974.

—— *The Great Admirals* [inc AFs Jellicoe, Beatty, Viscount Cunningham], London. 1977

—— *Mountbatten. Hero of our time*, London, 1980.

Howarth, David, and Howarth, Stephen, *Nelson, the Immortal Memory*, London, 1988.

Hubback, J.H., and Hubback, Edith C., *Jane Austen's Sailor brothers, being the adventures of Sir Francis Austen, GCB, Admiral of the Fleet, and Rear-Admiral Charles Austen*, London, 1906.

Humble, R., *Fraser of North Cape*, London, 1983.

James, William Milburne, *Old Oak: the life of John Jervis, Earl of St. Vincent*, London, 1950.

—— *A Great Seaman: the Life of Admiral of the Fleet Sir Henry F. Oliver*, London, 1956.

John, Rebecca, *Caspar John*, London, 1987.

Kemp, Peter K. (ed.), *The Papers of Admiral Sir John Fisher*, 2 vols., Navy Records Soc., 1960.

Keppel, Henry, *A sailor's life under four Sovereigns* [memoirs of AF Sir Henry Keppel], 3 vols., London, 1899.

Kerr, Mark, *Prince Louis of Battenberg, Admiral of the Fleet*, London, 1934.

Keyes, R., *The Naval Memoirs of Admiral of the Fleet Sir Roger Keyes, 1910–15*, London, 1934.

—— *Adventures Ashore and Afloat*, London, 1939.

Kurenberg, Joachim von, trans.Russell H.T. and Hagen, H., *The Kaiser. A life of Wilhelm II*, London, 1954.

Lambert, Nicholas, *Sir John Fisher's Naval Revolution*, Columbia, South Carolina, 1999.

Langdon, Jeremy, "Too old or too bold? The removal of Sir Roger Keyes as Churchill's first Director of Combined Operations", London, Imperial War Museum Review No.8 (undated).

Le Fevre, Peter, and Harding, Richard (ed.), *Precursors of Nelson: British Admirals of the Eighteenth Century*, Chatham, 2000.

Leach, Henry, *Endure no Makeshifts* [autobiography of AF Sir H.C. Leach], London, 1993.

Locker, H Algernon, *Memoirs of the distinguished naval commanders whose portraits are exhibited in the Royal Naval Gallery of Greenwich Hospital* [Anson, Jervis (St Vincent), Norris, Williams] Greenwich, 1842.

MacDonogh, Giles, *The Last Kaiser: William the Impetuous*, London, 2000.

McGeogh, Ian, *The Princely Sailor. Mountbatten of Burma*, London, 1996.

Macintyre, D., *Fighting Admiral. The Life of Admiral of the Fleet Sir James Somerville*, London, 1961.

MacKay, Ruddock, *Fisher of Kilverstone*, Oxford, 1973.

—— *Admiral Hawke*, Oxford, 1965.

Mahan, Alfred T, *Types of Naval Officers. Drawn from the History of the British Navy* [inc Hawke, Howe, Jervis (St Vincent)], London, 1902.

Marder, Arthur J., *Fear God and Dread Nought; the correspondence of Admiral of the Fleet Lord Fisher of Kilverstone*, 3 vols., London, 1952–59.

Marshall, John, *Royal Naval Biography* [1760–1823], 13 vols., London, 1823.

Mason, George, *The Life of Richard, Earl Howe*, London, 1803.

Masson, Madeline, *Edwina. The Biography of the Countess Mountbatten of Burma*, London, 1948.

May, William Henry [AF Sir W. H. May], *Memoirs, 1863–1930*, London and Beccles, 1934.

Molloy, Fitzgerald, *The Sailor King. William the Fourth, His Court and His Subjects*, London, 1903.

Moresby, John, *Two Admirals. Admiral of the Fleet Sir Fairfax Moresby and his son John Moresby*, London, 1909.

Mundy, George Rodney, (AF Sir George Mundy), *Narrative of events in Borneo . . . the operations of HMS* Iris, 2 vols., 1848.

—— *HMS* Hannibal *at Palermo and Naples during the Italian Revolution,* 1863.

Murfett, Malcolm H., (ed.), *The First Sea Lords: from Fisher to Mountbatten,* London, 1995.

Murphy, R., *Last Viceroy. Life and Times of Rear-Admiral The Earl Mountbatten of Burma,* London, 1948.

O'Byrne, William R, *A Naval Biographical Dictionary, comprising the life and services of every living officer in Her Majesty's Navy,* London, 1849, reprinted 1986.

Ollard, Richard, *Fisher and Cunningham. A study in the Personalities of the Churchill Era,* London, 1991.

Pack, S.W.C., *Cunningham the Commander* [life of AF Viscount Cunningham], London, 1974.

Patterson, A. Temple, *Jellicoe. A Biography,* London, 1969.

—— (ed.), *The Jellicoe Papers,* 2 vols., Navy Records Soc, 1946–48.

Penn, Geoffrey, *Fisher, Churchill and the Dardanelles,* Barnsley, 1999.

—— *Infighting Admirals. Fisher's Feud with Beresford and the Reactionaries,* Barnsley, 2001.

Perrett, Bryan, *The Real Hornblower. The Life of Admiral of the Fleet Sir James Alexander Gordon, GCB,* London, 1998.

Phillimore, Augustus, *The Life of Admiral of the Fleet Sir William Parker from 1781 to 1866,* 2 vols., London, 1876–79.

Ralfe, J., *The Naval Biography of Great Britain: consisting of Historical Memoires of those officers of the British Navy who distinguished themselves during the reign of His Majesty George III,* 4 vols., London, 1828.

Rawson, Geoffrey, *Beatty, Admiral of the Fleet,* London, 1930.

Rooke, P.E., ed., *Theobalds through the Centuries. The changing fortunes of a Hertfordshire house and estate* [home of AF Sir Hedworth Meux], Cheshunt, 1980

Roskill, Stephen W., *Churchill and the Admirals,* London, 1977.

—— *Admiral of the Fleet Earl Beatty. The Last Naval Hero. An Intimate Biography,* London 1981.

Seymour, Edward Hobart, *My naval career and travels* [memoirs of AF Sir Edward Seymour], London, 1911.

Simpson, M., (ed.), *The Somerville Papers,* Navy Records Society, London, 1995.

—— *The Cunningham Papers,* Navy Records Society, London, 1995.

Somerset, Anne, *The Life and Times of William IV,* London, 1980.

Southam, Brian, *Jane Austen and the Navy,* London, 2000.

Stephen, M., *The Fighting Admirals. British Admirals of the Second World War,* London, 1991.

Stuart (Finlay), Vivian Felix, *The beloved little admiral. The life and times of Admiral of the Fleet Sir Henry Keppel,* London, 1967.

Swinson, Arthur, *Mountbatten,* London, 1973.

Syrett, David, and Dinardo, R.L., (ed.), *The Commissioned Sea Officers of the Royal Navy 1660–1815,* Navy Records Society, London, 1994.

Terraine, John, *The Life and Times of Lord Mountbatten*, London, 1968.

Thompson, Grace E., *The Patriot King; the life of William IV*, London, 1932.

Tomalin, Claire, *Mrs Jordan's Profession* [William IV], London, 2000.

Tucker, Jediah Stevens, *Memoirs of Admiral the Right Hon.The Earl of St.Vincent, etc.*, 2 vols., London, 1844.

Vesey-Hamilton, Richard, *Letters and Papers of Sir T Byam* (Naval Records Society Journal, Vol XXIV)

Vian, Philip Louis, *Action This Day* [memoirs of AF Sir Philip Vian], London, 1960.

Walter, Richard, and Robins, Benjamin, (ed. Williams, Glyndwr), *A Voyage round the World in the Years MDCCXL, I, II, III, IV by George Anson*, London, 1974.

Warner, O., *Cunningham of Hyndhope, Admiral of the Fleet. A Memoir*, London, 1967.

West, Algernon Edward, *Memoir of Sir Henry Keppel, GCB, Admiral of the Fleet*, London, 1945.

Williams, Glyn, *The Prize of all the Oceans* [AF Lord Anson], London, 2000.

Winton, John, *Jellicoe*, London, 1981.

—— *Cunningham* [life of AF Viscount Cunningham], London, 1998.

Wright, George N., and Watkins, John, *The Life and reign of William the Fourth*, London, 1837.

Ziegler, Philip, *King William IV*, London, 1971.

—— *Mountbatten. The official biography*, London, 1985.

—— *From Shore to Shore. The Tour Diaries of Earl Mountbatten 1957–1979*, London, 1980.

——(ed.) *Personal Diary of Admiral the Lord Louis Mountbatten*, London, 1988.

GENERAL NAVAL HISTORIES

Andidora, Ronald, *Iron Admirals. Naval Leadership in the Twentieth Century*, London, 2000.

Arthur, Max, *The True Glory. The Royal Navy 1914–39. A Narrative History*, London, 1996.

Bennett, G., *Naval Battles of the First World War*, London, 1968.

Clowes, William Laird, *The Royal Navy*, 7 vols., London, 1897–1903.

Gardiner, Leslie, *The British Admiralty*, London, 1968.

Herwig, Holger H., *The German Naval Officer Corps. A Social and Political History 1890-1914*, Oxford, 1973.

Hill-Norton, Peter [AF Sir Peter Hill-Norton] *No Soft Options*, London, 1978.

—— *Sea Power*, London, 1982.

Hough, Richard, *Naval Battles of the Twentieth Century*, London, 1988.

—— *"Luxury" Fleet. The Imperial German Navy 1888–1914*, London, 1980.

Hughes, E.A., *The Royal Naval College at Dartmouth*, London, 1950.

Ireland, Bernard, *Naval Warfare in the Age of Sail: War at Sea 1756–1805*, London, 2000.

Jackson, William, and Bramall, Edwin, *The Chiefs. The Story of the United Kingdom Chiefs of Staff*, London, 1992.

Jellicoe, John [AF Lord Jellicoe], *The Grand Fleet*, London, 1919.

Kemp, Peter K. (ed.), *History of the Royal Navy*, London, 1969.

—— *The Oxford Companion to Ships and the Sea*, Oxford, 1976.

Lambert, Andrew, *Battleships in transition: The Creation of the Steam Battlefleet 1825–1860*, London, 1983.

—— *The Last Sailing Battlefleet: Maintaining Naval Mastery 1815–1850*, London, 1991.

—— *War at Sea in the Age of Sail 1650–1850*, London, 2000.

Lambi, Ivo Nikolai, *The Navy and German Power Politics 1862–1914*, Boston, Mass., 1984.

Lewis, Michael, *The Navy of Britain. A Historical Portrait*, London, 1948.

—— *England's Sea Officers*, London 1948.

—— *A Social History of the Navy 1793–1815*, London, 1960.

—— *The Navy in Transition. A Social History 1814–1864*, London, 1965.

Lloyd, Christopher, *The Navy and the Slave Trade. The Suppression of the African Slave Trade in the Nineteenth Century*, London, 1949.

Marder, Arthur J., *The Anatomy of British Sea Power*, New York, 1940 [also pub. as *British Naval Policy, 1880–1905*, London, 1946].

—— *From the Dreadnought to Scapa Flow: the Royal Navy in the Fisher Era, 1904–1919*, 5 vols., London, 1961–70.

Miller, Nathan, *Broadsides. The Age of Fighting Sail, 1776–1815*, New York, 2000.

Oswald, J.J.R., [AF Sir Julian Oswald], *The Royal Navy – Today and Tomorrow*, London, 1993.

Parkinson, C. Northcote. *Britannia Rules. The Classic Age of Naval History 1793–1815*, London, 1977.

Rodger, N.A.M., *The Admiralty*, London, 1979.

Roskill, Stephen W., *The War at Sea 1939–45*, 3 vols. London, 1954–60.

Willmott, H.P., *Grave of a Dozen Schemes. British Naval Planning and the War against Japan 1943–45*, London, 1996.

Winton, John, *The Forgotten Fleet* [The British Pacific Fleet, 1944–45], London, 1967.

INDEX

Basque Roads, 95, 230
Bathurst, Sir Benjamin, **22–23**
batons, naval, 92, 259
Battenberg *see* Mountbatten, Louis Alexander
Battle-cruiser Fleet, 27, 31, 62, 130, 140,146,
   183, 219; Force, 20
Beachy Head (10 Jul 1690), 195
Beatty, Sir David, Earl Beatty, 4, 15, **23–27**,
   34–35, 41, 85, 130, 145, 164, 244, 252
Begg, Sir Varyl, **27–28**
Beirut, 52, 118, 237
Belle-Ile, 46, 109, 205
Beresford, Adm Lord Charles, 34, 81- 82,
   120, 144, 172–74, 180–81, 218, 239,
   250, 267, 268
Berlin, Congress of, 54, 79, 111, 144
Bermuda, 15, 49, 70, 163, 213
Biscay, Bay of, 108-09, 211, 266
Black Sea, 53, 104, 111, 142, 179, 194, 224,
   227, 237, 241, 252
blockades, 17, 24, 37, 47, 48, 51, 57, 80,
   119, 130, 159; Confederate States, 72,
   160, 176; French Atlantic coast, 13, 19,
   94, 95, 100, 102, 105, 108-9, 123, 125,
   135, 136, 177, 207, 212 , 230, 236, 255;
   French Mediterranean coast, 134, 177,
   198, 211, 222, 254; Malta, 93, 101, 105,
   165; Montevideo, 53, 116; Netherlands
   coast, 94, 105; Spanish coast, 18, 45, 102,
   134, 166, 201
Boer War *see* Anglo-Boer South African War
Bonaparte *see* Napoleon Bonaparte, Emperor
   of the French
Borneo, 47, 110, 142, 191, 219 *see also*
   Brunei; Indonesia; Sarawak
Boscawen, Adm Edward, 123, 132
Boston, Massachusetts, 107, 124, 229, 249
Boulogne, 18, 70
Bowles, Sir William, **29–30**
Boxer Rebellion (1900-01), 24, 38, 74, 129,
   145, 228, 229
Boyle, Sir William, 12th Earl of Cork and
   Orrery, **30–32**, 217, 233
Brest, 95, 100, 108-09, 123, 125, 133, 136,
   167, 177, 198, 207, 211, 236, 255
Bridgeman, Adm Sir Francis, 182, 269
Bridport, Viscount *see* Hood, Sir Alexander
Bridport's Action (23 Jun 1795), 101, 253
British Columbia, 104, 119, 125, 133, 211,
   258, 265
British Expeditionary Force, 26, 37, 56, 83,
   148, 174, 217, 232, 269
British Guiana (Guyana), 16
British Honduras (Belize), 16
British Pacific Fleet, 15, 56, 61, 90–91, 138,
   149, 154, 187, 210, 213, 247
Brock, Sir Osmond, **34–35**, 164
Broke, Capt Philip, 249
Brooke, Rajah James, 142, 191
Brunei, 28, 47, 152, 191, 234 *see also* Borneo;
   Indonesia; Sarawak

Buenos Aires, Argentina, 225, 226
Burma War, second (1852), 17; third
   (1885–89), 221
Burney, Sir Cecil, **36–38**
Byng, Vice-Adm John, 87, 108

Cadiz, 18, 29, 93, 102, 106, 134, 166, 196,
   201, 226
Calabria (9 July 1940), 59, 242
Callaghan, Sir George, 20, **38–39**, 130, 145,
   158, 174
Calthorpe *see* Gough-Calthorpe
Candia *see* Crete
Canton (29 December 1857), 142, 171, 227,
   265
Canton (Guangzhou), 19, 71, 79, 142, 170,
   208, 227
Cape Helles landings (Apr 1915), 251 *see also*
   Dardanelles; Gallipoli
captain's servants (AFs joining the Navy as),
   47, 64, 100, 105, 165, 167, 200, 206
Carden, Vice-Adm Sackville, 66, 146, 251
Carlist Wars, Spain, (1835–39), 142, 226
Carolinas, North America, 11, 205 *see also*
   North Carolina, South Carolina
Carrington, Lord, First Lord of the
   Admiralty, 115, 139, 150
Chamberlain, Austen, First Lord of the
   Admiralty, 75, 76, 141
Chamberlain, Neville, Prime Minister, 21, 33,
   43, 44, 86, 147, 217
Chanak crisis (1922), 35, 41, 58, 137, 140
Channel Fleet, 82, 83, 105, 170, 173, 181,
   218, 228, 239, 267 *see also* squadrons,
   Channel
Charles, HRH Prince of Wales, 190
Charleston, South Carolina, 94, 198, 205,
   213
Chatfield, Sir Ernle, Lord Chatfield, 25,
   40–44
Cherbourg, 13, 102, 123
Cherimon River, 47
Chesapeake Bay, 46, 49, 124
Chile, 12, 45, 118, 121, 178
China Wars; first "Opium"(1839–42), 9, 46,
   53, 110, 142, 208; second "Arrow"
   (1856–60), 54, 71, 79, 111, 116, 118,
   142–43; 170, 220, 227, 265
Christmas Island, Indian Ocean, 169; Pacific,
   234
Churchill, Winston Spencer, Prime Minister,
   33, 44, 59–61, 86, 89–90, 99, 147–48,
   162, 185–86, 189, 217–18, 233, 242,
   247; First Lord of the Admiralty
   (1911–15), 24–25, 83–84, 127, 130,
   145–46, 170, 174, 182–83, 202, 215,
   239, 262, 269–70;(1939–40) 32–33 39,
   44, 86, 48, 147, 217; Secretary of State
   for War, 252
Clanwilliam, 4th Earl of *see* Meade

329

Nicholas II, Emperor (Tsar) of Russia, 4, 5, 98, **192-93**, 262
Nile, 23, 24, 101, 134; (1 Aug 1798), 101, 134
Noel, Sir Gerard, 81, 82, **193-95**
Normandy landings (Jun 1944), 56, 61, 99, 156, 186, 247
Norris, Capt Richard, 107, 197, 222
Norris, Sir John, 2, 3, 6, 11, 44–45, 86, 107, **195-97**, 222, 223
North Cape (26 Dec 1943), 89, 151
North Carolina, 49
North Sea, 11, 14, 17, 19, 25, 29, 93, 105, 122, 130, 132, 145, 158, 185, 205, 219, 220, 236, 239, 242, 244
North, Lord, Prime Minister, 72, 110, 124
Northern Patrol, 149
Norwegian campaign (1940), 14, 27, 32–33, 63, 86, 138, 147, 148, 154, 156, 185, 217
Nott, John, Secretary of State for Defence, 78, 152, 153, 158, 235
Nova Scotia, 29, 91, 200, 237, 248, 255, 257, 258, 266
Nugent, Sir Charles, 6, **198**

Ogle, Sir Chaloner, **199-200**
Ogle, Sir Charles, 3, 175, **200-01**
Okinawa (Apr-Jul 1945), 15, 247
Oliver, Sir Henry, 31, 127, **201-03**
Omdurman, Sudan (2 Sep 1898), 23
Orde, Rear-Adm Sir John, 134, 135
Oregon, 119, 231
Ostend, 17, 146, 199
Oswald, Sir Julian, **203-4**

Palestine, 52, 71, 118, 151, 237, 251, 264
Palmerston, Viscount, Prime Minister, 29, 119
Pantelleria (11–12 Jun 1943), 161
Parana River, 53, 116
Parker, Adm Sir Hyde, 48, 105, 207
Parker, Sir Peter, 3, 6, 198, **204-06**, 258,
Parker, Sir Thomas, Earl of Macclesfield, 11, 132, 133, 206
Parker, Sir William, 46, 79, 176, **206-08**,
Passaro (31 Jul 1718), 11
Patuxent River, 49
Peel, Sir Robert, Prime Minister, 30, 50, 94, 208, 230
Pei-ho River, 54, 111, 116, 129, 227, 229, 265
Peking (Beijing), 5, 38, 74, 116, 129, 145, 229
Peninsular War (1807–14), 18, 29, 49, 166, 207
Penjdeh Incident (1885), 80, 120, 128, 228
Philip, Duke of Edinburgh, 5, 11, 180, 188, 193, **209-11**
Philippines, 12, 227; Philippine Sea (19–20 Oct 1944), 148

Phipps-Hornby *see* Hornby, Sir Geoffrey Phipps
Piedmont, 48, 93
Pitt, the Hon William (Pitt the Younger), Prime Minister, 94, 95, 125, 135, 136, 258
Pitt, William, 1ˢᵗ Earl of Chatham (Pitt the Elder), Prime Minister, 13, 87, 108, 109
Plate, River, 29, 225
Pole, Sir Charles, 3, **211-12**, 260
Pollock, Sir Michael, **212-14**
polo, 25, 132, 147, 150, 257
Pondicherry (1778), 211
Port Arthur (Lushun), China, 81, 228, 266
Port Edgar, Edinburgh, 58, 242
Portland, Dorset, 22, 32, 36, 66, 73, 95, 195, 234, 245
Portuguese civil wars (1826–46), 94, 208, 226
Pound, Sir Dudley 56, 59, 86, 89, **214-18**, 216, 233, 242, 264
Power, Sir Arthur, 187, **218-20**
Pra River, 54
prisoners of war (AFs taken prisoner) 65, 94, 101, 177, 199, 248, 255
prize-money, 12, 46, 65, 102, 106, 199, 207, 211
Puerto Rico, 46, 167, 254, 255
Punto Obligado (20 Nov 1845), 53,

Quebec (1759), 132; Conference (1943), 186, 28
Quiberon, 46, 91, 109, 123; Quiberon Bay (20 Nov 1759), 109, 123
Quimper River, 167

Ramsay, Adm Sir Bertram, 21, 56, 217, 232
Ramsay MacDonald, James, Prime Minister, 21, 42, 75, 76, 140
Rangariri, New Zealand (20 Nov 1863)
Red Sea, 31, 36, 88, 181, 266
Red Sea Patrol, 31
Rhode Island, 92, 124, 198, 205
Richards, Sir Frederick, 80, **220-22**
Ripon, Marquess of, First Lord of the Admiralty, 72, 112
Roberts, Bartholomew, pirate, 199
Rochefort, 95, 108, 109, 123, 177, 212, 226, 230, 236
Rodman, Rear-Adm Hugh, USN, 25
Rodney, Adm Sir George, Lord Rodney, 254, 272
Rooke, Adm Sir George, 196
Roosevelt, President Franklin D, 70, 90, 218
Rosas (Nov 1802), 253; (Nov 1808), 236
Rota, 102
Rowley, Capt (later Rear-adm Sir) Joshua, 165, 223
Rowley, Sir William, 47, 165, 205, **222-223**
Royal Air Force, 1, 4, 16, 22, 26, 28, 42, 43,

Dunedin, 149; Dunkirk 1754–78, 123; 1945–65, 152; Durban, 27;
Eagle (1925), 147; 1946–78, 16, 22, 154; Echo, 105; Éclair, 177, 191; Eclipse, 72; Edgar 1688–1711, 195; 1779–1813, 200; 1858–70, 72, 119; 1890–1921, 38; Edinburgh 1702–71, 107, 199; (1925), 151; Effingham, 33, 89; Egmont, 93; Egyptienne, 201; Elephant, 19; Eltham, 122; Emerald 1795–1836, 165; 1856–69, 143; Emperor of India, 149, 231, 245; Empress of India, 37, 228, 250; Emulous, 249; Enchantress, 34; Encounter, 227; Endurance, 152; Endymion 1797–1860, 229, 240; 1865–85, 171; 1891–1920, 38; Espoir, 66; Essex, 123; Ethalion, 46; Euryalus 1803–26, 191; 1853–67, 9; 1901–20, 251; Eurydice, 1781–1834, 100; (1845), 240; Excellent, 64, 253; Exeter, 137; Exmouth, 267; Experiment, 132; Express 1934–56, 212;
Fame, 145; Fantome, 220; Faulknor, 241; Favorite, 191; Fearless 1912–21, 146, 263; 1963–2002, 16, 157; Fierce, 151; Fife, 16, 157; Firebrand, 53, 54, 116, 159; Firedrake, 205; Fisguard, 167, 225; Flamborough, 107; Flora, 92; Formidable 1777–1813, 255; 1814–69, 119; 1898–1915, 160; 1939–53, 247; Forte 1814–44, 46, 116; 1858–40, 142; 1893–1922, 139; Forth, 111; Fortunée, 230; Foudroyant, 133, 166; Fox, 31, 57; Foxhound, 161; Frobisher, 14, 32, 55, 156, 212; Furious 1850–67, 79; 1896–1915, 30; (1930), 137; Fury, 54;
Galatea 1810–36, 141; 1859–83, 9, 10; 1914–21, 85; 1934–41, 59, 217, 232; 242; 1964–88, 152; Ganges 1782–1811, 168; 1821–65, 175, 220; Garland, 11; Garnet, 72; Gibraltar, 62; Gipsy, 88; Gladiator, 265; Glasgow, 27, 189, 213, 218; Gloire, 249; Glorious, 89; Glory 1747–63, 122; 1788–1809, 17, 166; 1899–1920, 195, 263; Gloucester, 108, 132; Goliath 1781–1815, 101; 1898–1915, 88; Good Hope, 31, 35, 37, 40, 163, 243, 263; Gosport, 132; Grafton, 215; Grampus, 49; Grenville, 55; Greyhound 1703–11, 235; 1783–1808, 201; 1859–69, 119 ; Growler, 228; Guernsey, 87; Gurkha, 185;
Halcyon, 104; Hampshire, 11; Hannibal 1854–74, 191; 1896–1920, 57, 88; Hart, 145, 243; Haughty 1856–67, 71; 1895–1912, 31; Hawke, 36, 57, 140; Hawkins, 149, 245; Hazard 1837–66, 71; 1894–1918, 30; Hebe 1782–1811, 47, 253, 257; 1892–1919, 62; Hecla, 80, 238, 239, 250, 266; Hector, 126; Hercules 1868–81, 10, 79, 143, 169, 171;

1910–21, 39, 130; Hermes 1919–42, 137; 1953–86, 16, 77, 154, 157; Hermione, 38, 140, 267; Hibernia 1804–55, 136, 177, 208; 1905–21, 31; Highflyer 1851–71, 79; 1898–1921, 161; Highlander, 156; Hilary, 247; Hindostan, 69, 104, 263; Hood, 59, 62, 75, 219, 232, 242; Hornet, 171; Hotspur, 111; Houghton, 234; Howe 1805–19, 48; 1940–58, 114, 154; Hussar 1763–80, 211; 1807–33, 236; 1894–1920, 31, 251 ; Hydra, 29;
Icarus, 224; Illustrious 1789–95, 211; 1896–1920, 39, 62; 1939–56, 59, 186, 149; Immortalité 1859–83, 160, 193; 1887–1907, 36; Impérieuse 1804–38, 236;1852–67, 170, 227; 1883–1905, 66, 74, 84 104, 169, 225; Impétueux, 166, 167; Implacable 1805–55, 49, 167; 1899–1921, 57, 181, 250; 1944–54, 15; Impregnable, 168, 259; Inconstant 1783–1817, 48, 167; 1868–98, 169, 171, 180; Indefatigable, 62, 243; Indomitable 1907–21, 218; 1940–55, 56, 234, 247, 248; Indus, 93; Inflexible 1876–1903, 79, 228; 1907–21, 67, 229, 231, 239; Intrepid 1964-date, 16, 234; Invincible 1765–1801, 95, 100; 1907–16, 82, 239 ; Iphigenia 1808–33, 65; 1910–18, 62; Iris 1840–69, 191; 1877–1905, 228; Iron Duke 1870–1906, 40; 1912–32, 20, 25, 35, 39, 41, 85, 104, 130, 137, 164; Irresistible, 105, 165; Isis, 229;
Jackal, 241; Jalouse, 64; James Watt, 224; Jaseur 1813–45, 191; 1862–74, 121; Jason, 46; Javelin 1938–41, 185; (1944), 151; Julie, 236; Jumna, 73, 220; Juno 1780–1811, 167; 1895–1920, 24; Jupiter, 14;
Katoomba, 139; Kelly, 185, 186; Kempenfeld, 161; Kent 1762–84, 133, 254; 1798–1856, 177; 1926–48, 161, 210, 245, 263; 1961–80, 16, 115; Keppel, 246; King Alfred, 173, 241; King Edward VII, 34, 37, 39, 169, 215, 218, 239; King George V 1911–26, 67, 75, 149, 231; (1941), 242; Kingfisher, 230; Kingsale, 107; Kingston, 107, 199; Kipling, 186;
Lancaster 1797–1815, 64; 1902–20, 88; Lark, 17; Leander 1780–1806, 29, 248; 1813–30, 175; (1895), 215; 1931–49, 89; 1961–89, 16; Leonidas, 230; Leopard 1703–39, 107; 1790–1814, 18; Leviathan 1790–1816, 206; 1902–20, 39, 173; Liffey, 38, 169; Ligaera, 101; Lion 1709–38, 86; 1777–1816, 105; 1912–24, 20, 25, 34, 35, 41, 62, 183; Lively 1713–38, 222; 1756–84, 91; 1794–98, 133; 1804–10, 106; 1870–83, 228; 1900–22, 55; Liverpool, 119; Lizard, 30; Locust, 57;

333

334

submarine bases
  Dolphin, Gosport, 77, 214
  Neptune, Clyde, 77
torpedo schools
  Defiance, Devonport, 74, 75, 126, 263
  Vernon, Portsmouth, 55, 74, 75, 103, 104,
    126, 149, 157, 163, 169, 180, 215, 231,
    238, 263, 264, 266, 267
shore batteries, *see* coastal artillery
Shovell, Adm Sir Clowdisley, 195, 196
Sicily, 11, 39, 52, 60, 161, 166, 191, 210,
  219, 226, 247, 264
Singapore, 16, 21, 26, 43, 61, 142, 151, 152,
  187, 191, 216, 219, 227
Sirte (17 Dec 1941), 247; (21 Mar 1942),
  247
Smyrna (Izmir), 35, 45, 195
Somerville, Sir James, 33, 161, 187, 217,
  231-34
South Carolina, 11, 94, 198, 205, 213
South African War *see* Anglo-Boer South
  African War
South Atlantic campaign (1982) *see*
Falkland Islands
Spanish-American War (Apr-Aug 1898), 80
Spanish Civil War (1936–39), 43, 59, 216,
  232, 246
Spanish Succession, War of the (1702–14) 11,
  44, 196, 199, 222, 235
Spartivento (27 Nov 1940), 33, 233
Speed, Keith, Minister for the Navy, 152
Spencer, 2ⁿᵈ Earl, First Lord of the Admiralty,
  95, 212; 5ᵗʰ Earl, First Lord of the
  Admiralty, 172, 221
Spruance, Adm Raymond A, USN, 154
squadrons
  1ˢᵗ Aircraft Carrier, 247; 1ˢᵗ Battle, 21, 104,
    140, 215, 219, 239; 1ˢᵗ Battle-cruiser, 35,
    145, 203; 1ˢᵗ Cruiser, 32, 40, 55, 63, 161,
    189; 2ⁿᵈ Battle, 32, 67, 75, 231, 251, 268;
    2ⁿᵈ Cruiser, 104, 164, 181, 219, 239; 3ʳᵈ
    Aircraft Carrier, 15, 138, 150; 3ʳᵈ Battle,
    21, 37, 85
  3ʳᵈ Cruiser, 41, 164, 173, 239, 246; 3ʳᵈ
    Light Cruiser, 244; 3ʳᵈ Submarine, 77
  3ʳᵈ Training, 154; 4ᵗʰ Battle, 146, 149, 232,
    240; 4ᵗʰ Cruiser, 14; 5ᵗʰ Cruiser, 28, 31,
    37, 39, 77, 151, 263; 5ᵗʰ Frigate, 22; 6ᵗʰ
    Cruiser, 127; 6ᵗʰ Frigate, 15; 9ᵗʰ Cruiser,
    66
  12ᵗʰ Cruiser, 251; 15ᵗʰ Cruiser, 219, 247;
    17ᵗʰ Frigate, 157; 27ᵗʰ Escort, 152;
    Battle-cruiser, 25, 32, 34, 62, 75, 145,
    203, 216, 219, 244; Channel, 10, 20, 30,
    34, 36, 37, 54, 57, 65, 72, 73, 74, 84,
    111, 119, 139, 143, 144, 163, 169, 176,
    181, 193, 201, 202, 208, 215, 228, 241,
    250, 267 *see also* Channel Fleet;
    Dartmouth training, 157; "Flying", 97,
    119, 171, 180, 250, 265; German East
    Asiatic, 113, 239; Training, 30, 34, 74,

103, 139, 194, 203, 215, 243; Western,
  12, 13, 107, 109
squadrons, Naval Air; *No 4*, 99; *Nos 706, 723
  (RAN))*, *725 (RAN)*, *737*, *819*, and *820*,
  22; *No 825*, 137
Stanhope, 7ᵗʰ Earl, First Lord of the
  Admiralty, 21, 217
Stanley, Lord, 14ᵗʰ Earl of Derby, Prime
  Minister, 117–18, 119, 176, 237; 15ᵗʰ Earl
  of Derby, Colonial Secretary, 118
Staveley, Sir William, **234-35**, 240
Steuart, James, **235-36**
Stewart, Sir Houston Stewart, **236-37**
Stopford, Sir Robert, 117
Sturdee, Sir Doveton, 14, 82, 234, **238-40**
Suakin, Sudan, 36, 266
Submarine Service, 77, 145
Sudan, 5, 23, 36, 112, 144, 266
Suez, Egypt, 28, 36, 43, 69, 88, 138, 152,
  155, 163, 189
Sumatra, 247
Surinam, 46, 229
Suvla Bay landings (Aug 1915), 67, 251 *see
  also* Dardanelles, Gallipoli
Symonds, Rear-Adm William, 240
Symonds, Sir Thomas, **240-41**
Syria, 52, 71, 118, 237, 249

Tagus, 18, 134, 143, 208
Tahiti, 231
Taiping rebellion (1851–64), 117, 227
Taku Forts, China, 54, 79, 111, 116, 117,
  227, 229, 265
Taranto (11 Nov 1940), 59
Tatnall, Commodore Josiah, USN (later
  CSN), 117
Tel-el-Mahuta, Egypt (24 Aug 1882)., 36
Texel, 124, 230
Thames, 40, 110, 142, 211, 224, 229
Thatcher, Margaret, Prime Minister, 78, 152,
  153, 158, 159, 235
Thomas, J P L , Visct Cilcellin, First Lord of
  the Admiralty 162, 189
Ticonderoga, New York, 123
Tientsin (Tienjin), 24, 129, 229
Tomkinson, Rear-Admiral Wilfred, 76, 216
Toulon, 17, 47, 87, 93, 105, 107, 108, 134,
  167, 177, 197, 200, 205, 207, 211, 222,
  254
Tovey, Sir John, 56, 86, 232, **241-43**
trade protection, 11, 102, 123, 139, 199, 200,
  202, 205, 222 *see also* convoy protection
  operations
Trafalgar (21 Oct 1805), 5, 6, 18, 51, 96,
  102, 116, 130, 225, 230, 265
Treasury, parsimony of, 21, 26, 41, 42, 43,
  64, 76, 77, 78, 110, 125, 140, 252, 267
Truxillo, Honduras, 224
Tryon, Adm Sir George, 129, 267
Tsushima (27–28 May 1905), 192